Masculinity and Men's Lifestyle Magazines

A selection of previous *Sociological Review* Monographs

The Sociology of Monsters[†]
ed. John Law
Sport, Leisure and Social Relations[†]
eds John Horne, David Jary and Alan Tomlinson
Gender and Bureaucracy*
eds Mike Savage and Anne Witz
The Sociology of Death: theory, culture, practice*
ed. David Clark
The Cultures of Computing
ed. Susan Leigh Star
Theorizing Museums*
ed. Sharon Macdonald and Gordon Fyfe
Consumption Matters*
eds Stephen Edgell, Kevin Hetherington and Alan Warde
Ideas of Difference*
eds Kevin Hetherington and Rolland Munro
The Laws of the Markets*
ed. Michael Callon
Actor Network Theory and After*
eds John Law and John Hassard
Whose Europe? The turn towards democracy*
eds Dennis Smith and Sue Wright
Renewing Class Analysis*
eds Rosemary Cromptom, Fiona Devine, Mike Savage and John Scott
Reading Bourdieu on Society and Culture*
ed. Bridget Fowler
The Consumption of Mass*
ed. Nick Lee and Rolland Munro
The Age of Anxiety: Conspiracy Theory and the Human Sciences*
eds Jane Parish and Martin Parker
Utopia and Organization*
ed. Martin Parker
Emotions and Sociology*
ed. Jack Barbalet

[†]Available from The Sociological Review Office, Keele University, Keele, Staffs ST5 5BG.
*Available from Marston Book Services, PO Box 270, Abingdon, Oxon OX14 4YW.

The Sociological Review Monographs

Since 1958 *The Sociological Review* has established a tradition of publishing Monographs on issues of general sociological interest. The Monograph is an edited book length collection of research papers which is published and distributed in association with Blackwell Publishing. We are keen to receive innovative collections of work in sociology and related disciplines with a particular emphasis on exploring empirical materials and theoretical frameworks which are currently under-developed. If you wish to discuss ideas for a Monograph then please contact the Monographs Editor, Rolland Munro, at *The Sociological Review*, Keele University, Newcastle-under-Lyme, North Staffordshire, ST5 5BG.

Masculinity and Men's Lifestyle Magazines

Edited by Bethan Benwell

Blackwell Publishing Ltd/The Sociological Review

Blackwell Publishing
9600 Garsington Road, Oxford OX4 2DQ, UK

and

350 Main Street, Malden, MA 02148-5018, USA

First published 2003 by Blackwell Publishing Ltd

Library of Congress Cataloging-in-Publication Data

ISBN 1-4051-1464-9

A catalogue record for this title is available from the British Library.

For further information on Blackwell Publishing, visit our website:
http://www.blackwellpublishing.com

Contents

Acknowledgements

Grateful thanks must go to John Galilee who had significant input in the construction of the book in its early stages. I am also indebted to the team of reviewers who gave up their time to make invaluable suggestions about the chapters. Thanks also to Mark for his unstinting help and support in the final stages—it was greatly appreciated.

Preface

Jonathan Rutherford

In the age of the informational and service economy, certain traditional ways of being male, rooted in the industrial revolution and its domestic division of labour, are becoming obsolete. The debate over the changes in men's lives has been going on for three decades. It is not a unique historical experience. Whether it be the new man of feeling of the 1790s, the New Man of the 1890s or the New Man of the 1980s, there are moments in history when an epochal social life brings into existence new values and forms of living. Such meta-morphoses do not burst upon people in sudden revelation. They are uneven, and affect some classes and groups more than others. They are hard to measure and quantify, but we nonetheless feel them profoundly. The contemporary changes addressed in this book can be encapsulated in the paradigmatic shift from the historical ideal of manliness to the term 'masculinity' which became popular in the 1970s and 1980s. Unlike the ideal of manliness which was rooted in traditions of patriarchy, masculinity was conceived out of women's revolt against patriarchal relations, as an oppositional, critical and deconstructive term. We use masculinity to describe, define and problematize performances, representations and discourses of ways of doing and being a man. Unlike man-liness, it lacks an ethical dimension which can provide the moral resources to live by. Nevertheless, it has been a revolutionary term because it has named men as a gender rather than an unquestioned norm. Masculinity brought men into a new type of gendered subjecthood which was open to self reflection, criticism, analysis and debate.

Since the early 19th century, manliness had been associated with public duty, honour, moral obligation and emotional restraint. These virtues were imper-sonal ethical standards. How a man felt at any given moment was irrelevant to the question of how he should live. Manly codes of conduct gave order and meaning to men's lives. They expressed the values of the group and prescribed to the individual his role and what this required him to do. Manliness was a social role which provided society with its moral definitions. By the 1960s such ideals were being discredited. In the dawning era of self-fulfilment and women's struggle for sexual equality, such a definition of manhood was too rigid and oppressive to assimilate the new individualized emotions, sexual identities and aspirations. Patrimony, the communication of meaning and roles from one generation of men to the next (from father to son), underwent an historical disjunction. The aspirant nuclear family of the 1950s began to fail to reproduce a normative version of itself. The advent of a consumer society combined with new permissive legislation on divorce and sexuality challenged the styles of manliness and modes of power necessary to reproduce and sustain traditional heterosexual relations. Personal and love relationships were being democratized. By the early 1970s, divested of the institutional certainties of marriage, the language of love, trust and feelings took on a new importance in providing the framework within which people lived their lives. In socially significant sections of the educated metropolitan classes, being a good man was measured against the traditional feminine virtues of care, empathy and relatedness. Women's struggle for more independent lives meant that men began to negotiate their relationships with women and children on the basis of equality. It was a difficult transition which prefigured the broader changes in men's family lives and gender relations of the following decade. As Manuel Castells argues, the decade witnessed the emergence of trends which point toward the end not just of the nuclear family but of the family based on patriarchal domination.

Twenty years later, by the mid 1990s, a consensus of opinion had emerged in the media and popular literature about men as a gender. They were emotionally inarticulate, disoriented and demoralized. Numerous research projects and surveys catalogued a growing list of the failings of masculinity: the collapse of paternal authority, the rise of absent fathers, broken families and delinquent sons, the educational failure of boys, criminality, sexual immorality and promiscuity, rising rates of suicide, and violence.

In 1998, Marketing Consultants Mellors Reay and Partners produced a report, *The State of Men*, which explained to advertisers how best to represent today's insecure man. They concluded: 'The most successful way to communicate with men in today's environment is to reflect the soul of primal man. Man the warrior, the hero. In a world where men find their most basic instincts thwarted, an advertiser who indulges their favourite fantasies should prosper.' In the film *Fight Club*, the protagonist Tyler Durden says, 'We are a generation of men raised by women, I'm beginning to wonder if another woman is what we really need.' The men in the Club he has set up strive to punch and batter each other into a recovered sense of masculine dignity. Be hit hard enough, hit back hard enough, and everything that a man has felt himself to be robbed of and shamed by will be put to rights. Morality is effeminate. Nothing counts except the male desire for authenticity.

But what does it mean to be a man? Consumer culture has created a simulacrum of male experience. Men can dress in it, parody it, drink it, smoke it, watch it on TV and drive the latest model of it. The market has commodified, sequestered and substituted it for the tantalizing sensations of shock, newness, the glamour of appearance, action. The representations of individual desire, need and aspiration are articulated by the signs of commodities. And yet paradoxically we live in a culture which values authenticity and self-fulfillment. We are called upon to invent our own identities; to live in our own way and be true to ourselves. If we fail to achieve this, then our life might be considered wasted or ill-spent. But there is little to confirm what is an authentic experience or to say what it means to be self-fulfilled as a man.

Men's lifestyle magazines were a response to this predicament. They established a new hegemony of masculine thoughts, values and behaviours, incorporating the two contradictory forces of the consumer market and the ethic of self-realization. The first issue of *Arena* in the winter of 1986 featured actor Mickey Rourke on the front cover—iconoclastic, edgy, heterosexual, a loner and no follower of convention. It was an invitation to men to break ranks, pursue their individual desire and, what was more, express it through the consumption of expensive clothes, toiletries and leisure activity. Men could look at and read about themselves. *Arena* was the *Playboy* of the new media age. Cynical about duty and obligation, it encouraged a hedonistic celebration of men's bodies and heterosexuality without guilt; *Arena* was for the self assured. Riding high on Chancellor Nigel Lawson's consumer boom and using men's growing interest in couture as a Trojan horse, it prised open a notoriously conservative consumer market. The women's magazines followed with their own more downbeat supplements like *Cosmo Man* and *Elle Pour Home*. These were followed by *GQ* for the 30-plus and then, in the next decade, *loaded* and *FHM* broadened out the market, tapping into a younger generation. Like a court jester goading them into excess, *Viz* provided the mockery, pushing at the bounds of acceptable taste and the new feminist-influenced sexual conventions. Their appeal lay with men aged 18–30 whose lives were characterized by socializing, college and fairly frequent job changes. With few rituals and social practices to structure this transitional period, the move from dependency on parents to independence, adulthood and the establishing of their own relationships and families required the skills of self presentation, inter-personal communication and self possession. Men's lifestyle magazines were about styles of living, exuberant and cocky in the face of the official announcements about the deadbeat male. They provided a language and representation of male performativity which might ensure a young man's social acceptance by his male peers and his successful negotiation through this liminal period of his life.

The magazines and their preoccupations with how to be a man have their historical antecedents. Since the inception of capitalism in the 17th century, the market has always responded to significant changes in men's styles and sensibilities with improving and instructional manuals. We can find their modern origin in the possessive individualism of commerce and trade capitalism. Contracts established new forms of social relationships between men and replaced the rights, duties and reciprocities which had been a part of the family. While men's role of head of household remained constant during these changes, their power over women was made cultural and rational rather than divinely ordained. The effect was to expose it to its own logic of questioning and doubt. Young men were also increasingly independent from the constraints of the patriarchal household. Their behaviour became a source of concern to the religious authorities. Hundreds of improving tracts and pamphlets were published prescribing proper manly conduct. But it was the figure of Mr Spectator who became the most influential role model of male social improvement and aspiration. Adam Smith's archetypal rational citizen of the new capitalist market appeared in literary form in 1711, when Joseph Addison and Richard Steele published their journal the *Spectator*. Priced at one penny and running to 635 issues over a three-year period, the *Spectator* became the embodiment of a new form of middle- and upper class 'polite' society. The authors provided their readership with a guide to polite behaviour, recommending 'polite books', 'polite arts', 'polite songs'. Mr Spectator was Addison's *alter ego*, emulating a detached self-interest as he strove to make his way in the emerging metropolitan public culture. Politeness embraced every aspect of manners and morals. It was the style of a class culture in the making. Its language of tolerance superseded religious differences. Its symbol of belonging was etiquette rather than breeding. In the market place all men were the same before the new god of money.

The masculine refinement of Mr Spectator was a performance which required an audience, and this was to be found in the private drawing rooms, coffee houses and taverns of the city. Once ensconced in this newly emergent society, a man had to grasp the etiquette of conversation, particularly with ladies who were considered to be a source of moral improvement. However, the artifice of polite society, personified by the figures of the fop and the rake, increasingly became seen as a corrupting influence on English manliness. The word 'effeminate' came to suggest vanity, decadence, idleness, chatter and luxury which were traits associated with the aristocracy and the French. The rake in his cynical seduction of women promoted his private interests in place of public duty. The fop personified a man so wedded to polite society that he had surrendered the manly virtues of physical strength, hardiness and courage. He lacked sincerity and talked 'empty prattle'. Politeness was an art of deception which inevitably prompted a desire for an authentic 'language of the heart'. The Scottish philosopher David Hume's notion of sensibility which encouraged the open and spontaneous expression of feeling, provided the basis for alternative codes of behaviour for men. In *Treatise of Human Nature*, published in 1739–40, Hume claimed that feelings permitted the expression of social bonds upon which society was founded. His language of feeling was shared by the novelists Laurence Sterne and Samuel Richardson, and developed into the cult of Sensibility whose ideal was the spontaneous and 'natural' expression of emotion. In place of the public display of charm, sensibility was the private expression of sincerity. A man's emotions were a proclamation of his honesty and his soul.

The 18th century debates about the relationship of reason to emotion and its codification in manly performance were a consequence of the changing boundaries between the public and private realms. Similarly the contemporary antagonisms between the archetypes New Man and the New Lad reflect the increased commodification of culture and the changing relationship of the market to society. Concern with private life and the cultivation of the self are symptomatic of the revolutionary upheaval of the last decades of the 20th century. Preoc-

4

cupations with intimacy, friendship, the meaning of life, death, love, family, belonging, sexuality, pleasure, the body and emotions are a development of the transformations of Western societies. TV talk shows become public lessons in a newly emerging language of intimacy and ethical decision-making. What were once the private, domestic languages of women are being projected into the public arena. Men's lifestyle magazines are both a part of this trend and a reaction to it.

Methodologically we have used the concept of masculinity to try and analyse and map out the changes in men's lives. Yet it also marks the limit in our language and conceptual understanding of what it means to inhabit the body of a male. Male subjectivities are always 'in the midst of taking place'. In this respect masculinity places a limit on our understanding of the changes taking place in male subjectivities. There is a video work by the artist Sam Taylor Wood of a man dancing naked to Techno music in what looks like a small attic room. He gyrates and pirouettes, absorbed in the movement of his body, and the pounding repetitive beat. On a table next to him is a small plastic model of a brontosaurus. That is the name given to the work, *Brontosaurus*. Taylor Wood has cut out the sound of the dance music and replaced it with Samuel Barber's *Adagio for Strings*. As the dancer turns and twists, we hear the dark, mournful sound of an elegy for the extinct male. It is an image that epitomizes the contemporary opinion that men are the sex least able to change the times; the gender that lacks the ethical and emotional resources for self reflection. And yet this is only half the story—the part that has been repeatedly told. It is up to us to articulate the emergent subjectivity: what is coming into being; what we can bring into meaning. We need to find the intellectual resources which will enable us to throw up the important question—what are men to become in a post patriarchal society?

Introduction: masculinity and men's lifestyle magazines

Bethan Benwell

In 1994, a new magazine burst onto an unsuspecting market in Britain. It was brash, funny and sometimes surreal; it was tongue-in-cheek sexist; it celebrated working-class culture, male camaraderie and above all, masculinity. It deliberately presented itself as a challenge to the existing construction of the feminist-friendly, sensitive narcissist known as 'new man' embodied in the fashion-based publications founded in the 1980s such as *Arena*, *Esquire* and *GQ*, which were (according to one of its founding editors) by this time 'laughably out of touch' (Southwell, 1998). It was described by the same editor as 'an anti-men's magazine' (Southwell, 1998: 17); its brand of masculinity was quickly dubbed 'new lad' by the media; it was called *loaded*:

> ... men's lifestyles were [now] more concerned about good times than the stiff, fake 'new man' crap that the other titles had been peddling in the Eighties ... Britain was learning how to party ... *Loaded* was the men's mag that walked it like it talked it. It spoke the language of the bars and clubs of the UK. (Robb, 1999: 41: 44–5 cited in Beynon, 2002: 110)

In his book on the 'nineties', Jon Robb claims that the *loaded* effect has been one of the key cultural influences of the decade in the UK (cited in Beynon, 2002: 110). Whilst *loaded* is by no means the sole focus of this collection on masculinity and men's lifestyle magazines, it marked a crucial shift in cultural enactments of masculinity in late 20th century Britain and epitomizes the crucial and inextricable relationship that exists between men's magazines and broader cultural meanings of masculinity.

The modern incarnation of the men's lifestyle magazine was launched in the UK in the mid-80s and has continued to thrive both there and across the western world ever since. As an important site for the articulation of aspects of modern masculinity and addressal of the male consumer, they have been lauded in the market sector for their commercial success and lambasted in the broadsheet press and in academia for their negative contribution to modern gender politics.

This edited collection explores the burgeoning genre of men's lifestyle magazines and related constructions of masculinity. The selection of chapters aims to provide a broad-ranging interdisciplinary approach to the subject, reflecting the most recent scholarship in the field and drawing in contributions from sociology, media and cultural studies and linguistics. The book supports the view that men's lifestyle magazines are both representative site and mobilizing force of crucial cultural shifts in masculinity. It also subscribes to the belief that popular culture, in all its forms and instantiations, plays a key role in the constitution of modern identities. The focus on men's magazines, then, it is argued, is able to illuminate aspects of the condition of modern masculinity and recent discursive shifts associated with gender politics. At the same time, the book is committed to pursuing a thesis of a 'genealogy' of masculinity in the cultural sphere and therefore positions its view of men's magazines within a broader cultural context that includes other comparative modes or arenas of representation or communication which interact with magazines in telling ways (eg, TV, sport, film and 'real' men). Although the focus of the book is predominantly upon modern, British, heterosexual masculinity, it also involves discussion of men's magazines across a range of historical and cultural contexts and therefore includes contributions which address historical predecessors of modern men's magazines, Japanese and American magazines, specialist sporting magazines and gay lifestyle magazines.

The book as a whole is committed to addressing the following questions:

- What do constructions of masculinity in men's lifestyle magazines illuminate about current gender politics? How can we place this within the context of current debates within feminism or masculinity studies?
- What do such constructions suggest about the relationship between gender and sexuality? More specifically, what is the relationship between the constructions of masculinity and constructions of heterosexuality within and around these magazines?
- How can we best articulate the relationship between various sites within a broader circuit of magazine culture such as production, text, editorial identity, consumption and reception?
- How should we place men's lifestyle magazines within the larger context of popular culture and the relationship between popular culture and consumerism?

Masculinity and the men's lifestyle magazine

As we have so far suggested, a powerful and intimate relationship exists between popular culture and masculinity. But how do we define masculinity in such contexts? What are its forms and how is it mediated culturally? What is the relationship between cultural representations of masculinity, 'lived' male subjectivities and performances of masculinity? And is it actually possible to make such distinctions in the first place? As the introduction will go on to explore, any coherent account of the meanings arising from popular cultural forms needs to assume a fluid set of interconnections between the various sites within a 'circuit of culture' (Johnson, 1986; Du Gay *et al.*, 1997; Jackson *et al.*, 2001 and

Bethan Benwell

Stevenson *et al.*, this volume). Men's magazines may be conceived of as both 'cultural text' and 'cultural phenomenon' (Edwards, this volume); in other words, magazines produce representations of masculinity but are also a site within and around which meanings of masculinity circulate and are negotiated or contested. In this book, the emphasis is predominantly upon mediations of masculinity through the magazine as cultural text. Its relationship to other social forms of masculine practice, whilst addressed, are necessarily tentatively asserted. Clear exceptions allied more obviously to an ethnographic methodology are Stevenson *et al*'s chapter, which explores audience attitudes to men's magazines, Wheaton's chapter, which looks briefly at reader responses to a specific article, and Crewe's contribution which involves interviews with magazine editors.

Defining masculinity itself can be even more problematic. Variously conceived through theoretical models of biological essentialism, social constructionism (including both sex role analysis and a more Marxist-inspired separate-spheres analysis), psychoanalysis and feminism, approaches to masculinity and gender more broadly are now tending to favour the 'discursive turn' which currently dominates in cultural studies and critical theory. A discursively produced or performative account of gender has been most influentially articulated by Judith Butler (1990/1999). Butler's basic premise is that gender is neither something we have, nor is it something we are, rather, it is something that we, with variable degrees of volition, do. Gender is a discourse we both inhabit and employ, and also a performance with all the connotations of non-essentialism, transience, versatility and masquerade that this implies. In her theorizing, Butler is allying herself to a tradition of psychoanalytic-inspired French poststructuralist feminism which situates the gendered subject as endlessly produced through discourse and therefore lacking in existential coherence and stability. Such an account is appealing for studies of the way in which masculinity is produced in popular culture precisely because it acknowledges the reflexive process involved in producing gender in such contexts, the interconnections between and dependency upon various cultural 'scripts' or discourses, and the frequent ambiguity, contradiction, negotiation and fissure that accompanies such a process. It is unsurprising then, that so many of the chapters in this book draw attention to the instability and contingency of masculinity produced in and around men's lifestyle magazines, and either explicitly or implicitly adopt this discursive account.

Within a discursive account of gender, two main paradigms theorizing the condition of masculinity currently dominate and both are represented within this book:

- Masculinity as Power Project
- Masculinity as Identity Project

Power, whether bodily/material or imagined/representational has historically always been implicated in definitions of masculinity. Defined as a *relational category* (eg, Connell, 1995; Strathern, 1997; Brod, 2002) masculinity only really

8   © The Editorial Board of the Sociological Review 2003

makes sense in complementary or oppositional relationship to *femininity* and most commentators concur that such a relationship is defined hierarchically with masculinity as the superordinate category:

> 'Gender' encapsulates relations of difference which, although they are shifting and precarious, are always already structured through assumptions of the *dominance* of masculinity over femininity. (Segal, 1997: xxiii)

The understanding of masculinity as a position, mode or performance of power is one largely associated with a feminist (or pro-feminist, to use the intriguing term adopted in masculinity studies) perspective. Such a perspective necessarily entails some kind of critical interrogation or even deconstruction of masculinity, although theoretical opinion is divided as to the viability or even desirability of a total deconstruction of gender. Those advocating the abolishment of gender include Lorber (2000), whose recent rallying call for a 'degendering movement' appeared in the first issue of *Feminist Theory* and MacInnes, who radically asserts that 'gender does not exist':

> 'gender', together with the terms masculinity and femininity, is an ideology people use in modern societies to imagine the existence of differences between men and women on the basis of their sex where in fact there are none . . . (1998:1)

Whilst other commentators are sympathetic to notions of the tyranny of gender inscription, they are more sceptical of the possibility of reflexively stepping outside the discursive territory which informs both gender identity and subjectivities more generally or, indeed, of mobilizing such political endeavours effectively. Butler (1999), for instance, is keen to distance herself from those feminists who would rather transcend or overthrow gender; this is not because she eschews the political, feminist impulse behind this stance but that, in her premise that all forms of identity are discursively produced, she does not believe that it is possible for a coherent subjectivity to stand outside of gendered discourse:

> . . . there is no gender identity behind the expressions of gender; that identity is performatively constituted by the very 'expressions' that are said to be its results. (p. 33)

Nor does she believe that it is 'the critical task of feminism' to establish a point of view outwith constructed identities. (p. 187). Similarly, Connell (1995) provides a useful critique of 'exit politics' and Gardiner also argues that gender 'appears to be so deeply structured into society, individual psychology, identity and sexuality that eradicating it will be extremely difficult' (2002: 3). Whitehead, responding directly to MacInnes' work, argues that:

> [the] point at which political discourse emerges into private action is quite different for each individual. There can never be an assumption of collective political interest. Such a notion would require a homogenous coherent subjectivity, possibly grounded biologically, together with the subsequent ability of the individual to exist external to discourse/ideology . . . any communal-political alliances are inevitably riven with contingency, misinterpretations and the fluidity of transitory cooperations. (2002:80)

The disagreement about the practical possibility of abolishing gender can be broadly formulated around the familiar dichotomy between structure and agency, a notion that gender identity is either a matter of self-fashioning or a matter of positioning by institutional structures, discourse and ideology, and a dichotomy, interestingly, that Gardiner (2002: 12) proposes deserves some critical scrutiny. Whilst the impossibility of a *pre-discursive identity* or *pre-social integrity* due to our very situatedness within discourse is an important and valuable thesis, it perhaps rather sternly eschews the possibility of reflection, the confrontation and negotiation of oppositional ideologies, the importation of new paradigms from other cultures, or revolutionary leaps of imagination as well as historical changes in social and economic life which might make the dismantlement of gender a real possibility. Such a deconstructive project would in fact, at some level, seem to be suggested in the analysis of cultural texts (ie, men's lifestyle magazines) where dominant accounts of gender are usually foregrounded and celebrated and where gender continues to oppress. In such mass or popular texts, it also sometimes possible to identify the points of rupture, contradiction and ambiguity which Butler hopes might subvert conventional gender identity. For this reason, it is fair to say that this collection of essays, largely (though with some reservations) represent a political project of deconstructing or denaturalizing masculinity as a construction.

A different view of masculinity is suggested by an *identity project* account. Such an account is well represented by the men's-movement-end of the masculinity-studies' spectrum and is concerned with describing and shoring up accounts of men's subjectivities, often with a view to 'reclaiming' masculinity in the face of a hostile second-wave feminism. However, not all identity-aligned accounts are so essentialist or anti-feminist. In a ground-breaking text, *Female Masculinity* (1998) Judith Halberstam radically challenges the biological basis of gender by her investigation of women enacting or adopting masculine identities. Halberstam rejects accounts of masculinity that posit it as 'social, cultural and political effects of male embodiment and male privilege' (2002: 345) and also challenges the assumption of compulsory heterosexuality usually bound up in accounts of masculinity. In her separation of masculinity from power, she differs from Butler, who, whilst asserting the possibility of a fluid and transferable gender, still discusses the 'transferability of the phallus' (1993: 57–67, cited in Halberstam, 2002: 355) and thus still associates masculinity with power. However, a conception of gender as both unrelated to biology and unrelated to power poses serious problems of definition. For what is gender within this formulation? A style, a rhetorical set of tropes, an idiosyncratic, personalized identity, an historical consciousness only? Similarly, in proposing that when masculinity becomes separated from men and attached to women it loses its social power, Halberstam's thesis starts to look less radical; nevertheless its empirical work contributes greatly to our comprehension of the range of possibilities for gender realization.

Another contribution to the identity-project account is emerging in recent sociological theories of individualization and movements of counter-modernity represented in the work of Giddens (1991), Beck (1992) and Beck & Beck-Gernsheim (1995). For these writers, the project of reinforcing clear and dichotomous categories of gender is less about shoring up patriarchal power and more about a psychic response (described by Beck and Beck-Gernsheim as 'constructed certitude') to the fragmentation of traditional institutions such as marriage and the family. Such an account certainly provides a persuasive reason for the simultaneous single-minded pursual of *femininity* by parallel women's publications and the complicit mirroring of gender-reinforcing discourses. It is a thesis that interprets gender, *whether masculine or feminine*, as a form of 'cultural capital' (to use Bourdieu's term (1977)) for both men and women. It is also a paradigm favoured by Jackson *et al.* (2001, Stevenson *et al.* this volume) who are keen to explore 'alternative ways of theorizing cultural power that avoids out-moded ideas of dominance and resistance' (this volume). This thesis, captured in Beck's *Risk Society* (1992) is a persuasive way of examining the masculinity emerging from men's magazines, though not without its problems, and will be taken up later on this introduction.

MacInnes also formulates gender in terms of 'psychic insecurity' in the face of the 'terrors of modernity' (1998: 1). He argues that the 'fetishism of sex/gender' has replaced old securities such as religion and is linked to the social need for 'authentic identity'. This pursuit of 'authentic identity' is interestingly played out in discourses surrounding the inception of *loaded* magazine whose editors made much of notions of 'honesty', 'naturalness' and 'authenticity' in their branding of the magazine, which was then taken up in lived and media discourses surrounding the magazine. Crewe (this volume) discusses the central role that 'authenticity' plays in editorial constructions of identity in his interviews with Brown and Southwell, the founders of *loaded*. Jackson *et al.* (2001 and Stevenson *et al.*, this volume) find similar discourses of 'authenticity' in the responses and dispositions of their focus group participants when commenting on men's magazines.

However, MacInnes is far more critical of this account of gender rooted in the cult of the individual than some of the other writers. His concern relates to the fact that 'opportunities for political action have been lessened by the centralizing of the self, and the subsequent privatization of the political struggle prefigured by identity politics.' (Whitehead, 2002: 79). It is also possible that such a formulation of individualism constitutes a strategy for evading acknowledgement of the continued play of power within gender relations. In the introduction to her recent collection of essays: *Masculinity Studies and Feminist Theory: New Directions* (2002), Gardiner poses a crucial set of questions which relate to the practices of masculinity and which are not adequately addressed by an identity account:

> . . . who has a stake in retaining masculinity as a coherent category, of restricting it to men, and of valorizing it as a goal of individuals and a necessary component of society? (2002: 1)

Finally, in this section, before moving on to discuss the more precise set of accounts used to explain new forms of masculinity in men's magazines, it is worth briefly rehearsing the now-familiar arguments about visibility and invisibility in relation to masculinity and the consequences of this argument for a popular cultural sphere that sets so much store by openly and reflexively celebrating and foregrounding its gender identity.

In feminist accounts of gender, masculinity has usually been conceived of as the neglected or invisible gender. Representations of women are frequently marked in media and literary texts, usually by an often unnecessary emphasis on sexuality or physical attributes. Feminism has worked hard to deconstruct and analyse patriarchal constructions of femininity, but masculinity, until recently, has largely missed or avoided this kind of scrutiny. One reason for this is the way in which men's lives and experiences have, for social and historical reasons, tended to stand in for general or universal experience.

The very phrase 'masculine representation', so heavily implicated in this book on men's magazines, therefore embodies a kind of contradiction or paradox, since masculinity is and has been preoccupied with the evasion of clear definition and unequivocal subject positions. This tension between visibility and invisibility arguably both characterizes and preserves masculinity and is a theme that is taken up by a number of the contributors in this volume. (Stevenson *et al.*, Benwell, Taylor and Sunderland, Crewe, Osgerby, Tanaka). What is interesting to Tanaka, for instance, about the Japanese market in contrast to the British market, is the relatively *unmarked* status of men's magazines as a category. For instance, the *Japanese Publishing Yearbook* will classify lifestyle magazines addressed to and read by men as 'general lifestyle' or even 'women and fashion'. Stevenson *et al.* (this volume) argue that in the responses of their focus group participants, a movement exists between 'naturalisation of masculinity and reflexivity'—ie, masculinity is both backgrounded as common-sense and foregrounded as a construct. In the magazines themselves, a thrusting and overt self-presentation marking out a clear, differentiated territory co-exists with an inscrutable elusiveness, a repression of the bodily, a claim to ungendered 'humanity', so that a dialectic between 'self-hyperbole' and 'self-abolition' (Thomas, 1996: 23) is played out at the heart of masculine identity in and around men's lifestyle magazines.

A complication to this conflation of power and invisibility is presented by Robinson in her recent work, *Marked Men: White Masculinity in Crisis* (2000). Robinson goes against the grain of much current scholarship on masculinity in arguing that visibility may also be a way of securing power:

> Making the normative visible as a category embodied in gendered and racialized terms can call into question the privileges of unmarkedness; but visibility can also mean a different kind of empowerment, as the history of movements for social equality . . . has taught us. (2000: 2)

Robinson points out that both whiteness and masculinity have been made visible 'in both progressive and reactionary ways' and that 'what calls itself the normative in American culture has vested interests in both invisibility and visibility.' (p. 3) This formulation actually helps to illuminate the apparent paradox at the heart of magazine masculinity which oscillates between self-definition and evasion. Men's magazines, as this introduction will go on to elaborate, are simultaneously anxious to define their identities in terms of masculinity, but also to avoid a too-direct confrontation with its terms.

Changing masculinities

Recent theorizations within gender and masculinity studies posits that masculinity, whilst definable as an entity based on a formation of power and structure of relations with *femininity*, is nevertheless both continually evolving across time and space, and also realized *multiply* due its various intersections with other aspects of identity such as class, race and sexuality. It is a formulation neatly articulated by Beynon as 'a "singular-plural", much like "data" that can take many different forms' (2002: 2).

Within a framework of multiple *manifestations* of masculinity then, it is clear that dominant cultural meanings of 'what it means to be a man' have indeed shifted in the context of the men's lifestyle magazine, and that such shifts have played a central role in the articulation of magazine masculinities. The evolution of consumer masculinity in Britain from 'new man' to 'new lad' has been well documented (Nixon, 1996; 2001; Edwards, 1997; Jackson *et al.*, 2001) and is also thoroughly addressed in most of the chapters in this book, so for this reason I will not provide an elaborate account at this juncture. Put briefly, 'new man' emerged at about the time of the launch of the first contemporary UK men's lifestyle magazine, *Arena*, and by its more overtly sexualized codings, challenged the hitherto unmarked or invisible status of men. 'New man' was an avid consumer and unashamed narcissist but had also internalized and endorsed the principles of feminism including a reassessment of the traditional division of labour and a new commitment to fatherhood (Beynon makes the distinction between these two main strands as 'new man as narcissist' and 'new man as nurturer' 2002: 99). 'New lad' was a clear reaction to 'new man', and arguably an attempt to reassert the power of masculinity deemed to have been lost by the concessions made to feminism by 'new man'. 'New lad', most clearly embodied in *loaded* magazine but also by its competing successors (eg, *FHM*, *Maxim*, *Front*), marked a return to traditional masculine values of sexism, exclusive male friendship and homophobia. Its key distinction from traditional masculinity was an unrelenting gloss of knowingness and irony, a reflexivity about its own condition which arguably rendered it more immune from criticism. It was also a construct which drew upon working-class culture for its values and forms, was younger than 'new man', was little invested in the world of work, preferring to drink, party, holiday and watch football, made barely any reference at all to fatherhood, addressed women only as sexual objects and was ethnically white.

13

For the remainder of this section I wish to present a series of accounts for this particular shift from 'new man' to 'new lad' and for the condition of modern incarnations of masculinity in magazines and popular culture more generally. Why have the various manifestations of masculinity within and surrounding men's magazines evolved in the way they have? And how does this relate to broader theoretical conceptions of the workings of masculinity?

The following headings represent competing explanations for the practices of masculinity currently circulating about men's magazines, although on elaboration it will be seen that many of the accounts are actually complementary or overlapping:-

- 'Crisis' accounts
- Backlash to feminism
- Risk society, individuation, relationship conflict and constructed certitude
- Consumer imperative
- Haphazard/unreflexive account

'Crisis' accounts

The view that masculinity is currently 'in crisis' is a popularly prevailing one, but not without its detractors. Commentators both within and outside the academy have argued that recent shifts in patterns of production and employment, as well as the progress made by second-wave feminism, have unsettled traditional gender formations and led to changing gender roles which have tended to be seen as bolstering the social position and psychic security of women at the expense of the confidence and self-justification of men. Faludi's recent study of American masculinities, *Stiffed* (1999) for instance, eschews her earlier emphasis upon a 'backlash' to feminism in favour of a more sympathetic account which sees men assailed on all sides by the social advancement of women, unemployment, rampant consumerism and poor father role models.

The implications of a 'crisis' account for men's magazines arguably resonate in the widely observed regressive and adolescent tendencies acted out by 'new lad' magazines in which a nostalgic retreat to infantile forms of behaviour, including scatalogical obsessions, puerile humour, an absence of references to work or social responsibility, an obsession with 70s and 80s culture (reflecting the childhood eras of the magazines' reading constituency) and a kind of rebellious posturing against 'adult' authority (or possibly feminism) could arguably be seen as symptomatic of some sort of crisis of adult masculinity. This has been considered by Whelehan (2000), Nixon (1996: 382) and also by Rutherford in his revised introduction to *Male Order*, in which he argues that 'male redundancy has created cultures of prolonged adolescence'. (1997: 7).

Not only have 'lad' magazines been seen to reflect symptoms of masculine 'crisis', but they have also been seen by some commentators actively to contribute to this crisis by their sometimes bullying tone and ethos of low aspiration. Ordinary readers, it is implied, are a pretty worthless bunch of no-hopers[1] and whilst they may celebrate the skills of celebrity sportsmen or the charisma of cult actors, they cannot hope to emulate such achievements themselves. This perception may lead to rather dramatic charges of causality. For instance, whilst being interviewed by a Sunday broadsheet about my work on men's magazines, I was asked 'would you say that lad magazines are directly responsible for young men's high rates of depression and suicide?'.

However, the idea that this 'crisis' is a uniquely modern one emerging apocalyptically at the turn of the millenium is challenged by Kimmel (1987) who effectively demonstrates that moments of crisis have occurred historically for men ever since masculinity became an acknowledged category. Indeed, MacInnes argues that the very act of marking or 'fetishizing' gender itself arose from a 'crisis' for all men: the incompatibility between the egalitarian principles of modernity and the central tenet of patriarchy that men are naturally superior to women (1998: 11). Finally, Robinson (2000) considers how a rhetoric of 'crisis' in masculinity is not necessarily good news for feminists but may actually accommodate a range of narratives which actually shore up masculine power:

> While it is true that 'crisis' might signify a trembling of the edifice of white and male power, it is also true that there is much symbolic power to be reaped from occupying the social and discursive position of subject-in-crisis. (2000: 19).

However, whether wittingly symptomatic of a crisis discourse or not, men's magazines' nostalgic retreat seems rather to evade the position of 'subject-in-crisis' rather than revel in it. The 'wounded masculinity' posited by Robinson which can be strategically capitalized upon by groups of men, is little in evidence in the cocksure tone of *loaded*, *Maxim* and *FHM*. In fact the presence of literal wounds, curiously presented for visual consumption in these magazines (and commented upon by Rutherford, 2000), in the form of frostbitten limbs, gangrenous wounds, sceptic bites, diseased flesh, death, degeneration and assorted deformities, may actually represent a casting-out of the abject, a ritualistic rejection of fragile embodiment, because it does not directly implicate and therefore threaten the reader, and because it is presented as a voyeuristic fascination for the reviled 'other'.

Backlash to feminism

A backlash account has dominated descriptions of men's magazines, and in its assertion of a reaction to the encroachment of feminism upon the power and privilege of patriarchy has much in common with certain 'crisis' accounts. A backlash to feminism is arguably one possible response to a 'crisis' in masculinity. Faludi popularized the term 'backlash' in her book of that title (1991) in which she mapped out the evolving and hostile response, largely in the media, to the advancements of feminism and their associated negative effects on the well-being of men. Later, in *Stiffed*, as outlined above, she would shift her focus to the genesis of the modern crisis, rather than men's response to it. The 'backlash' movement was epitomized in a number of key anti-feminist publications, such as Neil Lyndon's *No More Sex War: The Failures of Feminism* (1992) as well as in political organizations such as the *UK Men's Movement*.

The omnipresence of a certain kind of sexism and misogyny in lads' magazines lends weight to the thesis that their ideology is, in part, motivated by a backlash to feminism; however this thesis has been rejected by many commentators, including some within this book, for a variety of reasons. First, it has been argued that a rejection of feminism is less to do with men's responses to women, but is bound up with 'new lad's' rejection of the feminist-friendly 'new man', in part a commercial response and also a rejection of the taint of femininity (and by extension homosexuality), rather than feminism. Second, it has been widely noted that 'new lad' discourse is actually very adept at incorporating discourses of feminism (eg, Benwell, 2002a, Jackson *et al.* 2001); this strategic move, however, will often lead to a later undermining of women's position. For instance, a feature in *Maxim* entitled 'This Woman Can Seriously Damage your Health' actively constructs a type of woman labelled the 'Elastic Band'—'the new breed of girlfriend who's as cute and forgiving as they come. Until one day she snaps.' This type is described within the article as a young, successful, intelligent and professional woman, 'pro-active in every area of their life'. Ostensibly this is a positive description and one that adopts elements from a feminist discourse. However, the article then goes on implicitly to blame such a progressive discourse for apparently psychopathic behaviour in the context of a heterosexual relationship:

> Used to feeling in control, the mid-nineties woman can't bear the powerlessness that comes with being dependent on another person's love and approval. When that support is withdrawn, the feelings explode. (Hughes, 1997: 49)

Other responses to feminism are less hostile, more tongue-in-cheek, and suggest that men's magazines' overwhelming strategy to deal with the power of women is not to fight it but to accommodate it (even if this leads to a later undermining, either by sexual objectification or ironic dismissal). However, a recent feature in *FHM*: 'Why Men Rule: Whoa There, Fella: You're Still in Charge You Know' (Simeon de la Torre, 2002), reveals a disturbing new discourse which is openly misogynistic, albeit apparently humorous, and has a very explicit anti-feminist agenda, eg: 'From the moment they started bunging themselves under horses—apparently in a bid to be taken seriously—women began to develop the sort of smug expression normally associated with cats standing next to empty bird cages' and 'A Lady Equals an Accident: Three reasons why the fairer sex should stay in the back seat'. It is obviously difficult to assert that a single feature represents an emerging trend and it may simply be an unforseen product of an idiosyncratic writer that slipped through the editorial net. Nevertheless, it prompts a certain kind of feminist vigilance about the content and power of men's magazines, with a reminder that the masculine discourse in such magazines is not always simply characterized by irony that is harmless and playful.

Risk society, individuation, relationship conflict and constructed certitude

Beck's theories of 'risk' and associated notions of individuation and constructed certitude have already been briefly introduced and provide a persuasive paradigm for explaining manifestations of masculinity in men's lifestyle magazines. One interesting observation to emerge from Beck's work which may be relevant to men's lifestyle magazines, is his contention that the fear generated by living in a society dogged by unknown and unquantifiable global risks, leads to an ethos of 'self-limitation'— '. . . one is no longer concerned with attaining something good, but rather with preventing the worst' (Beck, 1992: 49), an observation which resonates with our earlier discussion of the non-aspirational ethos of many current men's magazine titles. Perhaps even more pertinent, however, is Beck's description of the impulse of counter-modernity which responds to the loss of traditional certitudes accompanying the breakdown of industrial society with a new set of certainties.

'Constructed certitude' is a means of shoring up a clear and unified sense of identity or ideology partly by casting out or ignoring ambiguity or complexity. In men's lifestyle magazines this is most clearly realized as a form of gender certitude predicated upon a form of biological essentialism. A biological account of gender, whilst less fashionable and credible within an academic context, is still the most enduring and seemingly intractable orthodoxy within popular and media culture. The whole ethos of men's and women's lifestyle magazines, for instance, is entirely predicated upon the assumption that men and women occupy exclusive sub-cultures which are polarized in terms of values, behaviours and styles, and that such differences, whether emotional, linguistic or lifestyle, are entirely natural and essential. Sometimes this polarity is markedly and humorously enforced by features which consciously explore masculine and feminine behaviour. Witness, for instance, the title of a feature in *Maxim* magazine (April 1997): 'Twenty reasons why men are men and women aren't'. However, more commonly, this assumption is more subtly but ubiquitously encoded in presupposition and 'common-sense' statements or questions, eg, '. . . as painful as it might be to admit, if you pause for thought you'll realise that almost all of what men do in life is dedicated towards one common goal: physical pleasure in the form of full sex', (*FHM*, September 1998: 106) and 'Women have always assumed the nurturing role in society' (Red, May 1998: 23). Such a version of 'natural' gender difference is similarly epitomized in John Gray's best-selling *Men are from Mars, Women are from Venus* (1993), where masculinity and femininity are presented as racial characteristics of two entirely different species. In addition, the oppositional relationship in popular accounts is frequently conceived as hostile or competitive, what Beck describes as 'relationship conflict' (1992: 104); a conflict rooted in a female expectation of equality for gender relations coming head to head with male intransigence and a reluctance to change.

In a different sense, gender identity work also operates to delineate the limits of magazine masculinity, to **cast out** its 'other'; a process of identity work described by Stuart Hall as 'a constructed form of closure' (1996: 5), whereby identities are partially defined by *that which they lack*. Ethnicity, for instance, is rarely addressed in a reflexive way in men's magazines, so the assumption remains, due to the near-invisibility of black celebrities, writers, readers and positive or serious coverage of black culture more generally, that magazine masculinity is white in orientation. Work and fatherhood are rarely discussed and homosexuality is utterly taboo. Defining one's identity through exclusion, absence and closure rather than explicit classification can be a strategic (if tenuous) way of avoiding charges of discrimination, as John Perry, a writer for *loaded*, remarked when presented with the charge that men's magazines are homophobic: 'I cannot imagine us ever commenting on gay people' (Sunday Herald, 3/10/1999).

Consumer imperative

Edwards (1997) has argued that forms of masculinity in men's magazines 'have very little to do with sexual politics and a lot more to do with markets for the constant reconstruction of masculinity through consumption' (p. 82). This provocative argument, whilst perhaps neglecting the significance of men making forays into a traditionally female preserve, recognizes the powerful influence of advertisers and marketers in the realm of lifestyle magazines and their need continuously to regenerate new markets for their products. The style-conscious 'new man' is frequently cited as such a consumer-driven construction, as are (by some) the subsequent dramatic shifts to 'new laddism'.

Crewe (this volume), however, has pointed to the unusual editorial control exercised by writers for the 'new lad' magazines, especially in their early days, which marked a departure from the tyranny of the consumer imperative and represented a desire to vent a more 'authentic' masculinity, one which was less bound up in style-based consumer culture than the 'new man'. In fact, it is possible to say that advertisers have had to follow the editorial lead in adopting a kind of 'commodity laddism',[2] with an increasing number of adverts in men's magazines now looking indistinguishable from magazine features.

In their series of interviews with various magazine editors, Jackson *et al.* (2001) note an on-going tension between editorial integrity and the power of the advertisers; but their interviews seem to document a recent shift of control from the advertisers to the editors, with many editors claiming to eschew market research in favour of 'instinct' and their knowledge of street culture (a strategy arguably also adopted by advertisers). Jackson *et al*'s interviews also demonstrate, in the context of a 'rapid-action' capitalism, how intertwined the spheres of the 'culture industry' and civil society actually are, with magazines having both to respond to and stimulate shifts in culture. Crewe (forthcoming) also documents the shifting dynamics between publishing directors and editorial figures, and whilst presenting a slightly more complex picture (he notes for instance, that during times of commercial stability, editorial control is diminished), agrees that the 'scarcity of editorial knowledge in relation to publisher knowledge was a crucial aspect of the power relationship between editors and publishers'. In other words, the ability to gauge a large, diverse and unpredictable constituency of readers is a powerful piece of capital which creative editorial figures were able to exploit.

Haphazard/unreflexive account

Finally, our set of accounts would not be complete without acknowledging the possibility that the masculinity that emerges from men's magazines may be haphazard and unreflexive. Magazines are heterogeneous in form; ie, they are composed of unrelated parts (McLoughlin, 2000:2). Evidence from Jackson *et al.*'s readers (2001) is that their reading practices also reflect this disjointed, unsystematic form. Similarly Mort (1988) describes the 'bricolage' (p. 202) effect of consumer masculinity that emerged haphazardly and fragmented from various cultural spaces in the 1980s. Magazines are also multiply authored, and their editorial line, whilst usually coherent, is not strictly uniform. Furthermore, the range of reading responses to the text are similarly varied and sometimes contradictory. All these dimensions point to a masculinity that is more incoherent and accidental than existing accounts tend to assume. Jackson *et al.*'s monograph on men's magazines orients towards this unreflexive account, describing a 'heteroglossia of narratives' within magazine culture and a series of ambiguities, slippage and contradiction which may or may not be strategic and which complicate an account of where cultural power is situated. This will be further discussed in the next section.

Forms of 'new masculinities'

In this section our focus narrows to the more specific forms that masculinity takes in the contexts of text, reader response and editorial identity. I have identified four themes which characterize the new forms of masculinity emerging in men's magazines and which have also been discussed by most of the contributors to this volume:

• Certitude
• Strategic negotiation/accommodation of feminist discourses ('New Sexism')
• Irony
• Contradiction, ambiguity, ambivalence and double-voicing

Certitude

'Constructed certitude' has already been discussed in this introduction, and in the context of men's magazines tends to involve an exaggerated emphasis on the certainty of gender—both masculinity and femininity—and the preservation of male privilege through the exclusion of what is 'other'. Men's magazines are, for instance, notable for their almost entire absence of women's voices or of discussion of women as anything other than objects of desire. At the level of the text, we find strategies for shoring up identity which might involve in-group identifiers, such as slang or esoteric reference, inclusive pronouns and presuppositions involving shared knowledge. We also find methods of *exclusion*— elements of identity which are deliberately disavowed, such as femininity, obesity or vegetarianism, or sometimes simply notable by their absence. Taylor and Sunderland (this volume) adopt a useful framework of 'inclusion and exclusion' from van Leeuwen (1996) which illuminates such strategies in their analysis of the construction of a male sex worker's identity in Maxim.

Strategic negotiation/accommodation of feminist discourses ('New Sexism')

A common motif of the 'new lad' is the adoption of what have been termed 'new sexism' discourses. This involves the legitimation of male power in new and creative ways, often by the strategic accommodation or negotiation of liberal, progressive or feminist discourses and has been identified by a number of writers, many looking at spoken discourse within Discursive Psychology. See, for example, Gough (1998, 2000), Toerien and Durrheim (2001), Talbot (1997), Griffin (1989), Gill (1993), Riley (2001), Benwell (2002a). This sexism-by-subterfuge is explainable in terms of the hegemonic workings of masculinity which relies on consent and complicity rather than domination for its power and is also composed of diverse and sometimes competing practices of masculinity (Demetriou, 2001).

Typical manifestations of 'new sexism' discourses include the anti-sexist disclaimer ('I'm not being sexist but—') (Gough, 2001), construction of men as a 'new oppressed category' bewildered by the contradictory demands and perceived unfairness of feminism (Gough, 1998, 2000, 2001), essentialism discourses (Gough, ibid), use of irony (Benwell, forthcoming), synthesis of, or oscillation between traditional and new forms of masculinity (Toerien and Durrheim, 2002; Benwell this volume), articulation of progressive discourses which are then undermined (Talbot, 1997), appeals to 'individuality' over gender politics (Riley, 2001), a 'Jekyll and Hyde' construction of feminism positing a dichotomy between 'reasonable' and 'monstrous' feminism/feminists (Edley and Wetherell, 2001) and the rhetorical distinction between feminism (good) and feminists (bad) (Griffin, 1989; Riley, 2001).

Irony

Irony is perhaps one of the most common ways in which the accommodation (and transformation) of feminist discourses is achieved in men's magazines. As a non-literal trope that relies for its effects upon a combination of sender intention and receiver interpretation, irony can be difficult to pin down. This is a quality not lost upon those who wish their intentions to remain ambiguous. An expression of ironic intention ('only kidding!') is a frequent accompaniment to a politically-unpalatable sentiment since it allows the sender to save face whilst preserving the form (and therefore potentially the meaning) of the original, surface utterance intact. In fact the operation of irony in the context of expressions of sexism rarely works to subvert or oppose the object of irony, as we might assume the traditional function of irony to be, and indeed this kind of irony rarely has a clear object at all. Rather it operates as a preemptive disclaimer which places the burden upon the receiver to share the joke, regardless of their usual politics. This supports Hutcheon's observation (after Hayden White) that irony is 'transideological' (1994: 10)—it is capable of both a radical and a reactionary politics. This type of irony-as-knowingness is similar to Jackson *et al.*'s (2001) discussion of cynicism in men's magazines, 'a form of unhappy consciousness which has already been enlightened in terms of its unacceptability' (p. 104). Jackson *et al.* (2001) also argue that irony offers an *internal* defence to the sender against his or her own ambivalent feelings about masculinity.

Whilst the presence of irony in spoken interaction can be signalled by various paralinguistic and non-verbal cues, such as intonation or gestured quotation marks, it can be harder to detect reliably in written texts; absurd propositions, hyperbole or sentiments known to contradict those of the author may be the only suggestion. In fact it is probably true to say that the presence of irony in men's magazines is something which is rarely recoverable from the text at all but relies upon a more global knowledge that sexism in 'new lad' culture is ironically, nostalgically and harmlessly meant, a sentiment encapsulated in *loaded*'s by-line 'for men who should know better'. Of course, such a nebulous conceptualization of irony has a usefully slippery quality about it, and furthermore, it is worth considering that attributions of ironic intention are sometimes made charitably by those (often outsiders) who would find serious expressions of sexism implausible in a contemporary context. Crewe (forthcoming), for instance, documents the bewildered and defensive response of Southwell (founding editor of *loaded*) to the suggestion that *loaded* is an ironic magazine (Southwell, 1998). Crewe suggests that a commonly attributed tone of irony may be prompted by the many ambiguities and contradictions to be found within *loaded* which, he argues, are symptomatic of the uncertain identifications of the editors and ambivalent feelings regarding eg, sexual politics, class and aspiration (Crewe, this volume and private correspondence).

Contradiction, ambiguity, ambivalence and double-voicing

Bearing a close relationship to the workings of irony, a more general condition of contradiction or ambiguity is a commonly observed feature of men's magazines, not only in the textual construction, but also in responses to the magazines by both readers and editors. This condition might be thought of as simultaneously *strategy* and *symptom* of masculinity and a reflection of themes of reflexivity that have frequently been invoked to explain cultures of late modernity. McRobbie (1999) and Ballaster (1996), writing about women's magazines, both comment on the self consciousness and elements of contradiction which characterize their content. However, both writers are positive about this kind of knowing reflexivity; McRobbie comments that irony and self-parody allow its readers to enjoy 'the stereotypical rituals of femininity without finding themselves trapped into traditional gender-subordinate positions'. Irony, she says 'gives them some room to move' (1999: 53); Ballaster *et al.* argue that the glaring contradictions in women's magazines (eg, between adverts and editorials) which provoked savage charges of hypocrisy, are both acknowledged and embraced by editors, writers and readers alike (1991: 7).

Similarly, it could be argued that reflexivity in men's magazines acts as a kind of metatextual control over the topic of masculinity. Benwell (this volume) describes a textual ambiguity or contradiction at the micro-level of constructing either heroic or anti-heroic masculine identities within the text that fails to alight clearly on one construction, thus effecting a kind of strategic evasion of definition. Taylor and Sunderland (this volume) observe a similar pattern of contradiction between the ideal masculinity, embodied in the male escort who is the subject of the piece, and the ordinary masculinity of the positioned reader.

However, in a more symptomatic (rather than agentive) reading, contradictory, ambiguous and fragmented forms may also symbolize fragmented identities. Like the Freudian slip, contradiction fails to be suppressed by the 'regulatory fiction' of masculinity—which is haunted by that which it attempts to exclude. A curiously suggestive example of this occurred in a feature profiling the rock band *Dodgy* in *Front* magazine. Oscillating between hero-worshipping admiration and a self-checking cynicism, the writer describes the moment he meets his heroes in the toilets backstage:

> Unfortunately, I'm dying for a slash and can't wait, so I burst in positioning myself between Andy's thigh and Chris's head. I haven't got much room to play with and then it hits me. Dave, the new vocalist starts to sing. From his tousle-haired head comes a voice that is part Stewart, Winwood and Cocker (Joe, not Jarvis), all rolled into a cockney loudspeaker. How can you piss in the presence of that?

The homoeroticism of this moment in a discourse usually so carefully policed for such overtones is difficult to ignore and also difficult to dismiss as conscious irony.[3]

More prosaically, the discontinuity often observed to characterize masculine representations in men's magazines may be as much a reflection of production process as a clear reflection of masculine identity. Jackson *et al.*'s (2001) interviews with editors would seem to provide evidence of such a lack of clear strategy.

Approaching the analysis of masculinity in magazines

One of the key aims of this book is to synthesize a variety of approaches and methods for the study of men's magazines, and in doing so, acknowledge the importance of a global consideration of all moments in the broader context of the circuit of magazine culture and the ways in which they may connect up and interact with one another. Such an approach also gestures towards the complex relationship between public spheres/media and private spheres/lived masculinities.

This complexity of meaning and impossibility of singular interpretation in many ways compromises our earlier attempts to pin down the 'meaning' of magazine masculinity and so we may wish to caution against a too extreme form of 'radical relativism' which can lead to rather disempowering and toothless modes of analysis. Nevertheless, a consideration of broader contexts of culture may actually serve to support or refine intuitions gained from a more singular approach (eg, a close analysis of the language of the text). Benwell's and Taylor and Sunderland's contributions (this volume) for instance, both draw attention to the limitations of an exclusive focus upon the language of a text and stress that an ideal analysis of discourse would involve the contribution to meaning made by real readers' varied and subjective responses to the text.

Circuits of culture paradigm

The following contexts are all crucial to a comprehensive discussion of masculinity in men's magazines and are all represented in some way in the book.

- Cultures of production (including editors' identities)
- Cultures of consumption
- Audiences
- Intertexts
- History
- Discourse/language

Analysing *contexts of production* involves studying the relationship between editorial agenda, marketing and advertising, as well as the physical constraints imposed by time, budget and layout. Whilst not all aspects of cultures of production are considered in detail in this book, a useful discussion of editorial work and the sometimes vexed relationship with advertisers and publishers is considered by Jackson *et al.* (2001) and Crewe (forthcoming), and *editors' identities* provide the theme for Crewe's contribution (this volume). *Editors' identities* have come into sharp focus with the rise of the 'new lad' magazines, particularly *loaded* whose ethos and rationale have been inextricably bound up with the cult of particular individuals and their self-professed values and lifestyles. *Cultures of consumption* were the dominant and early focus of work on men's magazines represented in work by Mort (1996), Nixon (1996) and Edwards (1997) and demonstrated the key role that magazines have played in the evolution of consumer masculinity, particularly during the 1980s. This focus on the purchasers of the magazines has also led to a more ethnographic methodology in relation to the reading constituency of men's magazines and their reading practices and responses to the magazines represented in work by Jackson *et al.* (2001), Galilee (2002) and Stevenson *et al.* (this volume). Wheaton (this volume) extends this kind of *audience* analysis to a more detailed reader response methodology in which respondents comment on the specific content of magazines. A circuits-of-culture model is also interested in the synchronic *intertexts* which feed into the same 'lad' culture invested in by the magazines and many of the contributors make reference to other sites of popular culture such as TV shows and films (Gill, Edwards, Wheaton this volume) as well as the lived cultures of the men who buy men's magazines which both influence and draw upon elements of magazine culture. A consideration of *intertexts* also involves the reflexive media debates which circulate, often disapprovingly, around men's magazines and help to reify and disseminate key ideas and labels including that of 'new lad' itself. An *historical* perspective is crucial for understanding the evolution of consumer masculinity and for contextualizing aspects of its identity. By historicizing magazine masculinity, Osgerby's paper (this volume) allows us to see that many recent manifestations of masculinity are not terribly 'new' after all and illuminates the way in which hegemonic discourses have transformative potential whilst sustaining the 'patriarchal dividend' or privilege at the same time.

The *discourse* or *language* of men's magazines has only recently begun to receive scholarly attention and whilst existing approaches tend to involve an assumption that identities are produced through discourse, a more focused analysis of language makes provision for the *exemplification* of discourse as a social practice. A discursive approach to men's magazines is represented by a number of papers in this volume (Benwell, Taylor and Sunderland, Baker, Tanaka).

Whilst most of the contributors limit their analysis to a singular focus or methodology, it is acknowledged that the various spheres are mutually dependent, mutually defining and overlapping, a fact which is foregrounded in many of the papers, eg, Stevenson *et al.* point to the way in which readers (and non-readers) have internalized certain media discourses and Benwell discusses the dialogic format of men's magazines which presupposes the presence of the reader for its meaning. Indeed, a number of the contributions assume that most 'moments' within the circuit are highly interdependent and impose limits upon each other, eg, consumers are integrated into the production process itself by the ways in which they are imagined in the minds of producers (Crewe, private correspondence). The desirablity of synthesizing our analyses of all the contexts of culture continues to provide an exciting challenge for research in this area and, by juxtaposing a set of diverse methodologies with the same object of analysis, it is hoped that we have brought this ideal a little closer.

The future of men's lifestyle magazines?

Everyone in men's magazines has lost their nerve. All the magazines have just been in slow motion, free-wheeling, on remote control... (James Brown, *The Observer* 21/4/2002).

As this book goes to press, the future of men's lifestyle magazines looks uncertain. Gloomy headlines about the latest Audit Bureau Circulation figures abound in media journals and a corresponding decline in this particular incarnation of masculinity known as 'new lad' is assumed to follow: 'The Lads go Limp' asserts Jessica Hodgson in the *Media Guardian* (18/2/02); 'Men's Market faces Uphill Struggle' claims Jo Blake in *Mediaweek* (22/8/01) and James Brown, the editor credited with inventing the 'new lad' magazine niche practically single-handedly, has now turned his back on this market, condemning it as lacking 'soul or passion'[4] and being 'stale', 'pathetic' and 'embarrassing'[5].

Close examination of the evidence, however, reveals a more complex picture suggestive of both change and continuity. ABC figures have indeed reflected a decline in the market with an overall loss of 12 per cent between 2000 and 2001 but whilst the sales of some previous success stories, such as *FHM*, continue to fall, figures for the second half of 2001 actually showed a reversal of the general decline for certain titles, including *loaded*. All of this makes it very difficult to assert clear trends. Similarly, we might note the discontinuation of *loaded's* interactive website, *Uploaded*, and assume a waning interest on the part of both public and producers, yet *FHM's* website is still up and running and Brown's new magazine, *Jack*, also has its own website. Brown launched *Jack* in 2002 to a flurry of publicity—unsurprisingly including extensive derision of the existing market—and claimed that men have moved on and require more substance and seriousness in their reading materials[6]; but we can't help noting that Brown himself is ten years older, with new parental responsibilities, and that in fact his new publication may well be aimed at an older constituency. As Rod Liddle points out in an article in the *Guardian* ('So the lad is dead? Yeah, right,' 24/4/02):

> Could it be that those twentysomethings, whom he serviced so admirably with *loaded* are still . . . larging it big, with unfathomable quantities of lager and ecstasy and, indeed, cheerfully, chaotically available women? Isn't it Brown who has changed rather than the audience?

Finally, we can note with interest the explosion of lad culture (arguably a phenomenon with British roots) on to markets elsewhere in the world, particularly America[7]. Whilst the lad was proclaimed 'dead' by media pundits in Britain, he was busy flexing his muscles across the Atlantic. The launch of *FHM* in the States was described in the following triumphalist terms in an article in the *Sunday Times*:

> . . . A testosterone-charged British sperm is swimming across the Atlantic . . . If the American 'new man' was ever house-trained by feminism to be considerate, sensitive and interested in women's minds rather than their bodies, he is about to be led wildly astray. (Goodwin and Rushe 1/8/1999 cited in Beynon 2002, p. 114)

US versions of *loaded*, *FHM* and *Maxim*, but with remarkably few changes to in-house style and content, took off successfully at the end of the 20th and beginning of the 21st century and were mirrored too in TV broadcasting in programmes such as *The Man Show*, a flippant, ironic and unreconstructed celebration of laddish masculinity.

If we attempt to predict future incarnations of consumer masculinity, then, we may find little evidence for dramatic changes ahead. When we look at the first edition of *Jack*, the 'new' face of masculine consumption, we see, not only strong similarities to an early *loaded* (paeans to cult heroic figures, random surreal observations, a rhetoric of celebration and football writing) but in its front cover design depicting a giant bikini-clad woman in a watercolour design, based on the poster for the 1958 cult disaster movie, 'Attack of the 50 ft Woman', we are arguably witnessing a nostalgic retreat to the magazine era described by Osgerby in his chapter on the 'Pedigree of the Consuming Male', with a notable similarity in the styles of front covers from the 1930s, 40s and 50s. The men's magazine market, it would seem, has come full circle, and in our attempts to delineate an evolving masculinity, we might conclude that its various incarnations are cyclical, repetitive and parasitic upon its predecessors. Perhaps what the recent speculation about the declining markets for men's magazines and the various attempts to reinvent a male constituency point to most clearly, is the way in which the evolution of masculinity in the magazine context is so intimately bound up with the workings of consumer capitalism and its need to refresh the market once a product becomes 'stale'. With so little evidence of important or really radical change in masculine identities across the magazine market during its history, we could argue that the power and coherence of masculinity is well served by its strategic adaptability to new social, commercial and political imperatives whereby an *appearance* of change is in fact bound up with eternal renewal.

About this volume

The chapters in this book each address an aspect of the relationship between masculinity and men's magazines in complementary ways, so that what emerges is a comprehensive overview of the field. The range of chapters in the book broadly reflects two main methodological emphases, to borrow Edwards' distinction: analysis of magazines as a cultural phenomenon and analysis of magazines as a cultural text. This, however, should not imply that such a dichotomy is clear or even desirable; many of the contributors address the fluid nature of such boundaries, pointing for instance to the ways in which varied audience responses to men's magazines build and transform the meanings of the text. Other contributors (Wheaton, Osgerby) actually combine different methodological approaches within their chapters.

Nevertheless, what this methodological distinction does entail is that those analysing men's magazines as a cultural phenomenon tend to use traditional sociological methodology such as the interview or focus group discussion (Crewe, Stevenson *et al.*, Wheaton), or historical or intertextual methods of cultural analysis (Gill, Osgerby, Edwards); while those analysing men's magazines as a cultural text tend to employ linguistic or semiotic analyses (Benwell, Taylor and Sunderland, Baker, Tanaka, Wheaton, Osgerby). The book's *predominant* orientation to the textual forms and cultural intertexts of masculinity, in the context of the lifestyle magazine and other domains of popular culture, means inevitably that there are aspects of the *relationship* between these forms and meanings and the lived practices of masculinity that could be more fully elucidated in a future collection. There is clearly further ethnographic work to be done in exploring both the production and consumption contexts of men's magazines, as well as the incorporation/appropriation of some of these 'new lad' discourses of masculinity within the discourses and 'chat' of men and women in everyday settings. Nevertheless, the discursive or textual orientation to new forms of masculinity in and around men's magazines favoured by the majority of the contributors here, addresses an area of arguable neglect in sociology and provides crucial evidence of the forms of popular culture upon which practitioners of masculinity draw. The understanding of popular cultural texts is arguably a necessary precursor to the understanding of broader ethnographies of masculinity.

Whilst the collection of chapters represented here offers diverse approaches to and perspectives on the study of men's magazines, a number of common themes emerge independently across the collection which seem to suggest that certain motifs and strategies lying at the heart of new forms of masculinity have been persuasively identified and demonstrated. These support this introduction's earlier elaboration of 'forms of masculinity' and include the very common observation of **ambiguity, contradiction** and **fragmentation**; the **inseparability and overlap between sites of cultural production** (eg, texts and readers); and the **strategic accommodation of oppositional discourses** such as feminism. Whilst not every contributor is in agreement about the precise contribution such strategies make to a politics of male power, all would concur that they play a crucial role in the constitution of new forms and practices of masculine identity at the beginning of the 21st century in Britain and beyond.

Notes

1 This was reinforced by a comment made by *FHM* editor David Davies at a recent EMAP Men's Seminar (April 2002) that the magazine starts from the premise that 'men are crap'. (Peter Jackson, private correspondence)
2 Compare with Goldman's discussion of 'Commodity Feminism' in *Reading Ads Socially* (1992).
3 For a fuller discussion of this extract, see Benwell 2002b.
4 Stephen Armstrong (22/4/02) 'Jack the Mag' in *Media Guardian*.
5 Crewe (this volume).
6 Brown interviewed by John Arlidge: 'Loaded Lad Grows Up and Ditches Soft Porn', *Observer* 21/4/02.
7 Schirato and Yell (1999) also document the appearance of men's lifestyle magazines on to the Australian market in the second half of the 1990s including the very successful *Ralph* which seems close to *loaded* in its content and ideology.

References

Ballaster, R., Beetham, M., Frazer, E. and Hebron, S. (1991) *Women's Worlds: Ideology, Femininity and the Woman's Magazine*. London: Macmillan.

Beck, U. (1992) *Risk Society: Towards a New Modernity*. London: Sage.

Beck, U., Giddens, A. and Lash, S. (1994) *Reflexive Modernisation: Politics, Tradition and Aesthetics in the Modern Social Order*. Cambridge: Polity.

Beck, U. and Beck-Gernsheim, E. (1995) *The Normal Chaos of Love*. Cambridge: Polity.

Benwell, B. (2002a) 'Is There Anything "New" About These Lads? The Textual and Visual Construction of Masculinity in Men's Magazines': 149–174 in L. Litosseliti and J. Sunderland (eds) *Gender Identity and Discourse Analysis*. Amsterdam/Philapdelphia: John Benjamins.

Benwell, B. (2002b) 'Elusive Masculinities: Locating the Male in the Men's Lifestyle Magazine': 41–62 in A. Sanchez-Macarro (ed.) *Windows on the World: Media Discourse in English*. University of Valencia Press.

Benwell, B. (forthcoming) 'Ironic Discourse: Masculine Talk in Men's Lifestyle Magazines', *Men and Masculinities*.

Beynon, J. (2002) *Masculinities and Culture*. Milton Keynes: Open University Press.

Blake, J. (2001) 'Men's Market Faces an Uphill Struggle', *Mediaweek* 22nd August.

Brod, H. (2002) 'Studying Masculinities as Superordinate Studies', in J.K. Gardiner (ed.) *Masculinity Studies and Feminist Theory*. New York/Chichester: Columbia University Press.

Bourdieu, P. (1977) *Outline of a Theory of Practice*. Cambridge: Cambridge University Press.

Butler, J. (1999) *Gender Trouble: Feminism and the Subversion of Identity*, 2nd edition. London: Routledge.

Butler, J. (1993) *Bodies That Matter: On the Discursive Limits of 'Sex'*. New York: Routledge.

Castells, M. (1996) *The Power of Identity: The Information Age: Economy, Society and Culture*, Vol II. Oxford: Blackwell.

Connell, R.W. (1995) *Masculinities*. Oxford: Polity.

Crewe, B. (forthcoming) *Representing Men: Cultural Production and Producers in the Men's Magazine Market*. Oxford: Berg.

De La Torre, S. (2002) 'Whoa There Fella. You're Still in Charge You Know', *FHM* April.

Demetriou, D. (2001) 'Connell's Concept of Hegemonic Masculinity: A Critique', *Theory and Society* 30: 337–361.

Edwards, T. (1997) *Men in the Mirror: Men's Fashion, Masculinity and Consumer Fashion*. London: Cassell.

Faludi, S. (1999) *Stiffed: The Betrayal of the Modern Man*. London: Chatto and Windus.

Galilee, J. (2002) 'Class Consumption: Understanding Middle-Class Young Men and Their Fashion Choices', *Men and Masculinities* 5(1): 32–52.

Gardiner, J.K. (2002) 'Introduction', in J.K. Gardiner (ed.) *Masculinity Studies and Feminist Theory*. New York/Chichester: Columbia University Press.

Giddens, A. (1991) *Modernity and Self-Identity: Self and Society in the Late Modern Age*. Cambridge: Polity.

Gill, R. (1993) 'Justifying Injustice: Broadcasters Accounts of Inequality', in E. Burman and I. Parker (eds) *Discourse Dynamics: Repertoires and Readings of Texts in Action*. London: Routledge.

Goldman, R. (1992) *Reading Ads Socially*. London: Routledge.

Goodwin, C. and Rushe, D. (1999) 'Drool Britannia', *Sunday Times* 1st August.

Gough, B. (1998) 'Men and the Discursive Reproduction of Sexism: Repertoires of Difference and Equality', *Feminism & Psychology* 8(1): 25–49.

Gough, B. (2000) 'Biting Your Tongue: Negotiating Masculinities in the 1990s', *Journal of Gender Studies*. 10(2): 169–185.

Gray, J. (1993) *Men are from Mars, Women are from Venus*. London: Vintage/Ebury.

Griffin, C. (1989) 'I'm Not a Women's Libber, But—': in S. Skevington and S. Baker (eds) *The Social Identity of Women*. London: Sage.

Halberstam, J. (1998) *Female Masculinity*. Durham: Duke University Press.

Hall, S. (1996) 'Introduction: Who Needs "Identity?" ': in S. Hall and P. du Gay (eds) *Questions of Cultural Identity*. London: Sage.

Hodgson, J. (2002) 'The Lads go Limp', *Guardian*, 18th February.

Hughes, K. (1997) 'This Woman Can Seriously Damage your Health', *Maxim*, April.

Hutcheon, L. (1994) *Irony's Edge: The Theory and Politics of Irony*. London: Routledge.

Jackson, P., Stevenson, N. and Brooks, K. (2001) *Making Sense of Men's Magazines*. Cambridge: Polity Press.

Kimmel, M. (1987) 'The Contemporary "Crisis" of Masculinity in Historical Perspective': in H. Brod (ed.) *The Making of Masculinities: The New Men's Studies*. London: Allen and Unwin.

Liddle, R. (2002) 'So the lad is dead? Yeah, right', *Guardian*, 24th April.

Lorber, J. (2000) 'Using Gender to Undo Gender: A Feminist Degendering Movement', *Feminist Theory* 1(1): 79–95.

Lyndon, N. (1992) *No More Sex War: The Failures of Feminism*. London: Sinclair-Stevenson.

MacInnes, J. (1998) *The End of Masculinity*. Buckingham/Philadelphia: Open University Press.

McLoughlin, L. (2000) *The Language of Magazines*. London: Routledge.

McRobbie, A. (1999) 'MORE! New Sexualities in Girls' and Women's Magazines': in A. McRobbie, *In the Culture Society: Art, Fashion and Popular Music*. London: Routledge.

Mort, F. (1988) 'Boy's Own? Masculinity, Style and Popular Culture': in R. Chapman and J. Rutherford (eds) *Male Order: Unwrapping Masculinity*. London: Lawrence and Wishart.

Mort, F. (1996) *Cultures of Consumption: Masculinities and Social Space in Late Twentieth Century Britain*. London: Routledge.

Nixon, S. (1996) *Hard Looks: Masculinities, Spectatorship and Contemporary Consumption*. London: UCL Press.

Nixon, S. (2001) 'Resignifying Masculinity: From "New Man" to "New Lad" ': in D. Morley and K. Robins (eds) *British Cultural Studies*. Oxford: Oxford University Press.

Riley, S. (2001) 'Maintaining Power: Male Constructions of "Feminists" and "Feminist Values" ', *Feminism and Psychology* 11(1): 55–78.

Robinson, S. (2000) *Marked Men: White Masculinity in Crisis*. New York: Columbia University Press.

Robb, J. (1999) *The Nineties*. London: Ebury.

Rutherford, J. (1997) 'Introduction: Avoiding the Bends': in R. Chapman and J. Rutherford (eds) *Male Order: Unwrapping Masculinity*. 2nd Edition. London: Lawrence and Wishart.

Rutherford, J. (2000) Keynote address to 'Posting the Male' Conference, John Moores University, Liverpool.

Schirato, T. and Yell, S. (1999) 'The "New" Men's Magazines and the Performance of Masculinity', *Media International Australia incorporating Culture and Policy* 92: 81–90.

Segal, L. (1997) *Slow Motion: Changing Masculinities, Changing Men*, 2nd Edition. London: Virago.

Southwell, T. (1998) *Getting Away With It: The Inside Story of* Loaded. London: Ebury Press.

Strathern, M. (1997) 'Gender: Division or Comparison?': 42–63 in K. Hetherington and R. Munro (eds) *Ideas of Difference: Social Spaces and the Labour of Division*. Oxford: Blackwell Publishers/The Sociological Review.

Talbot, M. (1997) 'Randy Fish Boss Branded a Stinker: Coherence and the Construction of Masculinities in a British Tabloid Newspaper': in S. Johnson and U. Meinhof (eds) *Language and Masculinity*. Oxford: Blackwell.

Toerien, M. and Durrheim, K. (2001) 'Power Through Knowledge: Ignorance and the "Real Man" ', *Feminism and Psychology* 11(1): 35–54.

Thomas, C. (1996) *Male Matters: Masculinity, Anxiety and the Male Body on the Line*. Urbana: University of Illinois Press.

Van Leeuwen, T. (1996) 'The Representation of Social Actors': 32–70 in C. Caldas-Coulthard and M. Coulthard (eds) *Texts and Practices: Readings in Critical Discourse Analysis*. London: Routledge.

Whelehan, I. (2000) *Overloaded: Popular Culture and the Future of Feminism*. London: The Women's Press.

Whitehead, S. (2002) *Men and Masculinities*. Cambridge: Polity.

Part 1:
Genealogies of masculinity

Introduction: Genealogies of masculinity

The book begins with two broad genealogies of masculinity, one contemporary and one historical. Gill's contribution, 'A Genealogy of the Lad', charts the emergence of lad culture as both a sensibility and a discursive moment. Gill's methodology is a discursive and deconstructive one which assumes that 'new man' and 'new lad' are constructions controlled by and mediated through cultural and commercial industries. She uses a Foucauldian framework including notions of 'forms of knowledge' and 'dividing practices' to explicate the emergence or, perhaps more accurately, the production of these relatively stable and culturally familiar forms. Her chapter then explores in more detail the factors which were responsible for the production of this discursive moment, such as feminism, gay liberation, the style press, retailing trends and psychological movements. As a broad and intertextual overview of the particular form of masculinity being explored by this collection, it provides an ideal map of the terrain with which to guide and inform the reader's understanding of later chapters.

In the second chapter of this section, 'A pedigree of the consuming male: masculinity, consumption and the American leisure class,' Osgerby presents a genealogy of a slightly different kind. Dispelling the common myth that men's lifestyle magazines had their genesis in Britain in the 1980s, Osgerby's chapter offers a detailed exploration of the history of masculine consumption in America from the late 19th century to the present day. He presents a range of shifting masculinities associated with commodity culture and the male leisure class, including 'dudes', 'gangsters' and 'playboys'. Focusing in particular upon the rise of *Esquire* in the 1930s (despite the Great Depression of the preceding years), and in delineating their various rhetorical forms and common motifs, Osgerby demonstrates that the modern incarnation of masculinity known as 'new lad' is not particularly 'new' after all, but has a long and enduring pedigree within commercial culture. Osgerby's genealogy takes us right up to the present day and he concludes by reasserting the close and sympathetic relationship between the evolution of magazine masculinity and 'modern capitalism's demand for an endlessly re-generating consumer market'.

Power and the production of subjects: a genealogy of the New Man and the New Lad

Rosalind Gill

Introduction

Producing knowledge about men is big business. Where once men represented the invisible, unmarked norm of human existence and experience, today they are hyper-visible as a gendered group, with academics, marketing executives, journalists and others devoting considerable attention to masculinity or masculinities. In the past, forms of masculinity were studied only if they were regarded as a problem, with predictable classed and racialized pictures emerging and frequent moral panics about male youth and the 'dangerous classes'. Since the mid-1980s, however, masculinity in its own right has become a key focus of interest and interrogation as analysts queue up to explore and document shifts in men's values, tastes, aspirations, feelings, beliefs and behaviour. A whole army of cultural commentators now devotes its time and resources to identifying or picking over 'emerging trends' and to analysing, classifying, measuring and monitoring contemporary masculinities.

This process, as I shall argue, is not merely a descriptive one, but involves careful selections, exclusions and 'ontological gerrymandering' (Woolgar and Pawluch, 1985) in order to create persuasive accounts about new and changing forms of masculinity. Central to these accounts (whether produced by retail analysts, magazine editors or academics) is the production of new masculine subjects: the 'new father' and the 'superwaif', 'black macho' and 'soft lad', the 'new boy' and 'modern romantic'—these are just some of the terms that have been used over the last decade to capture the apparently novel ways in which contemporary manhood is lived.

Some of these new masculine subjects disappear quickly, leaving little trace. The 'new boy' and 'modern romantic', although generating many column inches of discussion and analysis, were ephemeral constructions who scarcely had a life outside fashion spreads, and were not widely taken up as ways of representing men's experience. Other subjects, though no less constructed, appear more solid and are certainly more long-lasting. The figure of the 'new father' is a case in point. Born out of the need for social scientists, retail analysts, market researchers and others to make sense of a variety of apparent changes in men's aspirations relating to fatherhood, the notion of the existence of the 'new father' was given substance by British Prime Minister Tony Blair's decision to take paternity leave for the birth of his youngest child, Leo, and by footballer David Beckham's assertion of his responsibilities to care for his son, Brooklyn, even when it conflicted with work. Both men were presented as examples of the 'new father', with other public figures offering further instantiations of 'new father-hood' in action. In this way, complex and contradictory findings about the changing domestic and emotional landscapes for heterosexual couples with children were rendered simple and knowable through the figure of the caring, child-centred 'new father'.

The aim of this chapter is to examine in detail the production of two other masculine subjects—the 'new man' and the 'new lad'. These two have been selected from the plethora of available alternatives because of their apparent power as ways of representing contemporary masculinity, their relatively enduring nature (over more than a decade) and because they can be found across many different sites. The chapter is divided into two broad parts. In the first, I elaborate my theoretical perspective—a Foucaultian and discourse analytic approach—and discuss how it differs in key respects from existing accounts. In the second—necessarily brief—part I sketch a tentative genealogy of 'new man' and 'new lad'—the aim being to demonstrate the production of these subjects across multiple sites, rather than to say anything in detail about each one.

Part 1: Power and the production of subjects

The approach taken here is a discursive one, which views 'new man' and 'new lad' as constructions. The starting point for the analysis is the Foucaultian (Foucault, 1979, 1980, 1987) idea that power works partly through the production of subjects—that is, rather than being neutral or descriptive terms 'new man' and 'new lad' are part of a power/knowledge nexus in which certain people, practices, ideas and way of living are normalized and others are rendered deviant. Writing about the development of distinctively modern forms of power in the 18th century, Foucault was concerned with 'dividing practices'—for example the spatial separation of different types of subject—and with the scientific classification of people by the emerging human sciences. Today, however, entire industries are devoted to defining and classifying new subjects: not only the academic disciplines of sociology and psychology but also journalists, futurologists and trend spotters, think-tanks, health analysts, psephologists, etc. These 'new cultural intermediaries' (Featherstone, 1995) interpret and mediate cultural and psychological questions about who we are, how we live and what we want. They represent us to ourselves, and, in doing so, make the world knowable in highly specific ways.

For example, it is now routine for marketing companies to release their 'findings' to the press, a short period after they have been reported to the client and are no longer deemed 'market sensitive'. Hungry for copy to fill the ever-expanding lifestyle sections of newspapers and magazines, journalists frequently produce detailed commentaries and 'think pieces' on such reports. The debates are then pushed through the 'media echo chamber' (Faludi, 1991) and observations about contemporary masculinity take on the status of truths about 'how men are'. These truths may then be imported into academic research—perhaps as 'evidence' that a project should be funded (eg, 'we are witnessing an epidemic of body dysmorphia among young men that requires urgent examination'), or to challenge a received wisdom. Meanwhile, retailing companies and magazines have also digested the findings and are already tailoring their products to take account of the new information about how men are changing: softer lines appear in car designs, fragrances are marketed to draw up on the 'new sensuality', beer adverts start using gay imagery, and so on.

This is a brief and oversimplified account, but it captures in essence the process by which various forms of knowledge including academic knowledge are involved not just in describing the world, but also in *producing it*. While writing this paper I came across a typical example. Under the headline 'Young men reject old image', an article in *The Observer* (26 August 2001) reports on a trend survey by *Informer* which documents a shift away from the 'new lad' to a form of masculinity described as 'nice bloke' (in brief: happy with equality, serious about work, juggling different commitments). In the same article the editor of the 'lad mag' *loaded* is quoted as saying that he intends to 'feminize' his publication in response to this shift. And so the reflexive cycle continues.

This moment is also reflexive in another way: individuals are being exhorted constantly to *reflexively monitor* themselves. We are invited to identify, measure and compare our desires, aspirations and behaviours against well-publicized but ever-changing norms that relate to every aspect of human life: our frequency and variety of types of sexual intercourse; the amount of time we spend with our children; the number of times we visit our doctor; the duration and nature of our experience of bereavement; the quantity of units of alcohol we consume in a week, etc. No area of life is immune. As Foucault pointed out, power in contemporary society operates increasingly through processes of *subjectification* in which self-regulation is paramount and the self is experienced as an ongoing *biographical project* to be worked on and disciplined (Rose, 1991,1999; Giddens, 1991; Beck and Beck-Gersheim,1995; Walkerdine *et al.*, 2001).

The 'new man' and the 'new lad': theoretical reflections

This chapter is concerned with exploring these processes of subjectification in relation to 'new man' and 'new lad'. 'New man' and 'new lad' represent perhaps the two dominant and most pervasive constructions of masculinity circulating in Britain over the past decade. Although, as I have already noted, there have been many other different attempts to label and classify masculinities, none have had the staying power of 'new man' and 'new lad', or their ability to capture or speak to changes in the landscape of gender. 'New man' and 'new lad' have become familiar and recognizable stereotypes. Despite the fact that constructions of them are always *occasioned*—that is, produced for particular purposes in specific interpretative contexts—there is considerable consensus about what constitutes each. The 'new man' is generally characterized as sensitive, emotionally aware, respectful of women, and egalitarian in outlook—and, in some accounts, as narcissistic and highly invested in his physical appearance. He is as likely to be gay as straight. By contrast, 'new lad' is depicted as hedonistic, post- (if not anti) feminist, and pre-eminently concerned with beer, football and 'shagging' women. His outlook on life could be characterized as anti-aspirational and owes a lot to a particular classed articulation of masculinity (see Crewe, this volume). A key feature of some constructions of 'new lad' is the emphasis on his knowing and ironic relationship to the world of serious adult concerns.

'New man' and 'new lad' are frequently represented as products of particular chronological moments, with 'new man' representing the zeitgeist of the 1980s and 'new lad' the 1990s (in the familiar journalistic tendency to map ideas and identities onto decades). Indeed, one of the most common cultural narratives of masculinity in the 1990s (alongside talk of its crisis) was the story of the *displacement* of 'new man' by 'new lad'. In such stories 'new lad' is a reaction against 'new man', as well as a backlash against the feminism that gave birth to him.

Such accounts are not limited to journalism, and indeed a striking feature of contemporary academic scholarship on the new man and new lad is the extent to which it draws on, borrows from and reworks other knowledges (eg, from market research or advertising or fashion retailing).

It is not simply that these domains constitute the *object* for academic researchers, but—in a more significant shift in terms of intellectual production—that academic research increasingly *resembles* the kinds of knowledges produced by other interested groups. John Hartley (2002) has argued that this shift in cultural studies more broadly represents a welcome (and postmodern influenced) recognition on the part of academics that they do not have the monopoly on useful knowledges or truths. An alternative, more sceptical, position, however, might point with concern to the political economy of universities or to the need increasingly to justify academic research by reference to wealth creation or innovation and to frame research in terms of potential 'users' (not infrequently business enterprises).

In relation to narratives of the shift from new man to new lad there are often considerable similarities between the accounts produced by market research agencies or journalists and those of academics. A lad-mag editor might point to the success of his publication being due to its recognition of the inauthenticity or dishonesty of portrayals of 'new man', together with its appreciation of the fact that straight men like looking at sexy photographs of young women. Tim Southwell of *loaded* tells us to 'get over it', while a Condé Nast press release widely reported in the broadsheets asserted:

GQ is proud to announce that the New Man has officially been laid to rest (if indeed he ever drew breath). The Nineties man knows who he is, what he wants and where he's going, and he's not afraid to say so. And yes, he still wants to get laid. (January 1991)

Meanwhile an academic points out that 'the most important lesson of the emergence of representations of the 'new lad'. . . concerns the way it points up the difficulty of reinventing masculine heterosexual scripts. This relates to a clear limited position within the shifts in masculinity associated with the 'new man' . . . [B]ecause no new heterosexual scripts were articulated—scripts that were both sexy and anti sexist—the opportunity for established scripts to re-emerge was always left open' (Nixon, 2001: 383–384).

The tone of these two accounts is very different, but they both stress the reality of the shift and its origins in the failure of discourses of 'new manhood' to address heterosexual men's sexuality.

One writer taking a very different position is John MacInnes. MacInnes is not interested in the putative shift from new man to new lad or in the pluralization of masculinities since 'just as there is no such thing as masculinity, neither are there any such things as masculinities' (1998: 40). For him, gender does not exist except as 'an ideology people use in modern societies to imagine the existence of differences between men and women on the basis of their sex where in fact there are none' (1998: 1). The key question for MacInnes thus becomes not what is masculinity and how is it changing, *but under what historical conditions did men and women come to believe that masculinity exists, what forms has this belief taken, and what consequences does it have?* (1998: 77).

MacInnes has made a powerful intervention into the field of masculinities studies and maintains a critical distance from the issues that have preoccupied most other scholars. I share his thoroughgoing 'culturalist' (Beynon, 2002) stance which refutes any essential, *a priori* psychological differences between males and females, and his assertion that gender is an ideology. Where I differ, however, is in the significance accorded to ideology. For me there is nothing 'mere' about ideology, it is not just an epiphenomenon, and nor can such a stark distinction between the real (material) and the discursive be maintained. Ideologies or discourses are real and have material effects, and it is these discourses that I take as my object of study.

This chapter, then, differs from both the perspectives outlined above. It does not assume the existence of a real and profound shift in men's sensibilities over the last two decades, presented in shorthand as the displacement of new man by new lad. But nor does it regard the discussion of different types of masculinity such as new man and new lad as essentially trivial. Instead it argues that new man and new lad are best treated as discourses (or interpretive repertoires, myths, or cultural constructions) for making sense of contemporary (largely white British) masculinity. These discourses are drawn on in different ways at different times in different forums for different occasioned practices. Rather than one displacing the other, they *coexist* as alternative formulations of masculinity which are constantly reworked and recycled and used to 'kick off' (Williamson,

1978) against each other. My perspective, then, takes seriously Beynon's point that: 'perhaps what we are currently witnessing at the start of the 21st century is nothing less than the emergence of a more fluid, bricolage masculinity, the result of "channel hopping" across versions of the "masculine"' (2002: 6).

New masculine subjects and real men

One advantage of this perspective is that it leaves open questions about the existence of a profound cultural shift in masculinity. Such changes have been remarkably difficult to document. While there have been a number of excellent and insightful examinations of new man and new lad as 'regimes of representation' or practices in advertising, fashion and photography (Nixon, 1996; Edwards, 1997; Mort, 1996), attempts to read off from these anything about the lived experience or sensibility of contemporary young men have proved problematic. There are no agreed-upon criteria for identifying new men or new lads among actual male populations. Indeed the one much repeated 'key index' of newmannishness is his contribution to domestic work—something that is usually only invoked to support arguments that the figure of the new man does not exist in the real world!

One problem, I would contend, is the tendency to think in rather static terms, with a kind of one-size-fits-all notion of masculine identity—itself surely a product of the marketing-led tendency to assert the existence of a limited number of 'types of man'. In fact, new man and new lad are not fixed identity positions or essences but are, as I have suggested, best thought of as discourses or cultural repertoires. Any of us—as skilled cultural actors in a society saturated by representations of new man and new lad—could '*do*' 'new man' or 'new lad', and indeed some accounts of the new lad makes precisely this point when they assert that the performance of a new man sensibility is something that they knowingly enact to get women into bed. For example Sean O'Hagan says that new lad 'aspires to New Man status when he's out with women, but reverts to old lad type when he's out with the boys. Clever, eh?' (1991).

Most contemporary empirical research on/with young men points to an extremely complicated relationship between the self descriptions made by real young men and the templates of masculinity on offer in magazines and other cultural forms. The important work by Peter Jackson, Nick Stevenson and Kate Brooks who interviewed groups of magazine readers, highlights the profound ambivalence of different investments and reading positions (Stevenson *et al.*, 2000a; 2000b; this volume; Jackson *et al.*, 2001). They point, for example, to the variety of distancing strategies deployed in accounts of magazine consumption, with the emphasis upon rebutting the potential charge that they take themselves or the magazines too seriously. My own recent research with Karen Henwood and Carl McLean, in which we interviewed 140 men aged between 15 and 35, found similar disavowals, such as claims that the magazines are only ever purchased for a train journey, or flicked through in a dentist's waiting-room, or just bought 'for a laugh'.

We also found that many of the men we interviewed were highly invested in independence and autonomy and in 'being different' (Gill *et al.*, forthcoming). Highly individualistic claims were often made persuasive through the construction of implicit and explicit contrasts with other men. Thus while men characterized their own decisions as independent, other men were described as 'fakes' or 'clones' or 'like sheep'. This can be seen in the focus group extract below with a group of Welsh men discussing (brand) labels.

Int: You mentioned Dolce & Gabbana there, I mean, do you think labels play a big part in it?
Paul: Yeah, I would have said so, definitely. It's all, it's all a big image thing, isn't it, really?
John: How to be [. . .] on a magazine.
Paul: Well, this is it.
John: And people treat it like the Bible. I'm not saying people do, but I reckon people do.
Jake: See something in it and they want to copy that.
Paul: Well, this is it, yeah. This is it.
John: It's in this magazine, it costs this much so it must be cool. Who cares what it looks like or smells like or whatever.

In this extract, the representation of magazine readers is that they use magazines like (life) style Bibles, slavishly copying the fashions displayed, regardless of what they actually look or smell like. The speakers construct their own identities contrastingly in terms of the intrinsic value of their own choices, and their defiant refusal to buy labels.

Our analysis of men's feelings about and reactions to eroticized magazine and advertising images of the male body points up similar complexities. While the producers of these images—such as the muscular torso that graces every month's cover of *Men's Health*—code these as *aspirational* and expect male consumers to regard them that way, our research found that this was a minority response. There were in total eight different kinds of response including feeling pressured, anger and resentment, desire, and indifference, and men are combined and moved between these in a subtle and fluid manner (Gill *et al.*, 2000).

At a very general level, then, our research makes a point made by most empirical research on 'ordinary' men: namely that lived identities are complex, contradictory and dynamic and do not have an unmediated relationship to any particular sites of cultural production (see also Stevenson *et al.* and Wheaton, this volume). It is noteworthy that discussions of the new man and the new lad have come out of analyses of fashion, retailing and magazines and have then tried to find evidence of these lifestyles among actual populations—rather than the other way round. Contemporary sociological and social psychological analyses, by contrast, seem to have found little evidence for large numbers of men straightforwardly inhabiting either a new man or a new lad identity—without a huge dose of irony (Frosh, Phoenix and Pattman, 2001; O'Donnell and Sharpe, 2000; Edley and Wetherell, 1997).

Recent studies have pointed instead to the significance of class, 'race', ethnicity and region in producing and fracturing young masculine identities. Stephen Frosh, Ann Phoenix and Rob Pattman point out that the cultural resources available to construct masculinities are racialized—a key point when thinking about the overwhelming whiteness of representations of the new man and the new lad (Frosh *et al.*, 2000; 2001). In their important study of boys in London secondary schools they found that black young men of African Caribbean descent are viewed as 'super masculine', embodying highly valued traits associated with toughness, a particular masculine style and dress, and physical ability. This rendered them popular/hegemonic figures, but also had major costs in terms of being trapped by what Majors and Billson (1994) call the 'cool pose', with little cultural capital in wider society. In fact the very traits that were admired, were also liable to produce fear and discrimination from authority figures such as teachers and potential employers.

Les Back's (1994) work on 'white Negroes' is also pertinent here as it explores the phenomenon of whites who wish to imitate and take on the powerful masculine image associated with black straight men. Back argues that far from challenging racism, this apparently admiring attitude to blackness actually appropriated it as a white artefact, without any necessary impact on the racist beliefs of the 'white Negroes'. This point about the racialized performance of masculinity is also made by Louise Archer whose study of 'Muslim brothers, black lads and traditional Asians' showed that the young Asian men could (and did) construct their identities in quite different ways, 'as a shared site of solidarity against racism, as a resistance to whiteness but also as a means of drawing divisions between black groups, and as an assertion of masculine power' (Archer, 2001: 98). Archer argues that the young men's identity discourses can be read as part of a process of 'imagined' construction which is fluid, flexible and constantly reinvented, thus challenging traditional notions of essentialised gender, cultural or racial identities. Against this backdrop, the persistent whiteness of representations of both new man and new lad is particularly striking.

Part 2: Outline for a genealogy

Having set out the theoretical perspective, it is time to move on to providing an outline for a tentative genealogy of the cultural discourses of new man and new lad. It is not possible to be either detailed or exhaustive here but merely to point to some of the varied influences on the construction of these figures, drawing on existing work and on my own analysis of influences that have been overlooked in other accounts. My starting point is Tim Edwards' assertion that the new man was not simply the product of the media or even of responses to second wave feminism, but 'he was rather the crystallization of consequences in economics, marketing, political ideology, demographics and most widely consumer society in the 1980s' (1997). This, I think, gives a very valuable sense of the multiplicity of different influences and determinations that produced the discourses about the new man and (equally) the new lad.

The 'new man'

1 Feminism and the new social movements

It would be impossible to make sense of the figure of the 'new man' without reference to feminism. Since the late 1960s feminism has had an enormous impact on every area of social life from paid employment to intimate relationships, and the transformations of gender relations that it provoked are still underway. Feminists interrogated many taken for granted aspects of traditional masculinity and laid at its door responsibility for atrocities from rape to nuclear war (Chapman, 1988). Early feminist criticisms of hegemonic masculinity as distant, uninvolved, unemotional and uncommunicative are still to be found reverberating through sites as diverse as talk shows, health forums and business think-tanks.

These critiques gave rise to a great appetite for a new kind of masculinity which would encompass many of the traits previously thought of as feminine— emotionality, intimacy, nurturing and caring (Chapman and Rutherford, 1988; Seidler, 1989, 1992; Connell, 1987; Kimmel, 1987; Hearn and Morgan, 1990) and it is partly against this backdrop that 'new man' must be understood.

Additionally, feminists sought to challenge the fiction of the unified and universal male subject, and to make masculinity visible as a gender. Moreover, some feminists—as well as other postmodernist thinkers—sought to deconstruct some of the binary ways of thinking that constructed masculinity as rational and instrumental against emotional and relational femininity. At its most basic, then, feminism started a conversation about gender, power, work, sex, intimacy, nature and culture—and opened up a space where gender relations could be progressively revisioned.

This revisioning was reinforced by a number of other social movements during the 1970s and 1980s—the peace movement, anti-racist organizations, environmental movements, movements for sexual liberation, postcolonial struggles and a variety of identity-based political organizations, eg, disability rights groups. What this loose categorization of groups share is both a disillusion with conventional, class-based, party politics and a commitment to new forms of organization and struggle, premised less upon representative democracy and more upon direct action. Taken together, the new social movements disrupted the very understanding of what 'the political' meant, expanding its definition to reach far outside the institutions of representative democracy and into everyday life. In this way, questions about domestic labour, childcare and consumption all came to be seen as irredeemably political. This redefinition also promoted a different model of the individual, as someone connected not simply to a family but also to wider communities and to the environment. In doing so it sowed the seeds for a revisioning of traditional masculinity, and helped to create a cultural milieu in which discourses of new manhood could emerge and flourish.

2 Popular psychology and masculinity

Another profoundly important set of influences on 'new man' can be found in the rise of a variety of different psychological perspectives in the last third of the 20th century—themselves influenced by feminism. The humanist psychology that was popularized in the UK and US throughout the 1970s took as its focus the 'whole person'. It promoted assertiveness in place of aggressiveness or passivity (which were popularly mapped on to men and women respectively), and it placed high value on good communication. Psychoanalysis also experienced an upsurge of interest at the same time, as evidenced by the growing number of different schools of psychoanalytic thought and training institutions, and increasing numbers of people seeking personal therapy and counselling. Moreover, a mounting disaffection with traditional science and medicine produced a flourishing alternative health movement, encompassing a whole range of natural and/or non-Western approaches to healing, many of which have a much more holistic view of the person than allopathic disciplines.

Taken together, these movements put the idea of the 'whole person' or 'self-actualized person' (Maslow, 1970) on the cultural agenda. Significantly, the whole person was often seen as an androgynous person, as extreme masculinity and extreme femininity came to be regarded not simply as socially restricting or damaging, but also as profoundly unhealthy (Chapman & Rutherford, 1988). Such concerns fed into the growing men's health movement which saw threats to men's health coming not just from coronary heart disease or cancer but also from patterns of behaviour and ways of relating that added up to a kind of 'toxic masculinity'.

Popular psychology and popular health movements, then, provided a supportive context for the 'new man' to emerge and develop.

3 The rise of the style press

A different site of production of new man imagery came from the rise of the style magazines in the 1980s (Nixon, 1996; Edwards, 1997; Mort, 1996; Stevenson *et al.*, 2000). For years, people working in the fashion, magazine, advertising and retailing industries had fantasized about the creation of a magazine which could be targeted at affluent male consumers—but it was seen as an impossible dream. The main reason identified for this was that men did not define themselves as men, in the same way that women defined themselves as women. Men lacked self-consciousness about their sex (the 'male as norm' problem, identified by feminists), and while they bought magazines about cars or fishing or cameras there was scepticism about whether they would buy a title organized around being a man, rather than a specific hobby. A second problem concerned the tone such a magazine should adopt—women's magazines had long adopted the formula of treating their readers like friends, with an intimate tone, but this was seen by people within the industry as potentially threatening to heterosexual men because of its implication of homosexuality.

In terms of understanding the emergence of new ways of representing masculinity Sean Nixon argues that *The Face*, launched by Nick Logan in 1982, was of primary importance. It promoted itself as a style magazine rather than a men's magazine, although the vast majority of its readers were male, and was organized around fashion, music and any kind of social commentary deemed to be chic enough to fit in its pages. Nixon (1996) argues that *The Face* developed a new aesthetic: it was not just about style, but it was emblematic of stylishness itself, creating a new vocabulary for fashion photography—a vocabulary, significantly, that extended the notion of style to include fashion spreads of menswear and advertising for body products targeted at men as well as women.

The style press exercised two key kinds of influence, then—first in opening up space for fashion/lifestyle magazines aimed at men and secondly in pioneering radically new ways of representing male bodies. Arguably, however, the two 'problems' that industry people had identified did not disappear. Their residues are clearly visible in contemporary men's magazines. Anxieties about how to address heterosexual men were resolved in two ways: first through the adoption of a 'laddish' tone which enabled male editors and journalists to address readers as 'mates', and secondly through an almost hysterical emphasis on women's bodies and heterosexual sex juxtaposed alongside avowedly homoerotic photographs. As Tim Edwards (1997) has argued, this allowed magazines to appeal directly to a gay readership whilst still defensively asserting the heterosexuality of their readers.

4 Retail power: masculinity goes to the mall

The rise of the style magazines can in turn be understood in terms of massive changes in the economy that were taking place in the 1980s. There was a dramatic decline in manufacturing and a rise in the service sector and retailing —itself producing a 'genderquake' (Wilkinson, 1994). The employment of increasing numbers of people within the retail sector was, however, just one of a number of factors that were changing the structure and meaning of shopping and consumerism (Mort, 1996). There was a significant trend towards conglomeration within clothes retailing, with five or six companies controlling the high street by the end of the 1980s; a growth in out-of-town shopping; and shopping began to be promoted as a major cultural or leisure activity—with the opening of large themed shopping centres, the provision of crèches and restaurants in shopping centres, and the promotion of trips to large out-of-town stores as a relaxing day out. Indeed, studies consistently find that shopping is the main leisure activity of the British (eg, Cultural Trends, 1998; Miller, 1995; Miles, 1996).

Another key shift was evident in the growth of marketing and the displacement of a selling orientation (selling what is already made) by a marketing orientation (making what will sell) (Edwards, 1997; Wernick, 1991).

In the 1980s the 'new man' became a new target for fashion companies—men were the new market (Edwards, 1997; Hession, 1997). This was heralded as a quiet revolution in fashion companies—as men had been considered a market that was difficult to crack, and shopping had hitherto been seen as a traditionally female pursuit. The move was associated with the meteoric rise of a few companies—most notably Next and the Burton group. Next, in particular, launched in 1986, borrowed images of the city and of share dealing and city gents for its clothes—striped shirts, brogues, double breasted suits. As such it was trading on images that were circulating elsewhere through the privatization campaigns, the Big Bang, as well as in major 'zeitgeist' films like *Wall Street* (1987). Frank Mort (1988) argues that Next was important for allowing men to *play* with these images without commitment. Where once clothes had been powerful and stable signifiers of social location, increasingly they were worn in more flexible and playful ways, such that men could 'try on' new identities through their apparel—perhaps working as a labourer throughout the week, but dressing like a share-room dealer to go out in the evening, and wearing 'outdoor casual' at weekends (Edwards, 1997; Mort, 1996).

5 Punk and after

Frank Mort (1988;1996) argues that this new playful relationship between clothes and identity was the result of a series of changes that took place in 1970s, provoked in part by punk music and style. With its emphasis on bricolage—the putting together of things that are normally kept apart, for example, Doc Martens and ballet dresses—punk created a space for men and women to be able to play with different self-presentations and broke down stable chains of signification, such that it was no longer straightforwardly possible to read off social location from particular ways of dressing.

There is little research exploring the connections of contemporary music with representations of masculinity, yet it would seem obvious that musical styles have a profound effect upon the ways in which masculinity is codified and lived. In relation to the 'new man' it is striking to note how the waves of music that gained popularity in the late 1970s and early to mid-1980s (ie, at the moment when 'new man' emerged as a discourse and regime of representation) all encoded challenges to traditional masculinity in the dress and style of their male artists, such as the sexual ambiguity of Boy George and Prince and the soft femininity of the New Romantic movement.

6 Gay liberation and the pink economy

As with feminism, it is hard to overestimate the impact of the gay liberation movement—post-Stonewall—on the construction of the figure of the 'new man'. One avenue for this influence has been on visual representations of the male body in popular culture. Magazines aimed at gay men, together with pinups and particular subcultural styles within the gay club scene, have had a profound effect upon representations of masculinity, through a routing that has gone from gay porn through art house photography to advertising (Parsi, 1997). Whilst there is considerable anger within parts of the gay community about the ways in which homoerotic images have been appropriated and commodified by straight media/marketing/retailing worlds, there has also been much excitement about the ways in which men are literally re-visioned in popular culture (Edwards, 1997; Simpson, 1994). In particular, the mainstreaming of selected gay representational practices served to cleave apart the automatic association of masculinity with heterosexuality, and the elision of masculinity with activity, by showing men not only as active sexual subjects, but also as objects of desire.

This in turn impacted upon the heterosexual scopic orders. Suzanne Moore (1988) has argued that it was precisely the growing visibility of eroticized representations of men outside the gay media that facilitated or gave permission for a new kind of gaze among women. She suggests that this constituted a major disruption to heteronormative politics of looking—in which old assumptions about subject/object, active/passive were challenged. Rather than simply being objects of the gaze, women have become active subjects who can look as well as being looked at. An important literature in film and photography studies deals with the ways in which representations of masculinity are designed to disavow homoeroticism: using the 'reassuring' presence of a woman as love interest, excessive violence or humour as their main means (eg, Neale, 1983; Cohan and Hark, 1993; Tasker, 1993). (And this constitutes perhaps an alternative reading of the preoccupation with 'gore' in magazines like *FHM*—see Benwell, introduction, and Rutherford, 2000). It also details the punishment meted out to women in film whose sexuality is deemed too active or independent. Moore's argument is that this shift made both the disavowal and the punishment redundant and facilitated more egalitarian sexual relations between men and women.

Another impact of gay politics upon the emergence of 'new man' is through its influence on retailing and consumerism. As Tim Edwards (1997) has pointed out, gay men tend to have higher disposable incomes than straight men and this can have a disproportionate effect on markets for all kinds of products. Their buying patterns also differ as consumption can be used to signify and reinforce sexual orientation.

Finally it is worth pointing to the significance of gay male culture in the wake of HIV/AIDS for any understanding of 'new man'. As well as having a devastating effect on the lives of tens of thousands of gay men, HIV and AIDS has also been important in generating new representations of masculinity in the West. One representation—seen best in the flourishing artistic and cultural activity which the crisis produced (see Griffin, 2000)—is of masculinity as loving, caring and nurturing, exemplified by the many men who have cared for partners and friends while they are living or dying with HIV. This offered a powerful alternative vision of masculinity—to heterosexual and bisexual as well as gay men—which differs markedly from hegemonic understandings of what it means to be a man.

The 'new lad'

1 A backlash against feminism

The dominant way of understanding the emergence of new lad is as part of a backlash against feminism. From this perspective the figure of the new lad, constructed around knowingly misogynist and predatory attitudes to women, represents a refusal to acknowledge the changes in gender relations produced by feminism, and an attack upon it. Imelda Whelehan argues that the new lad is 'a nostalgic revival of old patriarchy; a direct challenge to feminism's call for social transformation, by reaffirming—albeit ironically—the unchanging nature of gender relations and sexual roles' (2000: 5). He represents, then, a defensive assertion of masculinity, male power and men's rights against feminist challenges.

In a similar vein, Suzanne Franks has argued that as women's roles and identities have changed and expanded into domains previously thought of as male, 'new lad' represents a response which moves men further into the heartlands of masculinity—rather than blurring gender identities. In this sense, the new lad seems clearly to be part of a backlash against feminism across multiple sites and domains (cf Faludi, 1991). The growth of a number of conservative men's movements, organized around the assertion of fathers' rights after divorce, emerged at the same moment to attack feminism and use equal opportunities legislation to attempt to reinstate male power and privilege (eg, UK Men's Movement, Families need Fathers, Million Men movement).

As Peter Jackson, Nick Stevenson, and Kate Brooks (2001) point out, however, it would be a mistake to read 'new lad' *only* in terms of a backlash against feminism. They draw on Barbara Ehrenreich's analysis of the success of *Playboy* magazine to argue that new lad's individualistic, hedonistic, pleasure-seeking attitude must also be understood as a reaction to and rebellion against the figure of the male as 'breadwinner' and family provider (see also Segal, 1990). In this context the 'new lad' offers a refuge from the constraints and demands of marriage and nuclear family. He opened up a space of fun, consumption and sexual freedom for men, unfettered by traditional adult male responsibilities.

Jackson *et al.* (2001) suggest that 'new lad' may be a more ambiguous figure than straightforward backlash accounts suggest. Perhaps a useful analogy may be made with the rise of 'muscular heroes' in action cinema during the late 1980s and early 1990s (eg, Arnold Schwarzenegger, Sylvester Stallone and Bruce Willis). One reading of the state of action movies at this time was that they were classic 'backlash texts', which were concerned with bolstering hegemonic masculinity in the service of right-wing US foreign policy under Reagan and Bush. Moreover, they seemed to threaten to erase women from acting roles in films altogether. However, an alternative reading put forward by Yvonnne Tasker (1993) is that the films should be understood in terms of the difficulty of maintaining masculine physicality in the microchip era. Thus the muscular masculinities on offer *simultaneously reassert, mourn* and *hysterically state* male power, whilst also *parodying* it.

My own inclination would be to caution against going too far down this route of textual openness in relation to the new lad: we do not, after all, live in a semiotic democracy, and there are only so many ways in which new lad's misogyny can be read. Nevertheless, Tasker's insights about the *polysemic* nature of texts of masculinity and the *contradictory factors* that produce them are valuable ones to remember.

Another argument for not viewing new lad purely as a backlash against feminism is that his construction is also a response to and attack upon new man. That is, he is born of debates within/among masculinities as well as those between women and men. Elsewhere (Gill, forthcoming) I have looked in detail at 'obituaries' of the new man and the announcement of the birth of the new lad in newspapers in the US, UK and Australia throughout the 1990s. These birth and death announcements frequently occur in the same texts, given the prevalence of the cultural narrative that new lad displaced new man. What these texts (mostly written by new lads and their female champions) have in common—besides their viciousness and chillingly reactionary politics—is a widely shared analysis of the multiple problems or pathologies of new man. One set of criticisms is frequently directed at the *narcissism* of new man: 'grooming is for horses', opined James Brown in an early editorial of *loaded*. Interestingly, almost as common are attacks on new man's *lack of concern for his appearance* (see below). A further criticism (often made by female journalists) is of the asexual nature of new man. Jo Ann Goodwin, writing in the *Guardian*, pulls together these two criticisms in a scathing article about 'new man' as the 'toxic waste of feminism':

> The worst of it is that these men are so unappealing, so unaesthetic, so unsexy. Once you see through the dubious charm of someone 'who really understands women', what you are left with is a man whose clothes are appalling, and who is so busy trying to be supportive he has probably forgotten what an erection is for. (*Guardian*, February 13, 1993)

Finally, 'new man' is condemned as inauthentic. In these accounts, in a somewhat strange ontological move, the final nail in his coffin is the fact that he never really existed at all! He was, alternately, a media fabrication or marketing strategy or a calculating pose by ordinary men in order to get a woman (or women) to sleep with them. Against the duplicity of this figure, new lad is constructed as refreshingly honest and free from artifice: he knows what an erection 'is for' and he is not afraid to use it!

2 Media productions of new lad

Although new lad can be seen or heard across a variety of media, there seem to be three domains that have played a key role in constructing and promoting this form of masculinity: men's lifestyle magazines, the hybrid news/sport/quiz/talk shows on television, and 'zoo' radio. Most attention has been given to the role

of magazines in producing new forms of masculine subjectivity—examining ideologies, visual economies, and the kinds of subject position on offer.

There is now a growing body of work which charts the development of
'laddism' in magazines from 1990 onwards (Jackson *et al.*, 2001; Nixon, 2001;
Crewe, this volume). The shift first appeared in *GQ* and *Arena* in 1991, marked
by an increase in sexualized representations of women and a more 'assertive
articulation of post permissive heterosexual masculine scripts' (Nixon, 1996:
203). In a characteristically reflexive move, one of the first attempts to make sense
of this new masculine identity was itself published in *Arena* magazine (O'Hagan,
1991). Part sociological analysis, part 'ladifesto', this article sought to expose the
'myth' of the sensitive, caring and non-sexist new man, and celebrate the arrival
of his hedonistic, libidinous, postfeminist alter ego. The arrival of *loaded*
magazine on the scene in 1994, however, gave laddism its most distinctive voice,
dedicated, according to its first editorial letter, to 'life, liberty and the pursuit of
sex, drink, football and less serious matters' (*loaded*, Issue 1, May 1994).

Since *loaded*, *Arena*, *FHM* and *Maxim* are explored in detail elsewhere in this
book, I will not elaborate upon them here but merely wish to point to their
pivotal role in constructing a powerful discourse of 'laddism' which kicked off
against feminism, the figure of the new man and also older (unreconstructed or
Neanderthal) lad identities.

Radio has received far less attention than television or magazines as a site
where the new lad is produced and reproduced. Yet 'zoo' formats (imported from
the US in the 1980s and which break up the monologue of typical DJ shows)—
best exemplified in the UK by Steve Wright, Chris Evans and Chris Moyles—
were implicated early in new laddism using fast talk, multiple characters,
quizzes, true stories and many other postmodern devices to obscure or distance
themselves ironically from the underlying sexism. Many of the so-called 'talkie
bits' in shows were deliberate attempts to simulate male pub banter; the 'weath-
ergirl' could be used as a device for the new lad presenter to bounce his witty
remarks off; and the disparate, fragmented nature of zoo shows allowed a
myriad of politically reactionary ideas to enter the programme's discourse
unquestioned. Steve Wright, for example, regularly featured surveys that 'reveal
facts' like men's resentment of their family's dependence upon them (described
by Wright as 'meal ticket syndrome') or women's secret appreciation of being
whistled at by builders. In fact, close analysis of the (apparently merely) 'wacky'
or 'zany' fragments that make up zoo radio shows reveals that there was a clear
political subtext organized around right-wing populism, laddish sexism, homophobia and a highly exclusionary notion of (white) Englishness in shows broad-
cast in the period 1986 to 1990 (Gill, 1993) which clearly prefigured the rise of
the new lad in magazines.

3 Psychology: Neo-Darwinism and interplanetary communication

If psychology played a role in producing the figure of new man, then it has also
been equally important in the emergence of the new lad. Perhaps the biggest

shift can be seen in the rise of evolutionary thinking within psychology during the 1990s/noughties. Sociobiology and evolutionary psychology were previously confined to small, specialized fields of psychology and, in the wake of outrage over attempts to link 'race' and intelligence in the 1970s, were regarded as marginal and politically suspect. However, the promise of a 'genetics revolution' made possible by the mapping of the human genome, unleashed a wave of interest in evolutionary thinking in the 1990s. One effect of this was to threaten the entire basis of psychology as a discipline, as the topics associated with 'the mind' were recoded in terms of biochemical/neurological 'events' in the brain.

More significant—in terms of thinking about masculinity—is that an evolutionary psychology, often based on extrapolations from studies of animals, gained increasing prominence and publicity. Founded on the premise that all behaviour has an evolutionary basis, this social Darwinist work is preoccupied with gender and 'sexual selection'. It employs exaggerated and stereotypical descriptions of male and female behaviour and seeks to demonstrate how this is underpinned by sound evolutionary principles. The image of the male to emerge from this writing is not dissimilar from the new lad: testosterone driven and motivated by a desire to 'spread his seed' among as many women as possible. Moreover, it is notable that exponents of 'laddism' frequently draw upon evolutionary psychological ideas to justify their conviction that men are 'beyond reform' and need to simply accept the fact that they are subjects of their natural impulses (eg, lad magazines frequently invoke these discourses). In doing so, they draw support from writers like Robert Wright, who attacks feminism for 'doctrinal absurdities' and argues that in short 'human males "are by nature oppressive, possessive, the flesh-obsessed pigs"' (Wright, 1996, quoted in Segal, 1999: 82). In turn, Stephen Pinker explains the evolutionary basis for 'men behaving badly': 'A prehistoric man who slept with 50 women could have sired 50 children, and would have been more likely to have descendants who inherited his tastes. A woman who slept with fifty men would have had no more descendants than a woman who slept with one. Thus, men should seek quantity in sexual partners; women, quality—a source of protection, resources and good genes for their children' (Pinker, quoted in Bordo, 1999: 230).

Psychological writing at the populist end of the market has also played a major part in producing/allowing space for new lad. The last decade has seen a return to essentialist accounts of gender as a way of making sense of the apparently intractable problems between women and men. Bookstore shelves are groaning under the weight of these volumes which consider myriad aspects of human experience. The chief exponent is John Gray who has given traditional sexism a psychological gloss in his ever expanding *oeuvre* putting forward the view that men and women are creatures from different planets. Gray does not appear to believe that men and women share a single characteristic but, nevertheless, argues that they can form good relationships if they acknowledge their difference. This means accepting that when it comes to sex, for example, men are like blow torches (they heat up fast and turn off in an instant), whereas women are like conventional ovens, slow to heat and slow to cool down. Meanwhile, in emotional terms, men are like rubber bands (he needs to pull away before he can get closer), while women's self esteem follows the movement of the tides.

As Susan Bordo (1999) has pointed out, Gray's work has spawned a whole industry of men generously sharing the secrets of male psychology with women. From this perspective, the new lad appears archetypal of normal masculinity—simply a man who refuses to accept the false and feminized ideal of masculinity that women have sought to thrust upon him.

4 Publishing: lad lit and chick lit

The 'equal but different'/ Mars and Venus approach to gender has also been at the heart of a contemporary publishing phenomenon: the arrival of 'chick lit' and 'lad lit'. While gender and genre have long been interrelated, the late 90s saw the explicit codification of this in publishers' and booksellers' categories. Chick lit got its founding mother in Helen Fielding, whose *Bridget Jones* novel (1996) established the genre, and 'new lad' was hailed by Nick Hornby's *High Fidelity* (1995) and the work of Irvine Welsh and Tony Parsons. Today, there are any number of pretenders to the throne of 'lad lit', including Mike Gayle, Tim Lott and Nick Earl. Clearly, there are significant differences among these writers, and Hornby's later work, particularly *How To Be Good* (2001), with its female protagonist, no longer fits this genre.

Every aspect of such books, from the colour and design of the cover to where and how they are advertised, follows rigidly prescribed gender lines. The rise of chick lit and lad lit was underwritten by changes in the political economy of publishing—the collapse of the Net Book Agreement and the explosion of discount book 'clubs', increasingly using gender as the central tool in their marketing strategy and attempting to establish the clear blue water of gender difference between 'his 'n' hers' books.

The protagonists of lad lit are heterosexual men in their late 20s or early 30s who are 'on the make'—pursuing women, alcohol and football, looking back nostalgically upon childhood and youth and forward apprehensively to commitment, marriage and children. Anti-aspirational, inept, optimistic and self-deprecating, the heroes of lad lit mirror precisely James Brown's vision of *loaded* as 'for the man who believes he can do anything, if only he wasn't hungover' (*loaded*, 1994: 3). Elaine Showalter describes David Baddiel's second novel, *Whatever Love Means* (2000), thus:

> The novel begins on the day of Diana's death, with a statement meant to shock: 'Vic fucked her first the day Diana died'. Baddiel's laddish protagonist has hayfever and persuades the woman that his reddened eyes are tokens of his tears of grief; she goes to bed with him believing that he is a sensitive New Man who shares her emotions. In fact, Vic scores while England mourns. 'At first Vic thought he was just exploiting one individual's grief, but then he realized he was exploiting the whole nation's . . . he felt like each day was a bank holiday' (2002: 25).

This cynical and knowing performance of new mannishness notwithstanding, Showalter argues that Baddiel's novel and others in the lad lit genre represent a coming of age or settlement with 'adult' concerns, which is frequently expressed in terms that recognize that the 'freedoms' of the lad have costs or that the important things in life are difficult. In this sense, their discourse about hetero-sexual relationships can be seen to have clear resonances with the ambivalence expressed in the lad mags (see Stevenson *et al.*, 2000).

5 Football, television and masculinity

No discussion of the emergence of the new lad would be complete without an understanding of the role football has played in this. Football is not only one of the salient interests/pursuits of the 'new lad' as he is usually presented, but it is also implicated—as a multi-million pound industry—in the construction of this masculine subject.

Top-level professional football in Britain has undergone a number of wide-ranging changes over the last decade: the political economy of the League has been restructured; many grounds have been rebuilt to replace stands with all-seater stadia; and a set of deals have been established between football clubs and television companies with reverberations that led to the collapse of the channel ITV digital in 2002. These changes have transformed the meaning and experience of football and are complexly related to changing representations of masculinity.

The rebuilding of many stadia in the 1990s in the wake of the disasters at Heysel (Brussels) and Hillsborough (Sheffield) has transformed the experience of football for many fans. As the terraces or stands have been replaced by seating, many clubs have attempted to reinvent football as a 'family friendly' game, with particular efforts to attract more affluent audiences, more women and children. In fact, the size of female audiences has remained relatively static over the last 15 years but the image of the game has changed, meaning that many traditional male fans needed to find new ways to express their own dis-tinctive fandom. In this context an accentuated 'laddism' can form a bulwark against what may be perceived as 'feminisation' of the game.

If the association between football and a particular kind of masculine soli-darity is seen as under threat by these changes, the working-class audience has also found itself increasingly marginalized by dramatic increases in ticket prices. Together with a number of direct and indirect forms of exclusion and control (for example rationing of tickets, restriction of particular areas of the stadium, being forced to sit down when large groups had got up to cheer, etc.) this was experienced by many fans invested in 'masculine' identity as a betrayal of their love of their team (King, 1997). Against this, then, a series of attempts to defend particular styles of masculine fandom can be read as part of the project of preserving authentically masculine practices of football consumption (including singing, drinking and ecstatic solidarity) in the face of increasing commodification.

This too is evidenced in the commercialization of the game, heightened merchandizing activity, the growth of a 'celebrity culture' around Premiership players, and the globalization of the transfer market, challenging local affiliations. All these have impacted upon the meaning of football fandom and have offered different subject positions for male football fans to occupy. In this way, then, we can see that football is not simply one of new lad's interests but has also been profoundly important in his very constitution.

6 Libidinous heterosexuality after HIV and AIDS

Earlier in this chapter I explored the significance of HIV and AIDS in promoting a new model of masculinity: the new man. Here I want to argue that popular responses to HIV and AIDS also played a part in constructing new lad (see Baker, this volume). One important general representational shift in response to HIV and AIDS has been the production, since the late 1980s, of more explicitly sexualized and eroticized imagery of both men and women. This was partly a response to the inadequacy of early government health promotion campaigns (eg, Britain's 'Don't die of ignorance' promotion, dominated by large icebergs) and partly as a reaction against the sexual puritanism that HIV and AIDS seemed to threaten.

One impetus behind the emergence of the new lad in the late 1980s was the desire to retrieve sex-as-fun from the 'shadowlands' of HIV. In this sense it was part of a libidinous, life-affirming refusal to equate sex with death. One fact which may be read as a sobering outcome of this shift, however, is the steep decline in condom use among heterosexual men, compared with their gay counterparts. It is notable that campaigns directed at the heterosexual population have been much less successful in promoting safer sex practices, perhaps because of entrenched inequalities in gender relations (Holland *et al.*, 1997), the failure to produce an adequate 'erotics of health promotion' (Wilton, 1992), and also the discourses of risk-taking and hedonistic pleasure of 'new laddism' itself which are difficult to sustain alongside the notion of 'love safe, love sexy'—and may ultimately have devastating consequences.

Conclusion

In the first part of this chapter I set out a new theoretical approach for studying masculine identities, arguing that a Foucaultian emphasis upon power and the production of subjects was important if we were to avoid reifying or essentializing the figures of new man or new lad. I stressed the point that new man and new lad were best thought of as discourses, rather than as representations of any real men. In the second part of this chapter I attempted to follow this up by producing a tentative genealogy of new man and new lad discourses. This has been rather dissatisfying to write, since the attempt to give a sense of the range of different influences upon the production of new man and new lad discourses has rendered the account cursory and list-like. What I have tried to convey overall is the *diversity* of different influences upon discourses of new man and new lad, and to locate the studies of men's magazines that follow within this broader context.

More significant than any one of the influences discussed, however, to understanding the circulation of new man and new lad discourses, has been the rise of the new cultural intermediaries, discussed at the start of this chapter. We have become a culture preoccupied with interpreting itself—discovering or producing meaning in anything and everything. Legions of professionals now exist whose role it is to pick over and analyse every aspect of human behaviour from the bedroom to the street, to find or create a pattern in what they see, and to narrate the story of who we are back to us in compelling new terms. In this hyper-reflexive moment a single event may be random, but two instances of it are highly suggestive and three constitutes a major trend—whether that trend relates to male 'bad lad' pop stars getting married, celebrity women in their 40s having babies, or magazines closing down.

The new cultural intermediaries (of whom academics constitute one group) have been crucial to the emergence and persistence of discourses about the new man and new lad because they have obsessively searched for meaning in the changes in men's lives and sensibilities and refracted these repeatedly through stories of the dramatic tension between these two versions of masculinity. As the new lad is increasingly being represented as passé and tired, we can confidently expect new cultural intermediaries to be at the forefront of producing new masculine subjects for the 21st century.

Acknowledgedments

I would like to thank David Evans, Rachael Lille, Andy Pratt, Bethan Benwell and one anonymous referee for their help in the preparation of this paper.

References

Archer, L. (2001) 'Muslim brothers, black lads, traditional Asians: British Muslim young men's construction of race, religion and masculinity', *Feminism and Psychology* 2(1): 79–106.

Back, L. (1994) 'The "white Negro" revisited: race and masculinities in south London': in Cornwall, A. and Lindisfarne, N. (eds) *Dislocating Masculinity: Comparative Ethnographies*. London: Routledge.

Beck, U. and Beck-Gershiem, E. (1995) *The Normal Chaos of Love*. Oxford: Polity Press.

Beynon, J. (2002) *Masculinities and Culture*. Milton Keynes: Open University Press.

Chapman, R. and Rutherford, J. (1988) *Male Order: Unwrapping Masculinity*. London: Lawrence and Wishart.

Cohan, S. and Hark, T.R. (1993) *Screening the Male—Exploring masculinities in Hollywood Cinema*. London, New York: Routledge.

Connell, R. (1987) *Gender and Power: Society, the Person and Sexual Politics*. Cambridge: Polity Press.

Crewe, B. (2003) 'Class, masculinity and editorial identity in the reformation of the UK men's press' (this volume).

Edley, N. and Wetherell, M. (1997) 'Jockeying for position: the construction of masculine identities', *Discourse and Society* 8(2): 203–217.

Edwards, T. (1997) *Men in the Mirror: Men's fashion, masculinity and consumer society*. London, Cassell.

Faludi, S. (1991) *Backlash: The Undeclared War Against Women*. London: Chatto and Windus.

Faludi, S. (1999) *Stiffed: The Betrayal of the Modern Man*. London: Chatto and Windus.

Featherstone, M. (1995) *Consumer Culture and Postmodernism*. London: Sage.

Foucault, M. (1979) *Discipline and Punish*. Harmondsworth: Penguin.

Foucault, M. (1980) *Power/Knowledge: Selected Interviews and other Writings 1972–1977*. C. Gordon (ed.). Brighton and New York: Harvester Wheatsheaf.

Foucault, M. (1987) *The History of Sexuality*, Vol. 2. Harmondsworth: Penguin.

Franks, S. (1999) *Having None of it: Women, Men and the Future of the Work*. London: Granta.

Frosh, S., Phoenix, A. and Parrman, R. (2001) *Young Masculinities: Understanding Boys in Contemporary Society*. Basingstoke: Palgrave.

Frosh, S., Phoenix, A. and Pattman, R. (2000) 'Cultural contestations in practice: white boys and the racialisation of masculinities': in Squire, C. (ed.), *Culture in Psychology*. London: Routledge.

Giddens, A. (1991) *Modernity and Self Identity: Self and Society in the Late Modern Age*. Cambridge: Polity Press.

Gill, R., Henwood, K. and McLean, C. (2000) 'The tyranny of the "sixpack": understanding men's responses to idealized male body imagery'. In Squire, C. (ed.) *Culture in Psychology*. London: Routledge

Gill, R. (forthcoming) *Gender, Media Representations and Cultural Politics*. Cambridge: Polity.

Gill, R. (forthcoming) 'Mobile positionings in audience responses: not just a matter of gender, "race" and "class".' Under submission to *Media, Culture and Society*.

Gill, R. (1993) 'Ideology and popular radio: a discourse analytic approach', *Innovations in Social Science Research* 6(3): 323–339.

Gill, R., Henwood, K. and McLean, C. (in press) 'Body projects: masculinity, identity and body modification', *Body and Society*.

Griffin, G. (2000) *Visibility Blue/s: Representations of HIV and AIDS*. Manchester: Manchester University Press.

Hartley, J. (2002) 'The value chain of meaning: from cultural studies to creative industries?' Plenary address to Crossroads in Cultural Studies conference, Tampere, Finland June 29–July 2.

Henwood, K., Gill, R. and McLean, C. (1999) 'Masculinities and the Body: Mapping Men's Psychologies.' Report Prepared for Unilever.

Henwood, K., Gill, R. and McLean, C. (forthcoming). ' Transgressions', *The Psychologist*.

Hearn, J. and Morgan, D.H. (1990) *Men, Masculinities and Social Theory*. London: Unwin Hyman.

Hession, C. (1997) 'Men's grooming: The next growth catgeory.' pp. 57–60.

Holland, J., Ramazonoglu, C., Sharpe, S. and Thompson, R. (1997) *The Male in the Head*. London: Tufnell Press.

Jackson, P., Stevenson, N. and Brookes, K. (2001) *Making Sense of Men's Magazines*. Cambridge: Polity Press.

Kimmel, M. (1987) *Changing men, New direction on research on men and masculinity*. Newbury Park, CA: Sage.

King, A. (1997) 'The Lads: masculinity and the new consumption of football', *Sociology* 31(2): 329–346.

MacInnes, J. (1998) *The End of Masculinity*. Buckingham: Open University Press.

Majors, R. and Billson, J. (1992) *Cool Pose: The Dilemmas of Black Manhood in America*. New York: Lexington.

Maslow, A. (1970) *Motivation and Personality*. New York: Harper and Row.

Miles, S. (1996) 'The cultural capital of consumption', *Culture and Psychology* 12(3): 139–158.

Miller, D. (ed.) (1995) *Acknowledging Consumption*. London: Routledge.

Moore, S. (1988) 'Here's Looking at You Kid!': in Gamman and Marshment (eds) *The Female Gaze—Women as Viewers of Popular Culture*. London: The Women's Press.

Mort, F. (1988) 'Boys Own? Masculinity, style and Popular Culture': in Chapman and J. Rutherford (eds) *Male Order: Unwrapping Masculinities*. London: Routledge.

Mort, F. (1996) *Cultures of Consumption: Masculinities and Social Space in Late 20th Century Britain*. London: Routledge.

Neale, S. (1983) 'Masculinity as spectacle: reflections on men and mainstream cinema', *Screen* 24(6).

Nixon, S. (1996) *Hard Looks: Masculinities, spectatorship and contemporary consumption*. London: UCL Press.

Nixon, S. (2001) 'Re-signifying masculinity: from "new man" to "new lad"': in Morley, D. and Robins, K. (eds) *British Cultural Studies*. Oxford: Oxford University Press.

O'Donnell, M. and Sharpe, S. (2000) *Uncertain Masculinities: Youth, Ethnicity and Class in Contemporary Britain*. London: Routledge.

O'Hagan, S. (1996) 'Here comes the new lad': in Jones, D. (ed.) *Arena: sex, power, and travel*. London: Virgin Books.

O'Hagan, S. (1991) 'Here comes the New Lad!' *Arena*, May.

Parsi, N. (1997) 'Don't worry Sam, You're not alone: Bodybuilding is so queer': in Moore, P. (ed.) *Building Bodies*. New Brunswick: Rutgers University Press.

Rose, N. (1991) *Governing the South: The Shaping of the Private Self*. London: Routledge.

Rose, N. (1999) *The Powers of Freedom*. London: Routledge.

Segal, L. (1999) *Why Feminism?* Cambridge: Polity.

Segal, L. (1990) *Slow Motion: Changing Masculinities, Changing Men*. London: Virago.

Seidler, V. (1989) *Rediscovering Masculinity: Reason, Language and Sexuality*. London: Routledge.

Seidler, V. (1992) *Men, sex and relationships: writings from Achilles Heel*. London: Routledge.

Showalter, E. (2002) 'They think it's all over', *New Statesman*, August 12th.

Simpson, M. (1994) *Male Impersonators: Men Performing Masculinity*. London: Cassell.

Stevenson, N., Jackson, P. and Brookes, K. (2000a) 'The politics of "new" men's lifestyle magazines', *European Journal of Cultural Studies* 3(3): 366–385.

Stevenson, N., Jackson, P. and Brooks, K. (2000b) 'Ambivalence in men's lifestyle magazines': in Jackson, P., Lowe, M., Miller, D. and Mort, F. (eds) *Commercial Cultures: Economies, Practices, Spaces*. Oxford: Berg.

Tasker, Y. (1993) *Spectacular Bodies: Gender, Genre and the Action Cinema*. London: Routledge.

Walkerdine, V., Lucey, H. and Meldogy, J. (2001) *Growing up Girl: Psychosocial Explorations of Gender and Class*. Basingstoke: Palgrave.

Wernick, A. (1991) *Promotional Culture*. London: Sage.

Whelehan, I. (2000) *Overloaded: Popular Culture and the Future of Feminism*. London: Women's Press.

Wilkinson, H. (1994) *No Turning Back: Generations and Genderquake*. London: Demos.

Williamson, J. (1978) *Decoding Advertisements: Ideology and Meaning in Advertising*. London: Marion Boyars.

Wilton, T. (1997) *Engendering AIDS: Deconstructing Sex, Text and Epidemic*. London: Sage.

Woolgar, S. and Pawluch, D. (1985) 'Ontological gerrymandering: the anatomy of social problems explanations', *Social Problems* 32: 214–227.

A pedigree of the consuming male: masculinity, consumption and the American 'leisure class'

Bill Osgerby

'Esquire means simply Mister—the man of the middle class. Once it was the fashion to call him Babbitt, and to think of him as a wheelhorse with no interests outside of business. That's very outmoded thinking, however. For today, he represents the New Leisure Class'. (Arnold Gingrich, 'The Art of Living and the New Leisure Class', promotional pamphlet for the launch of *Esquire* magazine, 1933, cited in Arnold Gingrich, *Nothing But People: The Early Days at* Esquire—*A Personal History*, 1928–1958, New York: Crown, 1971: 102–3).

Masculinity and the 'Art of Living'

The Christmas of 1937 found Arnold Gingrich in buoyant mood. As editor of *Esquire*, the first American periodical to bill itself explicitly as a 'Magazine For Men', Gingrich used his preface to the seasonal edition to reflect on the title's runaway success. In the four years since its launch, Gingrich proudly announced, *Esquire*'s circulation had grown to over half a million, while the magazine regularly picked up five million additional readers who were captivated by its mix of 'love and laughter, vanity and variety, courage and curiosity, wonder and weeping and, even now and then, reverence and reflection' (*Esquire*, January 1937: 5). More than any of these, however, it was the magazine's consumerist agenda that stood out. *Esquire*'s forté lay in what Gingrich termed 'the Art of Living'. Combining colour illustrations of the latest men's fashions with regular features on foreign travel, cuisine and interior décor, *Esquire* encouraged its readers to think of themselves as autonomous men of taste who expressed their identities and status through the purchase of distinctive goods and signifiers.

The success of *Esquire* during the 1930s, however, sits somewhat incongruously alongside much recent scholarship dealing with the relationship between masculinity and consumption. In the late 1980s and early 1990s, on both sides of the Atlantic, many theorists highlighted what appeared to be new promotional cultures and commercial markets geared to a new generation of style-conscious male consumers. In America, for example, Diane Barthel (1988) identified a 'new', middle class man who was preoccupied with hedonistic pleasures and the purchase of consumer goods, while in Britain, influential work by Frank Mort (1988; 1996), Sean Nixon (1996) and Tim Edwards (1997) charted the rise of a narcissistic and self-conscious 'New Man' associated with an array of new, glossy lifestyle magazines and advertising campaigns. As Edwards observed, however, it was misleading to see the narcissistic masculine consumer as unique to Britain during the 1980s and 1990s, and there was a need to locate contemporary archetypes within a much longer history of men's active and overt practices of commodity consumption (Edwards, 1997: 92). This chapter, then, is an attempt to map out a broader pedigree for the consuming male, outlining configurations of masculine consumerism that anticipated (and in some respects laid the way for) the more recent archetypes of the 'New Man' and 'New Lad' discussed by the other contributors to this volume.

Models of masculine consumerism may have been especially visible at the end of the 20th century but this chapter argues that the distinguishing features of the consuming male had already taken shape a hundred years earlier and had become clearly recognizable by the 1930s. Moreover, while these developments were identifiable in Britain, it is argued that they were more pronounced and better established in the US. In America, masculine archetypes oriented around the personal pleasures of consumerism existed in embryonic form within the bachelor subcultures of the *fin-de-siècle* metropolis and subsequently found fuller expression among the fashionable bucks of the Jazz Age. It is argued, furthermore, that this rise of a hedonistic, masculine consumer was constituent in a wider transformation of American middle class life that saw the emergence of a new cultural habitus that privileged leisure, pleasure and personal 'liberation' through consumption—an emphasis on the 'art of living' that was to become increasingly pervasive amid the consumer boom of the 1950s and 1960s.

Men, women and chainstores: histories of gender and consumption

Since the 1980s a rich body of research has charted the historical relationship between consumption and female identity. Focusing on the late 19th century, authors such as Elaine Abelson (1992), Rachel Bowlby (1985; 2000), William Leach (1984), Erika Rappaport (2001) and Judith Walkowitz (1992) have all highlighted the pivotal role of women in the emergence of modern consumer culture. In this canon, the rise of the department store is seen as central to the 'commercial revolution' that transformed commodity consumption from a mundane act of subsistence into a spectacular bourgeois leisure pursuit. From this perspective, the grandeur and glamour of department stores provided the key context in which 'shopping' developed into a feminine realm of visual pleasure and public cultural practice:

> Their splendid new buildings and permanent exhibitions of lovely new things brought middle-class women into town to engage in what was historically a new activity: a

day's shopping. They were places of leisure and luxury, offering women the image of a life that they could then, in fantasy if not in substance, take home with them. (Bowlby, 2000: 7).

This developing world of consumerism is generally seen as having had a contradictory impact on women's lives. The new economic opportunities opened up by the expansion of retailing, for example, were often more apparent than real— many women finding employment only in low-skilled occupations or in deskilled jobs previously done by men. Modern consumerism's emphasis on desire and display also had mixed ramifications. Perceived by consumer industries as a commodified market, women were 'addressed as yielding objects to the powerful male subject, forming, and informing them of, their desires' (Bowlby, 1985: 20). At the same time, however, women were not simply the passive victims of the cunning commercial machine. The rise of department stores and the growth of shopping as a cultural practice also offered women an important dimension of public freedom that held possibilities for the articulation of more independent feminine identities. The interplay between the rise of the consumer society and the emergence of women's public cultures, therefore, is viewed ambivalently by critics. Yet there is one thing on which there has been strong agreement. Consumer practice developed as a pre-eminently *feminine* province. This gendering of modern consumerism has been widespread and influential—exemplified by Bowlby's avowed assertions that it is 'an empirical fact' that by the early 20th century women had emerged as the 'principal consumers' (1985: 27), and that 'the history of shopping is largely a history of women, who have overwhelmingly been the principal shoppers both in reality and in the multifarious representations of shopping' (2000: 7).

In contrast, men have been presented as relatively marginal to the development of modern consumerism. Bowlby, for example, identifies a bi-polar split between 'masculine' and 'feminine' forms of cultural practice that is 'constructed in terms of oppositions between work and leisure, rationality and emotion, practicality and the "instinct" for beauty' (1985: 11). This is a dichotomy between 'feminine' consumption and 'masculine' production that informs many accounts of the historical development of masculine identities.

Studies of the development of American masculinities during the 19th century, for instance, have dwelt heavily on the rise of the breadwinner archetype and the production-oriented ethos of the 'self-made man'. E. Anthony Rotundo, for example, presents the middle-class man of the late 19th century as a figure characterized by his pursuit of enterprise, productiveness and temperate respectability (Rotundo, 1993: 55). In family life, too, it is American men's *productive* role that has usually been highlighted. Many historians have contended that, while the 'separation of spheres' in the 19th century middle-class home demanded of women commitment to homemaking and domesticity, of men it required a dedication to providing for one's family.[1] Michael Kimmel, for example, draws attention to the emergence of the term 'breadwinner' between

1810 and 1820 (Kimmel, 1997: 20), the phrase denoting an ideal of mature and hard-working masculinity which dictated that men should deny themselves in order to provide for their wives and families.[2]

A similar set of preoccupations has also been highlighted in the historical development of British masculinities. A plethora of research on Victorian 'manliness', for example, has focused on the codes of hard work, self-control and vigorous independence that were central to dominant codes of British masculinity during the late 19th century.[3] For John Tosh (1994), meanwhile, masculinity has had multiple social meanings at various historical moments, though Tosh sees these as having been largely determined by the balance struck between three key cultural components—the home and maintenance of family life; work (the premier location for a man's expression of his individuality); and the array of all-male associations that provide men with privileged access to the public sphere. Again, then, it tends to be processes of production, work and responsibility (rather than consumption, display and pleasure) that are perceived as the defining characteristics of masculine identities.

In many respects this historical delineation between a 'feminine' realm of consumption and a 'masculine' realm of production is justified. The close affinity that developed during the late 19th century between constructions of femininity and modern consumerism ensured that the institutions and practices of commodity consumption were a problematic territory for men. At a time when, both in Britain and America, masculine ideals were widely perceived to be besieged by the rise of anonymous bureaucracies, declining opportunities for individual enterprise and the transformation of family structures and gender relations, any interest in the pleasures of consumption risked being interpreted as a socially unacceptable dalliance with the feminine 'Other'. Indeed, throughout the 20th century the feminine connotations to consumer desires and practices remained pronounced—a persistence which ensured that narcissistic and self-conscious consumption remained an uncertain field for masculine identities keen to establish their credentials of solid, heterosexual manhood.

Nevertheless, while the 'feminine' associations that have historically surrounded consumerism and its pleasures must be acknowledged, it would be misleading to see this as a field from which men have been totally (or even largely) excluded. Hegemonic masculine identities may have stressed production, the work ethic and the responsibilities of family life but, as Tosh points out (1994: 192–3), dominant articulations of masculinity have always had to contend with competing masculine identities. And in this narrative of negotiation and struggle over the 'meanings' of masculinity, a male personality predicated on narcissistic and leisure-oriented modes of consumption possesses a long and connected history. Absorbed in cultural codes so closely bound up with feminine associations, this consuming male sometimes came close to compromising his claims to sturdy 'manliness'. Yet his engagement with consumer pleasures and stylistic display was always carefully mediated, his milieu of hedonistic consumption painstakingly signposted as a bastion of robust heterosexuality.

The growing recognition that 'masculinity' is a multiform, mobile and historically variable construction has led the way for a number of studies spotlighting the development of masculine identities outside the hegemonic, production-oriented archetypes. In particular, a number of scholars have begun to uncover a degree of masculine involvement in the development of commodity culture much greater than hitherto acknowledged. In these terms, while feminist scholarship charting the pivotal role of women in shopping, department stores and other matrices of modern consumption has made an invaluable contribution to our understanding of the development of commodity culture, this work has tended to obscure the historical presence of men in the fields of fashionable display and consumer practice. In response, historians such as Christopher Breward (1999) have sought to reveal 'the hidden consumer'. In his analysis of menswear retailing in Victorian London, Breward clearly demonstrates the existence of a relationship between masculinity, fashion and hedonistic consumption during even the earliest manifestations of modern consumerism. As Breward himself points out, such research should not be seen as competing against, or overturning, established work on the historical construction of femininity, yet it certainly challenges any over-simplified account of fashionable consumption as an exclusively feminine domain (Breward: 1999: 8). Outside Britain, a history of other 'hidden consumers' can also be charted. In America, in fact, the greater pace and intensity of the development of a consumption-based economy ensured that men's immersion in the world of consumer experience was especially pronounced.

Dudes, gangsters and playboys: the perils and pleasures of masculine consumption

In the late 19th century American cities quickly grew into centres of commercial leisure and commodity consumption, offering many young, single women opportunities for carving out important cultural space. As Kathy Peiss argues, '[d]ancing sensual dances, attending cabarets and nightclubs, living as "bachelor girls" in apartment houses, these women expressed a new-found sense of freedom and possibility' (Peiss, 1987: 185). But men, too, enjoyed the fruits of Victorian commodity culture.

Masculine identities premised on hedonistic leisure and narcissistic display were not unprecedented. Geoffrey Ashe (2000), for example, chronicles a rich history of libertine, male excess in 17th and 18th century Europe, while during the early 19th century Beau Brummell and his fellow dandies enthralled fashionable English society and the *flâneur* meandered through Parisian arcades. In America, meanwhile, the late 19th century saw Thorstein Veblen (1899) identify a privileged 'leisure class'—men of substance who celebrated their cultural ascendance through proud displays of 'conspicuous consumption' in the spheres of fashion, leisure and social ritual. Beyond this 'leisure class' élite, however, there emerged other configurations of masculinity also distinguished by their predilection for hedonistic consumerism. By the end of the century, for example, many urban workingmen—both white and African American—were also embracing models of masculinity that privileged personal consumption. Making a virtue of stylish display, these 'mashers' and 'b'hoys' (as they were known) were prominent figures in urban centers of commercial leisure. Generally, however, consumption related to personal pleasure remained an uncertain territory for men. During the late 19th century, markedly feminine associations still surrounded consumerism, exemplified by the prominence of the dandy—or, as he was often known, 'the dude'—as a stock character in popular humour.

The dude was typically conceived as a young man, upwardly mobile and debonair, who sauntered through the bustling city streets. In some instances the term was used as an almost amiable epithet. Through his good looks and dapper clothes, for example, President Chester Arthur (holding office between 1881 and 1885) was dubbed 'The Dude President', while the turn of the century saw dilapidated Western cattle farms turned into 'Dude Ranches'—fashionable resorts where wealthy Easterners played at being cowboys. Yet a sense of ambivalence always surrounded the figure of the dude. The term itself probably stemmed from German-American usage, a likely derivation of the expression *duden-kopf*, meaning idiot or blockhead, and the dude was often configured as a negative stereotype whose flamboyance was absurdly effete. For example, a humorous trade card advertising a Michigan general store of the 1880s depicts the dude as a ridiculous ostrich—a study in foppish vanity as he preens before a mirror (see Figure 1). Distinguished by his flashy appearance and self-conscious urbanity, the dude was invariably a figure of ridicule and in popular culture was generally derided as an unmanly 'pussyfoot' (Paoletti, 1985: 129; White, 1993: 16). Over time, however, the dude's brand of style-conscious élan was to become more acceptable as the forces of commercialism and commodity consumption increasingly permeated middle-class masculine cultures.

By the late 19th century, America's developing urban centres were already drawing men into a diverse field of consumerism and commercial entertainment. Alongside the working-class 'mashers', many middle-class men were also embracing a culture based on personal consumption and there steadily emerged a variety of businesses geared to their interests. At the seamier end of the scale were brothels, bloodsports and other illicit pleasures but also significant were an array of businesses that catered to men's consumer demands. Indeed, Howard Chudacoff (1999) argues that an extensive 'bachelor subculture' formed around the network of eating houses, barber shops, tobacconists, tailors, city bars, theatres and array of other commercial ventures that thrived on the patronage of affluent, young 'men about town'. Mark Swiencicki (1998) paints a similar picture. For Swiencicki, traditional histories have been woefully inadequate in their elision of the male consumer. *Fin-de-siècle* American men, he maintains, were 'hardly the stridently ascetic beings that separate spheres historians presumed them to be' (1998: 781). Instead, Swiencicki draws on data from the 1890 US Census of Manufacturers to show that men incorporated a lavish brand of

Figure 1: *'The Dude at his Toilet'—Trade card advertising a Michigan general store, c. 1880s*

consumerism into their daily lives, men consuming about twice as many recreational and leisure goods as women and spending about 30 per cent of disposable family income in the process (1998: 796). At the same time, however, Swiencicki acknowledges a powerful 'gendering' in definitions of this consumer practice. Discourses of heterosexual masculinity dictated that men carefully distance themselves from the 'feminine' connotations of 'shopping'—so that whatever commodities women purchased and controlled were defined as 'consumer goods', whereas those purchased by men were accorded 'manly' (and more prestigious) status by being labeled 'expenditure' (1998: 792).

Generally, cultural codes that celebrated indulgent leisure were at odds with dominant values—particularly in the world of the 'traditional' middle class, where an emphasis on family life, the work ethic, moderation and probity were core values.[4] Developing during the 18th and 19th century, this worldview retained strong influence into the 20th century and found particular voice in the prohibition movement that prompted the Volstead Act in 1920. Yet Prohibition was always more of an ideal than a reality and, in the city nightlife of speakeasies and cabarets, a culture dominated by the pleasures of stylish consumption continued to grow. And, against this backdrop, there appeared a new masculine archetype that encapsulated both the allure and the perceived dangers of the developing consumer society—the gangster.

By the 1920s America had emerged as a fully-fledged consumer economy and in this context the figure of the gangster, like film stars and other glamorous celebrities of the age, showcased the possibilities for fulfilment and display offered by the new consumerism. With his expensive suits, tuxedos, spats and jewelry, his luxurious mansion and taste for fashionable nightlife, the gangster was, David Ruth argues, 'an oversized projection of the urban America seduced by the promises of consumption' (1996: 69). According to Ruth, throughout the 1920s and 1930s the gangster image was used by writers and filmmakers (and their audiences) as an avenue through which to explore the abundance of goods transforming American society—the gangster's stylish extravagance offering a glimpse of the new paths to individual fulfilment apparently opened up by the consumer economy. As well as embodying the promise of the new consumerism, however, the gangster also signalled its dangers. The gangster's prodigious wealth seemed to indicate that economic mobility was blurring distinctions of class, while the ease with which he mixed with leading citizens in restaurants, bars and night-clubs suggested an unnerving effacement of conventional distinctions between the respectable and the disreputable (Ruth, 1996: 81–5). As a masculine archetype, then, the 1920s gangster offered an ambivalent commentary on the rise of consumerism. Commodity consumption was constructed as offering the potential for sensual pleasure and individual fulfilment—though at the risk of undermining traditional value systems and social structures.

The gangster's combination of ostentatious display and deviant criminality underlined the suspicions that still surrounded consumerism during the 1920s.

Yet the popular fascination with his image and style also attested to a gradual acceptance of masculine identities predicated on consumer desires. The earlier archetype of the dude had invariably been an object of scorn, his commitment to fashion and the comforts of city life seen as effeminate and unmanly. But, as the 20th century progressed, a leisure-oriented consumer ethos became better established within dominant mores and lifestyles, a shift that brought with it articulations of masculinity whose associations with hedonistic consumption were more pronounced (and more socially acceptable) than their predecessors.

In the world of male fashion, for example, the early 20th century saw the development of a new, leisure-oriented aesthetic. Indicative was the rise of the 'Arrow Man' as a fixture in advertisements for Arrow shirts from 1905 onwards. A model of well-groomed and chisel-jawed masculinity, the 'Arrow Man' became the first in a series of youthful and stylish masculine archetypes whose virile muscularity guaranteed a fashionability untainted by suspicions of effeminacy. The Progressive Era also saw an identifiable 'collegiate' or 'Ivy League' style of dress take shape. Clothing firms such as Campus Leisure-wear (founded in 1922), together with the movie, magazine and advertising industries, gave coherence to this smart-but-casual combination of button-down shirts, chino slacks, letter sweaters, cardigans and loafers—a leisure-style that steadily reached out from the campus into the wider male population.

During the 1920s the ideal of a young, vibrant and avowedly consumerist masculinity was also a recurring *leitmotif* in American literature. *The Great Gatsby* (1925) is especially noteworthy. F. Scott Fitzgerald's most famous novel was an exploration of the power and pitfalls that accompanied American ideals of self-creation and success. Yet, in the enigmatic playboy, Jay Gatsby, Fitzgerald also created a character who personified important shifts in the dominant culture of 1920s America. In his palatial home, fabulous parties and expensive clothes, Gatsby was emblematic of America's growing fascination with consumption, glamour and opulent leisure, the character embodying the emergence of a new masculine style defined by a sense of youthful and narcissistic hedonism. Indeed, in all his literary creations, Fitzgerald caught the essence of a new, vivacious generation revelling in a world of consumer pleasure, sexual freedom and hectic leisure, while the author himself came to personify the lush, fast-paced lifestyles his novels depicted.

Consumption-oriented models of American masculinity, then, did not suddenly materialize in the late 20th century. Instead, there exists a much longer history of masculine identities formed around stylistic display and the pleasures of consumerism. His roots lying in the consumer society that arose in the late 19th century, the style-conscious, male consumer was given greater cultural definition and legitimacy during the 1920s as he was steadily codified and courted by the institutions of the expanding commercial market. Ironically, though, it was during the 1930s—a decade that saw the most severe economic depression in American history—that the 'consuming male' took fuller form.

'Talking shop with *Esquire*': consumption, style and masculinity in the 1930s

By the 1920s, strain was already detectable in the hegemony of the production- and family-oriented ethos that denoted respectable American manhood. Published in 1922, for example, Sinclair Lewis' satirical novel, *Babbitt*, portrayed an image of hollow, middle class convention in the character of George F. Babbitt. A Republican and Rotarian, Babbitt was a middle-aged, hard-nosed businessman whose individuality had been suffocated by the miasma of bourgeois conformity. In Babbitt, Lewis depicted a middle-class masculinity stultifying in its fixation with work and the trappings of decorum—his satire touching a popular nerve, as 'Babbittry' became a byword for a middle-class masculinity made shallow and banal through its obsession with respectability.

It was, however, the Great Depression that brought the 'breadwinner ethic' to its knees. Between 1929 and 1933, gross national product fell by roughly 30 per cent and industrial production was halved as unemployment levels soared to 13 million. For men whose identity cohered around their role as breadwinner, unemployment was an especially crushing, even emasculating, experience. Many came to see themselves as humiliated failures, robbed of the ability to support their families by forces beyond their control.[5] The masculine universe of style and leisure was also badly hit. As real income fell by 36 per cent between 1929 and 1933, the dollar volume of sales by men's clothing retailers dropped by 49 per cent and the number of actual stores plummeted by 40 per cent (Corbin, 1970: 340). Nevertheless, even during the Depression's darkest days, the ethos of the narcissistic male consumer endured—and in some respects positively thrived.

In Autumn 1933—a year in which a quarter of the American workforce were unemployed—the first edition of *Esquire* magazine testified to the survival of an up-market culture of fashion and leisure among those who had escaped the blight of the Depression. *Esquire*'s owners, David Smart and William Weintraub, had started out in publishing during the 1920s, producing promotional catalogues for men's fashion stores. But, as the economic downturn bit into their sales, the duo looked for business alternatives. In September 1931 they came up with *Apparel Arts*, a lavish quarterly magazine that combined high-class fashion pictorials with evocative editorial features and the occasional documentary photospread. Popular as both a trade paper and as a catalogue for clothes retailers, *Apparel Arts* also proved a hit with store clientele—customers sometimes walking off with copies after leafing through their pages. Encouraged by this response, Smart and Weintraub drafted in Arnold Gingrich (chief editor of their catalogues) and the trio began to envisage a magazine aimed more squarely at the store customer.

Billing itself as 'The Magazine For Men', *Esquire*'s high production values and large, colourful format ensured a hefty cover price of fifty cents. But industry expectations that the magazine would flounder were quickly defied. The 105,000 copies of *Esquire*'s first edition soon sold out and, though originally projected as a quarterly, the magazine went monthly with its second issue, circulation soaring to more than 728,000 by 1938 (Merrill, 1995: 45; 51).

As Kenon Breazeale observes, *Esquire*'s grand strategy was to 'organize a consuming male audience' (Breazeale, 1994: 1). From the outset, *Esquire* stood aloof from masculine identities predicated on hard work, thrift and production, Gingrich crafting the magazine into the peerless arbiter of cosmopolitan finesse. At the centre of the formula was a reverence for tasteful elegance. Alongside copious advertisements for high-class menswear, *Esquire* featured its own colourful illustrations of the fashionable man in his natural habitat—'A Day at the Anglers' Club, Key Largo'; 'To Palm Beach via the French Riviera'—the sharp captions and crisp text (mostly furnished by Gingrich himself) trumpeting the latest trends in masculine attire.[6] Around this core of sartorial *savoir-faire*, *Esquire* developed a wider universe of taste and refinement. Staple ingredients were coverage of fashionable nightlife, 'exotic' travelogues and features on gourmet cuisine and chic furnishings—all underlining the magazine's appeal to a readership of affluent and leisure-oriented middle-class men (see Figure 2). Prominent, too, were *Esquire*'s literary pretensions. The magazine's first issue included contributions from (among others) John Dos Passos, Erskine Caldwell and Dashiell Hammett, while subsequent editions featured bylines from numerous Pulitzer and Nobel prizewinners. Regular contributions from F. Scott Fitzgerald, meanwhile, further emphasized *Esquire*'s dedication to the spirit of 'living as an art'.

As Tom Pendergast (2000) recognizes, *Esquire* was not the first American magazine to address a consuming male subject. During the late 19th century, general feature magazines such as *McClure's*, *Munsey's* and *Saturday Evening Post* were initially based around the Victorian masculine ethos of hard work, thrift and production—though Pendergast argues they also tentatively embraced models of masculinity constructed around commodity consumption. The early 20th century, meanwhile, saw magazines such as *Vanity Fair* (originally launched in 1892) and *New Success* (1918) offer visions of masculinity based even more explicitly around a consumerist agenda that encouraged men to think of themselves 'not as objective cores of values but as . . . malleable potentialities, capable of achieving multiple expressions through the goods they purchased and the way they presented themselves' (Pendergast, 2000: 140–2). For Pendergast, the significance of *Esquire* lay in the way it successfully pulled together these earlier fragments of masculine consumerism into 'a coherent representation of a modern masculine ideal' (Pendergast, 2000: 28).

From the beginning, *Esquire* modelled itself as the antithesis of 'Babbittry'. In promotional material for his new magazine, Gingrich presented *Esquire* as the bible for 'a New Leisure Class' of insouciant males. The New Deal, Gingrich averred, had 'given leisure a new economic significance, and the five-day week has become not merely every man's right but virtually every man's duty. More time to read, more time to indulge in hobbies, to play, to get out of town—

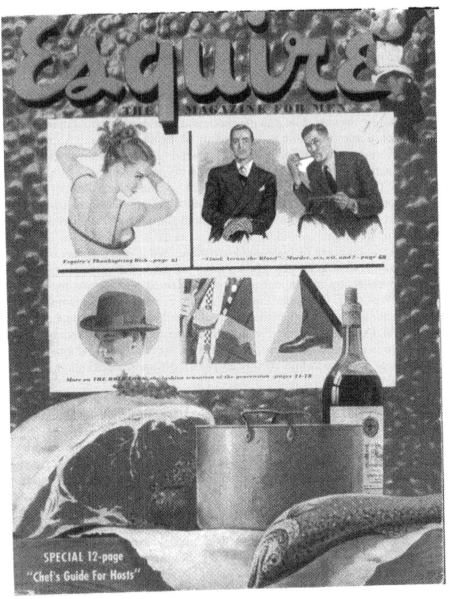

Figure 2: *'The Magazine for Men'*—Esquire, *Vol. 30, No. 5, November 1948*

more time, in short, to think of Living as an art, as well as a business' (cited in Gingrich, 1971: 102–3). And in this vein *Esquire* not only accorded routine coverage to the more exclusive avenues of relaxation (golf, motoring, game fishing and so on) but also included a regular 'shopping' department—'Talking Shop

With *Esquire'*—with advertisements for pipes, ties, ice-buckets and a variety of trinkets geared to the sybaritic man of means.

The realms of fashion and consumption, however, remained uncertain territory for men. Times had changed since the caricature of 'the dude' had caustically ridiculed the style-conscious male as unacceptably effete but the fields of fashionable consumption and display continued to have markedly feminine associations. As M.M. Lebensburger observed in 1939, in his trade manual, *Selling Men's Apparel Through Advertising*:

> Because women are so obviously and notoriously interested in personal appearance and style there is a feeling common among men that any demonstration of this same interest on their part is an indication of effeminacy [and] . . . an outward manifestation of distaste for style or indifference to style is, therefore, considered the mark of masculinity (cited in Merril, 1995: 32).

Esquire, moreover, not only potentially jeopardized its readership's self-image by venturing into fields closely associated with feminine social roles—fashion, cookery and home furnishing. The assiduous eye its style-spreads cast over the male form also risked charges of homoeroticism. Authors such as Denise Kervin (1991) have contended that it was only in the 1980s that the male body was constructed as an erotic spectacle in fashion advertising and features. And, certainly, the visual codes deployed by *Esquire* and its advertisers during the 1930s did not fetishize the male body quite as overtly as their 1980s counterparts. In fact, based around watercolour illustrations rather than photography, *Esquire's* fashion coverage can be seen as deliberately trying to disassociate itself from modes of 'direct' representation that might hint at a voyeuristic gaze. Nevertheless, while *Esquire's* fashion 'models' struck manful poses and looked out impassively from the pictorials, they remained the (sometimes quite sexualized) objects of the reader's gaze (see Figure 3). And the very act of configuring the male form as a visual exhibit created a space in which the heterosexual assumptions central to dominant articulations of masculinity were vulnerable to rupture.

Indeed, this was something of which *Esquire's* editorial team were well aware. There always existed potential for *Esquire's* representations of the male body to be co-opted by a homoerotic gaze, while the feminine associations of fashion and consumption made them precarious territory for articulations of masculinity anxious to avoid intimations of effeminacy. But Gingrich and his associates worked hard to limit the 'danger'. In his editorial introduction to the first edition of *Esquire*, for example, Gingrich was emphatic that the new magazine would 'never intend to become, by any possible stretch of the imagination, a primer for fops' (*Esquire*, Autumn 1933: 4). Instead, Gingrich reassured readers that his editorial judgments over content and presentation would allow *Esquire* 'to take on an easy natural masculine character—to endow it, as it were, with a baritone voice' (*ibid.*). And, in moulding the magazine's format, Gingrich went to great lengths to include elements that were (as the editor later euphemistically put it) 'substantial enough to deodorize the lavender whiff coming from the mere presence of fashion pages' (Gingrich, 1971: 81). In line with this policy,

Figure 3: *'The Riviera's Latest in Beach Undress'*—Esquire, *Vol. 4, No. 1, July 1935*

the 1930s saw *Esquire* carefully signpost its credentials to sturdy machismo through regular coverage of sports like baseball and boxing, together with frequent articles on daredevil pursuits such as big-game hunting and bullfighting. Indeed, significantly, the cover of the magazine's first edition made little overt reference to matters of style or fashion. Instead, a watercolour tableau depicted two flying-suited adventurers embarking on an exciting hunting expedition. Ruggedly masculine imagery also surfaced in many of the magazine's general articles and short stories—not least in those written by literary tough-guy Ernest Hemingway, a regular *Esquire* contributor.

Surveying *Esquire*'s early development, Breazeale notes other strategies through which the magazine strived to 'displace all the woman-identified associations so firmly lodged at the center of America's commodified domestic environment' (Breazeale 1994: 6). Risqué cartoons and titillating pin-ups, for example, underscored the magazine's claims to unwavering 'manliness' and established resolute heterosexuality as an incontrovertible given within the *Esquire* universe. Using its 'baritone' elements to secure its status as an unquestionably masculine and heterosexual text, therefore, *Esquire* was free to address its readers as unabashedly style-conscious consumers, steering them 'safely' through the provinces of visual pleasure and consumer practice.

Nor was *Esquire* alone in appealing to men as narcissistic consuming subjects. *Esquire*'s success prompted several imitations. In 1937, for example, the publishers Fawcett launched *For Men*, a pocket-sized magazine pitched at a middle-class, male market. Heavy on text, however, it lacked *Esquire*'s lively pizzazz. Closer to *Esquire*'s brand of glossy fashion and opulent leisure was *Bachelor*, also launched in 1937 (see Figure 4). *Bachelor* professed to be 'mirroring the varied interests of the discerning cosmopolite [sic]' (April 1937: 3) and, like *Esquire*, was replete with features on style and the glamorous good life. *Bachelor*, however, dispensed with the pin-ups, sports coverage and other 'baritone' elements with which *Esquire* secured its heterosexual status. Instead, *Bachelor* was more dilettante in tone, with close attention to the arts (especially photography and the theatre) and regular profiles of young men who were up-and-coming in the worlds of design and drama ('Presenting This Month's Bachelor of the Theatre'; 'A Portfolio of Bachelors of the Arts'). *Bachelor*'s fashion sensibilities, too, were less insistently 'baritone'. In contrast to *Esquire*'s subtle watercolours, *Bachelor*'s style coverage paraded the male form in chic photo features whose homoerotic codings were more candid (see Figure 5). In some respects *Bachelor* might even be seen, in part, as an early attempt to tap into an emerging gay consumer market. It was, however, a project ahead of its time. While a masculine consumer subject clearly existed in America during the 1930s, the feminine associations of fashion and commodity consumption remained pronounced. As a consequence, *Bachelor*—bereft of *Esquire*'s reassuringly heterosexual trademarks—struggled to win a significant market and survived for only a handful of editions.

During the 1930s, then, commodity culture remained an uncertain field for masculine identities in America. Nevertheless, as the success of *Esquire* demonstrates, providing the route was carefully signposted as masculine and hetero-

Figure 4: Bachelor, *Vol. 1, No. 5, August 1937*

sexual, it was quite possible for men to step into the world of consumerism and narcissistic style. There was, however, always a 'mythic' quality to *Esquire*'s visions of sybaritic consumption. Within its pages a fantasy was created that few readers could actually attain. Yet, as Graham Dawson perceptively observes, masculine identities 'are lived out in the flesh, but fashioned in the imagination'

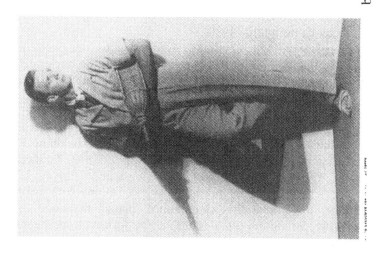

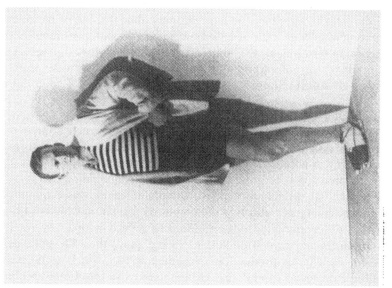

Figure 5: *'Late Vacation Styles'*—Bachelor, *Vol. 1, No. 5, August 1937: 39; 42*

(1991: 118). In these terms, *Esquire*'s world can be seen as an aspirational fantasy but one that registered material impact, through furnishing upwardly-mobile, male consumers with a repertoire of cultural codes and meanings—or an 'imagined identity', to use Dawson's (*ibid.*) term—which made intelligible their relationship with style, desire and commodity culture. In this way, therefore, *Esquire* served both to organize and to legitimate the growth of a consumption-oriented masculine self in America during the 1930s.

In Britain, a comparable—though perhaps less prominent—'imagined identity' also existed. During the 1930s British magazines such as the pocket-sized *Lilliput*, launched by the Hulton Press in 1937, blended humour, short stories, general features and discreetly airbrushed nude pictorials in a recipe geared to a male readership. According to Jill Greenfield and her associates, however, it was another pocket-sized title—*Men Only*—that represented 'the first British attempt at the commercial orchestration of masculinity via the medium of a men's lifestyle magazine' (Greenfield, O'Connell and Reid, 1999: 458). Launched by Pearson in 1935, *Men Only* had a format paralleling that of *Esquire*. Like *Esquire*, Greenfield *et al.* argue, *Men Only* combined style features with pictorials of female nudes and articles that championed 'heroic' manhood in a way that allowed the promotion of a consumption-oriented masculinity untainted by suspicions of effeminacy. Significantly, Greenfield *et al.* locate this construction of masculinity within a broader transformation of the British middle class, whose former emphasis on a public, masculine rhetoric of national pride they see as gradually giving way to a new, private discourse of domesticity and consumption (Greenfield, O'Connell and Reid, 1999: 461). In the US, the growing profile of the consuming male can also be related to wider shifts within the middle class as it adjusted to the growing pervasiveness of commodity culture.

Here, the work of French cultural theorist Pierre Bourdieu is instructive. In *Distinction* (1984), his analysis of changes in the fabric of French bourgeois culture, Bourdieu argues that after 1945, France saw the rise of a new form of capitalist economy in which power and profits were increasingly dependent not simply on the production of goods, but also on the continual regeneration of consumer desires. To sustain its survival, Bourdieu argues, this economic order demanded the emergence of a new socio-cultural formation which championed the cause of commodity consumption and judged people 'by their capacity for consumption, their "standard of living" [and] their life-style, as much as by their capacity for production' (Bourdieu, 1984: 310). Lacking the economic, cultural or social capital that distinguished the traditional petite bourgeoisie, this new class faction established its own distinctive status by colonizing new occupations based on the production and dissemination of symbolic goods and services—Bourdieu coining the term 'cultural intermediaries' to denote the new petit bourgeois cohort that rose to dominate fields such as the media, advertising, journalism, fashion and so on. Moreover, in its quest to secure its class position and status, the new petite bourgeoisie broke away from the puritanical, production-oriented 'morality of duty' associated with the traditional middle class. In its place was elaborated an 'ethic of fun', a new 'morality of pleasure as a duty', in which it became 'a failure, a threat to self-esteem, not to "have fun"' (Bourdieu, 1984: 367). Bourdieu's original study was focused on developments in French society during the late 1960s but it is possible to see a similar shift taking place with the structure of the American middle class—though during a historical period much earlier than that Bourdieu identifies for France.

In America, the 'traditional' middle class ethos that prioritized hard work, moderation and probity was already losing some of its authority during the 1920s. Between the wars, the American economy's growing dependence on consumer demand brought with it a major expansion in the number of salaried managerial and technical workers and 'culture producers' of all kinds—administrators, journalists, advertisers and other professions whose economic role centred on the production and dissemination of symbolic goods and services. Like Bourdieu's 'new petite bourgeoisie', this emergent middle class faction elaborated their distinctive cultural identity through their skills in 'the art of living', their values and codes of behaviour laying an accent on stylistic self-expression, self-conscious display and (to use Bourdieu's terminology) an 'ethic of fun'. And it was within this new, middle-class culture that masculine identities posited on consumer practice became both more fully-formed and increasingly acceptable. The gendering of consumption as a feminine (and feminizing) cultural arena remained powerful and masculine involvement in the realms of commodity culture still courted suspicion. But, once their status as incontrovertibly heterosexual and 'baritone' was clearly designated, models of hedonistic, style-conscious consumerism became an increasingly acceptable (even desirable) masculine terrain.

'Entertainment for Men': masculinity, magazines and consumption during the 1950s and 1960s

After the Second World War, the transformation of the American middle class intensified as it adjusted to growing levels of affluence. The scale of US economic growth in the postwar period was phenomenal, gross national product soaring by 250 per cent between 1945 and 1960 as a steady growth in national purchasing power pushed the economy forward. Concentrated in the growing suburbs, much of the explosion in postwar consumption was family-centred. In some respects this helped reinforce traditional middle-class values and their associated gender roles, giving a new lease of life to the archetype of the male breadwinner and his ethos of responsibility and rectitude.[7] At the same time, however, the consumer boom was also attended by an exponential growth of the advertising industry, the media and the service sector—developments that laid the way for a major expansion of the 'new petite bourgeoisie' whose habitus was anchored on stylistic expression and commodity consumption. And, as this cosmopolitan and hedonistic middle-class faction came into its own, models of masculinity rooted in personal consumption and an 'ethic of fun' increasingly came to the fore. The traditional gendering of consumption as a feminine cultural practice retained power—hence a degree of suspicion still surrounded the consuming male's 'manly' credentials—but, within the culture of the new middle class, masculine identities posited on consumerist appetites became more pronounced and acceptable.

During the 1950s, therefore, earlier masculine excursions into the field of personal pleasure and commodity consumption were amplified and extended. A benchmark of the ascendance of this form of masculine identity was the phenomenal success of *Playboy* magazine. Launched on a shoestring budget in late 1953 by its publisher and editor, Hugh Hefner, *Playboy*'s monthly circulation skyrocketed to nearly a million a month by 1959 and soared to in excess of 4.5 million over the next ten years. Billing itself as 'Entertainment for Men', *Playboy*'s mix of nude pictorials and up-market lifestyle features clearly took inspiration from the formula pioneered by *Esquire* during the 1930s—indeed, since his school days, Hefner had been an avowed fan of the earlier 'Magazine For Men' and in 1951 had briefly worked in *Esquire*'s subscriptions department. Nor was Hefner alone in imitating *Esquire*'s approach.

Esquire itself struggled to find a sense of direction during the 1940s and 1950s. The magazine maintained an affinity with the masculine consumer, but by the 1960s it had found a new niche as a quality features magazine. The postwar period, however, saw a range of other titles adopt *Esquire*'s consumerist leanings. *True*, for example, had originally been a down-market 'true adventure' pulp magazine when it was launched by Fawcett Publications 1936. The mid-1940s, however, saw *True* gradually reconfigured as a working-class equivalent to *Esquire*, repackaging the formula of masculine consumerism for 'the hunting, beer and poker set' in an attempt to cash-in on lucrative advertising revenue (Pendergast, 2000: 208). The move proved a commercial masterstroke and in 1948 *True* became the first men's magazine with a circulation in excess of a million. Others also jumped on the consumer bandwagon. In 1951, for example, the Publisher's Development Corporation launched *Modern Man*. With features that were red-blooded and resolutely 'macho' ('Hickok: Hell's Own Marshall'; 'How to Run a Submarine'), the magazine was chiefly geared to the 'action man', though *Modern Man* also tentatively embraced up-scale consumption through its glossy presentation, regular 'shopping' coverage ('Gadget Corner') and features that addressed more elegant sensibilities ('The Ten All-Time Classic Cars'; 'Modern Art For Men').

Nonetheless, there can be little doubt that it was Hefner who most successfully retooled the *Esquire* format for a new generation of male consumers. As Gail Dines (1995; 1998) observes, *Playboy*'s sexual content was intrinsic to the magazine's appeal, the success of the magazine helping to secure the acceptability of pornography within the cultural mainstream. At the same time, however, *Playboy* amounted to more than slickly packaged porn. The magazine's features on fashion, leisure and lifestyle celebrated a masculine universe of consumption and narcissistic display—a universe where an 'ethic of fun' was prioritized, while domesticity and puritanical abstinence were anathema. Nevertheless, while the hedonistic male consumer was certainly better established than he had been in the 1930s, the 'feminine' associations of commodity consumerism and its pleasures remained pronounced. Moreover, a heightened cultural emphasis on marriage and family life in America during the Cold War ensured that any rejection of homemaking 'togetherness' in favour of a cosmopolitan single life risked added suspicions of sexual 'deviance'. Like *Esquire* before it, therefore, *Playboy*'s sexual content helped stake out the magazine as an unmistakably heterosexual text. As Barbara Ehrenreich puts it, 'the breasts and bottoms were necessary not just to sell the magazine, but to protect it' (1983: 51). Any suggestion of effeminacy carefully neutralized, *Playboy* offered its readers 'safe' passage into the realm of narcissistic and self-conscious consumption.

For Ehrenreich, *Playboy*'s success was a barometer of wider change. *Playboy*, she argues, represented a 'visionary bible' for a new breed of consuming male, its images of 'cozy concupiscence and extra-marital consumerism' heralding the rise of a new 'playboy ethic' that prioritized personal gratification in a sparkling world of endless consumption, leisure and lascivious indulgence (Ehrenreich, 1983: 43; 170–1). Yet, while Ehrenreich is justified in seeing the 1950s as a decisive moment in the evolution of consumption-based masculine identities, her account is unduly truncated. As we have seen, the distinguishing features of her 'playboy ethic' had first condensed in America long before the 1950s—existing in nascent form in the bachelor subcultures of the postbellum cities, then developing more fully amid the prosperity that followed the First World War. But, while the masculine culture of leisure and personal consumption celebrated in *Playboy* was not unprecedented, the sheer scale of the magazine's success testifies to the growing pervasiveness and acceptability of male identities predicated on hedonistic consumerism.

More broadly, the magazine furnished an ideal for living that corresponded with the cultural orientations of the 'new' middle class—a rising faction whose habitus (like that of Bourdieu's 'cultural intermediaries') eschewed production and self-denial in favour of consumption, style and an 'ethic of fun'.

Alongside *Playboy*, other popular cultural phenomena also championed archetypes of hedonistic masculine consumerism in America during the 1950s and early 1960s. In showbusiness, for example, movie stars such as Rock Hudson and Tony Curtis established a niche in roles as jet-set playboys, while a boisterous clique known as the 'Rat Pack'—Frank Sinatra, Sammy Davis Jnr, Dean Martin and their cronies—carved out a reputation for high-living and licentious horseplay. Prosperous and independent, hedonistic and irrepressible, the icon of the 'swinging bachelor' came to personify a masculine identity reconciled with the demands and desires of modern consumerism. Indeed, this was a cultural trope that Hugh Hefner exploited to the full, his magazine's soaring circulation serving as the launchpad for an international *Playboy* business empire that embraced publishing, movie production and a chain of nightclubs, casinos and hotels.

During the 1950s and early 1960s the 'swinging bachelor' made his presence felt throughout American popular culture. But it was in magazine publishing that he registered particular impact. By 1957 *Playboy* was already bragging that it was 'The Most Imitated Magazine in America' (*Playboy*: July 1957), the late 1950s seeing the launch of a host of competitors. *Esquire*'s publishers, for example, responded with a revamped version of *Gentlemen's Quarterly*. Originally published during the 1930s as a menswear trade journal, the magazine was revamped in 1957 as a high-class fashion magazine for the 1950s man of style. Closer to *Playboy*'s format were a roster of other titles, all pitched to roguish men of means. Launched in 1956, for example, *Gent* touted itself as 'An Approach to Relaxation' and was followed by *Gay Blade* ('For Men With a Zest for Living', also 1956), *The Dude* ('The Magazine Devoted to Pleasure', 1956), *Escapade* ('Pleasure for Everyman', 1956), *Nugget* ('Entertainment in a Lighter Mood', 1956), *Rogue* ('Designed For Men', 1956), *Hi Life* ('The Live-It-Up Magazine for Gentlemen', 1958), *Bachelor* ('The Magazine for the Young at Heart', 1959) and *Millionaire* ('You Don't Need to be a Millionaire—Just <u>Think</u> Like One', 1964). These titles had a slick and colourful presentation and a higher quota of sexual content than *Playboy*—though their production values were poorer overall and their circulations were measured in hundreds of thousands rather than *Playboy*'s millions.

Nevertheless, while the hedonistic ethos of the 'new bourgeoisie' was in the ascendant during the 1950s and early 1960s, it was less than hegemonic. *Playboy*'s strongest circulation, for example, was chiefly in the east, California and metropolitan enclaves in between. Elsewhere, the magazine fared less well. In fact *Playboy* was a centre of controversy throughout the 1950s and 1960s, facing opposition from both moral crusaders, who viewed its nude pictorials as lewd and indecent, and the growing feminist movement, who objected to the magazine's sexual exploitation of women. Indeed, the short life of Stanley Publications' *Satan* magazine shows there were limits to how far the 'playboy ethic' could be pushed. Launched in 1957, *Satan* ('Devilish Entertainment for Men') offered a *Playboy*-esque mixture of nude pictorials, ribaldry and sybaritic lifestyle features ('Satan Sets Up A Bachelor's Den'; 'The Epicurean Satan'; 'The Sartorial Satan') (see Figure 6). Perhaps, however, the magazine's title and allusions flaunted the libertine ideal a little too brazenly. *Satan* folded after just six issues.

Libertarian consumerist lifestyles, moreover, were largely the preserve of the white middle class. During the 1920s and 1930s, the emergence of a consumption-driven economy had depended on a largely white consumer market, most African Americans prevented from participating in the consumer spectacle by a combination of white racism and trenchant economic inequality. African American cultural forms such as jazz were championed by *Esquire* (and later *Playboy*) as a talisman of exciting 'Otherness' but, for most of black America, active involvement in the world of hedonistic consumption was out of the

Figure 6: *'Devilish Entertainment for Men'*—Satan, *Vol. 1, No. 2, April 1957*

question. Nevertheless, as the economic growth of wartime and postwar prosperity delivered improved incomes to many African Americans, black consumers
were slowly linked to the commercial marketplace. And, as this took place,
notions of black masculinity began to be reshaped to conform to the logic of

consumer culture. In the sphere of magazine publishing, for example, the dynamics of consumerism gradually registered on the way African American men were framed and addressed. Launched in 1945, for instance, *Ebony* was a general features title (modelled on *Life* magazine) geared to a general readership but which 'brought black men into the realm of modern masculinity' through the special attention it gave to African American men's tastes and consumption patterns—while its pictures of semi-clad African American women imitated the titillating pictorials that were a mainstay of *Esquire* (Pendergast, 2000: 209).

While *Playboy*'s appeal was tailored fairly exclusively to a white market until the late 1960s, other publishers were willing to follow *Ebony*'s lead in addressing African American men as stylish and upwardly-mobile consumers. The foremost example was *Duke* magazine, launched in 1957. Based in Chicago, *Duke* was a *Playboy* imitator along the lines of *Nugget* and *Dude*, though in *Duke* the mix of pin-ups and consumerism was expressly geared to 'the Negro man-about-town' (*Duke*, June 1957: 38). *Duke*'s pitch, however, was a short-lived experiment. During the 1950s the black middle class remained a relatively small group and, although *Ebony*'s success showed that change was underway, a significant market of affluent black consumers was still some years off. Only in the late 1960s did the playboy ethic became an accessible option for African American men, advertisers and entrepreneurs gradually responding to the new consumer market created through rising black incomes.

Compared with America, British masculine ideals of personal consumption and stylish individuality reached fruition more slowly. As Frank Mort (1997) argues, the development of British consumerism was slower, partial and more uneven than the American experience. The emergence of a 'playboy ethic' in Britain, therefore, was more hesitant and much less dramatic than in the US. Nevertheless, amid Britain's consumer boom of the late 1950s and early 1960s, similar articulations of masculinity were discernable. Mort's research on the Burton's fashion empire, for example, shows how this chain of men's clothes shops underwent profound change from the mid-1950s—the firm's image of formal and gentlemanly manhood being eclipsed by decor, advertising and products that foregrounded discourses of individuality, hedonism and consumer pleasure (Mort, 1996: 134–145; Mort, 1997: 19–22; Mort and Thompson, 1994).

Similar developments were also afoot in British magazines. *Men Only* and *Lilliput* had sold well during the war and in 1950 were joined by *Pall Mall*, its title quickly changed to *Clubman*. Mixing 'artistic' nude pictorials with film star pin-ups, humour and general features, *Clubman* declared itself 'Britain's favourite entertainment magazine for discriminating men'. As its title suggested, however, *Clubman* had a stuffy, parochial ambience redolent of pipesmoke and tweed. More influential was *Man About Town*. Launched in 1951 by *The Tailor and Cutter* (a long-established menswear trade journal), *Man About Town* was originally a pocket-sized quarterly intended to provide 'The What, When and How of Men's Clothes'. The magazine articulated a version of masculinity that was sophisticated and urbane (exemplified by its restaurant guides, fashion advice and travel features), yet was still securely anchored in the conservative and temperate ethos of the traditional city gent. Gradually, however, the magazine's content and mode of address became more upbeat and lively (see Figure 7). In 1961 the title was sold to Haymarket Press who abbreviated the title to *About Town* (and in 1962 simply to *Town*) and the magazine was transformed into a beacon of masculine hedonism in a 'happening' world of hectic consumption.

American titles also courted the British market. A British edition of *Esquire* was launched in 1954, though disappeared three years later, the title lying dormant until its revival in 1991 amid the renaissance of British men's magazine publishing. American product fared better during the 1960s with the launch of a British edition of *Playboy*, its circulation growing to 90,000 by 1972. In 1964, meanwhile, a home-grown paean to masculine high-living appeared with the launch of *King* magazine, though by 1967 sliding sales had forced a merger with *Mayfair* (a more explicitly pornographic title).[8] *Club* was another British failure. Launched in 1970 by publishing giants IPC, *Club* was glossy and colourful, brimming with features on football, sex, fast cars and fashion ('If You're Not Interested in Girls, Cars, Clothes, Action, Sex, Money, Sport—Then Don't Dare Look Inside'). Overtaken by a burgeoning range of pornographic titles, however, *Club* soon faded away. More successful was *Penthouse*. Consciously modeled as a British equivalent to *Playboy*, *Penthouse* was launched by publisher Bob Guccioni in 1965. Such was the magazine's success that in 1969 Guccioni decided to tackle *Playboy* on its home turf, successfully launching *Penthouse* onto the US market—and effectively selling the 'playboy ethic' back to its country of birth.

Cultural politics and the male consumer

Recent models of masculine consumerism, then, are constituent in a much longer heritage. The desires and practices of modern commodity culture may well have developed as a distinctly 'feminine' realm but it was never a world from which men were excluded altogether. In America, particularly, a pedigree for the consuming male can be traced back to the late 19th century, the lineage finding fuller expression between the wars—texts such as *Esquire* working to defuse the feminine 'stigma' of consumerism and legitimating a masculine archetype oriented around the pleasures of personal consumption. During the 1950s and 1960s, moreover, this consumer-oriented archetype became fully established as key sections of the American middle class embraced a culture of consumerism and individual gratification.[9]

Furthermore, in locating the rise of the 'masculine consumer' within the broader transformation of middle class cultures, a picture emerges that is rather different from some commentators' emphasis on a 'progressive' dimension to the interface between masculinity and consumer practice. For Mort and Nixon, for example, the visual codes of the promotional culture that ushered in the

Bill Osgerby

Figure 7: Man About Town, *Autumn–Winter, 1959.* Used with permission from Haymarket Press.

1980s 'New Man' worked to 'rupture traditional icons of masculinity' (Mort, 1988: 194), their display of masculine sensuality and sanctioning of staged narcissism 'loosening the binary opposition between gay and straight-identified men' (Nixon, 1996: 202), thereby making space for a plurality of more provisional masculine identities. Edwards, however, cautions against reading style-conscious masculine consumption as a necessarily progressive force. For Edwards, models of masculinity premised on consumption have potential to veer towards aspirationalism and conservative individualism and are 'as equally personally destructive and socially divisive as they are individually expressive and democratically utopian' (Edwards, 1997: 2). Indeed, the growing presence of narcissism and consumer practice in American masculine cultures did not, of itself, constitute an unequivocally progressive challenge to power structures of gender and sexuality. Masculine identities oriented around consumption certainly challenged established masculine codes and archetypes—especially the production- and family-oriented ideals associated with the traditional middle class. But, rather than being radical or transgressive, the rise of the masculine consumer is better seen as a transformative phenomenon—part of wider changes in the American social structure that saw the emergence of a new, middle-class faction with a habitus whose reverence for hedonism and style was tailor-made to modern capitalism's demand for an endlessly re-generating consumer market.

Notes

1 Kerber (1988) offers a thorough overview of research in this field, while Davidoff and Hall (1987) present a penetrating analysis of 'separate spheres' ideology within a specifically British context.
2 Accounts of the rise of the American 'breadwinner ethic' are provided in Gordon (1980), Griswold (1993: 10–33), Kann (1991: 198) and Mintz and Kellog (1988: 50–5).
3 A number of analyses of these models of masculinity can be found in Roper and Tosh (eds) (1991). See also Beynon's (2001: 26–52) survey of related literature.
4 For discussion of the nature and development of American middle-class culture during this period, see the various contributions to Bledstein and Johnston (eds) (2001).
5 Discussion of the impact of the 1930s Depression on models of American fatherhood is provided in Griswold (1993: 46–50).
6 An illustrated survey of *Esquire*'s fashion features during the 1930s and 1940s exists in Hochswender and Gross (1993).
7 For discussion of the growth of ideologies of family 'togetherness' and their associated gender roles in the US during the 1950s see May (1999) and Weiss (2000).
8 A similar fate befell *Men Only*. In the early 1960s the title was bought by Paul Raymond and was subsequently transformed into a pornographic magazine.
9 A more extensive consideration of American archetypes of masculine hedonism can be found in Osgerby (2001).

References

Abelson, E. (1992) *When Ladies Go A-Thieving: Middle-Class Shoplifters in the Victorian Department Store*. Oxford: Oxford University Press.

Ashe, G. (2000) *The Hell-Fire Clubs: A History of Anti-Morality* (2nd edn.). Stroud: Sutton.
Barthel, D. (1988) *Putting on Appearances: Gender and Advertising*. Philadelphia: Temple University Press.
Beynon, J. (2001) *Masculinities and Culture*. Buckingham: Open University Press.
Bledstein, B. and Johnston, R. (eds) (2001) *The Middling Sorts: Explorations in the History of the American Middle Class*. London: Routledge.
Bourdieu, P. (1984) *Distinction: A Social Critique of the Judgment of Taste*, trans. R. Nice. London: Routledge.
Bowlby, R. (1985) *Just Looking: Consumer Culture in Dreiser, Gissing and Zola*. London: Methuen.
Bowlby, R. (2000) *Carried Away: The Invention of Modern Shopping*. London: Faber and Faber.
Breazeale, K. (1994) 'In spite of women: *Esquire* magazine and the construction of the male consumer', *Signs* 20(1): 1–22.
Breward, C. (1999) *The Hidden Consumer: Masculinities, Fashion and City Life, 1860–1914*. Manchester: Manchester University Press.
Chudacoff, H. (1999) *The Age of the Bachelor: Creating an American Subculture*. Princeton: Princeton University Press.
Corbin, H. (1970) *The Men's Clothing Industry: Colonial Through Modern Times*. New York: Fairchild Publications.
Davidoff, L. and Hall, C. (1987) *Family Fortunes: Men and Women of the English Middle Class, 1780–1850*. Chicago: University of Chicago Press.
Dawson, G. (1991) 'The blond Bedouin: Lawrence of Arabia, imperial adventure and the imagining of English-British masculinity': in M. Roper and J. Tosh (eds), *Manful Assertions: Masculinities in Britain Since 1800*. London: Routledge.
Dines, G. (1995) '"I buy it for the articles": Playboy magazine and the sexualization of consumerism': in G. Dines and J.M. Humez (eds) *Gender, Race and Class in Media: A Text-Reader*. London: Sage.
Dines, G. (1998) 'Dirty business and the mainstreaming of pornography': in G. Dines, R. Jensen and A. Russo (eds), *Pornography: The Production and Consumption of Inequality*. London: Routledge.
Edwards. T. (1997) *Men in the Mirror: Men's Fashion, Masculinity and Consumer Society*. London: Cassell.
Ehrernreich, B. (1983) *The Hearts of Men: American Dreams and the Flight From Commitment*. London: Pluto.
Fitzgerald, F. Scott (1950) (orig. pub. 1925) *The Great Gatsby*. Harmondsworth: Penguin.
Gingrich, A. (1971) *Nothing But People: The Early Days at* Esquire—*A Personal History, 1928–1958*. New York: Crown.
Gordon, M. (1980) 'The ideal husband as depicted in the nineteenth-century marriage manual': in E. Pleck and J. Pleck (eds) *The American Man*. Englewood NJ: Prentice-Hall.
Greenfield, J., O'Connell, S. and Reid, C. (1999) 'Fashioning Masculinity: *Men Only*, Consumption and the Development of Marketing in the 1930s', *Twentieth Century British History* 10(4): 457–476.
Griswold, R. (1993) *Fatherhood in America: A History*. New York: Basic Books.
Hochswender, W. and Gross, K. (1993) *Men in Style: The Golden Age of Fashion from* Esquire. New York: Rizzoli.
Kann, M.E. (1991) *On the Man Question: Gender and Civic Virtue in America*. Philadelphia: Temple University Press.
Kerber, L. (1988) 'Separate spheres, female worlds, women's place: The rhetoric of women's history', *Journal of American History* 75(1): 9–39.
Kervin, D. (1991) 'Advertising masculinity: The representation of males in *Esquire* advertisements', *Journal of Communication Enquiry* 14(1): 51–70.
Kimmel, M. (1997) *Manhood in America: A Cultural History*. New York: The Free Press.
Leach, W. (1984) 'Transformations in a culture of consumption: Women and department stores, 1890–1925'. *Journal of American History* 71(2): 319–342.

May, E.T. (1999) (2nd edn) *Homeward Bound: American Families in the Cold War Era*. New York: Basic Books.

Merrill, H. (1995) *Esky: the Early Years at* Esquire. New Brunswick: Rutgers University Press.

Mintz, S. and Kellog, S. (1988) *Domestic Revolutions: A Social History of American Family Life*. New York: Free Press.

Mort, F. (1988) 'Boys own? Masculinity, style and popular culture': in R. Chapman and J. Rutherford (eds), *Male Order: Unwrapping Masculinity*. London: Lawrence and Wishart.

Mort, F. (1996) *Cultures of Consumption: Masculinities and Social Space in Late Twentieth-Century Britain*. London: Routledge.

Mort, F. (1997) 'Paths to mass consumption: Britain and the USA since 1945': in M. Nava, A. Blake, I. MacRury and B. Richards (eds) *Buy This Book: Studies in Advertising and Consumption*. London: Routledge.

Mort, F. and Thompson, P. (1994) 'Retailing, commercial culture and masculinity in 1950s Britain: The case of Montague Burton, the "tailor of taste"', *History Workshop* 38 (Autumn) 106–127.

Nixon, S. (1996) *Hard Looks: Masculinities, Spectatorship and Contemporary Consumption*. London: UCL Press.

Osgerby, B. (2001) *Playboys in Paradise: Masculinity, Youth and Leisure-style in Modern America*. Oxford: Berg.

Paoletti, J. (1985) 'Ridicule and Role Models as Factors in American Men's Fashion Change, 1880–1910', *Costume* 29: 121–134.

Peiss, K. (1987) *Cheap Amusements: Working Women and Leisure in Turn-Of-The-Century New York*. Philadelphia: Temple University Press.

Pendergast, T. (2000) *Creating the Modern Man: American Magazines and Consumer Culture, 1900–1950*. Columbia: University of Missouri Press.

Rappaport E. (2001) *Shopping for Pleasure: Women in the Making of London's West End*. Princeton, N.J.: Princeton University Press.

Rotundo, E.A. (1993) *American Manhood: Transformations in Masculinity from the Revolution to the Modern Era*. New York: Basic Books.

Roper, M. and Tosh, J. (eds) (1991) *Manful Assertions: Masculinities in Britain Since 1800*. London: Routledge.

Ruth, D. (1996) *Inventing the Public Enemy: The Gangster in American Culture, 1918–1934*. London: University of Chicago Press.

Sinclair, L. (1922) *Babbitt*. New York: Harcourt Brace.

Swiencicki, M.A. (1998) 'Consuming Brotherhood: Men's Culture, Style and Recreation as Consumer Culture, 1880–1930'. *Social History* 31(4).

Tosh, J. (1994) 'What should historians do with masculinity?: Reflections on nineteenth century Britain', *History Workshop* 38(Autumn): 179–202.

Veblen, T. (1953) (orig. pub. 1899) *The Theory of the Leisure Class; an Economic Study of Institutions*. New York: Mentor Books.

Walkowitz, J. (1992) *City of Dreadful Delight: Narratives of Sexual Danger in Late-Victorian London*. London: Virago.

Weiss, J. (2000) *To Have and to Hold: Marriage, the Baby Boom and Social Change*. Chicago: University of Chicago Press.

White, K. (1993) *The First Sexual Revolution: The Emergence of Male Heterosexuality in Modern America*. New York: New York University Press.

Part 2:
Cultures of production and consumption

Introduction: Cultures of production and consumption

The focus of part 2 is upon particular sites of the production of cultural meaning within the broader circuit of culture of men's magazines. Men's magazines cannot be treated merely as textual products, unaffected by time and space, the intentions and motivations of producers and the wide-ranging and frequently divergent interpretations of readers. A series of interdependent 'moments' including contexts of production and consumption/reception all contribute to the cultural phenomenon of the men's lifestyle magazines. These contexts are mutually constitutive and combine to form what could be best described as the 'meanings' of men's magazines.

Crewe's chapter, 'Class, masculinity and editorial identity in the reformation of the UK men's press' draws upon a series of interviews that he conducted with the founding editors of *loaded* magazine, James Brown and Tim Southwell. Crewe's contention is that the identities of these specific editorial figures played a vital role in fashioning consumer marketplaces beyond the men's press as well as in forging the character of this sector itself at a time when the industry allowed a high degree of editorial autonomy.

In the course of delineating the fascinating intersections between the lived cultures of these editors and the production and content of *loaded*, Crewe draws attention to a series of interesting ambivalences and contradictions emerging from the editors' self-narratives, particularly surrounding issues of class, social mobility and education. Crewe argues that this rather defensive pattern of narrative is intimately bound up with constructions of heterosexual masculinity celebrated in the pages of *loaded*. Furthermore, the chapter reveals the tension between Brown and Southwell's assertions of the 'authentic' masculinity, engendered from personal autobiographies, that characterizes *loaded*, and the rather more reflexive and ironic qualities of the magazine which seem to disturb this claim to individualism and authenticity.

This tension is, interestingly, also played out within the responses to men's magazines of focus group informants in the next chapter, 'Reading men's lifestyle magazines: cultural power and the information society'. Stevenson *et al.* conducted focus group discussions with 15–20 groups of men (and a smaller number of women) some of whom were readers of men's magazines and a smaller number of whom were not, in order to draw out particular discourses surrounding consumption and reception of the magazines. The three discourses upon which the chapter focuses are 'honesty', 'naturalness' and 'openness', qualities interestingly paralleled in the narratives of the editors in Crewe's chapter, a point which supports the notion that these are culturally available discourses continually circulating around the phenomenon of the 'new lad'.

Stevenson *et al.* observe that an interesting tension emerges in readers' responses between 'a more uncertain and reflexive disposition' and 'more stable social markers'. They frame this tension within the context of Ulrich Beck's thesis of Risk Society (outlined within this volume's introduction), Beck's and Giddens' respective conceptualizations of 'reflexive modernity' and recent theorizations of a putative erasure of distance in the 'information society'. Ultimately they assign the male informants' responses (and by extension the meanings of men's magazines) to a liminal position between reflexivity (modernity) and constructed certitude (counter-modernity). The authors conclude that this analysis leads them to more interesting questions regarding the cultural importance of men's magazines in contrast to more conventional conclusions about the role of magazines within a commercial context or as the practice and affirmation of a 'conservative gender politics'.

Edwards' chapter, 'Sex, booze and fags: masculinity, style and men's magazines' provides both diachronic and synchronic readings of the relationship between representations of masculinity in magazine content, particularly relating to style and consumer markets. One of his key contentions is that issues of *style* (a key *raison d'être* of the lifestyle magazine) sit particularly uneasily with the defensive masculinity of 'new lad' and that men's magazines have had to rise to the challenge of accommodating this ambivalence by transforming it into a form of commercial capital.

Edwards offers a useful critique of existing literature in the field in which he foregrounds two dominant approaches to analysing the men's magazine market: magazines as cultural text and magazines as cultural phenomenon. An ideal analysis, he argues, would involve some kind of synthesis between the two approaches.

In the second part of his chapter, Edwards offers a tripartite scheme for analysing both changes and continuities in the representations of masculinity across various titles, using the typologies of 'Old Man', 'New Man' and 'New Lad'. By examining the way in which each construction engages with *work, sexuality* and *style*, he is able to problematize the notion that these types are clearly demarcated or oppositional categories and emphasizes the key role that earlier manifestations of magazine masculinities play in the constitution of the 'new lad'. Indeed, 'new lad', Edwards argues, manages successfully to reconcile the familiar tension between the 'playboy' and the 'narcissist' which had tended to characterize earlier magazine incarnations. Edwards' conclusions point to a powerful heterosexual imperative and thus disavowal of homosexuality, playfully suggested by the pun in his chapter title, which continues to shape and determine forms of magazine masculinity.

Class, masculinity and editorial identity in the reformation of the UK men's press

Ben Crewe

Media practitioners may be prone to inflating their creative importance, but there are certain times when individual practitioners are undeniably pivotal in fashioning new consumer markets and the identities that they engender. The following chapter will show that this was the case in the UK men's lifestyle magazine sector in the 1990s, where conditions were such that the terms of its reformation can be traced in significant ways to some specific editorial figures, and, in turn, to the cultures in which they were embedded.[1] The key protagonists here are James Brown and Tim Southwell, the founders of IPC's *loaded*: the magazine whose launch in April 1994 marked the watershed moment in the market's transformation and whose unanticipated success conferred upon its editors a commanding cultural authority over modern 'masculine knowledge'. Foundational in this authority was an assertion—expressed both in the magazine form itself and in the public pronouncements of its creators—that the 'new man' identity embodied in the 'style titles', *Arena*, *GQ* and *Esquire*, was insipid, over-aspirational and outmoded. It was against these magazines and their characterization of contemporary masculinity that *loaded* appeared to define itself, mobilizing an alternative identity that became known in wider consumer culture and public consciousness as the 'new lad'.

Loaded's popularity, and the rapidity with which the new lad superceded the new man as the dominant commercial representation of the modern male, undoubtedly conveyed real resonance with lived cultures of masculinity. At the same time, there was nothing inevitable about *loaded*'s emergence or the form in which it was articulated. It is in this respect that the personal motivations, knowledges and cultural resources of *loaded*'s editorial cabal merit further investigation, for they were critical in fleshing out the magazine, and thus in delimiting the development of the UK men's press as a whole. By charting some of the social and cultural roots of these identifications and ambitions—drawing partly on original interviews with Brown and Southwell—the renaissance of the sector and the emergence of the new lad discourse can be situated within a broader context of sexual and social politics.

The early 1990s

A review of consumer magazine markets written at the start of the decade in *Press Gazette* (3.12.90: 18) by Brian Braithwaite, one of publishing's elder statesmen, was a telling indication of the standing of the UK men's lifestyle sector in the eyes of most media practitioners. For, despite the highly fêted launches of *Arena* and *GQ* in the previous few years (see Mort 1996 and Nixon 1996), men's lifestyle magazines received no mention at all. Indeed, general-interest magazines for men were widely seen as niche products for a minor audience at the margins of the male public body. Although industry analysts and insiders recognized that the mass market represented an uncultivated terrain, they doubted that it would be fertile for many years.

Entrenched scepticism about the likelihood of the market being significantly extended was affected very little by the launch in 1991 of *Esquire*. Aimed at the affluent, professional, thirtysomething male, *Esquire*'s target market overlapped considerably with that of *GQ*. That both titles were keen to perch in news-stands alongside titles such as *Newsweek*, *The Spectator* and *The Economist* provides striking illustration of their self-images and the character of the sector at the time. The launch of *Focus* in November 1992 by Gruner and Jahr therefore raised industry hopes that a more advanced formulation of the market might be imminent. Elaborating the popular science, human interest, sport, nature and history format that had proved successful on the Continent, company MD Holger Wiemann was confident of the momentousness of the occasion: 'we haven't just created a magazine, I think we're creating a market' (*Media Week*, 16.10.92: 20). Publishing insiders were more sceptical, specifically about the magazine's 'downmarket' look and the lack of political and business coverage that would, according to the *Esquire* editor, make it 'escapist and marginal to what governs men's lives' (*Campaign*, 30.10.92: 15). Such reactions rehearsed the prevailing uncertainty amongst publishing companies about how to approach the mass market, and the generalized doubt that there existed an interested male public beyond the upmarket titles. *Focus*' failure to build a circulation much above 100,000 appeared to bear out the received wisdom that, as *Media Week* summarized in April 1993, 'ABC1 men and the phrase "mass market" are likely to remain strangers for some time' (16.4.93: 20). Only smaller launches for younger and more 'streetwise' audiences, including *Phat!* and *Zine*,[2] growth rates throughout the men's press in 1993 and, perhaps most portentously, *GQ*'s inaugural and successful use of a female cover star in August 1993, hinted at the developments that would occur over the following few years.

Although the style press was still, at this stage, broadly associated with the figure of the new man—a sexually progressive, affluent and style-conscious consumer—it was in its pages that the 'new lad' identity had first appeared as these titles sought to describe their editorial shifts from the dominant codings of the market's early years. This transition had been marked in both *GQ* and *Arena* in 1991 by an increase in sexualized imagery and the sexual scrutiny of women, and a more 'assertive articulation of the post-permissive masculine heterosexual scripts' already identifiable in both publications (Nixon, 1996: 203). Within the industry, Sean O'Hagan's article in *Arena*'s 1991 Spring-Summer issue had been one of the earliest and most influential attempts to identify this new male species. Seeking to lay bare the 'myth' of the 'sensitive, caring, emotionally balanced, non-sexist, non-aggressive New Man', O'Hagan depicted his emerging successor as 'a New Man who can't quite shake off his outmoded but snug-fitting laddishness' (p. 22). Informed by post-feminist discourse, intelligent, articulate and in tune with contemporary culture, new lads were 'not quite as boorish/tribal/drunken or loud as their prehistoric predecessors' but had neither the will nor the nerve to embrace the new man's more stringent behavioural demands (p. 24). They could defend their ideological shortcomings in socio-political terms (though they actually somewhat relished them), and 'tell you how misogynist the new David Lynch film is' but might well do so primarily as seduction strategies. Indeed, one of the new lad's defining characteristics was this ability to switch from old lad to new man as appropriate, albeit never quite descending to the sexist depths of the 'utterly unreconstitutable' male.

Other early sketches of the new lad had portrayed a similar figure. A feature in the *Independent on Sunday* by Alex Kershaw in April 1991 described him as 'a twentysomething, well educated urban male with cosmopolitan tastes—something of a sophisticate, but never pseudo or pretentious' (14.4.91: 19). His icons included 'Pat Nevin, the art-collecting Everton footballer, Roddy Frame, sensitive lead-singer with Aztec Camera, Terry Christian, the cocky Mancunian presenter of The Word and Gary Oldman, the film star', but not Gazza: 'too northern and too thick'. His value system was a conscience-free, pragmatic hedonism rather than the liberalism of the thirtysomething generation. He was cultured, style-conscious and interested in art, redolent of the sharpness of the Mod, and with many of his working-class overtones. Accordingly, he was keen on both the tribal and physical aspects of sport, particularly football, without being a lout. 'If anything, they're hooligan intellectuals', declared one new lad exemplar. Another, the comedian David Baddiel, outlined the new lad's post-feminist position on the opposite sex: 'he finds pornography funny. Of course he's aware of all the arguments about pornography. But he's capable of treating women as sex-objects without being sexist' (ibid: 19).

Three years on, *loaded*'s launch team enlisted the new lad label whilst signalling a rearticulation of some important characteristics. Having informed the press that the magazine would target 'the irreverent sensibilities of the new lad' (*The Guardian*, 11.4.94: G2, 16), launch editor James Brown reiterated the tone of his title by stamping 'superlads' upon the cover of the first issue. Addressing men who 'have accepted what we are and have given up trying to improve ourselves' (Brown, in *The Independent*, 8.9.94: 26), *loaded* seemed to be addressing a male public fairly similar to the conceptions of O'Hagan and Kershaw. However, the magazine's rendition of the new lad script was different in several ways from the model of the early 1990s: younger, louder, more hedonistic, not necessarily well-educated, well-groomed or cosmopolitan, and more likely to mock than admire 'sophistication' and earnest sensitivity. Whereas O'Hagan's new lad was knowing and even manipulative in his chameleon posturings, *loaded*'s was presented as unrestrained and without pretence. And whilst O'Hagan's portrait was of an urban intelligentsia distinct from the mass male population, IPC's was of the 'man-on-the-street': the '98 per cent of the male population' for whom the existing publications were 'totally unreal' (*Press Gazette*, 28.3.94: 9). Within months, *loaded* not only proved right IPC's assertion that it would serve a far broader male constituency than the prevailing men's magazines, but also began to redraw the boundaries of men's publishing.

The launch and impact of *loaded*

Highlighting the context in which *loaded* was launched is important, for its terms gave the magazine's co-founders, James Brown and Tim Southwell, the influence that justifies my focus on them in the second half of this chapter. Certain conditions demand particular attention. First, then, most publishers were eager to expand the men's market, yet doubtful about the viability of this proposition. Those who, in the early 1990s, had sensed dissatisfaction with the market incumbents were nonetheless hamstrung by their inability to identify an appropriate address for the mass male population. That is, although internal research at IPC, Emap and Dennis Publishing indicated that most men found the style press irrelevant, and preferred the celebratory tone of women's glossies to its restrained and self-conscious editorial pitch, such exercises were not considered capable of providing a coherent, alternative editorial formula. Consumers were regarded as useful sources for their critical but not their creative vocabularies. Instead, IPC brought former music press journalists Brown and Southwell onto its development team to provide a more positive and focussed editorial concept, one that both men claimed was based overwhelmingly on the cultures and interests that defined their lives (Brown, 1999; Southwell, 1998a; 1998b). Brown argued that *loaded*'s editorial composition simply expressed what would have come out 'if you'd picked me up and shaken everything out of my head' (Brown, 1999) and declared his aim to 'create a magazine that was for me and my friends, and an extension of my personality' (*The Independent*, 8.6.98: 13). With only tentative confidence about its likely success, but relatively little at risk financially in proceeding with its launch, IPC introduced *loaded* to UK news-stands in April 1994.

Aimed mainly at single men in their late teens and early twenties, unencumbered by family and financial responsibilities and into 'pub and club culture' (*Press Gazette*, 28.3.94: 9), the distinctions between *loaded* and its competitors were immediately apparent. *GQ*'s most recent issue had included articles on the Child Support Agency scandal, HIV, cricketer Michael Atherton, novelists Jay McInerney and Patricia Highsmith, fashion designer Giorgio Armani, and 'are you man enough to cope with PMT?' (*GQ*, March 1994). *Esquire* was fronted by Hollywood actor Tom Hanks and contained pieces on the Jamie Bulger case, boxer Mike Tyson's time in jail, Prozac, 'Dates from Hell', the 'real story behind Schindler's List', and 'why dogs are a man's best friend' (*Esquire*, March 1994). *Loaded* met consumers through British actor Gary Oldman who stared out from a front cover that highlighted articles inside on cult film *Withnail and I*, Italian football team Sampdoria, hotel sex, skydiving, cartoon characters Beavis and Butthead, rock star Paul Weller and footballer Eric Cantona.

James Brown used his first editor's letter to flesh out *loaded*'s identity further.

> *loaded* is a new magazine dedicated to life, liberty and the pursuit of sex, drink, foot-ball and less serious matters. *loaded* is music, film, relationships, humour, travel, sport, hard news and popular culture. *loaded* is clubbing, drinking, eating, playing and living. *loaded* is for the man who believes he can do anything, if only he wasn't hungover. (*loaded*, May 1994: 3)

The magazine continued to differentiate itself inside with a 'platinum rogues' table, 'charting the peaks, pratfalls and past form of a royal flush of bad boys', 'Great Moments in Life', recalling a football match pitch invasion by 'junior mods' in 1972, and a 'Greatest Living Englishmen' column commemorating 'Dave' from the Eighties UK television programme *Minder*. In coming editions, *loaded* would honour cult British gangster films *Get Carter* and *The Italian Job*, events such as 'John McEnroe doing his nut', 'growing a moustache' and 'the Blue Peter Garden getting vandalized', and men including *The Likely Lads*, 'mad newspaper vendors' and quiz show dummy 'Dusty Bin'. Compared to the list of 'places and things that made my life a life', from *Esquire*'s first issue in 1991—'Ben Webster, Ray Charles, W B Yeats, Mexico, Gabriel Garcia Marquez, Casablanca, Proust (unfinished), Hemingway, the World Series and so on' (quoted in *Media Week*, 15.2.91: 38)—the distinctive hue of *loaded*'s cultural references, in terms of generation, nation and class, was all the more evident. First then, its nostalgic yearnings were distinctively British, and rooted in more recent and more populist culture. Secondly, these references signalled an iden-tification with certain elements of working-class culture, in particular an empha-sis on street culture and self-gratification. Thirdly, *loaded*'s tone appeared markedly less earnest and more celebratory in its portrayal of masculine culture than its predecessors.

The speed of *loaded*'s success and scope of its wider impact came as a sur-prise to its creators as well as the publishing community at large. By August 1995, it was already the biggest selling magazine in the sector. Meanwhile, encouraged and assisted by *loaded*'s progress, other companies had joined IPC in producing titles that ignored the template of the first generation of men's titles. In May 1994, Emap had begun a revamp of *FHM* that owed much to IPC's gamble, and would eventually create the new market leader. By the end of 1995, the men's lifestyle press was, by some distance, the fastest expanding sector in consumer publishing.[3] A year later, whilst *loaded*'s circulation had reached 365,000, those of *FHM*, *Maxim* and *Men's Health* were over 150,000, 158,000 and 323,000 respectively (*ABC*, June–Dec 1996). In the frenzied market activ-ity that followed, *loaded*'s influence was ubiquitous. In previously 'specialist', adjacent and virgin sectors such as sports (*Total Sport; Total Football; Goal*), cars (*Petrolhead*), food, drink and travel (*Eat Soup*), multimedia entertainment (*Escape*) and 'the weird' (*Bizarre*), its editorial formula was repeatedly mobilized and its target market repeatedly pursued. Emap's *Total Sport* was a case in point, originating from the company's entertainment rather than specialist publishing division, using film and music writers as much as conventional sports journalists, and initially launching as a supplement to *FHM*.

Likewise, the market's fragmentation and expansion from 1996, spawning gadget magazines (*Stuff, Boys Toys, T3*), health and fitness titles (*XL, GQ Active, ZM, Men's Fitness, FHM Bionic*), and offerings for older, younger and less laddish male consumers (*Later, Mondo, Front, Deluxe*) owed a great deal to *loaded*'s initial path-finding.[4] By August 1998, when *FHM*'s circulation crested at over 775,000 monthly copies, those of *loaded, Maxim* and *Men's Health* were over 456,000, 300,000 and 245,000 respectively. Sales in the sector, narrowly conceived, topped 2.3 million, compared to 250,000, at a generous estimate, in 1990. And although declines at most titles at the end of the decade prompted cries that the lad mag bubble had burst (*The Independent*, 27.11.01), the market had, in fact, reached a predictable plateau after a period of extraordinary expansion, whilst many publishers now focussed resources on international brand expansion.[5]

If the paradigm shift that had occurred in men's publishing was not clear enough, Emap's estimated £20million buy-out of Wagadon in 1999 provided an arresting symbol of the period's transitions. As the publisher of *FHM* took over the company that, through *The Face* and *Arena*, had lain the earlier terms for the re-establishment of the UK men's press, the deal confirmed the triumph of the lad mags over the now floundering style titles and denoted the eclipse of the new man by the new lad throughout consumer culture. This shift was both corroborated and interrogated across commercial media. In the broadsheet press, the development of the market and its new masculine iconography was detailed and deconstructed with endless enthusiasm. Tabloids were more directly influenced by the self-evident success of this innovative mode of address. *The Daily Star*, in particular, appeared increasingly like a newsprint version of a lads' magazine towards the end of the decade, a congruence that was almost cemented in 1999 when new lad exemplar Chris Evans tried to take over the paper and install at its helm former *FHM* editor Mike Soutar. Evans was himself something of a new lad exemplar, his television show *TFI Friday* one of a number of programmes including *They Think It's All Over* and *Fantasy Football League*, that typified screen versions of the new lad script.

The advertising industry was perhaps even more powerful in embedding the new lad as a visual idiom for the condition of the modern man. Having struggled to capture shifts in sexual politics in the early 1990s, from 1994, agencies grasped the equation unexpectedly presented by the men's magazine market: irreverent, hedonistic, self-mocking, culturally self-conscious, laced with innuendo and unashamedly heterosexual. Press work for football goods producer Umbro pictured a young fan lying on his bed underneath a poster of a topless model whose body was covered only by a football top. With him smirking know-ingly at the camera, the tagline read 'Who says girls look better with their kit off?'. An acclaimed television advert for Supernoodles featured a man yielding to his girlfriend's pleas for a portion of his meal only after having spotted their dog, out of her sight, licking the plate. Such campaigns were designed for the viewer who recognized that he was fulfilling a male cliché. Others, such as Atlantic 252's 'Long wave radio has the biggest hits' advert, and Club 18–30's 'Beaver Espana' campaign were rather more heavy-handed, resulting in censures from the Advertising Standards Authority (*Campaign*, 1.11.96: 7).

Certainly, there were considerable differences between the tones of those cam-paigns bracketed together as 'New Lad ads' (*Campaign*, 11.10.96: 40). However, as in the press, the term had become a sweeping descriptor for modes of repre-sentation that both mocked and celebrated traditional stereotypes of the male role.[6] *Loaded* was consistently cited as the originator of the new stereotype; and it is thus to the producers of *loaded* that I shall now turn.

'Men who should know better'?

I have suggested already that the introduction of James Brown and Tim Southwell to the IPC development team in 1993 marked the point at which the company's plans for a mass-market men's title began to take shape as *'loaded'*. I noted furthermore Brown's claim that the magazine was, in essence, a repre-sentation of his own lifestyle and interests, and those of the people around him. Indeed, *loaded*'s pioneering status, and the freedom with which its producers were allowed consequently to work, did establish for Brown and Southwell con-siderable scope to fashion the magazine in accordance with their personal ambi-tions, concerns and identifications. As I will show in the following section, these were primarily anchored in issues around class and masculinity that were them-selves inter-related.

Perhaps the most revealing feature of Brown and Southwell's self-representations was a striking assessment of class identity, education and mobil-ity. Brown's ambivalence about such issues seemed to reflect his biographical details. His mother was a secretary and his father was a 'political travel writer', and it was their separation during his sixth-form that Brown considered respon-sible for what was certainly—given his social origins and intelligence—a pre-mature detachment from the educational ladder (Brown, 1999). Endowed with what Bourdieu would call 'strong cultural capital imperfectly converted into educational capital' (1984: 358), it was unsurprising that Brown soon found refuge for his abilities and ambitions in music journalism, an area that demanded little in the way of institutionally furnished knowledge and formal qualifications, but considerable levels of non-certified cultural capital. From his one-man fanzine covering local, alternative music and politics, Brown soon moved to *Sounds*, before becoming features editor at IPC's *New Musical Express* (*NME*) by the age of twenty. Southwell's professional background was also in music journalism, though his trajectory was slightly different. Raised by a porcelain artist and computer analyst and lecturer, he had co-founded a fanzine whilst studying social science at Central London Polytechnic and been employed at a variety of music magazines including *Smash Hits* and the *NME*, where he had briefly worked with Brown.

Such origins classified neither Brown nor Southwell in conventional terms as working class, yet both regularly presented themselves as spokesmen for the working-class male public. Brown's claims were largely implicit and indirect, connoted in references to football, drinking, 'the street' and 'boys behind the bike sheds' (*Press Gazette*, 28.3.94: 9). Southwell's were explicit and recurrent, requiring a strained interpretation of class. Although he acknowledged a distinction between himself and 'people who are in poverty, who are genuinely working class', Southwell also propounded the notion that 'whether you're working class or middle class, [if] you work all day, you're all working class aren't you? Working class just means that you have to work for a living' (Southwell, 1998b). Notably, this formulation allowed Southwell to present himself as a working-class man. Brown was openly equivocal about his class identity, recognizing that his mobility made any simple assessment impossible. Indeed, he dismissed the utility of class categories altogether—'people who talk about class are ostensibly people who have problems with their own class'—arguing that class labels obscured potential and had no real bearing on success or failure: 'everything comes back to the individual' (Brown, 1999). Such sentiments mirrored Brown's self-stylization as someone unclassifiable, unpredictable and uniquely talented. If this representation of individuality seemed to contradict Brown's assertions elsewhere that he was, like Southwell, an 'ordinary bloke', it also signalled his identification with middle-class notions of ambition and credibility that reflected what he might realistically have expected and to which he continued to aspire.

Indeed, the interruption of Brown's social and educational trajectory accentuated his conviction that his success was self-made, a view that Southwell shared in relation to his own achievements. Brown declared:

> Nobody ever gave me anything on a plate—I haven't got a leg up anywhere, so, you've got to do it for yourself—I didn't have any qualifications, didn't have influential parents who could get me a job anywhere; you've just got to get on and do it. (Brown, 1999)

In this context, Brown's scepticism about 'class' and his celebratory faith in social mobility were more intelligible. They derived from the narrative of his own life, with his unusually forceful ascent in the magazine industry and his ambiguous sense of his own class location. Many of his friends were described in the same terms, as ambitious 'subcultural entrepreneurs' (McRobbie, 1994) in fashion, film and sport who had created their own social pathways and careers: 'normal people' who had 'turned their passions and private lives into jobs' (Brown, 1999). Brown and Southwell considered such self-generated opportunism to have been aided and necessitated by a dissolution of class boundaries and certainties that was potentially liberating. In this respect, although politically left-wing, they endorsed a Thatcherite model of personal and social advancement, inflecting it with the democratic optimism of the post-punk ethic. Meanwhile, in analysing *loaded*'s success, they repeatedly cited the acid house dance movement and the resurgence of football culture, arguing that both had expressed and galvanized an ethos of possibility amongst a population no longer limited or defined by class (Brown, 1999; Southwell 1998b). In a variety of terms then, working class identity was given an ambiguous affect: as something that should be coveted, but also transcended through the mobility that attitude and ambition were able to advance.

This ambivalence around class was also palpable in Brown and Southwell's educational and professional self-narratives. Southwell declared himself a lazy, 'useless' student and appeared embarrassed by his 2:1 degree mark: 'god knows how the fuck that happened. Someone got my results mixed up with someone else's' (Southwell, 1998b). Asked 'are you your average reader?' in a trade press questionnaire he responded curiously: 'Christ no. Some of them have got degrees you know' (*Press Gazette*, 18.6.99: 19). Discussions of work were, likewise, striking in the pride with which luck, incompetence and lack of preparation were repeatedly emphasized (Southwell, 1998a; 1998b). Editorial staff were described variously as 'buffoons', 'berks', 'twerps out of their depth' and 'somewhere between the Bash Street Kids and Carry on Publishing' (Southwell, 1998a: 76, 111, 184, 111). Many were, like Southwell, highly educated.[7] Indeed, Southwell's efforts to portray them as this 'ship of fools' and to romanticize their idiocy were contrasted and compromised by an equally robust defence of his team as intelligent and skilled professionals, an argument used whenever the magazine was accused of yobbishness and sexism.

Such strains were echoed in Brown's explanation of why he did not continue his education:

> The teachers said 'go to university, you'll love it. You'll do all these things', and I thought 'well I can go and do them anyway'. I can play football for a club down the street, and I can go to watch the concerts anyway; I couldn't concentrate, I wanted to do something more important. A lot of the things that people found, when they're twenty-two, twenty-three, and they've come out of university, I knew that when I was seventeen. I knew that you got further educated and there weren't going to be any jobs. I understood that; so by the time that my friends were coming out of university, and they were going to functional, bureaucratic jobs at local councils, or DHSS's, or charities or whatever, and earning nine grand a year, I was in Hollywood with the Cult. I didn't go to university because I didn't want to go to fucking university. I'm quite interested now in studying a bit more, in studying for some stuff. But I always thought I'll study when I'm at a level where I'm interested in studying. I thought I would just waste the education. And also I knew that I would disrupt it for everybody else. (Brown, 1999).

At the same time, Brown stressed his cerebral qualities and his distinction from other male work identities: 'I'm a journalist. I don't fucking work on a building site—I'm extremely well read for somebody who's never had any further education'. Like Southwell, he was keen to be seen as subculturally erudite, informed and professional, but hostile to the connotations of formal education. More generally, the deferred benefits of education and 'thinking' were negatively compared with the immediate rewards of 'doing'. Brown invoked this particularly clearly in asserting that 'when other eighteen-year-olds were writing essays in university I was travelling the world and interviewing some of the hottest acts of the time' (*Financial Times*, 4.9.99: 7). Southwell's 'presentism' was equally pronounced when he mocked those who relied on experience and 'lionizing the past' and lauded the 'right here, right now' attitude to life (*The Guardian*, 21.8.99: Review 2). Reflection, deliberation and living life according to the terms of others were likewise condemned as 'inauthentic' and 'dishonest'; liberation was found in acting instinctively. If such sentiments around class, education and mobility hinted at underlying preoccupations with heterosexual and masculine credibility, this was no coincidence.

Masculinity, heterosexuality and the spectre of the 'new man'

Brown and Southwell's adherence to 'honest' masculinity took form partly in enthusiastic and unreserved modes of self-expression that were unreservedly heterosexual, without being macho, overbearing or aggressive. Both were candid in stating passion for their work and interests—Southwell, for example, declaring that 'The day we got the magazine back from the printers I felt like I'd given birth—I was close to tears' (1998a: 59–60)—and, in Brown's case, in admitting personal fragility. In this respect, the emotional reserve of certain conventional masculine subjectivities (for example, the men within management studied by Roper (1994)) was notably lacking. Brown's demeanour was described by one press interviewer as 'almost feminine' (*The Independent*, 8.6.98: 13), a profile he accepted by announcing 'I'm a great admirer of women, both intellectually and of the feminine form. If people think I've got feminine attributes then that's fine' (Brown, 1999).

Brown's response signalled the casual and unrestrained sexual subjectivity that was central to his identity and the distinctions he sought to emphasize between himself and other masculine identities. The figure of the 'new man', with his more hesitant and questioning stance on sexual relations, was marked out as the most immediate antithesis of his and Southwell's identifications. Both derided what they saw as his 'miserable liberal guilt' (*The Times*, 18.12.98: 40–41) about sexual affairs and labelled him insipid, unappealing and 'dishonest'. Axiomatic in such dispatches was a presupposition that, at least in the sphere of sexual relations, equality had already been achieved. Brown heralded a 'post-sex, post-politics' society, declaring that he had no interest in the 'politics of gender' and that 'All that men versus women stuff is rubbish' (*The Guardian*, 21.4.97: Media 6–7).[8]

Such celebrations of a post-feminist settlement were naive, but nonetheless distinguished *loaded*'s founders from traditional forms of chauvinism. Indeed, disdain for the new man was insignificant next to the contempt reserved for the 'truly Neanderthal' louts and misogynists from whom *loaded*'s editors distanced themselves (Southwell, 1998a: 214). Events on a national 'loaded tour', when the editorial team was surprised to encounter a constituency of 'truly sexist', 'mindless' readers (pp. 234, 237), had brought these dissociations into particular relief. 'It made your stomach twist when you realized what you were up against', recalled Southwell (1998b), who had expected the audience to share his post-political assumptions and ambitions. Again, though, Brown and Southwell's 'everyman' identifications had reached significant limits. Meanwhile, despite their antipathies about the new man, Brown and Southwell were relatively fluent in the language of feminism and keen to prove their emotional competence and enlightened attitudes towards women's work and the domestic division of labour: 'I've always done the washing up and I'm sure I could handle changing the baby's nappies. I certainly don't see it as an embarrassing thing to do or purely a woman's domain' (Southwell, 1998a: 214). Both men presented their laddishness as a further illustration of progressiveness, as a sign of a refreshingly uncomplicated appreciation of liberated, 'unrepressed' women. From this perspective, new men were seen as cool but insincere, tediously sensitive or awkward and inept. Worst of all, for Brown and Southwell, they were repressed, judgemental and inauthentic, trying to prescribe a role for men whose inauthenticity was self-evident in the efforts required to inhabit it. Thus, according to Brown (1999), checking one's instincts was a betrayal of one's true self, whereas laddish hedonism was the honest expression of a masculinity that was innate: men might change 'on the surface', but 'the animal, the mammal, or whatever we are, stays the same'.

Casting themselves as subjects of their natural impulses and urges meant that *loaded*'s editors could be unapologetic about their hectic consumption of drink, drugs and women. They were unembarrassed about their ineptitudes, flaws and incompetences for the same reason. Southwell stated, 'men haven't got a clue what is going on', maintaining that they did not want more responsibility in their lives and relied on women to make sense of the world (*The Times*, 18.6.99: 28). Here, then, he assumed a masculinity that did not demand deference or claim inherent, authoritative superiority. Instead, he suggested an awe for the opposite sex that was almost childlike. Ultimately, however, this represented a well-worn masculine discourse that absolved men of responsibility for their actions. *Loaded*'s tagline, 'For men who should know better', acknowledged this with remarkable clarity.

However, Brown and Southwell's aversion to the new man requires further comment. It was the 'Guardian journalist' whom they repeatedly attacked as the ultimate embodiment of his 'narrow-minded', value-laden, 'self-reprimanding' and joyless liberalism. Brown argued that this identity:

> didn't relate to anybody's lives, apart from a few people who'd come out of Oxbridge or who were writing columns in newspapers—I've got a friend, one of *loaded*'s editors, he brings up his kid on his own, but he's not a 'new man'—But you can do all those

things that are perceived to be feminine and [not] wear dungarees, read *The Guardian*, and lose your character and your sexuality. (Brown, 1999).

These references were significant. *The Guardian* itself connoted the left-wing politics of the middle-class intelligentsia, contrasted with the mass populism of the tabloid press with its more lustful irreverence and its inflections of working-class culture. Indeed, Brown's comments flagged his conviction that the middle-class identity that the new man signified was incompatible with masculine heterosexuality. His antipathy was, in this respect, based largely on the inferences of femininity that he felt were intrinsic to the new man's class properties. For him and Southwell, such intimations were particularly preoccupying, for the new man identity was associated not just with the editorial representations of the style press but also with its journalists. It was in relation to this conventional occupational identity within men's publishing that Brown and Southwell would need to define and differentiate themselves.

Occupational identity and the *loaded* team

MONDAY: . . . I celebrate my appointment to the editorship of *GQ* by driving to a benefit for Striking Liverpool Dockers at the Mean Fiddler in Harlesden with two Scouse rascals . . . THURSDAY: Meet *GQ* staff for first time. Lunch with newspaper mogul. Electricity cut off at flat. FRIDAY: Wash in hot water from pan. Travel the mile from the loaded office to the BBC studios at Bush House in Jason's fibreglass bomb of a Lotus Esprit. (Brown in *The Independent*, 27.4.97: 27).

As Brown's diary entry reiterated, his dual affinity with a lifestyle of glamour and success and the alternative credibility of a more ordinary, 'gritty' existence was immanent in professional as well as personal concerns. Southwell's portrayals of the *loaded* work culture exhibited even more strongly his and Brown's investments in jobs that were not part of the 'serious' professions, with their associations of moral earnestness, service and sobriety. Thus, *loaded* staff were presented as invariably and hilariously drunk and out-of-control as well as dedicated professionals: 'we were either in the pub having a laugh or slogging our guts out in search of the impossible deadline' (Southwell, 1998a: 44). In this adaptation of work-hard, play-hard culture, commitment was demanded not only in the office but also in the accompanying lifestyle of hedonistic excess. Indeed, drinking was defined as integral to the job rather than something done only after the office closed,[9] allowing work to be characterized as 'not really work'. Southwell's proud citation of one journalist's remark that '*loaded* was like being down the pub' (p. 40) illustrated the fulfilment he drew from understanding editorial production as a synthesis of graft and gratification.

This glamorization of labour was given more concrete form in Brown and Southwell's admiring references to 'new journalism', the body of North American literature from the 1960s and 70s that included writers such as Tom Wolfe, Hunter Thompson and Norman Mailer (see Wolfe and Johnson, 1975).

Brown referred to Wolfe's books noticeably as his 'further education' (*The Guardian*, 16.11.98: Media 2–3). There were several features of new journalism that had resonance for *loaded*'s founders. What appealed in particular was the way in which writers were placed at the centre of their own narratives through subjective, first-person reportage and inner dialogue, a style that contrasted sharply with conventional notions of objective and impersonal description. New journalists likewise considered it vital to be at the centre of the action, to view things with originality and to report with what Wolfe summarized as 'personality, energy, drive, bravura—style' (1975: 31).

Drawing on these conventions, Brown and Southwell demanded that journalists were spirited and provocative participants in their own stories rather than the detached observers that many style press journalists appeared to be. The obligation of the *loaded* journalist was, in Southwell's words, 'to get into the most interesting situation possible—and if there isn't a situation, create one' (Southwell, 1998b). By identifying themselves as heirs to the movement that had challenged the American writing establishment, Brown and Southwell were also able to put themselves forward as the new missionaries of their field. Their sense of cultural marginality and their self-proclaimed struggle for cultural democratization were informed in part by the belief that they were conferring value on cultures of masculinity that were widely practised but given little recognition: 'we took it to the level of the street, the nightclub and the pub, where guys were used to being ignored' (Brown on 'Midweek', Radio Four, 23.9.98). They also came from backgrounds in fanzine journalism and the music press that were uncommon in the men's magazine market at the time. Brown's initial proposal for *loaded*, which he had pitched initially as '*Arena* edited by Hunter S. Thompson' (*Guardian*, 16.11.98: Media 2–3), also drew on changes he had helped implement at the *NME* by bringing humour and irreverence to a title perceived to have become pompous and po-faced. Brown argued that the music press's tone of spiky but inclusive enthusiasm could be successfully exported to a men's lifestyle sector that had been dominated by a more conservative voice originating in news and fashion journalism. At the same time, then, new journalism's endorsement of an alternative, 'subjective' editorial address was reproduced in Brown and Southwell's aversion to what they perceived as the normative and 'objective' judgements of the new man.

Brown's ambitions, 'to create some generational tension—to make the men's magazine editors feel old and scared [and] other publishing houses feel out of date', were thus couched in almost revolutionary terms (Brown, 1999). He extolled *loaded* as proof that 'you didn't have to go to Eton or Oxford to run a magazine'.

Southwell's comments signalled the underlying salience of class to his professional aims:

> if you'd met the editor of any of these [style] mags down the pub—or more likely the gentleman's club—he wouldn't have time for you, unless you knew someone with a *chateau* he could stay in during Paris Fashion Week. The best I could offer was a week in my uncle's caravan in Tenby. (Southwell, 1998a: 128).

103

He applauded *loaded* for being the first 'successful working-class magazine', and an 'accurate reflection of working-class dreams' (*Campaign*, 4.12.98: 12; Southwell, 1998a: 210). Brown was more equivocal about *loaded*'s class character, communicating his suspicion of class categories: '[It's] about a devil-may-care attitude, not demographics' (*The Independent*, 8.9.94, Living, 26).[10]

The new journalist's ethic of 'making the story happen' also appealed to Brown and Southwell's preferences for action and spontaneity over cautious reflection. More significantly also, it allowed them to give to their work an impression of action, risk and agency. The passive and desk-based aspects of editorial production were played down considerably, whilst the heroism and talent of the individual journalist were foregrounded (Brown, 1999; Southwell, 1998b). The tradition of *NME* journalists, such as Charles Shaar Murray and Nick Kent, who had frequently presented themselves as more interesting than their interviewees, was palpable here. There was also a distinctly gendered edge to these occupational narratives, borne in an established discourse of romantic masculine individualism (MacKenzie, 1987). This focus on individual accomplishment certainly contrasted with Brown and Southwell's emphasis on the importance of teamwork, the collective 'gang' culture of their team at *loaded* and their self-proclaimed ordinariness.[11] But what such apparent contradictions underlined were familiar tensions in the self-identities of *loaded*'s editors, in which issues of class, masculinity and mobility loomed large.

Fundamental in Brown and Southwell's self-narratives was, in fact, an anxiety about how to retain masculine credibility in the context of career commitments and achievements that they perceived to undermine it. In seeking to be seen as ordinary and yet unique, erudite yet not formally 'educated', and as hard-working and aspirational yet not professionally solemn, *loaded*'s editors showed recurrent tensions between investments in two different masculine identities. The first was an assertively heterosexual masculinity anchored in working-class values of collective solidarity, anti-authority bravado, immediate gratification, hedonism, humour and a confident sexual agency. The second was a script that endorsed middle-class notions of individual accomplishment, success and competence, but which was felt to lack the desirable sexual identity that Brown and Southwell demanded.

This latter discourse was plainly encapsulated in the 'new man' identity about which Brown and Southwell were highly ambivalent. Although they defined their *professional* ambitions against the editors and iconography of the style press, as 'men who should know better', they acknowledged that the new man discourse was also appropriate to many of their attitudes and identifications. Recycling his favourite critique of the magazine, Brown summed up that '*GQ* and *Arena* tell me how I should be, but—unfortunately, *loaded* tells me how I am' (Brown, 1999). The most powerful reason for his and Southwell's repudiation of the new man was their feeling that it was marked as inherently asexual through its middle-class qualities. It was by constituting their work instead as a version of manly labour—edgy, active, brave and almost physically demanding (Brown even referring to the *loaded* office as the 'shopfloor')—without being merely *manual* labour, that *loaded*'s creators negotiated some key personal tensions. Crucially then, by offsetting the 'unmasculine' connotations of the existing journalist identity of the men's magazine market, Brown and Southwell were able to conceptualize their occupational practices and ambitions in a way that felt suitably and sufficiently 'masculine'.

Loaded

A full description of the identity of *loaded* itself is not possible here but it should suffice to highlight some key areas in which the preoccupations, motivations and cultural repertoires of its editors were played out in the magazine. *Loaded*'s editorial voice, for example, reflected Brown and Southwell's occupational experiences and identifications. Seeking to emulate the clubbish intimacy between readers and writers of the weekly music press, they promoted an expansive letters page and a tone of self-mocking enthusiasm whilst peppering the magazine with pictures of and references to the antics and accidents of the journalists. Advancing the idea that the magazine's producers were no different from its consumers, such policies spoke of Brown and Southwell's commitments to seeing themselves as 'ordinary blokes' and their attachment to the new journalist ethic. The influence on *loaded* of *The Sun* was also significant. In its attention to captions and headlines, its 'scrapbook' design (Chippendale and Horrie, 1990), its short lead-times, and its swaggering, irreverent confidence, *loaded*'s look and pitch were distinctive from those of the existing magazines, and signalled its editors' identification with the mass male public.

The terms of *loaded*'s sexual identity were also manifest from its first edition, with actress Elizabeth Hurley photographed in a pose somewhat more risqué than the style press convention. A homage to hotel sex included upfront references to porn channels, 'soggy prophylactics' and 'rampant sex' (*loaded*, May 1994: 39–41). The main travel feature, recounting 'cheap cocaine, cheap women' and the Miss Guyana bikini contest, comprised the drink, drugs, football and women recipe that would characterize the magazine's future reports: 'Venezuela is not very good at soccer. So its lads take pride in the next best thing: the quality of the totty' (pp. 61–64). Whereas interview subjects in the style press had always been pressed on areas such as the nature of stardom, the politics of popular culture and the rituals of daily dress (Nixon, 1996: 147; Nixon, 1997), *loaded*'s were more likely to be pressed on their consumption of alcohol, drugs and women.

The launch edition's leading articles bore the imprints of its editors even more markedly. The first was an interview with Paul Weller, former lead singer of 1970s band The Jam and 'godfather of mod', for whom mutual adoration had forged Brown and Southwell's early friendship (Southwell, 1998a). References to Weller's 'barely concealed aggressive discontent' and the influences of mod and punk culture alluded to familiar interests (*loaded*, May 1994: 21–24). The issue's other principal subject was actor Gary Oldman, one of the new lad role-models cited in Alex Kershaw's 1991 article. In an addendum to the main feature, Brown paid a revealing tribute to an evident personal icon:

> Dangerous, sexy, wild, disturbed, disturbing, out of control, in control, too talented and with character too . . . But the real passion and excitement that makes him so damn attractive as a role model, a hero, is in his pursuit of excellence—he's deadly serious about his art. But not at the expense of humour. (*loaded*, May 1994: 51)

Weller and Oldman were apt inaugural icons. Mod's roots were in the post-war encounter between 'working-class puritanism and the new hedonism of consumption' (Cohen, cited in Turner, 1990: 172), in which the tensions of white-collar mobility were symbolically resolved through the retention of the language and rituals of the parent culture alongside the embrace of the dress and music of the 'affluent consumer'. Oldman's upward social mobility was, for Brown, an explicit part of his appeal: 'His brother-in-law was shot by villains, his father died by the bottle, his teachers told him he was thick—if he hadn't become an actor he'd probably have become a criminal' (*loaded*, May 1994: 51). As the magazine championed footballers, boxers, rock stars and alternative comedians in subsequent months, its choices were germane in selecting some of the most glamorous and 'masculine' routes out of the working class. Brown and Southwell's admiration for notions of arduous but enjoyable labour and the achievement of success through unique talent in an 'everyday' field, re-emphasized the masculine intonation of their occupational identifications (Southwell, 1998a).

In his respect for the transformation of personal interests into careers, Brown was able to conceive of hedonism and ambition—defined as living life to the full—as non-contradictory ideals. He denied that *loaded* was nihilisitic and unambitious, claiming instead that the magazine encouraged enthusiasm, the maximization of potential, and the pursuit of one's ambitions—'whether it's collecting toy cars or pencils, or having sex with women—or going rock-climbing'—in a deliberately non-directive way (Brown, 1999). Unlike most competitors, *loaded* offered no explicit lifestyle guidance (such as sex tips or advice about how to negotiate a payrise) or product reviews. The magazine was presented as a vehicle for the legitimation of the enthusiasms of its producers but not one that was actively prescriptive or assumed the innate superiority of certain practices over others. Although *loaded* was normative in all sorts of ways, including in its plea to 'seize the day' and its indefatigable libertinism, the values of its editors were again discernible here.

Loaded did, however, endorse the legitimacy of not striving and a less dutiful, self-sacrificial and conservative version of the masculine career script than *GQ* and *Esquire*. Whilst *The Face* published a list of the most important people in fashion, Brown co-wrote '*loaded*'s least important people: the slobs, the no-marks, the people who are going nowhere', including cartoon characters Homer Simpson and the renowned actor, drinker and womanizer Oliver Reed. Such initiatives were interventions designed 'to galvanize a nation of men into realizing that you didn't have to be ashamed of being a bloke any more' (Southwell,

106

1998a: 214). In thus seeking to be inspirational whilst also assuming that 'men are useless. Everyone knows men are useless' (Brown, in *The Daily Telegraph*, 20.10.97: 34), *loaded* exhibited one of the critical tensions of the identities of its producers.

In interpreting such contradictions, many cultural commentators branded Brown and Southwell as middle-class men posing as working-class, a simplistic analysis that underestimated the genuine, albeit ambivalent, nature of their commitments. The '*loaded* lad' was also often described as 'ironic', suggesting a 'studied political incorrectness', an 'awareness of his own clownish nature' (Moore, in Southwell, 1998a: 205; Bancroft, 1998). Benwell (forthcoming) has argued that the use of irony in men's lifestyle magazines serves to 'continually destabilize' the notion of a coherent and monolithic masculinity. The authorial voice oscillates between those identities against which it defines itself without allowing its own nature to be fixed. Benwell concludes that this evasiveness 'accommodates multiple audiences', 'provides multiple and fluctuating identities for its readers' and becomes 'ideologically inscrutable'. My analysis in this chapter argues that, in *loaded*'s case, such vacillations and instabilities ultimately conveyed the straining masculine subjectivities of its producers.

Conclusion

By the end of the decade, Brown, Southwell and *loaded* had all moved on in interesting ways. Brown's success at *loaded* resulted in a move to *GQ*, where he remodelled the magazine's conservative-metropolitan identity (Nixon, 1996) into something much closer to his own, targeting the 'black market yuppie who used to be a ticket tout and organize raves' (*Press Gazette*, 4.7.97: 3). The redefined reader was assumed to have moved on in ways that paralleled Brown's changing lifestyle, the man who had read *loaded* four years earlier but whose income and interests were now more advanced. Brown explained that, whilst he had grown up, was better dressed and now had proper responsibilities, he had also retained some key characteristics: 'when you find yourself wanting to chin someone because they've gazumped you on a house, you know something's up' (*The Guardian*, 21.4.97: Media 6). In his first full issue, in November 1997, he stamped his mark on the title, interviewing Paul Weller and penning coverlines including 'one off the wrist' (for a photo-feature on watches) and 'There's more to Colombia than meets the nose' (p107).

Three years later, having parted from *GQ* and launched his own publishing house, Brown disavowed the sector that he had effectively forged, describing it as 'stale', 'pathetic' and 'embarrassing': 'If I'd known when I started *loaded* that the men's sector would descend into a conveyer belt of old soap stars in bikinis, I assure you I would not have done it' (*Press Gazette*, 17.11.00:1). Meanwhile, having once asked, rhetorically, on Channel Four's *Girlie Show*, 'who could get bored of drinking and women?', Brown had become a married teetotaller. In 2002, he re-rentered the market with *Jack*, 'an orgy of war, animals, fashion, genius and cool' (*Jack*, spring-summer 2002: 1), which Brown described as 'a personal celebration that I've found another way to live my life' (*The Observer*, 21.4.2002: 15), a life in which he was now a father, 'glued to the History, Biography and Discovery channels' and enjoying *National Geographic* magazine as much as *Viz.* (*The Sunday Times*, News Review, 21.4.2002: 5): 'we're gripped by the same sense of excitement', he reported, 'but our sensibilities have definitely altered'. Southwell had moved into multimedia ventures, having left the editor's position at *loaded* early in 2000, unhappy with the commercial imperatives and focus groups that he felt were compromising his editorial autonomy. A rather tart IPC press release announcing his departure suggested that, as a thirtysomething father, Southwell was 'not the *loaded* lad that he used to be' (*Campaign*, 17.3.00: 5).

Such events and developments were instructive in a number of ways. First, they illustrated the shifts in masculine identity that accompanied the ageing process and, in doing so, forced job movements upon the many editors in the men's magazine market who relied upon 'instinct' to edit their titles. Secondly, they highlighted an increasingly competitive market in which, as commercial pressures intensified and mass-market formulae became more entrenched, the kind of editorial autonomy afforded to Brown and Southwell in 1994 was no longer available to most editors.[12] It was the relative absence of such imperatives, and the initial elusiveness of relevant knowledge about how to address the mass male public, that gave to *loaded*'s editors the kind of cultural authority that has merited my focus on them in this chapter.

To highlight the influence of these practitioners on the development of the men's magazine market during the 1990s is clearly not to say that these practitioners somehow 'created' it out of nothing, or that the analysis of its roots need not go beyond them. Not least, many of the discourses upon which Brown and Southwell's self-narratives drew—anti-intellectualism, entrepreneurialism and classlessness, for example—were well-established. Likewise, Brown's self-consciously constructed claims of authenticity and uniqueness were betrayed by his own assertions that, with *loaded*, he merely gave form to widespread masculine lifestyles that had been hitherto ignored: 'we didn't have to invent a scene—we were taking a culture and putting it into a magazine. So we created a magazine to report on that culture' (Brown, on 'On the Ropes', Radio Four, 16.7.2002).[13] To see Brown and Southwell as bearers, rather than originators, of these cultures is important here. It is equally critical, however, to emphasize the key point of this chapter, that it was *through* these personnel, the cultural resources that they deployed to interpret and re-present a rather amorphous masculine culture, that the market took on the particular characteristics that it did. Just as the informal knowledges and personal missions of a cabal of 'talented individualists' (Mort 1996: 34) at *The Face* initially defined the sector in a particular manner in the 1980s (Mort, 1996; Nixon, 1996), a decade later, it was around the aspirations, commitments and identifications of Brown and Southwell that *loaded* and the mass market *crystallized*.

To illustrate that this was the case is to suggest, more generally, that cultural intermediaries and production personnel occupy key positions in the 'circuit of culture' (see du Gay, 1997) alongside consumers and texts, and within the broader structures of media regulation and ownership. Studying the backgrounds, ideologies, lifestyles and practices of these practitioners, and the cultures within which they operate, must be central to the analysis of cultural goods such as men's magazines. That it was against the expertise and identities of the style press editors that Brown and Southwell's professional motivations took shape supports Nixon's observation that the failure of the new man to elaborate an adequately heterosexual male identity made it all the more likely that less progressive sexual scripts, such as the new lad, would resurface (Nixon, 1996: 206). Here then, the interior life of the industry, its masculine culture, was highly significant. What this also therefore highlights is the need for the close reading of occupational discourses, rivalries and vocabularies within creative fields and for further enquiry into the relationship between the sexual politics of production cultures and the cultural products that they generate.

Notes

1 This chapter is based upon ESRC-funded PhD research carried out at the University of Essex from 1997–2001.
2 *Phat!* was an unsuccessful attempt in July 1993 by independent publisher C21 to target 'streetwise boys' aged 13–16 through urban, youth culture including films, women, computer games and television (*Media Week*, 2.7.93: 8). *Zine* was a youth lifestyle title and student magazine spin-off, launched in November 1993, which claimed to sell over 70,000 copies of its first three issues but failed to make any further headway (*Media Week*, 26.11.93: 8).
3 The expansion rate of 130.8 per cent during the year was over 100 per cent more than the next best sector (*Media Week*, 20.10.1995: 16).
4 This is not to say that all launches were successful, indeed a great many were not, including *Eat Soup*, *Escape*, *XL*, *GQ Active*, *ZM*, *Mondo*, *Deluxe*, and *Later*.
5 Between 1994 and 1998 alone, the men's lifestyle magazine market had grown by 674 per cent, compared to 4 per cent in the women's market (Mintel 1998).
6 Undoubtedly the most striking example of the new lad's hegemony as a signifier for the state of young masculinity was *The Independent's* main article on April 17th 1998, describing the government's concern about teenage boys involved in crime and drugs whom it had dubbed 'the *loaded* generation'.
7 Of seven *loaded* editorial staff who returned questionnaires in 1999, all had Honours degrees, from institutions including University College London, Sussex University and the University of Liverpool.
8 Several staff on other 'lad mags', interviewed by the author in 1998–1999, displayed similar outlooks. *Front* editor, Piers Hernu, reasoned, 'I don't think many people count bare breasts as pornography nowadays, do they? You've got bare breasts in virtually any magazine you look in—you get it in the *Sunday Times* magazine; so that's not pornography'. A commercial executive at *Maxim* declared his response to accusations of sexism thus: 'I think that's a bit of politically correct bullshit really. I just don't see it. Actually we have had many, many letters—and I'm quite sure that this would be the case with other magazines as well—from women saying how much they appreciate men's magazines in educating men about what women want and so on'.

9 It was rumoured that *loaded* was the first magazine to pay drinking expenses to its writers, since it saw alcohol as a potent source of ideas and an essential component of pursuing a story.

10 Brown made the following, seemingly contradictory, statements in consecutive interviews.

> *loaded* was primarily created by working-class people. It was created by a working-class magazine company. The topics covered in it were ostensibly working-class interests: football, music, drinking, bagging off with girls, whatever; and wanting to improve, better yourself.
>
> *loaded* wasn't set up as a working class magazine. . . . The mixture of people on the staff, some were from up north, some were from out in Essex, some had gone to public school, some had gone to comprehensive schools, some had gone to corrective institutions; some had done degrees, others had got O-levels, others hadn't got O-levels. Some had had very successful jobs, others hadn't. *loaded* was [just] a product of the people who created it. It wasn't an attempt to be working class. (Brown 1999).

11 Such incongruities were also evoked in Brown and Southwell's identifications with films such as *The Dirty Dozen* and *The Magnificent Seven*, where themes of individual flair stood out against those of heroic masculine toughness and team spirit.

12 Brown was proud to recall that twenty-four of *loaded*'s first thirty-six front covers had featured men (Radio Four, 16.7.2002). By the end of the decade, with the commercial implications of not having female coverstars far more significant than five years earlier, there was little hope of a *loaded* editor persuading IPC to support a male coverstar. In fact, the appointment of Keith Kendrick as *loaded* editor in 2001 marked a new point in the magazine's editorial history, with Kendrick's overhaul clearly taking *loaded* in the direction of *FHM* and *Maxim*, titles that had not considered male coverstars since the mid-90s.

13 The purpose of Brown's occasional insinuations that he did, in fact, 'invent' the market—like his celebration of the notion that his magazines simply tumbled from his mind—was partly rhetorical. Such claims did much to enhance Brown's status within the industry, and, indeed, were supported by a trade press that frequently glamorized the creative process.

References

Bancroft, A. (1998) 'The model of a man: masculinity and body image in men's lifestyle magazines', paper given at the British Association for the Advancement of Science conference, 10–11 September 1998, University of Cardiff.

Benwell, B. (forthcoming) 'Ironic discourse: evasive masculinity in British men's lifestyle magazines', *Men and Masculinities*.

Bourdieu, P. (1984) *Distinction: A Social Critique of the Judgement of Taste*. (translated by Richard Nice). London: Routledge.

Brown, J. (1999) unpublished interviews.

Chippendale, P. and Horrie, C. (1990) *Stick It Up Your Punter! The Uncut Story of The Sun Newspaper*. London: Heinemann.

Du Gay, P. (ed.) (1997) *Production of Culture/Cultures of Production*. London: Sage.

McRobbie, A. (ed.) (1994) *Postmodernism and Popular Culture*. London: Routledge.

MacKenzie, J. (1987) 'The imperial pioneer and hunter and the British masculine stereotype in late Victorian and Edwardian times': in J.A. Mangan and J. Walvin (eds) (1987) *Manliness and Morality: Middle-Class Masculinity in Britain and America, 1800–1940*. Manchester: Manchester University Press.

Mintel (1998) *Men's Lifestyle Magazines*. Mintel Intelligence.

Mort, F. (1996) *Cultures of Consumption: Masculinities and Social Space in Late Twentieth-Century Britain*. London: Routledge.

Nixon, S. (1996) *Hard Looks: Masculinities, Spectatorship and Contemporary Consumption*. London: UCL Press.

Nixon, S. (1997) 'Advertising executives as modern men: Masculinity and the UK advertising industry in the 1980s': in M. Nava, A. Blake, I. MacRury and B. Richards (eds) *Buy this Book: Studies
in Advertising and Consumption*. London: Routledge.

Roper, M. (1994) *Masculinity and the British Organisational Man since 1945*. Oxford: Oxford University Press.

Southwell, T. (1998a) *Getting Away With It: The Inside Story of* Loaded. London: Ebury Press.

Southwell, T. (1998b) unpublished interview.

Turner, B. (1990) *British Cultural Studies: An Introduction*. London: Routledge.

Wolfe, T. and Johnson, E.W. (1975) *The New Journalism*. London: Picador.

Reading men's lifestyle magazines: cultural power and the information society

Nick Stevenson, Peter Jackson and Kate Brooks

Introduction

This chapter is based on an inter-disciplinary research project that investigated the social significance of the recent commercial success of men's 'lifestyle' magazines. The project included an analysis of the visual and verbal content of a range of magazines (including *loaded, FHM, Maxim, Men's Health* and several other titles), interviews with editorial staff at the magazines and focus group discussions with 15–20 groups of men (and a smaller number of women).[1] The project aimed to explore what the commercial success of these magazines had to say about changing constructions of masculinity in the 1990s. In this chapter we aim to provide an assessment of the place of men's 'lifestyle' magazines within the information society, casting our analysis in terms of the concept of cultural power. We focus on the economic and cultural significance of the magazines and try to draw out some lessons for those who are seeking to develop a more political response to the magazines. Our analysis is considerably strengthened in this regard by our attempt to capture the public forms of talk that are available to magazine consumers, forms of talk which are significantly drawn upon in the focus group discussions. We aim to provide an analysis of the magazines which focuses upon their ability to make money and to encode popular subjectivities.

When we began this project there was very little academic interest in men's magazines, apart from some work by Frank Mort (1988, 1996), Sean Nixon (1993, 1996, 1997) and Tim Edwards (1997). There was, of course, a well-established feminist literature on women's magazines including important work by Angela McRobbie (1978, 1991), Janice Winship (1978, 1987), Janice Radway (1987), Joke Hermes (1995) and others. The feminist literature highlighted the contradictory nature of women's magazines (especially for feminist readers). Many women described their guilty pleasure in reading the magazines, enjoying them as a source of entertainment and distraction but conscious, too, that the magazines perpetuated dubious ideas about romantic love, compulsory heterosexuality and other patriarchal values. These ideas of ambivalence and contradiction fit well with our own search for alternative ways of theorizing cultural power that avoid outmoded ideas of dominance and resistance (cf. Stevenson *et al.*, 2000a). To give just two examples, Ros Ballaster and her co-authors emphasize the need to go beyond a stark choice between magazines as 'bearers of pleasure' and 'purveyors of oppressive ideology'. As they argue:

> The identification of 'contradiction' fails to embarrass either editors, writers or readers. The success of the women's magazine is no doubt connected with its ability to encompass glaring contradiction coherently in its pages (Ballaster *et al.*, 1991: 7).

Similarly, in Hilary Radner's account of the ambivalent appeal of women's magazines, she suggests that:

> Perhaps the women's magazine does a better job of speaking for women, of empowering their voices, than does the feminist scholar who has set this as her task. I am not suggesting that we see women's magazines as an emancipatory institution, as the site of authentic resistance to the patriarchal norm [but that] . . . as feminists we might learn from the women's magazine as a pedagogical model, one that meanders yet remains contained, that offers information within a heteroglossia of narratives rather than from a univocal position, that accumulates rather than replaces, that permits contradiction and fragmentation, that offers choice rather than conversion as its message (Radner, 1995: 135).

So, too, with men's magazines, we are interested in the 'heteroglossia of narratives', in the dispersed and fragmented nature of cultural power, rather than in the kind of unitary view of power implied in traditional models of dominance and resistance associated with the Frankfurt School and their 'mass culture' thesis.

'Mass culture' in the information age

The 'mass culture' thesis within media studies was based upon the idea that culture had been converted into an industry. In Adorno and Horkheimer's (1973) original formulation, the sphere of culture was argued to be becoming increasingly like that of production with instrumental reason coming to administer and control a superficial media and consumer culture. The culture industry, it was thought, had a negative effect on the audience: repressing difference, manufacturing sameness and reproducing conformity. More recently, through the work of John Fiske (1987), David Morley (1988), Ien Ang (1991) and others, media and cultural studies has made us aware of the semiotic complexity of modern audiences. While this remains a major advance it leaves open the question of the ideological power of modern media cultures, a critical idea of cultural power (and ideology) being dependent upon the notion that certain linguistic signs symbolically reinforce or leave unquestioned material relations of domination.

Our argument here is not intended to lead back into a study of media that returns to discredited notions of the 'culture industry'. However, it is evident that the media continue to have the power to define 'what everyone is talking about'. The images, discourses and frameworks of understanding that we borrow from the media to make sense of our everyday lives are embedded in wider cultures of production and media circulation. In this respect, we have found the metaphor of 'circuits of culture' to be helpful (Johnson, 1986). By this we mean that ideologies and cultures disseminated by the media draw upon a multitude of sources and simultaneously influence and are influenced by civil society. Yet what is absent from these debates is any attempt to link the organization of the economy to that of culture (cf. Paul DuGay's argument for a critical approach to 'cultural economy' in DuGay (1997; DuGay and Pryke, 2002)). The main problem here is that any attempt to rethink the connections between these dimensions can easily revert to earlier notions of economic determinism and thereby undermine the specificity of the cultural. Similar problems beset more culturalist frameworks where the production of meaning goes on outside any recognizable social context.

Economic success or failure is now increasingly determined by product innovation, retailing and design rather than by traditional concerns with processes of production. Flexible specialization means that cultural institutions are better able to pick up on the shifting patterns of consumer spending and lifestyle. As Sean Nixon (1997) points out, the role of information in the design process helps shape the cultural meanings and values that become associated with a product and leads to the segmentation of mass culture into niche markets. Design-intensive, flexible capitalism provides both opportunity (with a number of commercial operators cashing in on the considerable success of the magazines) and uncertainty (in terms of job insecurity and mobility). New technology has also allowed organizations to achieve increasing flexibility in terms of more knowledge-dependent and less hierarchical structures. Information networks have enabled large corporations to co-ordinate their activities worldwide, while building in reflexive inputs to enable them to respond quickly to the current state of the market and to benefit from economies of scale. Hence, whereas industrialism was orientated towards economic growth, informationalism is more concerned with the development of knowledge and the creation of networks. The digitalization of knowledge bases allows information to be processed and stored across huge distances. Thus capitalism is becoming less dependent upon the state and more upon the ability of a common informational system to transmit knowledge across distanciated networks (Castells, 1996).

These features have all helped construct an information-based society. As Beck (1992), Castells (1997) and Melucci (1996) have all argued, the 'cultural' dimension can no longer be conceived as an add-on after the 'real' dimensions of politics and economics have been satisfactorily explained. Whether we are talking about the risk society, network capitalism or the concerns of social movements, ideas of symbolic challenge and exclusion remain central. The power to name, construct meaning and exert control over the flow of information within contemporary societies is one of the central structural divisions today. Power is not solely based upon material dimensions but also involves the capacity to throw into question established codes and rework frameworks of common understanding. We need to appreciate how dominant systems and institutions seek to establish the power of master codes, rendering some perspectives meaningless while asserting the dominance of other viewpoints. The cultural power of men's lifestyle magazines can be seen in terms of particular circuits of information which are genuinely mediated by a diversity of media forms and popular experience. As Castells argues, modern media cultures operate in:

> a system in which reality itself (that is, people's material/symbolic existence) is entirely captured, fully immersed in a virtual image setting, in a world of make-believe, in which appearances are not just on the screen through which experience is communicated, but they become the experience (1997: 373).

In a global, fast moving, semiotic culture, power is increasingly exerted through the material dimensions of semiotic cultures. In network systems, power comes through the inducement and persuasion of information and images generating new opportunities, risks and desires (Urry, 2000).

These changes in the way power is mediated in modern societies have also shifted the ground upon which social movements are obliged to operate. Castells (1997) characterizes a variety of social movements as developing highly skilful media techniques in largely reactive and defensive responses to economic globalization. By this he means that such movements do not so much articulate a vision of a future emancipated society but a more conservative attempt to preserve current social identities. The task of any oppositional movement must be to connect local experiences to a more global agenda. Defensive reactions to globalization can be seen in a range of fundamentalist and communalist political movements and cultural struggles across the world. As the democratic state becomes increasingly reduced to an empty shell the new sites of power lie in images and information codes. In Castells' (1997: 359) words: the 'sites of this power are people's minds'.

These considerations point towards not only a new politics but a new society in the making. For example, Castells (1997) argues that the patriarchal family, the focal point of patriarchalism, is being progressively challenged. The combined forces and increased visibility of different sexual practices, the massive incorporation of women into paid work, growing control over biological reproduction and the new self-definitions offered by new social movements are redefining gendered relations. The shaking of heterosexual norms and the disruption of the patriarchal family (primarily through the emergence of 'single' lifestyles and households, divorce, the practice of 'living together' and greater autonomy in reproduction) has meant that there is an increasing diversity of family types on offer. Castells perceives that, despite the fact that men continue to be more economically and socially privileged, a reactive politics is unlikely to serve their long-term interests. Hence to begin the process of rebuilding society in the face of exclusion and fundamentalism, the emergence of more egalitarian families is crucial to the remaking of civil society.

The renegotiations of heterosexual relations have also proved to be an important focus of attention in the recent work of Ulrich Beck (1992, 1997) and

Anthony Giddens (1991, 1992). Both point to processes of detraditionalization and individuation as being the key focus for the unfreezing and increasingly open nature of previously established patriarchal relations. Industrial society was based upon a strict separation between public and private with women largely excluded from the public sphere and their identities being shaped by a rigid gender system. However, with women entering the workforce in growing numbers after the second world war, we are beginning to witness the break up of the gender system in both economic and cultural terms. This also releases men from being the sole supporter of the family and thereby weakens the previous connections between work, family and gender. The partial deconstruction of public and private worlds inevitably means that love becomes a more contingent social arrangement. Love, no longer colonized by economic necessity, becomes an empty sign that has to be filled in by the participants within the relationship. In this, argue Beck and Beck-Gernsheim (1995), love has taken the place of religion in that it is the central way through which modern subjects attribute meaning to their lives. Love relationships are the places where we can be ourselves, gain intimate contact with others and find a place where we can belong. Yet, whereas more equal relationships imply more freedom for women, for men it implies more competition, more housework, less 'control' and more time with their children.

Beck brings these questions together through what he calls 'reflexive' modernization, which he contrasts with the idea that modernity has become more reflective. Simple reflection theory holds that the modernization of society leads to the increasing capacity of subjects to ask questions about the society within which they are living. Instead, 'reflexive' modernization can lead to reflection on the forces that are threatening to plunge modernity into self-dissolution, although this is not necessarily the case. Hence Beck is clear that this is not a theory of progress or decline, but one that takes up the ambivalence of modernity by focusing upon 'deep-seated institutional crises in late industrial society' (Beck, 1994: 178). Reflexive modernization is about unintended self-confrontation rather than reflection. However, Beck (1997) has consistently sought to argue that the 'age of side effects' or the 'break up of industrial society' does not necessarily lead in one direction rather than another. 'Reflexive' modernization may not lead to a reflection upon modernization and its consequences, but onto forms of counter-modernization. Whereas 'reflexive' modernization dissolves the boundaries of class, gender and nation, counter-modernity seeks to re-naturalize these questions by recreating boundaries and repressing critical questions. Counter-modernity, then, represents the partial repression of doubt, ambiguity and ethical complexity.

Whether we understand contemporary cultural processes as 'reactions' to globalization or as more reflexive responses to the break up of tradition, these contours all place a new emphasis on the cultural and symbolic power of modern communication systems. Hence to consider men's lifestyle magazines through the rubric of the information society has a number of advantages over previous waves of theorizing. First, the organization of culture is central to the idea of the information society, whether this is through the creation of new media markets or through the shaping of the perceptions of consumers. Secondly, the information society thesis holds that there is no one central conflict within society that effectively determines all other social relations. This means that the frameworks of knowledge we have available to understand contemporary shifts in gendered and sexual relations are no more or no less important than other features. Thirdly, the cultural aspects of everyday life can indeed be linked to broader questions connected with both the economy and culture. In this respect, men's lifestyle magazines make visible a number of contemporary questions in respect of masculinity and gendered social relations. Money can be made quickly out of the commodification of masculine anxieties and new ways of coding shifts in contemporary gender relations. As we shall see, men's lifestyle magazines become a legitimate area to debate the pleasures and identities of contemporary subjects. Finally, the domains of 'public' and 'private' have become partially deconstructed through the entry of women into the 'public' and the media's invasion of the 'private'. This has helped to both politicize personhood by making visible a number of previously excluded questions concerning health, death, sexuality and gender. Such dimensions increasingly become part of the common culture of modern media societies. Viewed in terms of the information society perspective, new forms of identity politics may find their way into the public sphere through commercial cultures. Cultural power in this context flows from the ability of the magazines to make new subjectivities and ideologically code intimate human relations in contradictory ways (cf Stevenson *et al.*, 2000b).

The men's magazine market

Until the 1990s there were no 'general interest' magazines written specifically for men. There were some 19th-century precursors like *Blackwoods Magazine*, some gay magazines like *Spartacus* which flourished in the late 1960s, and some men's tailoring magazines like *Man About Town* which ran under various titles from 1953 to 1968. But, in general, the British publishing industry was distinctly cautious in its attitude to men's magazines. While the major publishers prevaricated, a small independent publisher, Wagadon, entered the market in 1986 with *Arena*, edited by Nick Logan. Once its success was established, the main publishers all followed suit, aiming to get a share of the burgeoning men's market and to provide men's titles to match their established women's magazines (see Table 1). Until the late 1980s, however, the received wisdom in the publishing industry was that 'men don't buy magazines', or at least that:

> men don't define themselves as men in what they read [but] as people who are into cars, who play golf, or fish . . . Successfully launching a general interest men's magazine would be like finding the holy grail (*Campaign*, 29 August 1986).

117

Table 1: The British men's magazine market in the late 1990s

Title	Date launched	Publisher	Publisher's related titles
Arena	1986	Wagadon	The Face
GQ (Gentlemen's Quarterly)	1988 (GQ Active, April 1997)	Condé Nast	Vogue, Vanity Fair, House & Garden etc.
Esquire	1991	National Magazine Company	Cosmopolitan, Harpers & Queen etc.
Attitude	1994	Northern & Shell	Penthouse
FHM (For Him Magazine)	1994	EMAP	Q, Mojo, Select etc.
Loaded	1994	IPC	Marie Claire, Homes & Gardens, Woman etc.
Men's Health	1995	Rodale Press	
XL for Men	1995	EMAP (formerly Stonehart)	Q, Mojo, Select etc
Maxim	1995	Dennis Lifestyle	Stuff for Men
Stuff for Men	1996	Dennis Lifestyle (acquired by Haymarket 1999)	Maxim

Within ten years men's magazines had become 'The fastest growing of all consumer magazine markets [with] currently the highest profile' (*Key Note*, 1996). From the early 1990s, the market developed in a truly spectacular way. A Mintel report on men's lifestyle magazines (1997) describes a 400 per cent growth from 1991 to 1996 in a sector that it estimated to be worth £30.9 million in cover sales revenue, predicted to grow to £68 million by 2000.

While there are some similarities in content and style among the magazines included within our study, there are also some significant differences. Some titles (including *GQ* and *Esquire*) are more 'upmarket' in terms of content and readership; others are resolutely 'downmarket' (including the market leaders, *FHM*, *loaded* and *Maxim*). Some have a specific focus: on 'extreme' sports (*Xtreme*), health (*Men's Health*) or computing (*Escape*). Others have spun off from the success of their 'parent' magazines to address a more specific niche (such as *Stuff for Men* from *Maxim*, or *GQ Active* from *GQ*). All are addressed, at least implicitly, to a heterosexual readership with the exception of *Attitude* which is specifically targeted at gay men. Some of the magazines, notably *loaded* and *FHM*, have achieved a genuinely mass circulation (with monthly sales of several hundred thousand, outselling the most popular women's magazines like *Cosmopolitan* and *Marie Claire*); others have a much lower circulation. The titles included here are all monthly (or in some cases, bi-monthly) magazines, costing between £2 and £3. They vary from around 120 to 300 pages in length, with advertising accounting for between 20 and 40 per cent of their pages.

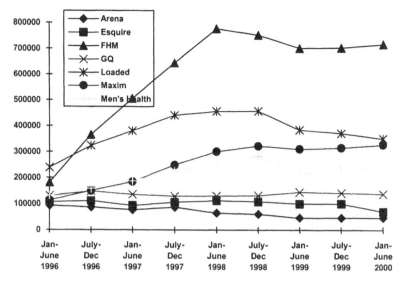

Figure 1: *Magazine circulation. (Source: Audit Bureau of Circulations)*

Circulation figures confirm the growth of the sector, initially dominated by the rise of *loaded* and later by *FHM* (see Figure 1). They also show significant expansion among some of the more 'upmarket' titles, such as *Men's Health*, as well as the relatively static or declining sales of some of the longer-established titles (such as *Arena* and *Esquire*) as they have faced increasing competition.

The market has clearly begun to segment into a small number of mass-circulation titles and numerous specialist or niche markets. The figures for the last couple of years might even suggest that the expansion of the men's maga-zine market has peaked, with sales of all the leading titles (with the exception of *GQ*) showing a decline. In the second half of 2001, for example, the circula-tion of *FHM* dipped to 570,719 (a year-on-year decline of 20.4 per cent), sending shock waves throughout the industry ('The lads go limp', *The Guardian*, 18 February 2002). Other leading titles, including *loaded, Maxim* and *GQ*, all experienced a drop in year-on-year sales of over 10 per cent. While sales may now have peaked, the rapid growth of this sector during the 1990s clearly sug-gests that significant social change was taking place.

Having analysed the growth of the men's magazine market in the 1990s, we now go on to discuss the content of the magazines and to offer an interpreta-tion of the diverse ways in which the magazines are read. Our particular focus here is on the magazines' stylistic and narrative construction and on how readers make sense of the magazines. We focus on how the magazines look and how they adopt a particular storytelling approach, including the provision of lists and snippets of advice as devices for the discussion of sexuality (Pfeil, 1995). In particular, we explore the different discourses and fantasies that the magazines make available to their readers. In general, the magazines address the reader as a 'mate', offering to become the 'reader's friend' by providing handy hints, pointing out obvious pitfalls and providing useful advice. This is all done in the language of 'common sense', with irony being used as a warning against taking anything that is said too seriously.[2] In this sense, the magazines are careful to avoid talking down to their readers. The language employed by the magazines is 'familiar', producing a sense of mediated intimacy between the 'lads' who run the magazine and their (assumed to be equally 'laddish') readers. For example, *FHM* publishes the phone numbers of its staff, runs a regular section on bar room jokes, letters to the editor (where they invite ugly readers to write in to be fixed up with a 'shag'), various sections offering advice (from sex to how to fix 'your own motor') and flirtatious interviews with fashion models and soap opera stars. Despite the fact that men's magazines have a disjointed narrative flow, the overall mode of address is friendly, ironic and laddish.

We can, however, also point to differences between the magazines within this genre. During the late 1990s, *loaded* was much more likely to celebrate male stars of British popular culture like George Best, Phil Daniels, Liam Gallagher, Jack Dee and John Cleese. This was coupled with a concerted focus upon the downmarket, outrageous and bizarre. By comparison, *FHM* and *Maxim* set a different tone for the development of the market. *FHM* is a thicker and glossier publication than *loaded*. Whereas *loaded* championed a 'birds, fags and booze' lifestyle, *FHM* featured well-known women celebrities on the cover and had a more commercial focus on the consumption of music, films and fashion. Both *Maxim* and *FHM* also ran 'advice' sections (*Maxim* called theirs 'How to do absolutely everything a whole lot better') which would have been too 'preachy' for *loaded*. Furthermore, *GQ*, *Arena* and *Esquire* all featured 'eye catching' women on the cover while attempting to maintain a more literary and discerning image (through the use of columnists such as Paul Morley and Tony Parsons). The fashion advertisements in these publications tend to be both more upmarket and more prominently displayed than within the other titles, including status brands such as Ralph Lauren, Hugo Boss, Armani and Moschino. These magazines have a more luxurious and exclusive image than is evident within titles such as *Maxim* and *FHM*. Finally, the men's magazine market expanded at a rapid rate during our study opening out space for a number of more niche marketed publications like *Attitude*, *XL*, *Stuff for Men* and *Escape*.

While there is not the space here to explore the complexities of these various titles, our argument is that they can all be positioned in relation to the major players within the field. For instance, whereas *Attitude* was a gay (and less laddish) version of *GQ*, *Escape* provided internet tips for *loaded* lads. On the other hand, *Men's Health* has also incorporated many of these features but is much more concerned with technical detail. In this respect, there is a clear division between the 'expert' status of the magazine and the person in need of advice (the 'reader'). It is assumed that the flow of knowledge is overwhelmingly one way (from the magazine to the reader), but that the magazine can be trusted (like a good doctor) not to mislead the reader. Consequently, the set of social relations presumed by a magazine like *Men's Health* is hierarchical and invites a believing rather than an ironic disposition. This distinction should help us draw some conclusions as to how we might understand the magazines politically.

In particular, we would like to emphasize the impact that *loaded* had on the visual style and content of the other men's magazines. *Loaded*'s arrival in 1994 radically reshaped the field of men's magazine journalism. According to Tim Southwell (the magazine's second-in-command):

> For issue one we played to what we believed were our strengths. We went on tour with Paul Weller, [journalist Mick] Deeson wrote about how great hotel sex was and I'd gone skydiving in California. We also had the famous pictures of Liz Hurley in that pair of pants—the pair that showed a little too much of what it should have been concealing. Plus Rod Stewart, George Best, Dave from Minder, Beavis & Butthead, Vic Reeves, Withnail and I, Gary Oldman, Eric Cantona and the first-ever UK magazine interview with Tiger Woods. All for an introductory price of £1 (Southwell, 1998: 55–56).

To mark the magazine's distinctiveness from the other (more upmarket) men's titles, *loaded* deliberately focused on football, cars, drinking and music. In an early editorial, James Brown commented:

> *Loaded* should be rammed full of the things that people go on about in the pub and that stuff like health and perfume should be left to the adult mags. Remember, grooming is for horses (July, 1995).

The use of laddish irony which became common currency within *loaded* changed the face of men's magazine publishing. Both *Maxim* and *FHM* borrowed from and reinvented the visual and verbal economy of *loaded*, blurring the distinction between lads' mags like *loaded* and more upmarket titles like *GQ* and *Esquire*.

The general distinction between 'upmarket' magazines aimed at slightly older men (*GQ, Esquire, Arena*) and 'downmarket' magazines (*FHM, Maxim, loaded*) has become increasingly blurred (with James Brown's editorial move from *loaded* to *GQ* in 1997 acting as a key signifier in this respect). So, for example, Peter Howarth (as editor of *Esquire*) sought to defend his magazine's reliance on a diet of 'babes and boobs' by arguing against the idea that there had been a 'dumbing down' of men's magazines. Yet he went on to say that 'any good magazine must offer a balance of content, and part of that balance, if it is to reflect the interests of men, will inevitably be articles on beautiful women' (*The Guardian*, 25 November 1996).

The popularity and commercial success of *loaded* undoubtedly had an impact on the other magazines. 'Softer', more caring, versions of masculinity (associated with the 'new man') were displaced by a 'harder' image whereby other aspects of masculine behaviour such as drinking to excess, adopting a predatory attitude towards women and obsessive forms of independence (read: fear of commitment) became the new focal point. As Sean Nixon (1996) pointed out, the emergence of the 'new lad' signified the difficulty of reinventing heterosexual scripts, with irony being used to 'distance' the reader from these difficulties. However, we would argue that whereas the function of irony in relation to the 'new man' was to provide a safe distance between the reader and less traditional scripts, with the new wave of 'laddism' irony began to operate to subvert political critique. To offer a political critique of the magazines was to miss the point of the joke and place yourself outside a mediated laddish community. However, irony in men's magazines continues to function in a similar way to the new wave of women's magazines (discussed by McRobbie, 1999) in that it allows men to experience the contradictory nature of the magazines (and masculinity) at a safe distance.

We also wish to suggest that the public appearance of the magazines has brought into the open a number of anxieties and fantasies about men and masculinity in a changing society. As Peter Middleton has argued in relation to another form of popular culture:

[comic books] offer powerful fantasies in a graphic mode which does not intrude too much disruptive reality either in the storyline or in the sketchy visual representation. Above all, comics offer the inside story on the adult world. Hyper masculine action comics are offered to boys as the inside information on men's lives, information they find hard to get from anywhere else (1992: 25).

The knowing sexism of the magazines also operates within a wider culture which has introduced the idea of 'relationships' as a central concern for both sexes. The changing sociological context within which the magazines have appeared means that they are a far more complex phenomenon than is implied in simplistic arguments about a feminist 'backlash'. The magazines are caught between an attempt to construct masculinity as a form of fundamentalist certitude while simultaneously responding to a world where gender relations are rapidly changing. In sociological terms, we argue, the magazines can be made sense of by identifying the social and cultural contradictions that they are trying to handle, caught between an awareness that old-style patriarchal relations are crumbling and the desire to reinscribe power relations between different genders and sexualities. In terms of the information society thesis spelled out earlier, they are economic and cultural responses to gender quake.

Making sense of men's magazines

Drawing on focus group discussions with a wide range of men (and a smaller number of women) we seek, in this section, to understand the magazines in the context of men's changing identities and gender relations.[3] In particular, we explore how our focus group participants attempt to 'make sense' of recent changes in masculinity and consumer culture through their reactions to the magazines, including previously neglected topics such as fashion, health and relationships. Though our analysis focuses on 'men's talk', the inclusion of some mixed gender focus groups and one all-women group provided additional

Table 2: Discursive repertoires

Harmless fun	Laddishness
Honesty	Trash
Naturalness	Irony
Openness/visibility	Change/backlash
Seriousness	Women as Other

insights into contemporary constructions of masculinity and gender relations. Indeed, the group that was most openly hostile to the magazines and most critical of the resurgence of 'laddish' forms of masculinity was the only all-female group. Given that the magazines are mostly aimed at men, it is men's voices that we sought to capture in the focus groups. At the end of this process, we identified a range of discursive repertoires ('discourses' for short) through which our respondents attempted to 'make sense' of the magazines (see Table 2).

All of these discourses, we suggest, can be understood in terms of the ambiguities of contemporary masculinities, which are resolved (discursively at least) through notions of 'constructed certitude'.[4] Here, however, we shall illustrate our argument by reference to just three of the discourses: honesty, naturalness, and openness. These discourses arguably have a particular relevance to our understanding of the magazines' political dimensions.

1 'honesty'

Several groups distinguished *loaded* from the other magazines, claiming that, while the others pretended to be sophisticated, cultured and intelligent, *loaded* was 'more blatant', with 'no pretensions'. Magazines like *GQ* were described as 'art' or 'aspirational' (for people with 'lashings of dosh'), presenting a superficial or glossy image of the 'new man'. By contrast, *loaded* was more 'honest': 'a celebration of the unacceptable face of men'. Even among those who preferred 'classier' magazines like *Arena*, with 'more cultural integrity', a contrast could still be drawn between magazines like *GQ* and *Esquire*, 'dressing themselves up in a glossy cover', and *loaded* which was 'a bit more basic'. Similarly, those who found *Arena* too high-brow ('pseudo arty'), like the Sunday broadsheets, would read *loaded* 'just for a laugh', like the tabloids.

Some groups were sceptical concerning *loaded*'s way of addressing its readers, seeing it as 'manipulative' or as appealing to the 'lowest common denominator'. For the majority of respondents, however, *loaded*'s blatant emphasis on women, sport and entertainment was a welcome contrast to the 'airs and graces' of the more style-conscious magazines: 'They make no qualms about it ... they're not hypocritical'. Other groups also spoke about the 'honest and open view' of 'shameless' magazines like *loaded* which don't feel any need to justify themselves, celebrating 'a kind of freedom to ... shout and be kind of loud and get pissed'.

Loaded's founding editor James Brown was singled out for praise by many readers. Unlike the other magazines, whose editors had to strive for success in a calculated manner, James Brown was said to embody the magazine's values in a more natural way. Although he studiously cultivated this image (via biographical material on the UpLoaded website and in media interviews, for example), many readers appeared to take the image at face value: 'He seemed to live and breathe it . . . in an honest way'.

Notions of 'honesty' among the magazines and their readers are also interestingly at odds with the use of irony that is so pervasive in the magazines themselves and among their readers as revealed in our focus group discussions. For example, there is a significant contradiction between the claim to be returning to more 'authentic' forms of masculinity—less forced or contrived than discourses of the 'new man'—and the adoption of ironic modes of address which are, at the very least, double-edged if not wholly duplicitous (cf Hutcheon, 1994).

2 'naturalness'

Many of our focus group participants argued that the image of the 'lad' was a more natural form of masculinity than the contrived image of the 'new man' which it replaced as a dominant media construction during the 1990s. The magazines were welcomed as promoting an image of masculinity that was more 'natural' in at least two senses: more authentic (true to men's real selves) and less contrived (unlike images of the 'new man'). The idea that the 'new man' was a media fiction was widely shared: 'The new man went too far . . . [he was] unrealistic [and] didn't exist except on television'; he was 'a fiction created by Richard and Judy [day-time TV presenters]'; 'all about image'; 'a mythical creation . . . completely unrealistic and artificial . . . I think the media makes a lot of it up'.

Unlike the rather diffuse image of the 'new man', none of our respondents had any difficulty in identifying the characteristics of the 'new lad', reeling off a familiar list of traits and consumer goods: 'beer, shoes, cars, stereos and women'; 'big chunky watches, suits, haircuts'; 'beer, football, women, clothes, music and films' and, later in the same group, 'football, booze, women, films, what was the other one?'. The list of characteristics was sometimes qualified, as in the following discussion:

Eddie: I think [the magazines] are aimed at the average lad . . . have a few beers, watch the footie, trying to, er, pull girls [laughs] . . .
Tom: It's like getting away from the 'new man' image.
Eddie: But at the same time it's not going back to like the . . .
Tom: It's like you've got to look good, but you've still got to have your traditional attitudes, like having beers and watching footie . . . you can go out and have a good laugh, a few beers, but you can also, like, be civil you know, like sensitive.

The apparent ambiguity of contemporary masculinities was taken up by several other groups, describing forms of masculinity that were 'not sexist, not racist but interested in drinking, getting drunk' or 'being a boy, liking your beer, but also being quite aware, do you know what I mean? It's OK to be a bit of a lad . . . you can have your politics and respect women'.

If laddish masculinity was only too 'natural' for some men, others were grateful for the support that the men's magazines gave them in legitimizing behaviour that might previously have been criticized. Whereas previously men had been in constant danger of 'slipping up and making some mistake', there was now more cultural approval for 'being yourself'. The magazines have played a crucial role in this: 'giving you permission . . . to be the man you want to be . . . You know, whether I want to start screwing around or whatever . . . it's ok to be actually who I am'; 'it's sort of allowing you to say and talk about things that you might have thought but you didn't really talk about too much and you might feel slightly embarrassed about'. In response to this widely felt sense of insecurity, the magazines were seen to offer 'a palliative for all the things that you're unsure about'. The magazines were there 'to assure your identity . . . how you're supposed to look'; their success 'plays upon those things that you're going to feel inadequate about . . . because you want to make up the deficit'; 'you need that kind of support'.

The repertoires of 'honesty' and 'naturalness' are also significant in that they imply the existence of a more 'balanced' form of masculinity—in between the extremes of the 'new man' and the 'new lad'—neither a 'traditional' form of masculinity nor a simple response to the alleged extremes of feminism and 'political correctness'. This more 'authentic' form of masculinity was felt by some groups to be most closely approximated in *loaded* (in terms of its 'honesty' and lack of pretentiousness). Other groups felt that such 'balance' was potentially available in new and more 'open' forms of masculinity, an opportunity which had failed to materialize or a moment that had been lost.

Media constructions of 'laddishness' have come to seem so 'natural' that for many respondents there was no need to defend them or to consider alternative forms of masculinity. While some participants were critical of the magazines' celebration of 'laddish' masculinities, many more revelled in the lack of restraint implied by what they construed as a return to more 'natural' expressions of masculinity. This included, for example, the opportunity to look at pictures of 'sexy' women in an unselfconscious and relatively guilt-free way. One group argued that *loaded* 'does something dead simple', reflecting 'how blokes are'. While images of the 'new man' were commonly recognized as a cultural construction, 'laddish' forms of masculinity were generally regarded as more 'honest' and 'natural'. As one focus group participant suggested: 'New Laddism is a sort of honest and open view about blokes between the ages of 17 and 35'. By the late 1990s, then, 'laddishness' had become so taken-for-granted as a form of masculinity that it was widely regarded as 'natural', in contrast to other versions of masculinity, such as the 'new man', which were commonly perceived to be a media construction.

3 'openness'

Returning to a more 'honest' or 'natural' expression of men's 'true selves' is partly contradicted by some of the magazines' encouragement of their readers to be more 'open' to different forms of masculinity. These might include a more open attitude towards men's health, sexuality or fashion, for example. Magazines like *Men's Health* encourage men to be more 'open' about themselves (to talk about their feelings, for example), while bringing into the open certain (previously repressed) aspects of masculinity including more public discussion of men's relationships, fashion and health. However, the magazines constantly monitor this process, using humour and other devices to help 'distance' their readers from any embarrassment they might feel at being seen to take these issues 'too seriously'.

Being 'open' about sexuality raised particular problems for the magazines and for the men in our focus groups. While the magazines are dominated by images of conventionally 'sexy' young women, their fashion pages also provide readers with a publicly acceptable way of looking at images of beautiful young men without the stigma that attaches to reading or viewing more explicitly homoerotic images. As one respondent put it: 'most gay magazines you couldn't read [in public, but] I wouldn't feel embarrassed reading this on the train'; 'there's lots of gorgeous blokes in it and perhaps they appeal to both [gay and straight] markets, you know'. While, for some readers, the magazines might open up a space to desire differently, in other respects they simply reinscribed traditional notions of gender and sexual difference ('Who's gay, who's straight?' *Maxim*, January 1997). Apart from the sheer predominance of female models in the magazines, the fashion sections in which male models are featured are usually relegated to the back pages. Even there, male models tend to be shot in very active, sporting poses (doing kung fu or judo moves for example) or alongside female models, apparently confirming their heterosexuality. As one reader argued:

> they've managed very subtly to avoid the gay . . . because there is a hetero and gay distinction here . . . but it's absolutely [clear], you know, these are guys' guys, this is about a hetero guy. It's quite interesting the way that that's been stressed and a lot of taboos have been very very carefully scooted around.

Other readers were more ambivalent about representations of sexuality in the magazines, talking about having 'a sneaky glance' and referring to their 'illicit aspect'. One participant worried about reading *Men's Health* on the bus while travelling through Manchester's gay village, fearing that people would assume he was gay. More common, however, was the suggestion that 'gay people have led fashion in our lifetimes and we can see that the gap between the straight scene and the gay scene has sort of closed'. Nor was this view restricted to gay men. Whereas men were previously 'very coy', now they were 'opening up', one man told us: 'I think people are more open, it's socially more acceptable to say that you are different, you can sort of desire openly as a man'.

Our aim here has been to demonstrate the discursive complexity of men's magazines once they have been translated into popular forms of talk. These discourses need not represent men's private feelings about the magazines but aim to represent the popular forms of understanding that are available in respect of the magazines and masculinity. That many seek to 'champion' the magazines at a time of gender uncertainty is not surprising. Yet what should be evident is the cultural power of the magazines to limit the range of responses available and their relative success in coding some of the contradictory aspects of modern masculinity. Our argument is not that the audience responses reveal a cultural domain going on 'behind the backs' of the magazines but that their popularity, within an entertainment culture, is partially explained by the variety of subject positions they make available with respect to modern masculinities.

Men's magazines and informational politics

As the extracts from our focus group discussions suggest, the modern self is seemingly caught between a more uncertain and reflexive disposition and more stable social markers. Taking the example of changing masculinities, many of these features soon become apparent. Reviewing the sociological literature, Segal (1990) points towards the 'slow change' of masculine identities in respect of men's participation in child care, the declining importance of the 'breadwinner' role and adherence to heterosexual norms and practices. Yet the commodification of masculine anxieties, the growing awareness of health issues and a more reflexive disposition towards fashion and the body (all evident in the magazines) articulate more ambivalent frames.

If modernity is characterized by the rapid pace of change and the increased risks entailed by the undermining of traditional social scripts, it should be no surprise that one form of media power involves the construction or reinscription of earlier forms of certainty. This process is what Ulrich Beck (1997) refers to as the construction of certitude. If modernity has meant increased questioning of tradition, doubt, reflexivity and the unfreezing of gender relations, the construction of certitude is a form of counter-modernity that attempts to dismiss such issues or to render them more manageable. The attempt to replace questioning and doubt with more certain frames of reference can be related to a number of fundamentalist currents that are articulated in terms of certainty rather than risk. Beck writes:

> Certitude arises from and with the prevalence of a 'magic of feelings' (to use a modern term), an emotional praxis that sweeps away the trembling and hesitation of questioning and doubting with the instinctive and reflex-like security of becoming effective and making things effective in action (1997: 65).

According to Beck, the construction of certitude offers a 'magical' solution to questions of identity, eradicating doubt and the need to orientate oneself in a world that is increasingly perceived as being fragile and uncertain. In terms of masculinity, the more 'certain' world of patriarchal relations is not only part of a wider nostalgia for a social order that protected men's material interests, but one that offered more straightforward codes in terms of what passed as 'acceptable' masculine behaviour. However, wider economic changes, the questioning of sexuality by lesbian and gay groups, the undermining of traditional notions of public and private, and the political role played by feminism more generally have all served to destabilize modern masculine identities. Hence, in a situation where certainties and tradition are being progressively undermined, they have (somewhat paradoxically) to be 'constructed'. The construction of certitude in cultural forms need not, however, be read simply as a 'backlash' against feminism. Instead, we suggest that, while such formations have political implications, they may be understood as a more complex response to changing gender relations. Arguably, the construction of certitude gives both men and women a sense that the social world is more stable than it actually is. That is, images of phallic masculinity promote a cultural 'comfort zone' giving the masculine self (however temporarily) a sense of fixity and psychic security.

How, then, might this analysis be applied to our understanding of men's lifestyle magazines? Constructed certitude is most apparent in the profusion of 'how to' sections that are carried in many of the magazines, offering advice (often in a semi-ironic tone) so that readers can brush up on a variety of techniques from the monitoring of sexual performance to changing a car tyre. For example, *Maxim* (July 1997) carried a typical feature called 'How to be better than her last lover'. In many respects the article reaffirmed binary divisions between men and women: whereas she needs to feel relaxed, intimate and that she can trust her partner, he simply wants to have sex. However, the article stopped some way short of simply reaffirming old-style patriarchal relations as the reader is made aware that he is likely to be compared to his partner's former lovers. Unless he 'proves himself' a good lover the relationship may founder. In stories like these the magazines can be read as offering a space of both reflexivity and certitude, as simultaneously a material force seeking to re-work gender relations and a cultural fantasy with few if any practical implications. These constructions are politically important as such cultural practices continue to mark contemporary culture's 'distance' from modern feminism, while remaining pertinent as fantasies, allowing temporary forms of closure from men's current gender troubles.

Similarly, our focus group discussions with younger men moved between the naturalization of masculinity and reflexivity. In this sense, contemporary consumer culture positions male subjects in terms of a number of different and contradictory locations. In terms of the information society thesis, the choice between reflexivity and counter-modernity is not as straightforward as it might appear. The magazine's political significance in terms of content and meaning may, in fact, lie between these two tropes. It is the magazines' capacity to be able to accommodate both more 'open' and reflexive aspects of modernity along with the certitude of tradition that most convincingly explains their appeal. This enables male consumers to 'open up and close down, to move into and withdraw from the flow of messages' (Melucci 1996: 51).

In terms of the information society, the magazines represent the commodification of contemporary gender anxieties. They are sources of cultural power in respect of the speed at which network capitalism stimulates new markets and helps inform the changing definition of contemporary masculinity. From this perspective, we are not forced into making a choice between viewing the magazines as either forms of flexible accumulation or a largely conservative gender politics. Rather, we would argue, they pose more interesting questions for contemporary social movements that would seek to offer a critique of men's lifestyle magazines. From our perspective, such a critique would need to take the magazines more seriously (accepting that they are a genuinely popular intervention into the field of contemporary gender relations) while acknowledging the extent to which the 'new lad' is as much of a discursive fiction as the 'new man'. Following Melucci (1996), the democratization of public space is dependent upon our reflexive capacity to view our current identities as socially constructed. This not only opens up the possibility of critique, but also introduces the possibility of creativity and change. Social movements seeking a progressive politicization of contemporary masculinities might have a great deal to 'learn' from the magazines. They might learn, firstly, that attempts to interrupt powerful discourses that seek to code 'how men really are' will mean interrupting the ideological flow of the magazines to help suggest more complex alternatives. They would also be advised to 'work with' the magazines and the extent to which they occupy the grounds of health, relationships, definitions of success and male friendship — all of which are key components within any new men's politics. That the magazines may attempt to present themselves and their readers as engaged in a form of 'harmless fun' should not discourage others from seeking to unravel more subtle understandings of modern masculinities.

Notes

1 The project was funded by ESRC under award number R000221838. An earlier version of this chapter was presented as a paper at a seminar organized by the Centre for Gender Studies in Europe at the University of Sheffield. A more extended discussion of magazine content can be found in Stevenson *et al.* (2000a). The focus group discussions are analysed in more depth in Jackson *et al.* (1999) and in our book: *Making sense of men's magazines* (Jackson *et al.*, 2001). Our argument about ambivalence and contradiction is outlined in Stevenson *et al.* (2000b).

2 The editor of FHM once declared that everything in his magazine should be funny, useful or sexy, parodied in the *Guardian* as 'funny, useful and selling' (17 February 1997).

3 These arguments are developed further in Jackson *et al.* 1999, 2001.

4 These discourses are, of course, articulated in various ways, some of which endorse and some of which repudiate conventional notions of 'what men are like'. Elsewhere (Stevenson *et al.*, 2000b; Jackson *et al.*, 2001) we elaborate on the different dispositions that lie behind the articulation of each discourse. This is particularly germane in situations such as that reported here, where popular discourses (as reflected in the focus groups) themselves reflect wider discourses that were already

available in the magazines themselves and in the extensive media commentaries about the magazines that were particularly prevalent in the mid-1990s. An account of discourses and dispositions inevitably involves an exploration of the ambiguities and ambivalences of contemporary masculinities such as can only be hinted at in the space available to us here.

References

Adorno, T. and Horkheimer, M. (1973) *The Dialectic of the Enlightenment*. London: Allen Lane.

Ang, I. (1991) *Desperately Seeking the Audience*. London: Routledge.

Ballaster, R., Beetham, M., Frazer, E. and Hebron, S. (1991) *Women's Worlds: Ideology, Femininity and the Woman's Magazine*. London: Macmillan.

Beck, U. (1992) *Risk Society: Towards a New Modernity*. London: Sage.

Beck, U. (1994) 'The Reinvention of Politics: Towards a Theory of Reflexive Modernization': in Beck, U., Giddens, A. and Lash, S. (eds) *Reflexive Modernization*. Cambridge: Polity Press.

Beck, U. (1995) *Ecological Politics in the Age of Risk*. Cambridge: Polity Press.

Beck, U. (1997) *The Reinvention of Politics: Rethinking Modernity in the Global Social Order*. Cambridge: Polity Press.

Beck, U. and Beck-Gernsheim, E. (1995) *The Normal Chaos of Love*. Cambridge: Polity Press.

Castells, M. (1997) *The Power of Identity: The Information Age: Economy, Society and Culture*, Vol. II. Oxford: Blackwell.

DuGay, P. (ed.) (1997) *Production of Culture/Cultures of Production*. London: Sage.

DuGay, P. and Pryke, M. (eds) (2002) *Cultural Economy*. London: Sage.

Edwards, T. (1997) *Men in the Mirror: Men's Fashion, Masculinity and Consumer Society*. London: Cassell.

Fiske, J. (1987) *Television Culture*. London: Methuen.

Giddens, A. (1991) *Modernity and Self-Identity: Self and Society in the Late Modern Age*. Cambridge: Polity Press.

Giddens, A. (1992) *The Transformation of Intimacy: Sexuality, Love and Eroticism in Modern Societies*. Cambridge: Polity Press.

Hermes, J. (1995) *Reading Women's Magazines*. Cambridge: Polity Press.

Hutcheon, L. (1994) *Irony's Edge: The Theory and Politics of Irony*. London: Routledge.

Jackson, P., Stevenson, N. and Brooks, K. (1999) 'Making sense of men's lifestyle magazines', *Environment and Planning D: Society and Space*, 17: 353–68.

Jackson, P., Stevenson, N. and Brooks, K. (2001) *Making Sense of Men's Magazines*. Cambridge: Polity Press.

Johnson, R. (1986) 'The story so far: and other transformations': 277–313 in D. Punter (ed.) *Introduction to Contemporary Cultural Studies*. London: Longman.

McRobbie, A. (1978) '*Jackie*: an ideology of adolescent femininity': 96–108 in Centre for Contemporary Cultural Studies Women's Group (eds) *Women Take Issue*. London: Hutchinson.

McRobbie, A. (1991) *Feminism and Youth Culture*, London: Macmillan.

McRobbie, A. (1999) *In the Culture Society*. London: Routledge.

Melucci, A. (1996) *Challenging Codes: Collective Action in the Information Age*. Cambridge: Cambridge University Press.

Middleton, P. (1992) *The Inward Gaze: Masculinity and Subjectivity in Modern Culture*. London: Routledge.

Morley, D. (1988) *Family Television: Cultural Power and Domestic Leisure*. London: Routledge.

Mort, F. (1988) 'Boy's own? Masculinity, style and popular culture': 193–224 in R. Chapman and J. Rutherford (eds) *Male Order: Unwrapping Masculinity*. London: Lawrence & Wishart.

Mort, F. (1996) *Cultures of Consumption: Masculinities and Social Space in Late Twentieth Century Britain*. London: Routledge.

Nixon, S. (1993) 'Looking for the holy grail: publishing and advertising strategies for contemporary men's magazines', *Cultural Studies* 7: 467–92.

Nixon, S. (1996) *Hard Looks: Masculinities, Spectatorship and Contemporary Consumption*. London: UCL Press.

Nixon, S. (1997) 'Exhibiting masculinity': 291–336 in S. Hall (ed.) *Representation: Cultural Representations and Signifying Practices*. London: Sage.

Pfeil, F. (1995) *White Guys: Studies in Postmodern Domination and Difference*. London: Verso.

Radner, H. (1995) *Shopping Around: Feminine Culture and the Pursuit of Pleasure*. London: Routledge.

Radway, J. (1987) *Reading the Romance: Women, Patriarchy and Popular Literature*. London: Verso.

Segal, L. (1990) *Slow Motion: Changing Masculinities, Changing Men*. London: Virago.

Southwell, T. (1998) *Getting Away With It: the Inside Story of* Loaded. London: Ebury Press.

Stevenson, N., Jackson, P. and Brooks, K. (2000a) 'The sexual politics of men's lifestyle magazines', *European Journal of Cultural Studies* 3: 366–85.

Stevenson, N., Jackson, P. and Brooks, K. (2000b) 'Ambivalence in men's lifestyle magazines': 189–212 in P. Jackson, M. Lowe, D. Miller and F. Mort (eds) *Commercial Cultures*. Oxford: Berg.

Urry, J. (2000) *Sociology Beyond Societies*. London: Routledge.

Winship, J. (1978) 'A woman's world: Woman—an ideology of femininity': 133–145 in Centre for Contemporary Cultural Studies Women's Group (eds) *Women Take Issue*. London: Hutchinson.

Winship, J. (1987) *Inside Women's Magazines*. London: Pandora Press.

Sex, booze and fags: masculinity, style and men's magazines

Tim Edwards

Men's magazines are, it seems, all about sex, booze and fags. A cursory glance at the newsagent shelves stacking magazines for men reveals a raft of blatant front cover images of scantily clad young women and headlining of articles concerning sex or alcohol-induced practical jokes. Images of cigarette smoking are also common, whilst male homosexuality is either rarely or poorly represented. In addition, New Lad, in contrast with New Man, is often deeply concerned not to appear 'faggy' or effeminate and the tobacco, alcohol and sex industries are well represented in terms of the advertising space they occupy. My concern here is to unpack this situation and demonstrate that contemporary men's magazines often invoke issues of lifestyle and sexuality, particularly as they relate to masculinity. Much of this also centres, I will assert, on their uneasy relationship to matters of men's fashion and style.

The meteoric rise of the new so-called 'men's magazines' in the UK has also created much interest in academic as well as media circles (Edwards, 1997; Mort, 1996; Nixon, 1996). The fact of their growth is pretty much without contention. As measured in terms of circulation through annual Audit Bureau of Circulation (ABC) studies and readership figures through National Readership Surveys (NRS), the market for men's magazines in the UK has grown from a mere four titles in 1990, each with a circulation of well under 100,000, to currently at least a dozen titles, depending on one's definition of a 'men's magazine', with top sellers such as *FHM* (*For Him Magazine*) hitting circulation figures of 500,000 (Beynon, 2000). In addition, only two titles—*Arena* launched in 1986 and *GQ* launched in 1988—existed at all in the 1980s. The accuracy of such figures, particularly those related to readerships, are open to question but the overall expansion of this particular market has been undeniable.

Further evidence for this expansion is provided in the overall diversification of the market for men's magazines and its increasing tendency to sub-niche within its own niche. For example, *Arena, FHM, loaded* and *Maxim* now all produce related fashion titles of their own whilst *GQ* and *FHM* have also spawned their own health and fitness magazines. The market has also tended to sub-divide into health-oriented titles such as *Men's Health* and *Men's Fitness*, up-market glossies such as *GQ, Esquire* and *Arena*, and the slightly more downmarket yet nonetheless consumerist world of the re-vamped *FHM, Front, loaded* and *Maxim*.

What is in contention here of course is what all this actually means. Whilst in no way wishing to take away from what is clearly an easily quantifiable and indeed quantum impact, there are certain initial qualifying factors to take into account when assessing the importance of men's magazines. First, men's magazines have a longer history than is often suggested, arguably originating in the rise of *Playboy* which was launched in 1953 or the relatively extended longevity of *Esquire* and *GQ* in the USA. In addition, what one might call 'men's interest' magazines including titles for motoring, hobbies and pornography generally have a far longer history still (Osgerby, 2001). Second, the rapid expansion of men's lifestyle magazines is in some ways a peculiarly English phenomenon. Other parts of Europe and the USA have a well-established history of producing magazines for men and have not necessarily developed the same exponential cult of 'laddism' which has often informed their expansion in the UK, although *FHM, loaded* and *Maxim* are now also imported into the USA. Third, this expansion also crucially depends upon a question of definition. Whilst magazines organized around 'masculine' themes such as cars, technology or sports may be classifiable as 'men's magazines' or, perhaps more aptly, as men's interest magazines, the current crop of men's magazines has more to do with the rise of a whole new genre of lifestyle titles in the 1980s such as *i-D* and, most famously, *The Face*, launched in 1984. This genre has its origins in development of such image conscious titles as *Harper's & Queen, Tatler* or *Vogue* and continues today most strongly in the form of *Wallpaper*, a decidedly up-market glossy magazine that self-consciously confuses the previously distinct areas of interior design and fashion, in the form of dress, within an overall miscellany of 'lifestyle'. The new men's magazines, then, are precisely men's lifestyle titles as opposed to men's interest magazines. However, as I will explore shortly, the term lifestyle is almost synonymous with style itself and men's lifestyle magazines still incorporate men's interests. As a result, I will use the term men's style magazines from now on to denote the contemporary form of men's magazines more generally.

Questions of definition notwithstanding, what remains constant and interesting here is the on-going promotion of magazines through which men can affirm their sense of masculinity without necessarily recognizing or confronting it. Historically, this was achieved most simply and directly through constructing the magazines around assumed 'men's interests'—whether cars, women or sport—whilst never addressing them as men or consciously acknowledging their role in constructing a masculinity for them. The problem, then, for the new crop of men's style titles in the UK in the 1980s lay precisely in trying to square the circle of producing a 'men's magazine' that somehow wasn't one at all. In short, men's magazines, past and present, have always been for men but rarely about men, other than male celebrities.

In the following analysis, then, I wish to consider quite how and why men's style magazines in the UK have now developed to such an extent and then to explore some of the implications of this phenomenon for our understandings of contemporary masculinities. As a result, there are three key sections: first, a discussion of the preceding literature on men's style magazines and how we may understand their significance; second, an unpacking of their development using the now common iconography of the New Man and the New Lad; and third, a consideration of how this relates to contemporary western masculinities more widely and, in particular, an assessment of the increasing importance attached to men's style itself.

Cultural texts/cultural phenomenon: men's style magazines and representation

Men's style magazines are cultural texts and, as such, any analysis of their significance in terms of masculinity is essentially an analysis of representation. As is now well known, sociological and cultural understandings of representation have grown exponentially in recent decades (Hall, 1997). Despite this, many of the themes and points invoked remain relatively constant. First, in terms of understanding the meanings of a cultural text, it is now recognized that this is a matter of interpretation and therefore meaning lies as much if not more with the subject or reader as it does with object or text. Moreover, there is no one-way determination of the meaning of cultural texts from producers to consumers. Second, this renders any discussion of meaning temporally and spatially specific so that a magazine does not necessarily mean the same thing now as opposed to then or here as opposed to there. Third, there remains a complex series of power relationships in making sense of these meanings as producers and consumers of cultural texts are not necessarily equal yet also vary enormously in terms of the economic and cultural capital they possess (Bourdieu, 1984).

When these issues are applied to the unprecedented expansion of men's style magazines in the UK, several important points arise. First, the question of supply and demand is contentious, as it is not necessarily clear that men's style magazines were either merely commercial initiatives in the market place or solely something men were demanding or wanted. Second, it is difficult, to say the least, to apply any certainty to their meaning for the men who read them and who may take them very seriously and at face value or alternatively view them ironically and with scepticism. Third, and as a result, their importance for an understanding of contemporary masculinities is therefore fundamentally and necessarily tentative and contingent rather than demonstrative and fixed.

We are then immediately presented with something of a conundrum for, if the meaning and significance of men's style magazines is so contested and difficult to measure, then how and why are we doing it? This situation is complicated further when one also considers that most of the preceding literature on men's magazines is theoretically led rather than research driven and yet tends to postulate a series of fairly grandiose points related to the sexual politics of the 1980s and 1990s. These include: first, the notion that men's style magazines have arisen due to various cultural and historical developments and, in particular, entrepreneurial and commercial initiatives rather than as any direct result of shifts in sexual politics; second, that the images presented are often pluralistic and polyvalent in their importance with the implication that the magazines tend to blur various boundaries relating to masculinity, most particularly in relation to sexuality; and third, that men's style magazines are then understood mostly fully as part of a series of wider developments in visual and or consumer culture (Chapman & Rutherford, 1988; Mort, 1996; Nixon, 1996). All of this primarily theoretical work highlights the sense in which the expansion of men's lifestyle titles is not an isolated or random development but part of or, at least, connected with, a wider set of processes whether in relation to masculinity and sexual politics or marketing and consumer culture. As such, it provides important understandings of men's style magazines as a cultural phenomenon. What tends to remain lacking is an engagement with them more as representations or cultural texts. In particular, the absence of analysis of the audience or the consumption patterns of men themselves is problematic precisely because it tends to assume a pre-given set of meanings. Conversely, however, an analysis of men's style magazines as cultural texts alone runs the risk of missing their significance as a far wider cultural phenomenon. The key difficulty that remains then is precisely that of trying to reconcile the two.

In addition, most of these works have focused strongly on the iconography of the New Man as the organizing factor in their analyses with varying outcomes. Chapman and Rutherford's pioneering collection *Male Order: Unwrapping Masculinity* primarily framed its analysis of the New Man in terms of responses to feminism yet ended up mostly admitting that this development was more the result of ploys in marketing than progress in sexual politics (Chapman & Rutherford, 1988). The journalist Jon Savage similarly wrote that the New Man was simply the same old wolf in designer clothes (Savage, 1996). Frank Mort's *Cultures Of Consumption* provided a somewhat eclectic analysis of the phenomenon as a form of cultural history. For Mort, the rise of the New Man was the result of series of shifts within commercial culture itself since the second world war, including the rise of tailoring *en masse* for men and the development of various entrepreneurial initiatives in the 1980s, as well as the reinvention of the *flâneur* in areas such as Soho, London (Mort, 1996). Sean Nixon's analysis centred more upon developments in visual culture and the New Man was seen precisely as a figure of spectatorship constructed at the level of advertising itself, as well as in retailing, marketing and the media more widely, which were in turn supported through the expansion of flexible specialisation in mass production (Nixon, 1996). Mort and Nixon remained tentatively positive concerning these developments in terms of their capacity to reconstruct new forms of masculinity within consumer culture along less traditional and less divisive lines. My own work previously challenged some of these points, particularly in relation to the supposed pluralism of some of the imagery, yet remained an analysis of men's style magazines in relation to a much wider set of developments in fashion, consumer culture and masculinity. A key concern here was the extent to which men's style magazines were socially divisive through their often heavy emphasis upon a form of consumer culture that tended to target the young, white and affluent or city man which had the effect, intended or not, of excluding many older, rurally located or simply poorer men (Edwards, 1997, 2000).

One exception to these more theoretical texts is the recent work of Nick Stevenson, Peter Jackson and Kate Brooks (Jackson *et al.*, 2001). This provides an empirical investigation, via interviews and discussions, into men's consumption of the new crop of men's style magazines in the UK. Whilst limited to a fairly small sample, the work undermines any simplistic or deterministic understanding men's relationship with the magazines. Rather it often highlights men's ambivalence towards them and their sense of almost simultaneous engagement and disengagement with the both the existence and content of the magazines. This reiterates the important point that preceding analyses of men's style magazines have mostly constituted discussions of them as a phenomenon rather than as cultural texts. There is, I think, still some support for this in the sense that an analysis of men's magazines as cultural texts alone, whilst potentially strongly detailed and nuanced, precisely runs the risk of losing sight of their importance as a wider cultural phenomenon with implications for our understanding of contemporary masculinities. For example, a detailed deconstruction of the content of *loaded*, whilst arguably very valid, may tend to miss its wider significance as an entrepreneurial initiative or its part in wider processes of media constructions of masculinity. As a result, I wish to continue here with an analysis of men's style magazines more as a cultural phenomenon whilst still recognizing their significance as cultural texts. As outlined earlier, the difficulty remains one of reconciling the two dimensions, something that is not truly within the scope of a single chapter.

From Old Man To New Lad: masculinity and men's style magazines

In this next section I wish to address the question of how men's style magazines relate to issues of masculinity. In so doing I hope to illustrate that this relationship is not set in stone and, in particular, has changed over time. More importantly, I do not wish to do this through the perhaps more common route of simply delineating the ideal type of man or masculinity appealed to and/or constructed through a given magazine. Rather I wish to provide a more schematic analysis of the changes and continuities in the representations of masculinity as well as the variations and commonalities across the titles in plural. This reflects my concern, already outlined, that an analysis of men's style magazines solely as cultural texts runs the risk of missing understanding them as a far wider cultural phenomenon. More particularly, as I will highlight shortly, it also starts to reveal the sense in which such distinctions are potentially superficial if not artificial.

My analysis here centres upon the now well-known iconography of New Man and New Lad to which I wish to add the iconography of Old Man to delineate a third form of representation of masculinity in men's magazines that existed prior to New Man. What I hope this starts to do is to unpack notions of the Old Man, New Man, and New Lad and highlight some of their key distinctions. Yet it is also quite apparent that these 'ideal types' are defined strongly in relation to each other and are, in essence, mutually reinforcing. As a result, such an analysis is understood as much horizontally through the differences and variations across the notions of masculinity as it is vertically as a more insular definition of what constitutes an Old Man, New Man, or New Lad.

The three iconographies are most predominantly defined in temporal and spatial terms and, more specifically, in relation to the launch of specific men's style magazines in the UK. As a result, New Man is temporally located in the launch of the first men's style magazine, *Arena*, in 1986 and New Lad in relation to the launch of *loaded* in 1994. It is harder to identify a fixed starting point for Old Man. However, one could see the launch of *Playboy* in 1953 as key or, more widely, the rise of a more consumerist masculinity throughout the 1940s and 1950s in the USA (Osgerby, 2001).

One concern here is the sense in which all three of these forms may now perhaps co-exist. This is undermined, however, in relation to the currently enduring popularity of New Lad iconography and its influence across all of the titles and in popular culture more widely. Whilst New Man iconography primarily existed at the level of various forms of media journalism and media promotion of Old Man was necessarily more restricted, as the mass media per se was less developed, New Lad became a far wider phenomenon found in prime time television and mainstream film as well as the press and magazines. The BBC situation comedy *Men Behaving Badly*, game shows such as *They Think It's All Over* and *Never Mind The Buzzcocks*, as well as movies such as *Reservoir Dogs*, *Snatch* and *Lock, Stock And Two Smoking Barrels*, plus the latter's TV spin-off, in very different ways play upon and invoke the theme of the New Lad. Loud and sexist humour often tied in with rudeness and bad behaviour, if not extreme violence, characterize all of these representations of masculinity that, for the most part, appear to have a direct appeal to a young, aggressive and self-consciously working class male audience and or its admirers.

We can also discuss the three forms in terms of sexual politics, since all three notions of masculinity are defined strongly according to their attitudes towards women that vary from pre-feminist sexism (Old Man) to something supposedly more progressive (New Man) to the so-called 'ironic' sexism and use of mockery and humour in relation to feminism that characterizes New Lad culture. The significance of the irony of New Lad culture within men's style magazines has, however, recently come into question as an avoidance of feminist criticism of men (Benwell, forthcoming; Greer, 2000; Whelehan, 2000). The irony associated with any of these media is ambiguous as there is no *forcible* compulsion to read the New Lad ironically and it remains possible to take it seriously or at face value. In short, one is perhaps equally encouraged to laugh with and not at the

New Lad. This is precisely an illustration of the sense in which men's style magazines remain cultural texts that are open to multiple ironic, and non-ironic, interpretations.

More seriously, in the film examples mentioned above, men and the masculine are defined in pretty unsavoury and unreconstructed terms as equally the signifier and the signified in a world where women and the feminine become symbolically if not literally annihilated. Consequently, the films of Guy Ritchie possess no major female characters and render women almost non-existent whilst the feminine is itself merely a signifier that the men defensively resist. Similarly, magazines such as *FHM, Front, loaded* and *Maxim* often reduce not only the representation, rather the very *incorporation*, of women to the sexual. The frequent inclusion of soft-core pornographic material, in the form of supplements such as calendars, is an example of this process at work. One may make the assertion, then, that New Lad representations of masculinity do indeed represent a retreat from the real world where women do exist and may compete with men whether at home or at work. This occurs either through inverting feminism into female rather than male obsolescence or in presenting modes of masculinity that don't even pay attention to, let alone depend upon, the importance of secure work or long term relationships with women. Instead the emphasis is placed upon men-only worlds of wheeling and dealing, heavy drinking, one-night stands and male bonding. Only the BBC situation comedy *Men Behaving Badly* gives any importance to its actresses or a female audience, as its women characters are often portrayed lampooning their male counterparts quite successfully. Whelehan has however argued that, even here, the New Lad represents a form of nostalgic retreat or what she calls 'retrosexism' (Whelehan, 2000).

In addition to a discussion of sexual politics, we can note the complexity of the relationship of these notions of masculinity with questions of class and paid work. Whilst Old Man was clearly defined through his pursuit of a regular job or career for life and New Man was the archetype of an aspiring yuppie, work is curiously either unimportant, absent or simply invisible in the world of the New Lad which appears mostly defined as one enormous alcohol-induced party. There are perhaps a couple of ways of interpreting this situation. One is to say that it is a direct reflection of increased insecurities in employment patterns, particularly for young working-class men, and it is therefore an attempt to redefine masculinity without direct relation to work. The difficulty here is that the lifestyle of the New Lad still costs. A more accurate point to make is that New Lad, unlike Old Man or New Man, is not necessarily defined through his financial independence and is perhaps the youngest of the trio. What this potentially also highlights is the success of New Lad iconography in beginning to open up a market in magazines for teenage boys to parallel that which has existed for teenage girls for some time (McRobbie, 1991; Nava, 1992; Winship, 1987).

The question of sexuality is equally complex in relation to these representations of masculinity. Whilst Old Man was defined rigidly through his heterosexuality, either through the ideal of marriage or the promiscuous iconography of the playboy and New Man was the most worryingly ambiguous of the three, as potentially new age, caring and loving, or even gay, New Lad would seem to represent a retreat from both of these options into some kind of pubescent world of masturbation and drunken one-night stands. In addition, Greer and Whelehan have argued that the development of parallel cultures amongst young women or the rise of the New Ladette in tandem with the New Lad does not necessarily demonstrate a growing equality of the sexes so much as the collapse of each into a regressive form of masculinity; whilst the power of women with otherwise successful careers is undermined through salacious spreads of them stripped of their clothes (Greer, 2000; Whelehan, 2000).

At the same time, the denial of the homosexual and homosexuality itself often remains uncontested. Consequently, gay male sexuality is often not represented or incorporated at all and, where mention is made, it is often in very negative terms. For example, the editors of *loaded* have been outspoken and vociferous against the sexual ambivalence of the New Man and magazines such as *Front* regularly castigate what they call 'lady boys'. As I and others have pointed out previously, much of this may be due to the increasing turning of the male into the object as well as the subject of the gaze, particularly in advertising, resulting in a near neurotic denial of the homoeroticism which necessarily ensues in men looking at other men (Dyer, 1993; Edwards, 1997; Neale, 1983). In this sense, the New Lad is not necessarily a new invention and perhaps a very regressive one in terms of any form of sexual politics.

What are we to make of this overall? In the first instance, there is a strong sense in which the three iconographies are mutually reinforcing: a New Lad is precisely a New Lad as he is not a New Man and vice versa. In addition, the main parameters of development across these iconographies seem to centre on the relationship of masculinity to two key factors: work and sexuality. Old Man was most fundamentally defined according to the fixity of his work and sexuality alike, whilst New Man in some ways and to some extent tended to undermine each of these in variant forms of aspirational individualism that perhaps also implied that his sexuality was as mobile as his career. New Lad in turn reasserted, with some defensiveness, a form of sexual certainty and appeared to implode the emphasis upon work completely. If these two factors are removed, very little distinction seems to exist at all across the three categories.

There is also, perhaps, as much sense of continuity here as there is change as all these representations of masculinity are intensely media driven and more 'hyper-real' than they are 'real' (Baudrillard, 1983). They all also crucially depend upon and are, indeed, constructed around, a series of commodity signifiers and consumerist practices, whether in the form of sharp suits and designer label culture or classic cars and the latest technology. If one removes such accessories, distinctions between Old Man, New Man and New Lad in the representation of masculinity start to implode. Indeed, does a New Man still exist without a designer suit and a mobile phone, or is a New Lad complete without export strength lager and a shirt with a logo?

Therefore, in addition to work and sexuality, we can also argue that relationships with fashion and style are equally complex. Whilst Old Man style was perhaps characterized as classical or conservative in its emphasis upon the clean cut, and New Man culture was often downright narcissistic given its focus upon designer clothing, moisturisers and increasingly the naked male form as epitomized in the advertising for Calvin Klein underwear, the New Lad's position was, and is, harder to define. An interest in matters of style clearly exists as evidenced in an often label-driven obsession with casual and sporting styles ranging from Ben Sherman to Burberry logos on shirts and jeans. Yet this interest is decidedly defensive against any association of narcissism or invocation of homosexuality. Consequently, 'fashion' becomes 'clobber' and, whilst the New Lad clearly values his Ralph Lauren shirt as a sign of conspicuous consumption, equally he must be man enough not to worry too much if it gets ripped in some pub brawl or if he regurgitates his chicken vindaloo down it. What is often at work here is a process of counteracting any association of femininity, as frequently invoked in a concern with how one looks, with heightened displays of masculinity or even violence in often all-male arenas. This is illustrated in the tendency of New Lad fashion advertising to undermine the New Man's sense of preciousness concerning clothing and accessories. Consequently, expensive suits are often represented in the context of pubs and football pitches as opposed to sumptuous hotels and offices or, alternatively, designer labels become associated with aggressive and sporting celebrities such as Vinnie Jones. This would seem to demonstrate the tendency of New Lad representations of fashion to avoid any invocations of effeminacy or sexual complexity. I will return to these contradictions in the presentation of men's style in the final section.

In addition, the new men's style magazines, whether in the form of the older, glossier and fashion-conscious *Arena* or newer mid-market and laddish *loaded*, are similar to the original men's interest titles except, precisely, for their emphasis upon visual style. All of the titles mentioned, past and present, are stuffed with 'men's stuff'—indeed one is called *Stuff*—and are still organized according to the same assumed men's interests whether in the form of cars and alcohol or sport and women. What marks the newer titles out as distinctive compared with their predecessors is the addition of articles and advertising for fashion, grooming and appearances or, in short, the inclusion of what was previously perceived as exclusively 'women's stuff'. As I have illustrated previously, a simple content analysis of the magazines tends to demonstrate that most of these newer and more feminine concerns are concentrated within advertising and/or heavily promotional content, whilst the assumed and traditional men's interests still dominate features and articles (Edwards, 1997). This is reflected in the editorial content of men's lifestyle magazines that tend to focus upon men's interests such as sport, cars, or interviews with stars, and not discussions of grooming and fashion which are mostly confined to advertising for clothing, accessories and aftershaves or short editorial summaries situated low down in the contents list. This serves as a way for men's magazines to simultaneously incorporate yet undermine the importance of issues of fashion and grooming. More widely, this also illustrates a tension within all the titles, between a progressive re-defining of new content for men's magazines and the maintenance of more traditional sexual divisions. Headline discussion of, for example, how men may look younger or look after their skin has yet to exist on any scale to parallel the prominence of fashion and adornment in women's magazines, whether in more upmarket titles such as *Vogue* and *Marie Claire* or in mass market youth-driven magazines such as *Cosmopolitan*. The inclusion of more traditionally feminine concerns primarily at the level of advertising suggests that this is perhaps more of a commercial initiative and less of an editorial one, and that gender divisions are in fact maintained rather than undermined.

More importantly, the development of parallel bi-annual fashion-orientated titles such as *Arena Homme Plus* and *FHM Collections* illustrates not only the commercial success of the sector overall but also an increased tendency to separate out potentially more gender transgressive areas and to maintain a strong sense of division within an overall schema of assumed men's interests. Whilst the older, glossier and more up-market titles such as *GQ* and *Arena* still pay some attention to matters of men's fashion, this is now often severely reduced in the more mid-market worlds of *FHM*, *Maxim* and particularly *loaded*. As I will illustrate shortly, this is perhaps explained mostly as a result of the unease in terms of masculinity and sexuality that still surrounds men's fashion and style.

In the final instance, it seems the New Man and the New Lad are perhaps niches in a market that is defined more than anything else by an array of lifestyle accessories. The iconography of Old Man, interestingly, is more diffuse, though still has consumerist dimensions whether in the form of Brylcream, scooters or classic suits. We are left, then, with the question of what is still distinctive here concerning the rise of the New Lad or the expansion of men's style magazines more generally. In particular, no mainstream magazine of any kind is invented, exists or survives without the commercial revenue of advertising. The success of New Lad iconography therefore is at least partly due to its provision of a vehicle for securing advertising revenue which in turn raises the question of what has caused the iconography of the New Lad to succeed where that of the New Man had previously failed. The success of New Lad culture would seem to centre largely upon a matter of how consumer culture is sold to men. As I shall go on to argue in the next section, New Lad 'style' is often predicated upon a wider understanding of masculine identity and 'lifestyle' that exists beyond the textual confines of the magazine in a variety of popular cultural domains and which eschews overt narcissism, elitism and sexual uncertainty. By subsuming the more narrow concern with designer labels and grooming associated with the New Man within a broader set of masculine signifiers, the New Lad has been able to resolve some of the tensions surrounding male consumption.

The narcissist and the playboy: masculinity and men's style

Style, in the sense of fashion and grooming or personal adornment, remains in essence a phenomenon more associated with the feminine and femininity than the masculine and masculinity. In this purist sense, then, the entire phenomenon of style is in contradiction with the masculine and the notion of men's style is antithetical if not an outright oxymoron. As various commentators have pointed out, this is a peculiarly modern and western phenomenon famously once called the Great Masculine Renunciation in the work of Flügel (Craik, 1994; Flügel, 1930; Hollander, 1994). At the same time, recent analyses have demonstrated the persistence of men's style, often in very subtle forms, whilst alluding to a constant unease if not tension surrounding masculinity and style within modern western societies (Cole, 2000; Breward, 1999; Edwards, 1997).

The notion of lifestyle, which came into increasingly common parlance in the 1980s, is perhaps less gender specific. Lifestyle in its original sense referred simply to an individual's or group's way of living and was concerned primarily with social practices such as work, interests, or leisure pursuits. In the 1980s, however, the term rapidly started to imply more strongly issues of aesthetics and image or style in the sense of visual culture, which was also simultaneously increasingly commodified and centred upon products such as cars, interior furnishings and indeed fashion. In addition, central in this was the move within marketing and advertising to make increased use of psychographic, as opposed to demographic, data, related more to attitudes and values than to income and geography (Nixon, 1996). Also key was the marketing of products or services in miscellaneous clusters. For example, the designer suit went with the personal organizer that then complemented the sports car and so on. Consequently, lifestyle was often style writ larger and in more consumerist terms (Chaney, 1996).

To take the specific issue of men's style, then, there was perhaps a new or distinctive sense of slippage through which men's *style*, as fashion, could enter a more populist arena under the wider auspices of *lifestyle* and thus resolve some of the tensions surrounding masculinity that issues of men's style have historically tended to invoke. However, the unease concerning men and style still remains. A well-dressed, well-groomed and 'stylish' man still tends to arouse anxieties concerning sexuality and masculinity or the terrifying twosome of the homosexual and the effeminate. Stereotypically, 'real' men don't care what they look like and just 'throw things on' whilst women go shopping and agonize over matters of self-presentation. Men themselves are more concerned with *doing* things, like work or sport, rather than with *looking* like anything. This tension around men's style, then, is precisely an echo of a far wider active-passive, production-consumption gender division well documented in many recent analyses of consumption (Bowlby, 1993; Edwards, 2000; Lury, 1996). However, as I have argued elsewhere, the cultural validation of men's style is not without precedent (Edwards, 1997). One only has to think of dandies, Italian stallions, gangsters, the glamour of Hollywood idols, mods, rockers and other subcultures to realize the relationship of masculinity to men's style has a long history that is more complex than one of simple antithesis. In this final section, then, I wish to further unpack this tension or contradiction in relation to men's style and indeed men's style magazines.

As I have already highlighted, what remains distinctive for our analysis here is precisely the rise of men's *style* magazines that were concerned to develop in varying forms a primarily more consumerist and image-conscious masculinity. This also underpins much of the concern, popular and academic alike, in shifting the gendered notions of masculinity away from more traditional concerns such as cars and DIY into areas such as fashion, grooming and the body that are areas more traditionally associated with women and femininity. Consequently, whilst well-groomed women are often seen as stylish, well-groomed men often face accusations of narcissism. This also at least partly accounts for some of the anxieties concerning sexuality that this apparent gender transgression in terms of representation invokes. Exploring the 'feminine side' of masculinity within modern western society has traditionally been associated with the derided preserve of the homosexual and perhaps it still is.

What also exists, however, within the history of male consumption, is the legacy of a sharp dressing, heterosexually promiscuous and equally highly consumerist masculinity associated with, amongst other things, gangsters, youth culture, Hollywood and the world of bars and nightclubs (Osgerby, 2001). Interestingly, men could get away with being consumerist and stylish if they were heterosexually promiscuous enough or plain-and-simply violent enough. For example, the intense interest in matters of personal style often associated with the mafia is precisely excused accusations of narcissism due to its equal association with promiscuity and aggression. Sport stars and celebrities are also potentially mitigating of negative consequences as in the case of football superstar David Beckham whose interest in matters of style and willingness to invoke sexual ambivalence is now well known. However, the outcry concerning his wearing of a sarong, or even the degree of media interest invoked, demonstrates the limits or boundaries involved, even for celebrities. The more recent problem, then, for the new crop of men's style magazines in the 1980s and 1990s was precisely this sense of slithering between the sexual ambivalence of the narcissist and the sexual potency of the playboy.

The problem of sexual ambivalence often invoked in advocating a visual and personal consumerism to men was also a peculiarly Anglo-American problem as other parts of Europe have far longer histories of marketing fashion and style to men, for example in France and Italy where men's style has historically aroused less anxiety and men's style magazines have a longer history. The problem has also historically been negotiated in the United States through an appeal to various iconographies of masculinity including the Wild West, sport and, most potently, corporate virility and the phallic power of Wall Street. The US version of *GQ*, for example, has a stronger emphasis upon corporate masculinity, and suited style in particular, than its UK counterpart.

However, in the UK the answer only came belatedly in the form of New Lad, a supposedly ironic slap in the face of New Man. Central in this was the launch of *loaded* in 1994, subtitled as a magazine for 'men who should know better' and the brainchild of ex-music journalists James Brown and Tim Southwell. As John Beynon points out, *loaded* celebrated British working class machismo in the form of football, the pub and masturbation, setting new records in the circulation figures for men's style magazines, whilst the then loss leader *FHM* reinvented itself on a similar theme and promptly outsold all its competitors (Beynon, 2002). Of critical significance here is the sense in which it was the iconography of the New Lad, and not the New Man, that gave men's style magazines in the UK the means to go truly mainstream.

As I highlighted earlier, what perhaps in turn tends to account for the uniqueness and success of the New Lad phenomenon in the UK is its relationship to social class. If the New Man was a primarily an aspirational and individualist middle-class invention (and working class only through default or origin, as in the case of the City Boy), the New Lad offered a new form of masculinity to the young working-class male whose aspirations were now curtailed through the decline in manufacturing and the recession of the early 1990s. As a result, its appeal became wider and a broader umbrella of masculinities not necessarily defined in terms of aspiration and career was incorporated. On top of this, it sidestepped the issue of employment and men's style magazines found their ideal vehicle for promoting consumerist masculinity *en masse*.

Moreover, whilst New Man imagery, centred upon designer clothing, personal grooming and aspirational individualism encapsulated in Armani suits, Clinique skin care and Calvin Klein underwear, was clearly strongly consumerist and commodified, it failed to resolve either the elitism or the sexual ambiguity that photographs of men in their boxers or immaculate suits invoked. In contrast, New Lad iconography, centred upon shirts with logos, premium lager and sport, although equally commodified, invoked none of the sexual uncertainty of the New Man precisely because so much of its style was bound up with a strictly delineated identity—one that was unequivocally heterosexual, hedonistic and non-aspirational. In short, it let young working-class men use moisturiser, dress up and go shopping without appearing middle-class, effeminate or homosexual. Ultimately, the contradictions and tensions of masculinity, sexuality and consumer culture were papered over in the invention of a multi-media driven phenomenon called laddism. This laddism was, in turn, also supported through the directives of the alcohol, sex, sport and other industries in providing its revenue. In the final instance, then, one of the main reasons why the New Lad has succeeded so well where previous invocations of consumerist masculinity have failed is precisely because it reconciled, at least artificially, the tension of the Playboy and the Narcissist.

Conclusions: sex, booze and fags

Within the scope of my remit here, I have primarily made three points: first, that men's style magazines and the phenomena that they represent and tap into are not necessarily as new or without precedent as they may first seem; second, that the phenomenon of men's style magazines, in the UK more specifically, is in some senses unique as a peculiarly class- as well as media-driven concern; and third, that men's style magazines are most fully understood as commercial initiatives which have much in common with all similar titles and, more particularly, as cultural texts representing differing ways of articulating the tensions and contradictions of masculinity and sexuality with style and consumer culture.

What remains of particular concern here, however, is the unprecedented success of New Lad iconography in terms of its increasing sales of men's style magazines and its wider significance for popular culture alike. I have suggested that a key concern here is its reconciliation, albeit artificially, of the tension between the playboy and the narcissist in relation to men's style and consumer culture. In its vociferous emphasis upon heterosexual promiscuity and drinking, it avoided both the élitism and the sexual ambivalence often present in representations of men's style within consumer culture. Consequently, men's style magazines are not only about sex and booze (whether 'shaken but not stirred' or simply 'well-bladdered'), but also the fear of fags.

References

Baudrillard J. (1983) (orig. pub. 1981) *Simulacra And Simulation*. New York: Semiotext(e).

Benwell, B. (forthcoming) 'Ironic discourse: Masculine talk in men's lifestyle magazines', *Men and Masculinities*.

Beynon, J. (2002) *Masculinities And Culture*. Milton Keynes: Open University Press.

Bourdieu, P. (1984) *Distinction: A Social Critique Of The Judgement Of Taste*. London: Routledge and Kegan Paul.

Bowlby, R. (1993) *Shopping With Freud*. London: Routledge.

Breward, C. (1999) *The Hidden Consumer*. Manchester: Manchester University Press.

Chaney, D. (1996) *Lifestyles*. London: Routledge.

Chapman, R. and Rutherford, J. (eds) (1988) *Male Order: Unwrapping Masculinity*. London: Lawrence and Wishart.

Cole, S. (2000) *'Don We Now Our Gay Apparel'*. Oxford: Berg.

Craik, J. (1994) *The Face Of Fashion: Cultural Studies In Fashion*. London: Routledge.

Dyer, R. (1993) *The Matter Of Images: Essays On Representation*. London: Routledge.

Edwards, T. (1997) *Men In The Mirror: Men's Fashion, Masculinity And Consumer Society*. London: Cassell.

Edwards, T. (2000) *Contradictions Of Consumption: Concepts, Practices And Politics In Consumer Society*. Buckingham: Open University Press.

Flügel, J. C. (1930) *The Psychology Of Clothes*. London: Hogarth Press.

Greer, G. (2000) *The Whole Woman*. London: Anchor.

Hall, S. (ed.) (1997) *Representation: Cultural Representation And Signifying Practices*. London: Sage.

Hollander, A. (1994) *Sex And Suits*. New York: Knopf.

Jackson, P. *et al.* (2000) *Making Sense Of Men's Magazines*. Cambridge: Polity.

Lury, C. (1996) *Consumer Culture*. Cambridge: Polity.

McRobbie, A. (1991) *Feminism And Youth Culture: From 'Jackie' To 'Just Seventeen'*. Basingstoke: Macmillan.

Mort, F. (1996) *Cultures Of Consumption: Masculinities And Social Space In Late Twentieth-Century Britain*. London: Routledge.

Nava, M. (1992) *Changing Cultures: Feminism, Youth And Consumerism*. London: Sage.

Neale, S. (1983) 'Masculinity as spectacle: Reflections on men and mainstream cinema', *Screen* 24(6): 2–16.

Nixon, S. (1996) *Hard Looks: Masculinities, Spectatorship And Contemporary Consumption*. London: UCL Press.

Osgerby, B. (2001) *Playboys In Paradise: Masculinity, Youth and Leisure-Style In Modern America*. Oxford: Berg.

Savage, J. (1996) 'What's so new about the New Man? Three decades of advertising to men': in D. Jones (ed.) *Sex, Power And Travel: Ten Years Of* Arena. London: Virgin.

Whelehan, I. (2000) *Overloaded: Popular Culture And The Future Of Feminism*. London: The Women's Press.

Winship, J. (1987) *Inside Women's Magazines*. London: Pandora Press.

Part 3:
Discursive constructions of masculinity

Introduction: Discursive constructions of masculinity

The next two essays are united by a shared focus on the language of men's lifestyle magazines and argue that a detailed examination of the micro patterns of linguistic representation can usefully illuminate macro patterns of gender ideology. In focusing on discourse, each contends that the linguistic choices made by a writer are not accidental or arbitrary but work to present a particular view of the world. One of the most fruitful aspects of close textual analysis is the way in which it is able to reveal otherwise unnoticed patterns of lexis and grammar which contribute to a particular mode of representation.

Benwell's chapter, 'Ambiguous masculinities: Heroism and anti-heroism in the men's lifestyle magazine', examines a particular site of tension or ambiguity prevalent in the writing of many features between firstly, a traditional masculinity within which attributes such as physicality, violence, autonomy and silence are celebrated (often a profiled celebrity or iconic hero), and secondly, a more ironic, humorous, anti-heroic and self-deprecating masculinity (often allied to the ideal reader). Through an analysis of clause relations and the positive or negative connotations assigned to parts of the text, she argues that the textual identity of 'new lad' is actually situated in this oscillation between the two identities rather than being allied to one or the other.

Central to the discussion of this oscillation is the thesis of masculine invisibility (discussed and problematized in the introduction to this volume). By continually moving between multiple constructions of masculinity, negating or denying what has just been marked and identified, the magazine male achieves a kind of invisibility—an instability that ensures that a position for him is never available for clear definition and thus also unavailable for critical scrutiny.

Taylor and Sunderland's contribution, ' "I've always loved women": the representation of the male sex worker in *FHM*' adopts a Critical Discourse Analysis methodology in order to expose assymetrical patterns of power in the representation of gender relations in a profile of a male sex worker, Peter. Using an analytical framework developed by van Leeuwen (1996) for interpreting the representation of 'social actors' the authors are able to draw attention to processes of exclusion and inclusion in the construction of the sex worker's masculinity. By systematically examining the choices of lexis and their positive or negative associations, patterns of transitivity (who has agency in clauses, who is affected), as well as identifying the inclusion of broader scripts and discourses of masculinity, they are able to demonstrate that Peter's identity has been carefully monitored by these representational resources in order to shore up his masculine power and exclude any hint of ambiguity, transgression or weakness.

These linguistic choices and patterns of 'exclusion' arguably work most forceably in the service of making normative what might otherwise be considered to be transgressive within the dominant model of masculinity espoused by these magazines: ie, a man who is paid to serve women sexually. In addition, Taylor and Sunderland arrive at similar conclusions to Benwell regarding the opposition that is set up between the heroic masculinity of the profiled individual and the ordinary and implicitly deficient masculinity attributed to the reader or other men.

Ambiguous masculinities: heroism and anti-heroism in the men's lifestyle magazine

Bethan Benwell

The focus of this chapter, like many within this book, is upon the identification of an emergent manifestation of masculinity celebrated within and around men's lifestyle magazines and popularly dubbed, 'new lad' (see introduction and other contributions: this volume). The particular approach I wish to adopt here, however, is a *discursive* one, one that engages in close detail with the workings and strategies of the language of the text.

The discourse of men's lifestyle magazines operates through both textual representation and a more dialogic direct address to its (largely) male readers to shore up a certain social group identity in which dominant cultural ideals of masculinity are nurtured and perpetuated. However, whilst the ubiquitous nature of mass media creates the potential for more dominant, hegemonic constructions of gender, commentators on popular culture are frequently able to locate sites of ambiguity within what are frequently fluid, transient and unstable genres. The discussion developed within this chapter, and supported by close textual analysis, will focus on a particular site of tension or ambiguity prevalent in much of the features writing. This tension exists between first, a traditional masculinity within which attributes such as physicality, violence, autonomy and silence are celebrated and, second, a more ironic, humorous, anti-heroic and self-deprecating masculinity. In the course of my discussion I shall debate whether such ambiguity reflects an unwitting schizophrenia at the heart of magazine masculinity, or whether it has a more deliberate and strategic function.

In addition, the chapter seeks to raise awareness of the benefits of a linguistic approach within a socio-cultural study and demonstrate how close analysis of the ruptures, contradictions and ambiguities of the text can be revealing of what, at first glance, appears to be a more confident, homogenous and uncomplicated version of gender.

The discursive construction of gender

The work of the influential gender theorist, Judith Butler (Butler 1999; 1993), has recently revolutionized language and gender studies by its key contention that gender is not a stable, pre-discursive entity, inherent in individuals, but that it is something constituted, mobilized and negotiated through the enactment of discourse. Gender, she argues, is something, not that we are but that we *do* or 'perform'. Butler's project is broadly deconstructionist in the sense that one of her main objectives is to expose the constructedness of gender and the processes by which a gender order and its attendant heterosexuality comes to seem 'natural' and stable. This 'performative' principle has been taken up with enthusiasm by language and gender theorists (Hall and Bucholtz, 1995; Cameron, 1998; Coates, 1998; Livia and Hall, 1997; Bucholtz *et al.*, 1999; Litosseliti and Sunderland, 2002; McIlvenny, 2002), some of whom had previously worked on the assumption that gender could be treated as a pre-discursive social variable and used as a stable correlative against which to measure patterns of linguistic behaviour (eg, the talk produced by a group of women talking is labelled as a special linguistic category: 'women's talk', simply by virtue of the sex of the speakers). At the same time, similarities between Butler's theories and the work of Discursive Psychology (eg, Potter and Wetherell, 1987; Edwards and Potter, 1992) whose work was premised upon the principle of 'action-oriented' analysis of participants' practices, started to be noted and capitalized upon (Speer and Potter: 2002). Such enthusiasm from linguists is unsurprising; Butler's appropriation of the term 'performativity' has its roots in Pragmatics, a branch of linguistics founded chiefly upon the work of philosophers Austin (1975), Searle (1969) and Grice (1975), and alludes to the understanding at the heart of this theory that utterances are not merely encoders of meaning, but *acts* which impact upon the world.

In addition, linguists and discursive psychologists, working broadly within a detailed Conversation Analytical framework, have considered not just what Butler's theories can offer them, but what they can contribute to Butler's work. One of the shortcomings of Butler's work has been its limited engagement with actual texts and the detailed analysis of processes of discursive production so crucial to her hypothesis (Speer and Potter, 2002). Thus, a collaboration between Butler's theory of performativity (hitherto reliant upon abstract and decontextualized examples of idealized discursive behaviour), and a more detailed analysis of real, instantiated discourse which pays particular attention to the orientations of the participants involved, is a tremendous breakthrough for Gender Studies and one which promises to be both fruitful and instructive.

The role of the written text

The focus of this chapter is upon the linguistic or discursive representation of masculinity in men's lifestyle magazines and here, we encounter a particular difficulty with the existing paradigm shift within the field of language and gender: its relative neglect of written and textual realizations of gender. Discursive Psychology is exclusively oriented to naturally occurring spoken interaction and, whilst accounts of gender discursively constructed through written texts (particularly media texts and popular fiction) are relatively common (eg, Mills, 1995; Caldas-Coulthard, 1996; Gough and Talbot, 1996; Harvey and Shalom, 1997; Talbot, 1995, 1997; Litosseliti and Sunderland, 2002), their relationship to the constitution of gender in the social world has rarely been explicitly theorized. For theorists working more abstractly upon identity formation within a post-structuralist framework (eg, Butler, Foucault, Derrida) the distinction between *modes* of discourse is rather inconsequential. Since the boundary between text and context within this paradigm has been effectively collapsed and all meanings or 'truths' are discursively mediated through endlessly circulated scripts, schemas and 'discourses', there is no theoretical distinction between forms of text, nor indeed the public/private sphere (McElhinny, 1997, Bucholtz, 1999), which has otherwise been so crucial to discussions of mass communication versus 'naturally occurring' interaction. Theoretical accounts of written engagements with gender identity have tended to focus upon their *representational* function: men's magazines, for instance, are seen as a site of the representation of culturally dominant or idealized versions of masculinity. They are also, however, *constitutive* of gender (Litosseliti and Sunderland, 2002) in the same way that spoken discourse is. The meanings of popular cultural forms are starting to be viewed not simply as ideological artefacts, imposing their meanings on susceptible groups, but also increasingly in terms of the ways in which these texts are *consumed* (eg, Bucholtz, 1999; McLoughlin, work in progress). Audiences of cultural texts are beginning to play a more prominent role in our understandings of the meanings and identities that arise and circulate around such texts, often in local, contingent and unenduring ways, and sometimes in ways that resist the intended ideology of the sender. What has tended to contribute to the relative neglect of this analytical approach is the practical and methodological problems theorists have encountered in attempting to engage with the dialogue between producer, text and reader. Whilst conversation analysts are, to an extent, able to provide an analysis of spoken interaction which attends to (and is thus accountable to) the orientations of the participants involved, a thoroughly context-sensitive analysis of how *written* texts for mass consumption operate within socio-cultural practice involves an almost Holy Grail-like quest in pursuit of 'real reader' responses, the modes of production within which the texts are situated, an analysis of the contexts within which they are likely to circulate and an attempt to wed all these various dimensions, which, ultimately, can only be speculative[1].

The dialogic mode of men's magazines

Nevertheless, the constitutive potential for gender identity is particularly relevant with respect to the phenomenon of the men's lifestyle magazine. Here masculinity is not merely *attributed* to actors within the text or even the passive, unresisting 'ideal' reader; the very format and rationale of the magazines encourages and even relies upon an active dialogue and a positive affiliation by readers to the normative identities set out within the magazine. A dialogic principle is at work at two levels in relation to the men's lifestyle magazine. First, *loaded*, the magazine commonly charged with the development and reification of 'new lad' identity (see Crewe: this volume), was very explicitly set up by its founder editors (James Brown and Tim Southwell) to engage actively in dialogue with readers. This aim is also supported by Brown and Southwell's well known and now apocryphal tale (set out in Southwell's account of the founding of *loaded: Getting Away With It*, 1998) of how the seeds of the *loaded* concept were sown at a football match he and Brown attended, at which they expressed the ambition to 'recreate the feelings of euphoria' experienced within the largely male celebration of sporting heroes and masculine camaraderie. Brown and Southwell claimed that *loaded* was born of a desire to offer readers a discourse with which they were already familiar (Southwell, 1998:2), a claim also reproduced in *loaded*'s marketing/media pack which states that *loaded* 'write(s) about topics and issues our readers talk about amongst themselves—and we write about them in their own language'.

In this way, the relationship between producer, text and consumer, inherent in any cultural transaction (see Introduction and Stevenson *et al.* on 'circuits of culture': this volume), is perhaps even more salient in a genre which, in its very rationale, sets so much explicit store by the circulation of meaning, discourse and discursive identities between the editorial team and community of readers. The stuff of *loaded*, it is suggested, is the stuff of friendship, banter and talk down at the local pub with your mates. The meanings, styles of discourse, catchphrases and dominant ideologies circulate freely between magazine text, 'real' interaction and website (now defunct for *loaded*, but available for other magazines), and any notion of 'origin' is nebulous and fruitless to pursue.

Second, the interactive format of *loaded* (and its many imitators, eg, *Maxim*, *FHM*, *Front*) further reinforces this dialogic principle. Readers' letters play a prominent and informing role and editorial staff leave the anonymous safety of their usual role as objective authors to become the *protagonists* of the magazine articles by volunteering themselves for intrepid field trips or exotic masculine pursuits (both of which will, in fact, constitute the data for the analysis later in this chapter) offering self-revelatory insights in their accounts as they do so. In addition, the language used (in common with much popular media, such as women's magazines and tabloid papers) has an *interpersonal* quality (Halliday, 1978; Fairclough, 1989; Talbot, 1995; Benwell, 2001) realized by language features such as *direct address* ('you') *commands/exhortations* (eg, 'Get a Life!') and *questions* (eg, 'Does he play around?'), as well as colloquial and slang items, which in men's lifestyle magazines often amount to a form of exclusive, ingroup code (Benwell, 2001). This privileging of the interpersonal dimension of meaning in mass media has been described by Fairclough (1989) as 'synthetic personalization'—an attempt to address a mass audience in a more individual, personal and intimate way—and is recognized, amongst other things, as a rhetorical mode of persuasion (Fairclough, 1989; Talbot, 1995).

The analytical approach adopted in this chapter might best be described as 'textually oriented discourse analysis' (Fairclough, 1992), which is grounded in the cultural contexts of men's magazines but which is essentially an in-depth qualitative linguistic analysis of two short extracts of data. Whilst an account of men's magazine discourse which is able to explicate all possible points along a 'circuit of culture' (eg, producer intentions, consumer response) and their relation to one another is beyond the scope of my analysis here, I acknowledge, where possible, a range of possible reading positions and intertexts upon which the discourse is likely to draw. In addition, my analysis draws attention to the ways in which ambivalent meanings and meanings potentially *oppositional* or *resistant* to magazine masculinity are accommodated and negotiated within the text.

A detailed and qualitative engagement with the patterns and choices of language which form cultural texts has frequently been neglected in cultural studies; therefore an approach such as this should be seen as complementary to others within the book whose emphasis is upon a different *aspect* of the study (eg, readers, producers) but whose object of study is essentially the same (Edwards, Stevenson *et al.*, Crewe: this volume). A textually-oriented approach such as this one should be seen as both a self-contained analysis and one part of a larger project investigating the discourse of men's magazines.

In the next section I go on to develop the theme of 'masculine invisibility' (also discussed in the Introduction: this volume) which is central to my thesis about masculine discourse in men's magazines.

'Invisible' masculinity

The burgeoning field of language and gender studies has been slow to broaden its focus to masculinity and indeed has, by its almost exclusive attention upon femininity and 'women's talk', been arguably complicit in perpetuating the invisibility of men in cultural representation.[2] The historical tradition of men being constituted in terms of universal, normative values has led to the phenomenon of 'invisible masculinity' (Coward and Black, 1998; Mort, 1988; Nixon, 2001; Benwell, 2002) whereby 'there is a discourse available to men which allows them to represent themselves as people, humanity, mankind' (Black and Coward, 1998, p. 118) and a reluctance for discursive practices around men to engage explicitly with their status as gendered.

In recent years, this discourse of gender neutrality has been challenged from two rather disparate quarters: first, the rapid rise of consumer markets anxious to capitalize on the male consumer in the mid-eighties (Mort, 1988; Nixon, 1996; Edwards, 1997; Faludi, 2000) and second, by the scrutiny of a feminism, largely within academia, keen to challenge and problematize the dominance and normativity of masculinity within gender relations (Coward and Black, 1998). Arguably, of course, there is a certain kind of dialectical relationship between the two; consumer markets have always been responsive to the injunctions of dominant contemporary ideological thought, and it is no coincidence that the identity of the feminist-friendly narcissist, 'new man' (Chapman, 1988; Mort, 1988; Nixon, 1996; Jackson *et al.*, 2001) is as firmly rooted in the discursive sphere of second wave feminism (particularly in the 1980s) as it is in the raft of men's lifestyle magazines and accompanying consumer markets of menswear and male grooming (Mort, 1988; Nixon, 1996, 2001).

The backlash to 'new man' in the form of 'new lad' (see also Introduction: this volume) led to a withdrawal by masculinity from centre stage and a diffidence and ambivalence about excessive displays of vanity or physicality (Nixon, 2001). Crucially, the heterosexist imperatives of magazine masculinity were starting to dictate that putting male bodies on display led to the possibility that they would be appreciated by an 'undifferentiated male gaze' (Simpson, 1994), and thus be potentially homoerotic in force. The impermeability of masculinity, the wholeness of masculinity, it could be said, is threatened by the penetrating gaze of the subject. The imperative to remain whole, uncontaminated and unambiguously homogenous is translated in visual terms as the male as focalizer and subject of gaze. Seeing operates as a metaphor for consumption and colonization. What this means for the visualization of the male in such magazines is a relative scarcity of images of men (particularly in comparison to images of women in women's magazines), especially desirable, sexualized or commodified men (Benwell, 2002).

Paradoxically, men's magazines are one of the few arenas in which masculinity is regularly addressed, discussed and *scrutinized*. One of the main preoccupations of this chapter will be to analyse how it is that the magazine simultaneously constructs its own brand of masculinity and avoids a direct confrontation with its terms and description.

The articulation of the backlash to 'new man' masculinity suggested that dominant masculinity was feeling itself to be weakened, not only by the perceived 'taint' of femininity (and by extension, homosexuality, with which male consumerism had always been traditionally associated) but also by the language of aspiration associated with consumer culture, which had its male readers in its grip (Faludi, 2000).

The rejection of 'new man' however did not lead to an unproblematic return to traditional, pre-feminist masculinity. Such a return would have been perceived as regressive and conservative in an industry obsessed with 'new markets' and 'new identities'. Arguably, the one great trump card played by the new lad magazines anxious to reclaim the power of masculinity but simultaneously to preserve an intelligent post-feminist political identity was the clouding of masculine identity with a certain measure of *ambiguity*. Ambiguity usually takes the form of ironic distancing—the strategy by which activities, allegiances, ideologies, sentiments may all be expressed with absolutely no commitment from the writer or, at the very least, a certain degree of equivocation about such commitment. Irony in this way acts as a defence against critical scrutiny. Similarly, the male image *meets* the probing gaze with an ironic gaze of its own. Adverts and features that focus on health, beauty and grooming are invariably laced with liberal helpings of irony, humour or protest (Benwell, 2002).

Another manifestation of ambiguity in men's lifestyle magazines comes in the form of a perpetual oscillation between two forms of masculinity: traditional, heroic masculinity and ironic, fallible and anti-heroic masculinity. Traditional, ideal masculinity tends to be represented by muscularity, physical labour, outdoor settings, heroic activities, sport and violence. 'New lad' magazines such as *loaded* have retained a soft spot for traditional masculinity and its icons, and regular tributes to celebrities, such as footballers, boxers, actors and also individuals associated with dangerous spheres or pursuits such as war-photographers, Mafia members or IRA informers appear in their pages. Profiles or interviews with such celebrities or individuals tend to be unequivocal in their praise and admiration, and detail particular feats of violence or bravery in support of their perceived status as heroes. Anti-heroic masculinity, on the other hand, defines itself in opposition to heroic masculinity and is resolutely and good-humouredly self deprecating. Anti-heroism is associated with ordinariness, weakness and self-reflexiveness and is arguably a phenomenon particularly associated with a British sensibility. These qualities have an attractive appeal to a masculinity elsewhere defined as ironic and non-narcissistic. However, the identity of 'new lad', the ideal reader, the voice and ethos of the men's lifestyle magazine, as constructed textually, allies itself neither with traditional heroic masculinity, nor with ironic anti-heroic masculinity, but subtly oscillates between the two. Traditional masculinity is aspired to by the magazine male; anti-heroism is what he inevitably falls back on, when this ambition either fails or is deemed by the magazine producers, in anticipating the likely responses of their readers, to be too narcissistic or insufficiently ironic.

The first extract under discussion (from *GQ* magazine) of a tribute to Clint Eastwood (or at least the uniform *persona* created for almost all his film roles in Westerns) is a good example of the celebration of traditional masculinity juxtaposed with the fallibility of the 'ordinary' man. The author of the piece actually describes him as: 'the most powerful masculine icon of our era'[3] (see Appendix 1 for full transcript). In linguistic terms (and to use Burton's adaptation (Burton, 1982) of Halliday's transitivity framework (Halliday, 1978, 1994)), this masculinity is manifested in terms of a high proportion of *material action intention processes* (verbs denoting intentional physical action) with a clear *affected* (someone or something affected by the process), eg, 'He stabbed Nazis in the neck', 'he slaughtered multitudes of Swastika-draped swines'. 'shot people in the back'. In other words, Eastwood is subject-agent of his processes, which are all physical acts and have an effect on something in the world. In addition, the vocabulary and metaphors are violent and excessive. The author clearly derives inspiration from his hero but is not identified with the same kind of heroism. Heroes are unique, they are idealized and we admire and celebrate them but we cannot be like them, otherwise there would be nothing extraordinary to worship; an observation made by Steve Neale:

While the ideal ego may be a 'model' with which the subject identifies and to which it aspires, it may also be a source of further images and feelings of castration, inasmuch as that ideal is something to which the subject is never adequate. (Neale. 1983: 13)

This position for the author (and by extension, the ideal reader, who is implicitly encouraged to identify with the narratorial perspective) is made manifest by the high proportion of *mental processes* (verbs of perception, 'I saw', 'it seemed to me', verbs of cognition, 'I knew', 'I surmised' and verbs of reaction, 'I liked'), and the position of the author as *affected* in passive processes. For instance, the author is defined in relation to Eastwood within passive constructions as the bearer of impressions, both perceptual and emotional: 'I was spellbound, haunted, exhilarated and shattered', 'To a pimpled teenager this was intoxicating', 'my destiny changed forever'.

This version of masculinity is a useful template by which to compare other more ambiguous versions in other texts. Men's lifestyle magazines frequently contain features in which the writer (again as a standard-bearer for the qualities of magazine masculinity) is initiated in a traditionally or ideally masculine pursuit. The following two extracts (both taken from the same issue of *loaded* magazine—see appendices 2 and 3) are typical examples which reveal remarkably similar patterns in the way masculinity is constructed. The first reports on an Outdoor Pursuits weekend and the second on an audition to be a male porn star.

In 'Dirty Weekend' it is the rhetorical structure that creates ambivalence through a continual oscillation between heroism and anti-heroism. Expressions of fear in the face of some of the highly physical and risky pursuits are continually countered. This may be done simultaneously with the *prestige* use of humour or slang, eg, 'We were putting our lives and our *swanky new gear* in the hands of Chris, Mark and Derek . . .'; 'The hard bit was *having the bollocks* to step out backwards over the edge of the cliff' (my emphases). Anti-heroism may also be countered shortly afterwards by a relational proposition of concession signifying a more traditional heroism, eg.:

> I was shivering—the cold or fear, who knows? I wasn't even scared of heights. I was scared of falling off one. But even through the fear and panic, I was aware of being surprised and impressed by the simplicity of the belay system. ('Dirty Weekend')

In reverse, straightforward and sincere expressions of heroism or even self-congratulation are similarly countered with self-mockery or expressions of anti-heroism:

> Over the lip of the cliff, when I'd got used to the idea of being horizontal, the descent was relatively enjoyable, apart from the bit where I forgot I was supposed to move my legs in time with my descent and ended up with my head lower than my feet and an upside-down view of most of South Devon. ('Dirty Weekend')

The fact that the shifts move equally from heroism to anti-heroism as well as vice versa lends support to the view that the text is able to accommodate more than one reading position. Those more invested in traditional masculinity will be able to orient to those sentences in which the heroism of the protagonist survives intact. Those less invested will be able to enjoy the undermining of heroism.

In 'Stiff Competition' we have what resembles at times a pastiche of pornographic discourse. Our point of identification, the writer, initially seems to promise to be the bearer of a supreme male sexuality. He is auditioning for the role of 'Superdick' for a porn film. Our expectation of his phallic omnipotence is, however, swiftly disappointed as we recognize again the role of the anti-hero, this time literally impotent:

> Berk number one swaggers onto the set exhibiting all the haughty, self-assurance of a toddler on his first day at infant school. Stopping beside the bed I look them both in the eye, raise an appreciative eyebrow and can think of precisely nothing to say. ('Stiff Competition')

The text employs different voices which are incongruously juxtaposed and unexpected collocations (eg, 'self-assurance of a toddler') to convey the movement from heroism to anti-heroism. The writer is both James Bond suaveness ('raise an appreciative eyebrow') and tongue-tied teenager ('can think of precisely nothing to say'). This pattern is repeated elsewhere in the text:

> Dutifully, I reach my hand behind Kerry and 'ping', in one gloriously fluid motion, her straining bra springs open unleashing its considerable cargo not six inches from my face. Deric's delighted and I find myself wondering if I'd look better in a Porsche or a Merc.

> Tentatively I squeeze her left breast but am immediately flummoxed about what to do with it.

Turning back to 'Dirty Weekend', I now wish to analyse in more linguistic detail the precise workings of ambiguity within a small sample of text. My analysis, relying as it does upon my own interpretation of the cultural significance of certain items, is acknowledged to be limited, and a more 'reliable' (and also pluralistic) discussion may be forthcoming were focus groups of magazine readers employed to support my reading. Nevertheless, the analysis is grounded in a long-term and in-depth acquaintance with a large corpus of magazine discourse in which the cultural connotations of particular phenomena are regularly negotiated and reified.

Looking at the second and third sentence of the article extract we see the familiar pattern of an expression of heroism countered by one of anti-heroism:

> What we were about to embark on could have been called an Outward Bound course, a bonding exercise or, at a push, a survival weekend. But I knew that no poncey name could disguise the grim reality: a group of blokes wearing expensive gear they'd blagged for free, getting pissed on Bacardi Spice in between jumping into rivers, plunging off cliffs and crawling down potholes.

This pattern is created by the use of the modal phrase, 'could have been'—a theoretical possibility, in this context an ideal state, and the connotatively pos-

Table 1

Item 1	Connotation	Item 2	Connotation	Relation
sentence 2 (ideal)	Positive	sentence 3 (reality)	Negative or positive?	Antithesis
'outward bound course', 'bonding exercise', 'survival weekend'	Positive (though see endnote 4)	'poncey name'	Negative	direct reference (anaphoric)
'poncey name'	Negative	'grim reality'	Negative	Antithesis
'grim reality'	Negative	'blokes wearing expensive gear they've blagged for free getting pissed on Bacardi Spice..'	Positive	direct reference (cataphoric)

itive vocabulary within discourses of heroic, traditional masculinity, 'Outward Bound Course', 'bonding exercise' and 'Survival weekend'[4], followed by the relation of antithesis in the third sentence, signalled by 'but'.

However, the relationship between heroism and anti-heroism is actually far more complex and ambiguous than a simple relationship of antithesis. Although the vocabulary in the second sentence is connotatively positive, this is countered by its description in the following sentence as 'poncey'—slang which is connotatively negative within almost all masculine discourses, since it is regarded as antithetical to masculinity. A further tension is set up later on in the line where 'poncey' is set in antithesis to 'grim', also a connotatively negative term in most cultural contexts. The negative connotation of 'grim reality' is again disrupted by the positive connotations (within masculine culture) of a series of slang words: 'blokes', 'blagged' and 'getting pissed'. Although the qualities suggested by these items are not conventionally heroic, (a bloke, for instance is an ordinary man rather than a hero) they have a certain covert prestige, especially in modern, fratriarchal (Remy, 1990) discourse. The meanings of the discourse items being used to describe these men and their activities are, in this way, endlessly deferred throughout the process of the text. We can see the workings of these various tensions, deferrals and ambiguities in the Table 1.

In other words, where a relationship of *antithesis* is suggested (two elements within the text constructed as exclusively oppositional by conjunctions such as 'but' or other cues, eg, 'disguise'), we would expect a *contrast* between negative and positive but find there is no contrast. Similarly, where a relationship of *direct reference* is suggested (one element stands in for another, eg, 'grim reality' refers directly to 'blokes wearing expensive gear'), and we would expect to find the connotation to be the same, we find a *contrast*. The myriad of textual contradictions, deferral of meaning and rapidly shifting sentiments in relation to constructions of masculinity seem to offer a variety of possible reading positions. In such a text, a reader may regard 'Outward Bound' activities as simultaneously heroic, 'poncey' or simply good fun; the text hedges its bets and accommodates all eventualities.

Both articles focusing on the magazine producers' forays into masculine spheres are typical of the way in which the magazines construct for their readers a position which acknowledges and recognizes a traditional masculinity but to which the reader is not allowed to aspire. This position can be interpreted in a number of ways. At one level the magazine is acting out the drama at the heart of psychoanalytic accounts of masculinity; the notion that traditional masculinity is characterized by aspiration rather than full possession (Segal, 1997). Roper and Tosh usefully discuss this:

> Despite the myths of omnipotent manhood which surround us, masculinity is never fully possessed, but must perpetually be achieved . . . Masculinity is always bound up with negotiations about power, and is therefore often experienced as tenuous. (Roper and Tosh 1991: 18)

The magazine's position seems to suggest in an unusually explicit way, that the power and privilege associated with traditional masculinity is unreachable or at least a struggle to attain.

Conversely, the power of the magazine male is tenuously held on to by what is arguably a very ambiguous (and thus, unknowable and strategically evasive) attitude to the explicit engagement with masculinity that we see in these extracts of data. Both pursuits ('survival' activities and starring in a porn movie) are traditionally associated with the aspirations or fantasies of an older model of masculinity, and the failure by the 'new lad' protagonists to inhabit this role successfully produces two possible readings. On the one hand, we have the rather masochistic construction of masculinity as a poor shadow of its former self, but, on the other, the more knowing, even satirical rejection of an outmoded, politically dubious, masculine predecessor. This second reading is strengthened by the recognition of a further value of 'new lad' masculinity appearing in conjunction with the repudiation of traditional masculinity (particularly apparent in 'Dirty Weekend'), which rewards specific qualities, eg, opportunism, humour and the ability to have fun.

Conclusion

Whilst an analysis of such a small sample of data can only allow a tentative discussion about the way in which masculinity is constructed in men's lifestyle magazines, the pattern of ambiguous oscillation between two positions is one which I have, in my exploration of a large corpus of magazine data, come to recognize as a very common strategy.

It could be said that the imperative of many feminists and gender commentators to scrutinize masculinity, to make it marked and visible, is ironically acted out by men's lifestyle magazines. By offering a reflective insight into masculinity, they specifically mark it and open it to this kind of scrutiny. At the same time this process of objectification is deeply threatening and often specifically resisted. Therefore we can observe a fascinating tension within men's magazines—a process of marking and identifying which is simultaneously negated or denied. This in turn is reflected in what might be termed, a 'politics of irony'. An ironic knowingness, a self-reflexiveness is used as a shield against the explicit marking of masculinity. By distancing himself from masculine constructs, either through anti-heroism, shifting connotation (deferred meaning), or through an ironic gloss, the magazine man achieves a kind of invisibility—his self-awareness pre-empts critical (feminist) scrutiny. Similarly, the continual oscillation between aspiring hero and anti-hero ensures that a position for the magazine male is never stable enough to be available for clear definition.

Whether such patterns are *strategic* on the part of the magazine producers, or whether they are *symptomatic* of a real kind of struggle between these different masculine identities, experienced by the writers and anticipated in their readers, remains unclear. Such ambiguity, tension and self-contradiction is certainly well documented in Crewe's interviews with magazine editors (this volume; forthcoming), and any notion of a 'politics of irony' paying out a clear patriarchal dividend is not terribly persuasive in the textual examples we have examined here. The anti-heroism constructed in these extracts becomes meaningful through its opposition to heroism, and in this context anti-heroism is a condition of failure rather than a radical position from which to critique traditional masculinity. What is clear is that these texts under discussion reveal, in consistent ways, a very interesting discursive struggle between contradictory masculine identities. Whether or not this is a construction which is skilfully and deliberately deployed by the magazine producers, or whether it reflects a more haphazard and confused attitude to gender, we can at least conclude that the oscillation between heroic and anti-heroic positions is one that has come to characterize certain manifestations of 'new lad' masculinity.

Notes

1 Fairclough's formulation within Critical Discourse of a three-dimensional conceptualization of discourse (text, discursive practice and social practice), goes some way to addressing this need for a situated analysis. (Fairclough 1992)
2 Even a recent collection, Bucholtz's *Reinventing Identities* (1999) has no paper devoted especially to an exploration of masculinity or 'men's talk'.
3 It is perhaps no coincidence that such a relatively unironic, unabashedly 'hero-worshipping' piece should appear in GQ, which, despite its attempts to reorient itself more along the lines of 'new lad' magazines, still retains the flavour of the older 'new man' model.

4 At the same time, there is potential for an alternative reading position here, since activities such as 'outward bound courses' have connotations of middle-class culture and self-improvement, both of which 'new lad' identity does not particularly espouse. 'Male bonding' might be said to be directly associated with 'men's movement' masculinity which is arguably quite compatible with 'new lad' identity; but whilst male bonding is something which is implicitly enacted by men's lifestyle magazines, the explicit articulation of it is quite taboo and thus in this context likely to be ironic. The simultaneous celebration and rejection of terms is a good example of the 'double voicing' which occurs again and again in men's lifestyle magazines and which renders this particular manifestation of masculinity almost impossible to pin down.

References

Primary Sources

loaded, June 1997
GQ, June 1997

Secondary Sources

Austin, J.L. (1962) *How to Do Things With Words*. Oxford: Clarendon Press.
Benwell, B. (2001) 'Have a go if you think you're hard enough: Male gossip and language play in the letters pages of men's lifestyle magazines', *Journal of Popular Culture* 35(1): 19–33.
Benwell, B. (2002) 'Is there anything 'new' about these Lads?: The textual and visual construction of masculinity in men's magazines': in Litosseliti and Sunderland (eds) *Gender Identity and Discourse Analysis*. Amsterdam/Philadelphia: John Benjamins Press.
Bucholtz, M. (1999) 'Purchasing power: The gender and class imaginary on the shopping channel': in Bucholtz *et al.* (eds), *Reinventing Identities: The Gendered Self in Discourse*. NY/Oxford: Oxford University Press.
Bucholtz, M, Liang, A.C., and Sutton, L. (1999) *Reinventing Identities: The Gendered Self in Discourse*. NY/Oxford: Oxford University Press.
Burton, D. (1982) 'Through glass darkly: Through dark glasses': in Carter (ed.), *Language and Literature: An Introductory Reader in Stylistics*. London/NY: Routledge.
Butler, J. (1999) *Gender Trouble: Feminism and the Subversion of Identity* (2nd edition). NY: Routledge.
Butler, J. (1993) *Bodies that Matter: On the Discursive Limits of 'Sex'*. London: Routledge
Caldas-Coulthard, C. (1996) 'Women who pay for sex. And enjoy it: Transgression versus morality in women's magazines': in Caldas-Coulthard and Coulthard (eds), *Texts and Practices: Readings in Critical Discourse Analysis*. London: Routledge.
Cameron, D. (1997) 'Performing gender identity: Young men's talk and the construction of heterosexual masculinity': in Johnson and Meinhof (eds), *Language and Masculinity*. Oxford: Blackwell.
Coates, J. (1998) 'Thank god I'm a woman: The construction of differing femininities': in Cameron (ed.), *The Feminist Critique of Language*. London/NY: Routledge.
Coward and Black (1998) 'Linguistic, social and sexual relations: A review of Dale Spender's Man Made Language': in Cameron (ed.), *The Feminist Critique of Language*. London: Routledge (2nd edition).
Crewe, B. (forthcoming) *Representing Men: Cultural Production and Producers in the Men's Magazine Market*. Oxford: Berg.
Edwards, D. and Potter, J. (1992) *Discursive Psychology*. London: Sage.
Edwards, T. (1997) *Men in the Mirror: Men's Fashion, Masculinity and Consumer Fashion*. London: Cassell.
Fairclough, N. (1989) *Language and Power*. London: Longman.
Fairclough, N. (1992) *Discourse and Social Change*. Cambridge: Polity Press.

Faludi, S. (1999) *Stiffed: The Betrayal of the Modern Man.* London: Chatto and Windus.

Gough, V. and Talbot, M. (1996) 'Guilt over games boys play: Coherence as a focus for examining the constitution of heterosexual subjectivity': in Caldas-Coulthard and Coulthard (eds), *Texts and Practices: Readings in Critical Discourse Analysis.* London: Routledge.

Grice, H.P. (1975) 'Logic and conversation': in Cole and Morgan (eds), *Syntax and Semantics 3: Speech Acts.* New York: Academic Press.

Hall, K. and Bucholtz, M. (eds) (1995) *Gender Articulated: Language and the Socially Constructed Self.* London/NY: Routledge.

Halliday, M.A.K. (1978) *Language as Social Semiotic: The Social Interpretation of Language and Meaning.* London: Edward Arnold.

Halliday, M.A.K. (1994) (2nd edn.) *An Introduction to Functional Grammar.* London: Edward Arnold.

Harvey, K. and Shalom, C. (eds) (1997) *Language and Desire: Encoding Sex, Romance and Intimacy.* London/NY: Routledge.

Litosseliti, L. and Sunderland, J. (eds) (2002) *Gender Identity and Discourse Analysis.* Amsterdam: John Benjamins.

Livia, A. and Hall, K. (eds) (1997) *Queerly Phrased: Language, Gender and Sexuality.* Oxford: Oxford University Press.

McIlvenny, P. (ed.) (2002) *Talking Gender and Sexuality: Identities, Agencies and Desires in Interaction.* Amsterdam: John Benjamins.

Mills, S. (1995) *Feminist Stylistics.* London: Routledge.

Mort, F. (1988) 'Boy's own? Masculinity, style and popular culture': in Chapman and Rutherford (eds), *Male Order: Unwrapping Masculinity.* London: Lawrence and Wishart.

Neale, S. (1993) 'Masculinity as spectacle: Reflections on men and mainstream cinema': in S. Cohan and I.R. Hark (eds), *Screening the Male: Exploring Masculinities in Hollywood Cinema.* London: Routledge.

Nixon, S. (1996) *Hard Looks: Masculinities, spectatorship and contemporary consumption.* London: UCL Press.

Nixon, S. (2001) 'Resignifying masculinity: From "new man" to "new lad"': in Morley and Robins (eds), *British Cultural Studies.* Oxford: Oxford University Press.

Potter, J. and Wetherell, M. (1987) *Discourse and Social Psychology: Beyond Attitudes and Behaviour.* London: Sage.

Remy, J. (1990) 'Patriarchy and fratriarchy as forms of androcracy': in Hearn and Morgan (eds), *Men, Masculinities and Social Theory.* London: Unwin Hyman.

Roper, M. and Tosh J. (1991) *Manful Assertions: Masculinities in Britain since 1800.* London: Routledge.

Searle, J. (1969) *Speech Acts: An Essay in the Philosophy of Language.* Cambridge: Cambridge University Press.

Simpson, M. (1994) *Male Impersonators: Men Performing Masculinity*, London: Cassell.

Southwell, T. (1998) *Getting Away With It: The Inside Story of* Loaded. London: Bury Press.

Speer, S. and Potter, J. (2002) 'From performatives to practices: Judith Butler, Discursive Psychology and the management of heterosexist talk': in McIlvenny (ed.), *Talking Gender and Sexuality: Identities, Agencies and Desires in Interaction.* Amsterdam: John Benjamins.

Talbot, M. (1995) 'A synthetic sisterhood: False friends in a teenage magazine': in K. Hall and M. Bucholtz (eds), *Gender Articulated: Language and the Socially Constructed Self.* London/NY: Routledge.

Talbot, M. (1997) 'Randy fish boss branded a stinker: Coherence and the construction of masculinities in a British tabloid paper': in S. Johnson and U. Meinhof (eds), *Language and Masculinity.* Oxford: Blackwell.

Appendix 1

(*GQ* June 1997)
HEROES
Our heroes define us. They are the men we would most like to be. . . .
A LAW UNTO HIMSELF (Tim Willcocks on Clint Eastwood)
The first time I saw Clint Eastwood I was about twelve years old; the film was Where Eagles Dare. In the first hour of the movie, Eastwood did almost nothing and said even less; in the second hour, he started killing. He stabbed Nazis in the neck as if brushing his teeth; he said 'Hello' and smiled, as a prelude to pumping silenced bullets into their thoraxes; and using two machine pistols at once, he slaughtered multitudes of Swastika–draped swines with the bored insouciance of a man shelling peas. As I reeled from the cinema—my destiny changed forever—my father smiled at me and said: 'That's what he's like, that Clint Eastwood. He always knows what he's doing.'

Next I saw *The Good, The Bad and The Ugly*. It made *Where Eagles Dare* look like an episode of 'The Magic Roundabout'. This time Eastwood said 'Hello' and shot people in the back. He gunned down the wounded as they begged for mercy. He lied, swindled and betrayed. He abandoned his partner to a slow death. It was even clear that he had no intention of spending the fortune in gold for which he had killed so many.

I was spellbound, haunted, exhilarated and shattered. Eastwood had not only wiped out most of the cast, he'd wiped out every idol I had. I knew that even if Randolph Scott, Yul Brynner, Steve McQueen, Gary Cooper and John Wayne had all been banded together against him, Eastwood would have cleansed them from the desert as easily as breaking wind.

Today, when most stars could be cleansed by Basil Brush, it is hard to remember Eastwood's impact. He was a monument to unhinged individualism. He never admitted the possibility of error. His self-knowledge was so complete, so taken for granted, that he was never required to conquer doubt, anxiety, or insecurity of any kind. Such neuroses simply did not exist. My father was right: Eastwood was a man who, at any and all times, knew exactly what he was doing.

To a pimpled teenager this was intoxicating. I must say, it still is. But back then it threw into painful relief the humiliating weediness and compromise of real life; it exposed emotion, sexuality, social obligation and family as the vile encumbrances they often are; and from these there was no escape. But in the sanctuary of an Eastwood movie it was possible to believe oneself free. Not merely free to do as one pleased, but free of all the shaming and tedious shackles of being human. Eastwood was never a fascist, as simpering fifth-raters claimed he was. He was the supreme anarchist: an unsmiling Dionysus for a flabby and hedonistic age.

This central image of Eastwood—the man who needs no one and does as he wants—is for me the most powerful masculine icon of our era, more so even than Presley. Presley was the King: but like all kings he as never more—nor less—than a man, Eastwood, who had the discipline not to contaminate his

Bethan Benwell

creation with personal displays of weakness, did not seem human at all; nor even merely superhuman. He was, rather, the unholy spirit of pagan God.

Appendix 2

(*loaded*, June 1997)
DIRTY WEEKEND (Trevor Ward)
Seven brave men were set to battle the elements. But they couldn't make it so we sent this lot . . .

. . . There were seven of us carrying the honour and reputation of *loaded* before us as we were put through our paces during the next couple of days. What we were about to embark on could have been called an Outward Bound course, a bonding exercise or, at a push, a survival weekend. But I knew that no poncey name could disguise the grim reality: a group of blokes wearing expensive gear they'd blagged for free, getting pissed on Bacardi Spice in between jumping into rivers, plunging off cliffs and crawling down potholes.

We were putting our lives and swanky new gear in the hands of Chris, Mark and Derek from Mountain Water experience. In the past they've dealt with unruly schoolkids, hormonal, claustrophobic women and the odd stag party of rugby players, so they didn't even blink at the name *loaded*.

We set off in two carloads to the edge of Dartmoor National Park, as our compilation CD unwittingly provided the soundtrack for the capers to come: Iggy Pop's 'Lust for Life', XTC's 'Senses Working Overtime' and the Jam's 'Going Underground'.

. . . Devil's Rock didn't strike me as a great name for a place to be taught how to abseil, so I was glad it was already congested with climbers and we had to drop our ropes from nearby Cyclops Crag instead. We were to abseil down a 90 foot cliff, but the sensation was even more terrifying, as we were actually nearer to 300 feet above the river Plym below. With our harnesses hooked to a safety line, we made our way one by one along a tiny ledge to the point where Mark would talk us through general abseiling etiquette and then expect us to walk backwards over the cliff edge.

Me and Big Piers—so-called as much because of the flattering effect his harness had on his package as for the fact that he was taller than the other Piers—were the last in line, and neither wanted to be left up here alone. Before us, we'd already seen Miles take one step backwards over the cliff and then terrifyingly lose his footing, sending him plunging several feet before the safety line kicked in. I claimed seniority as the writer and took my place ahead of Piers. With my back to the drop below, Mark clipped me to the line and explained how the belay brake system worked. I could control my rate of descent by simply swinging my right arm in and out. That was the easy bit. The hard bit was having the bollocks to step out backwards over the edge of the cliff. It was very windy and cold up there. I could see the grey haze of Plymouth in the distance to my left, and the green, smudgy expanse of Dartmoor to my right. I had no idea

166

© The Editorial Board of the Sociological Review 2003

what was directly below me, and didn't want to look. I slowly shuffled my feet backwards until I could feel the firm ground give way to nothingness. <u>I was shivering—the cold or fear, who knows? I wasn't even scared of heights. I was scared of falling off one. But even through the fear and panic, I was aware of being surprised and impressed by the simplicity of the belay system as it prevented me from plunging head first to the ground.</u>

<u>Once over the lip of the cliff, when I'd got used to the idea of being horizontal, the descent was relatively enjoyable, apart from the bit where I forgot I was supposed to move my legs in time with my descent and ended up with my head lower than my feet and an upside–down view of most of South Devon.</u> Near the bottom, I crashed into a tree and had to be helped out by the others.

'Alright, but not brilliant. Walking backwards over a cliff—not a good thing,' read my notes, in shaky script.

Appendix 3

(*loaded* June 1997)
STIFF COMPETITION (Piers Hernu)
loaded goes off half cocked at porn auditions
'Superdick Auditions This Way' says a large sign taped to the front door of The Fantasy Channel offices. I push it open only to hear a gaggle of secretaries giggling behind me. We squeeze into the lift and four tortuous floors of tittering later, I've begun an afternoon of abject humiliation.

Eight names are put into a hat—guess who's called out first?

<u>Berk number one swaggers onto the set exhibiting all the haughty, self assurance of a toddler on his first day at infant school. Stopping beside the bed I look them both in the eye, raise an appreciative eyebrow and . . . can think of precisely nothing to say.</u> I stand there under the spotlight, a rabbit caught in the headlights, motionless, dumb and quivering.

'H-hi girls,' I stammer eventually. 'Umm . . . I'm Superdick.'

'Sam pats the bed beside her. 'Sit down Superdick,' she simpers. I perch awkwardly on the edge of the bed, my eyes swimming in a sea of long legs, lace and cleavage. Kerry unbuttons my shirt to reveal a dome-like protuberance, utterly devoid of ribbed muscle, closer to Peter Stringfellow than Peter André. In the shadows I spot Deric playing porno charades to give me a clue. Dutifully, I reach my hand behind Kerry and 'ping', in one gloriously fluid motion, her straining bra springs open unleashing its considerable cargo not six inches from my face. Deric's delighted and I find myself wondering if I'd look better in a Porsche or a Merc.

Tentatively I squeeze her left breast but am immediately flummoxed about what to do with it. I lean forward . . . a dry lizard's tongue darts out of my mouth and flickers like a beached anchovy around her erect nipple.

Sam starts to unbutton my flies and my last dregs of self-confidence drain away like dirty bathwater as Kerry places her head gently on my beer gut and slides a finger under the elastic of my boxers. Helpless, I watch as both girls squint into the dark recesses of my underpants.

All three of us are greeted by the sight of what appears to be a newborn weasel crashed out on an old brillo pad. Reaching inside, Kerry prods the prostrate pink creature with a painted fingernail. It rolls over but remains deep in slumber, unaware of the ordeal its owner is going through. Kerry starts giggling and then, reaching deep inside the bottom drawer of female cruelty, pipes up: 'Superdick? More like Drooperdick!'

Everyone in the room laughs. The one person who isn't laughing lies there like the main attraction at some circus freakshow. In a room full of people I am suddenly completely and utterly alone.

Mark, a burly, blond Brummie is appointed the new Superdick. Grudgingly, I wish him well and flee. Never, in my whole life, have I felt less super and more of a dick.

'I've always loved women': the representation of the male sex worker in *Maxim*

Yolande Taylor and Jane Sunderland

Introduction

Magazines are a promising genre to examine in the study of gender identities and relations because, arguably, they have the potential both to maintain and to affect cultural values and norms in society (see also Caldas-Coulthard, 1996). The emergence in the 1980s of a new genre—the men's 'lifestyle' magazine—has also opened up new avenues of research in the hitherto relatively unexplored domain of masculinity. Linguistic analysis of magazines, although not a new phenomenon, is still fairly uncommon, particularly in relation to masculinity (as indeed is the linguistic study of masculinity more generally). Talbot (1992, 1995) and Caldas-Coulthard (1996), for example, have both analysed magazines or magazine articles but have concentrated on femininity. Partly for this reason, we have chosen to look at masculinities, and to do so by analysing an article from the men's lifestyle magazine, *Maxim*, about a male 'escort'.

Critical Discourse Analysis can be seen as a useful tool in language and gender studies for exposing asymmetrical patterns of power. Its recognition of the importance of studying language use in a social context, in which there exist social practices, allows gender to be studied as a fluid, dynamic entity, rather than as a fixed and unchanging masculine/feminine duality. In this chapter, we draw on Critical Discourse Analysis to establish how masculinities are represented (and perhaps constructed) in this magazine article, and whether the article signals a shift in cultural representations of masculinity and indeed of sexual relations.

Gender and language use

West, Lazar and Kramarae (1997: 119) suggest that '[what] we think of as "womanly" or "manly" behaviour is not dictated by biology but rather is socially constructed'. There are numerous factors which contribute to this social construction, for example the school, the family, the media and language. Language use must, of course, be distinguished from language *as an abstract system*—the focus of early language and gender studies, which addressed what was seen as the inherent systemic sexism of certain words and phrases. Critiqued, for example, were the supposedly generic *he* and *man*, and the way that some words had come to acquire a negative and/or sexual connotation when referring to women, for example *professional* and *tramp* (see Cameron, 1990). Efforts were made in many institutional settings to eliminate such linguistic sexism, for example the Code of Practice produced by the University of Strathclyde's Programme of Opportunities for Women Committee on 'gender-free language' for reference by staff and students. Cameron (1994) points out, however, that gender inequalities are apparent not so much in individual words as in meaning as a whole:

> sexism in language exists below the surface, so that superficial reforms (like proscribing some finite set of offensive forms or making all texts formally gender neutral) are insufficient to combat it. Many instances of sexism are manifested not in single words or specific constructions but through an accumulation of discursive or textual choices; this kind of sexism will always elude the mechanical application of a standardizing rule. (Cameron 1994: 32)

More important than the specific linguistic items, then, must be language use. In most early (1970–1990) studies of gender and language use, women were the main subjects of research, contributing to them being seen as the 'other' and men as the 'norm' (see also Cameron 1996; Johnson 1997). Such problematization of women implies not only women's *deviance* but also that the onus for change lies on women's shoulders. Cameron (1995) in fact explores the ways in which women have been encouraged to change their way of speaking to be more like men in order to succeed in traditionally male-dominated fields. Margaret Thatcher, for example, was famously advised to deepen the tone of her voice and to regulate her 'female' intonation to compete in the male-dominated world of politics.

With the change in the fundamental questions being asked in language and gender research—ie, 'instead of "how do women and men behave linguistically?" we can ask how particular linguistic practices contribute to the production of people as "women" and "men"' (Cameron, 1996: 47)—the preoccupation with talk (and with 'gender differences' in talk) has now been complemented by, and has largely given way to, a focus on the way in which gender is both represented and constructed in language use. This includes written texts such as men's lifestyle magazines, which are, of course, just one of the many text types which can be investigated in this context.

Language use varies with genre, which affects the kind of discourse and discourse practices available. The language of magazines (like that of other written and spoken texts) can be seen as the result of a series of *choices* which are available to its writers. Choices made by writers present just one version of 'reality' and, as van Leeuwen (1996: 43) points out, although it is difficult to tell how accurately a given text reflects reality, we can at least:

> investigate which options are chosen in which institutional and social contexts, and why these choices should have been taken up, what interests are served by them, and what purposes achieved.

This is the purpose of our study.

This study

The data for the study is an article entitled 'What's it like to . . . be paid to have sex: tales of a male escort' from the June 1998 edition of the magazine *Maxim* (see Appendix for a typescript of the original article). We chose *Maxim* because it is a best-selling glossy men's lifestyle magazine and therefore potentially widely influential in terms of its content. Launched in 1995, *Maxim* is targeted at young men with a high disposable income. For many years, the men's magazine market was dominated by pornography and magazines dealing with hobbies and leisure pursuits such as golf, fishing and motoring. The launch of *Arena* and *GQ* in the 1980s heralded the start of a sudden, successful influx of glossy men's lifestyle magazines looking at issues such as health, fashion, sex and sport.

We selected the article about a male 'escort' (in fact, a sex worker) for analysis because of its potential as an epistemological site which could lend special insights into gender, gender identities and gender relations, dealing as it does with the transgression of a social practice traditionally associated with masculinity ('men pay women for sex'). In the interests of depth and richness, we chose to study one article in detail as opposed to several articles more superficially. We recognize that, in consequence, the study is essentially *illustrative*, but feel that what it does illustrate is important.

Kimmel and Messner (1995) point out that although many social processes play a part in constructing masculinity, sexuality is central to that process. 'Lifestyle' magazines make an explicit link between gender and sexuality because they consider a person's identity to be bound up with their sexuality: 'The real self is the self revealed in personal intimacy and in the modern women's [and men's] magazines this real self is understood as sexual behaviour' (Caldas-Coulthard, 1996: 250).

Linguistic analyses of written texts about masculinity is not entirely new, and texts on masculinity and sex have also been analysed. Jewitt (1997) investigated the way in which images in sexual health leaflets informed the social construction of masculinity, using a framework put forward by Kress and Van Leeuwen (1996). Jewitt found a 'conventional representation of male sexuality' (1997: 1), informed by discourses of sexual competence, competitiveness and individuality. Benwell (2002) analysed a large corpus of magazine data to see whether the social construction of masculinity pointed to a 'new' version of masculinity which was a reaction against the 1990s 'new man'. She concluded that the 'new lad', in rejecting feminist-friendly masculinity, did not offer a newer, more forward-looking version but, in fact, reflected a return to more traditional (patriarchal, misogynous, homophobic) models of masculinity. Closest to our own study, however, is probably the work of Caldas-Coulthard (1996), whose textual analysis was of an article which appeared in the women's lifestyle magazine *Marie Claire*, about women who pay for sex. She showed that although the article was quite progressive in terms of sexuality, for example including a strong discourse of sexual liberation, the article was nonetheless underscored by a fairly traditional view that women can only find happiness in a 'long-term heterosexual relationship'. Our study, in contrast, focuses on a man who *sells sex to* women, for whom a long-term relationship of any sort is simply not represented in the text at all.

Analytical framework

As indicated, Critical Discourse Analysis (CDA) (eg, Fairclough, 1989, 1992) provides an analytical framework which is eminently suitable for analysing written (and spoken) texts in which power or asymmetry appears to be relevant. It sees meaning residing not in individual words but in whole socially-produced discourses, recognizing that texts are produced and read in context rather than in isolation (Huckin 1997). CDA can bring to light patterns of unequal power relations which are embedded in a text—useful not only for drawing attention to social imbalances but also for encouraging corrective action. Talbot (1998: 150) explains that CDA's success lies in 'unearthing the social and historical constitution of naturalized conventions (in other words, of ways of doing things that are so apparently natural they are just "common sense")'. Language and gender researchers thus can, and often do, draw on CDA approaches in order to see how language contributes (often negatively) to the representation and possible social construction of men and women, for example, highlighting the fact that in many societies it is still men who fairly consistently play the more powerful roles, at least institutionally (see also Sunderland and Litosseliti, 2002). The writer's choice of particular linguistic items, grammatical structures, discourses and/or subject positions above others has been one focus of critical discourse analysis (see also van Leeuwen 1996, 1997). A writer can make a magazine article, its characters and their actions appear in a particular way, positive or negative, not only through the choice of vocabulary and grammatical structures, but also, importantly, by *not* using other vocabulary or grammatical structures which logically could have been used. A critical linguistic analysis, whilst revealing asymmetrical patterns of power, cannot however account for the differing ways in which a given text can be interpreted or 'consumed' (Fairclough, 1992). CDA can and does appreciate and draw on context, but meaning for a given reader will be influenced by that reader's own subjective reading of that text.

The analysis presented in this chapter will consist of examining both the language (individual words, phrases and whole sentences) and the content of the article which the language 'carries'. The questions below provide the framework for our analysis:

- Is the representation of the protagonist, Peter, in the magazine article made to sound positive or negative?
- How are Peter and the other characters represented, in general terms?
- What topics have been focused on out of the pool of topics available?

- Who is 'activated', who 'passivated' and who 'benefits' here?
- What lexical choices have been made?
- What (gendered/gendering) discourses 'run through' the text?

But before addressing these questions, it will be valuable to comment on various aspects of the production process and the analytical framework.

The reader may be expected to assume (if he or she gave it some thought) that the article has been written on the basis of an interview. However, with no access to the original tapescript nor the journalist's notes, it is impossible to know in what ways the writer's 'data' has been processed, or 'mediated', as it has passed through the production processes. Let us assume, though, that an interview of some sort was carried out. Firstly, the wording and questions of an interview can direct the interviewee's responses (Mills, 1994). The way the questions were understood by 'Peter' and the way in which his responses were in turn subsequently recorded/documented and interpreted (not necessarily in this order) will all have an effect on the final text. Secondly, it is usual for copy to go from writer to sub-editor to editor; at any point during this process certain elements will be selected and others (including parts of responses) discarded for a variety of reasons such as available space, the tone of the magazine, house style, accompanying images and personal preference. Whether or not the original text has been manipulated is, however, for our purposes, relatively immaterial; what is more important is why the writer/sub-editor/editor has chosen to include/discard/amend certain parts of the interview in order to achieve a particular representational effect.

To build up a picture of the gendered identities constructed through the discourses in the article, we have drawn upon the analytical framework developed by van Leeuwen (1996) to analyse how 'social actors' are represented. Van Leeuwen uses the terms *inclusion* and *exclusion* to refer to instances in a text when a social actor is present or has been left out, how this is achieved linguistically, and why. Here we have adapted the terms to include whole topics and any explicit justification of these. Inclusions and exclusions build up a particular version of reality and it is interesting and perhaps revealing to speculate not only why the author/sub-editor/editor has selected one topic over another but also what effect a different choice would have had on the meaning potential of the text.

Van Leeuwen (1996: 43, 44) defines *activation* as 'social actors' being represented as the 'active, dynamic forces in an activity' and *passivation* as social actors '"undergoing" the activity, or as being "at the receiving end of it"'. By taking away the subject of a sentence, or by turning the subject of a sentence into the object, a writer can change the power balance and salience/importance of different events. Cameron (1990), for example, uses an article from *The Daily Telegraph* to illustrate how rape can be portrayed as a crime against the victim's husband rather than against the victim herself:

> A man who suffered head injuries when attacked by two men who broke into his home in Beckenham, Kent, early yesterday, was pinned down on the bed by intruders who took it in turns to rape his wife. (Cameron, 1990: 17)

By making the husband the grammatical subject of a passive construction ('was pinned down'), and by mentioning him first, the impression may be given that it is he who really suffered rather than his wife. Similarly, analysis of the data in our study might reveal whether Peter or his clients are in control, or, more subtly, in what ways.

Through choice of content and language, a writer builds up a picture of a character. The particular representation favoured is not accidental; it is the writer's way of making a judgement about that person and 'positioning' them. It is possible that a character may be positioned in multiple (and perhaps conflicting ways) in the same text, for example as a wife, mother, daughter, student and friend. When describing an event or action, a writer normally has a fairly wide range of lexical choices available, depending on the effect they hope to create. To describe a person as 'intelligent and witty', for example, gives a very different impression to 'know-it-all and acting the fool'. Lexical choices cannot be analysed in isolation; rather they have to be studied contextually with the subject of the article, genre (here, a men's lifestyle magazine), co-text (words, sentences and paragraphs preceding and following them) and intended audience in mind. Here, we look at the choice of nouns and adjectives used to describe the social actors (Peter and his clients).

Discourse, as Mills (1997) points out, is a term employed across many fields, including linguistics, sociology, philosophy and social psychology. Its meaning is often left undefined. The most basic linguistic understanding is probably 'language beyond the sentence', that is to say, stretches of text or speech rather than individual words; more productively, a discourse can also be seen as a 'recognizable way of seeing the world' (see also Sunderland and Litosseliti, 2002). Certain social contexts tend to be associated with particular linguistic conventions and vocabulary, for example medical discourse and academic discourse, but it is also possible to recognize more precise discourses; in parentcraft texts, for example, a specific and specially named discourse such as 'mother as main parent/part-time father' discourse (see eg, Sunderland, 2002). It is possible, even likely, for more than one discourse to be evident within a given text; a hierarchy of discourses may, in fact, be apparent, some of which may conflict or support one another (see eg, Sunderland and Litosseliti, 2002).

Analysis of 'What's it like to . . . be paid to have sex: tales of a male escort'

The title of this feature sets the story up as something light and entertaining, something for other heterosexual men to envy—having sex with lots of women and getting paid for it. An initial reading of the text reveals a story told as if Peter were talking informally with a group of male friends. Through the use of a first-person narrative, ie, the use of *I* and *me* as opposed to Peter being referred to in the third person (*he*), it might seem that Peter is boasting to his friends about his great job (the later linguistic analysis does not uncover anything which contradicts this). This male 'focalization' (Mills, 1995), which here refers to the way that a seemingly neutral narrative voice conceals a gendered perspective, means here that Peter is, in fact, controlling the perspective of the text. The experience is made to sound positive on the whole: Peter is represented as successful, in control and sexually expert and the reader is allowed to see only an 'ideal' type of masculinity.

We will begin with an analysis of the content of the article.

Is the representation of the protagonist, Peter, in the magazine article made to sound positive or negative?

For the most part, Peter's experiences are represented in a positive manner. The title 'What's it like to . . . be paid to have sex: tales of a male escort' may have been chosen to give the impression that the character is in the *lucky* position of having sex with lots of women and getting paid for it. This continues as Peter describes a particular client as wealthy and attractive; escorting her is compared to a real date: 'To be honest, the mood of the evening wasn't that different from a night out with someone you fancy; passionate but quite relaxed.' (18–20) (see Appendix for full line-numbered text). The work may be hard: 'It's 2am, there's a long night ahead and the meter's got quite a way to run . . .' (24, 25), but, on the other hand, this is offset by the earnings: 'I clocked up £50k last year' (27). It is portrayed as easy money because Peter only has sex with the women he wants to and enjoys it: 'You could say I love my work—I've certainly always loved women' (64, 65). Not only do the clients pay to have sex with Peter but they also pay for the night out. He gets to visit 'all sorts of expensive show-off places' (39), but this is not portrayed as entirely positive because Peter apparently finds too much of a good thing boring: 'You do get blasé about it' (40, 41).

Peter is also represented as a product to be sold and used: 'I'm an expensive commodity really' (55, 56). Read ironically, this could be seen as Peter being happy to be a 'commodity', as long as he is an 'expensive' one; there is no self-deprecation here. One way Peter says he is 'used' is as a tool for revenge for women who believe their husbands are being unfaithful: 'she's just hired you to "get back" at him by turning up to a function with a young toy-boy in tow' (54, 55). Nevertheless, the writer still manages to portray Peter as benefiting from these encounters because he makes money, decides who he will and will not have sex with, and can have sex with lots of women with no emotional ties (the stereotypical heterosexual male fantasy?).

How are Peter and the other characters represented, in general terms?

Peter is represented overwhelmingly as a man who has fallen on his feet; not only does he have sex with lots of women but he also gets paid to do it: 'most clients pay me about £100 an hour on top of what they pay for the night out' (26, 27). Added to which he gets tips such as 'a £90 Armani shirt' (14, 15).

With regard to the client, Peter is represented as the sexual expert who is able to give women what they want: 'at some stage she's probably thinking, "I want my money's worth." And I'm there to give it to her. Whichever way she wants' (33–35). He is represented as being good at what he does and aware of the clients' individual needs: 'an all-nighter who I knew needed drinks and dinner' (6). This representation ties in with the findings of previous research (Tiefer, 1993) that dominant Western conceptions of masculinity revolve around sexual competence, and with Jewitt's (1997) claim that 'There is a cultural expectation that men are sexually knowledgeable'. Peter's sexual competence also encompasses protection: 'I use condoms every time, I'm not taking any risks' (35–36). Whilst mentions of such practicalities may detract from the glamour and the world of masculine fantasy, it does help to set him up as the one in control, the expert.

Peter's 'expertise' is contrasted with that of 'ordinary' men, and indeed he is represented as sexually expert in relation to the reader. The reader is addressed directly and advised by him to: 'Nuzzle the neck, move down slowly but surely, make sure she's really aroused, spend just the right amount of time—ten minutes is my advice' (30–32). This advice is further exemplified by the inclusion of 'trade secrets' which Peter divulges to the reader: 'The golden rule is not to try and be too seductive' (77). These titillatory instructions serve to construct a soft-porn image, typical of many men's lifestyle magazines (Benwell, 2002); arguably, these magazines and articles are themselves soft-porn.

Another way in which Peter is represented is as 'man in control'. According to the text, Peter works for himself, and chooses who he will have sex with: 'The way I deal with really ugly clients is to explain that I do the escorting for the night but that I never actually have sex because I'm married, my wife knows what I do and the agreement is: no sex at the end' (104–107). It is unlikely that a female prostitute could enjoy the same degree of choice—but such comparisons are absent (and the female-associated word *prostitute* never used in this text). Having sex with unattractive women would of course make the job seem less enviable and, therefore, fail to fulfil a male fantasy of being able to have commitment-free sex with attractive women and be paid for it. The reader's suspicions as to the veracity of Peter's freedom to choose whom he has sex with may however be raised by such contrary observations as 'your preferences don't matter.'

Peter is depicted as in total charge when the situation goes wrong. If, for example, a client's partner arrives unexpectedly on the scene: 'I tend to be very logical in situations like that: I just kept calm and looked for somewhere he wouldn't spot me' (62, 63). Although the clients are paying him and he is there to meet their needs, he is shown, James Bond-like, to mastermind all situations, including protecting his own face at all times.

Interestingly, Peter is also positioned as superior to other men as though he is competing against them. Other (would-be) escorts are represented as not successful: 'Some guys can't make it as escorts' (36, 37). The implication here is that although other men may fall short of the mark, this is not the case with Peter.

This is also implied with reference to his technique: 'If a client doesn't have an orgasm, you're not doing the job properly. At the end of the day, women pay good money for good sex. They can get crap sex anywhere' (143, 144). The implication is that sex will not be 'crap' with Peter.

Positive representations of social actors stop short when the writer describes his/Peter's clients: 'She wasn't the usual after-dinner shag' (5). This could be understood to mean that Peter sees and experiences the majority of his clients as part of a series of uninteresting women with whom he has predictable sex. This is echoed when the writer describes some of the clients in an unflattering way: 'To be honest, a lot of my clients look better from behind' (103, 104). The clients, on the other hand, are represented negatively, either sexually or with regard to their appearance, particularly in the section 'Sex: the ins and outs', where they are classified according to the headings of: 'Oldest' (117), 'Ugliest' (119), 'Fattest' (120), 'Kinkiest' (121), 'Smelliest' (123) and 'Most Expensive' (125). Such simplistic and reductive classifications have an obviously controlling function; by compartmentalizing women into these pigeon-holes, Peter renders them more manageable. The inclusion of women who change their minds also contributes to the negative positioning:

> You do get women who decide to hire you then change their mind. You have to be 100 per cent understanding, you can't afford to be forceful about it. If they change their mind and have already paid you, you have to do the honourable thing and offer a refund. (107–110)

Peter's women clients are thus represented as potentially capricious and not knowing their own minds. This echoes the wider gendered discourses of the pernicious 'No means Yes' and the patronising 'it's a woman's prerogative to change her mind' kind. Conversely, Peter is represented as magnanimous and obligingly pandering to their whims.

What topics have been focused on out of the 'pool' of topics available?

There are seven main topic areas which the writer has chosen to focus on: a client, earnings, sexual technique, the clients' partners, Peter's previous relationships, what his job as an escort entails, and those clients he will not have sex with. We wish to concentrate now on what has not been included (and what, from a feminist perspective, arguably should have been) and to speculate on how inclusion of these might have changed the representation of Peter and of what he does in the text.

There is no mention of whether Peter is currently in a committed long-term relationship or not. This absence is important because Peter is depicted as having no ties and as free to do as he pleases. To describe him in terms of a serious relationship would create a new (for this article) discourse of 'man as long-term partner' which would be contrary to the dominant discourse of *Maxim* and indeed other men's magazines where men are invariably represented as single and involved in non-committed sexual, rather than emotional, relationships. In the same edition of *Maxim*, there is only one feature about stable relationships—

and that is concerned with 'how to follow your partner if you suspect her of having an affair'.

Another perspective noticeable in its absence is justification for being an escort. No reason is given by the writer as to why Peter decided to become an escort (an unusual job for a man) other than the money and that he likes the job: 'You could say I love my work' (64). Why not? If the writer were to provide justification for Peter being an escort, this might suggest to readers either that the writer saw the job as being wrong in some way or, perhaps, that Peter was doing this because he couldn't get other types of (better) work and/or was unemployed. The absence of explanation may mean that the writer views male escorting in terms of masculine desire as completely unproblematic and 'common sense'—not normative for men, by any means, but (or therefore) 'nice work if you can get it' (Talbot, 1998), as opposed to a 'degrading' job—prostitution—for women.

And it is this omission that is in fact the most striking: not only is the word 'prostitute' never used in the lexicalization of Peter (see later), there is no reference to the situation of female prostitutes, or even female 'escorts'. The article is at pains to distance Peter's 'enviable' occupation with one associated with exploitation in general (Peter is in control!) and exploitation of women in particular. Thus what might be read as transgression is carefully negotiated, and the fantasy is maintained.

The second part of our analysis involves a close analysis of language choices, both grammatical and lexical.

Who is 'activated', who 'passivated', and who 'benefits' here?

Our close linguistic analysis includes an examination of the grammatical relations in the text to see who is the subject of the sentence and whether that subject is activated or passivated. Such an analysis might reveal where power within the grammatical structure lies and, therefore, whether it is Peter or his clients who are represented as being in control. The results, for Peter and for his clients, are presented in the following lists[1].

1 Peter is activated in relation to the clients:

    SVO (B) before I could even contemplate taking her back (7, 8)
        (B) I picked her up at the office (17)
        (B) I'd 'escorted' her (17, 18)
        (B) I'm there to give it to her (34, 35)
        (B) if you're going to . . . give a client her money's worth (48, 49)
        (B) in the situations where you escort clients to functions (56)
            I shocked her (67, 68)
            I never agree to have sex with someone (79)
            if I don't know them (79, 80)
            I tell them (80)
            if I meet them in a bar I walk up (83)
            [I] look them straight in the eye (84)

(B) it's my job to make them feel relaxed (88)
    the way I deal with really ugly clients (104)
(B) you have to do the honourable thing and offer a refund (110, 111)
    beating off total dragons (113)

2 Peter's clients are activated in relation to him:

SVO (B) she bought me a £90 Armani shirt (14, 15)
    (B) a cool £1000 . . . that she handed over (16, 17)
    (B) [she was] licking my earlobes (21, 22)
    (B) [she was] telling me (22)
    (B) she couldn't wait to get me home (22)
    (B) most clients pay me (26)
    (B) she's just hired you (54)
    when they start abusing you (93)
    (B) if someone's paying me good money (94)
    (B) who decide to hire you (108)
    (B) [if they] have already paid you (110)
    I was terrified she would get on top of me (121)
    This one wanted me to put on (122)
    She wanted me to go down (124)

PASS you tend to get briefed [by the client] (56, 57)
    I've been whipped, scratched, bitten [by the client] (91, 92)
    I have a problem with being insulted [by the client] (94, 95)

The grammatical analysis reveals, unsurprisingly, that as the subject of the sentence, Peter is in complete control of the situation: 'I'm there to give it to her' (34, 35). Added to which, whilst Peter overwhelmingly benefits financially in the text, his clients are represented as benefiting sexually. It is interesting to note that in the instances where Peter does not actually *benefit* from the actions of his clients, for example: 'I was terrified she would get on top of me' (121) and 'when they start abusing you' (93), the words 'terrified' and 'abusing' create a negative effect in terms of the client's representation. Conversely, when the clients do not benefit from encounters with Peter, he is not represented unfavourably: 'I tell them' (80) and 'look them straight in the eye' (84).

What lexical choices have been made?

Tables 1 and 2 below list the ways in which the social actors are lexicalized in the text, with frequencies. Although the article tells the story in the first person and therefore may be how 'Peter' lexicalizes himself, the clients and sexual practices, we cannot be sure that these are his original choice of words or even those of the writer. Table 1 presents the lexicalization of Peter; Table 2 gives the ways in which the clients are lexicalized.

An examination of the lexical choices reveals that both Peter and his clients are, in the majority of cases, described in terms of physical appearance. But

Table 1: Lexicalization of Peter

Lexicalization of Peter	*Frequency*
escort	3
25-year-old who left school at 16	1
pretty fit	1
athletic	1
6ft 3in	1
fair haired	1
blue-eyed	1
confident	1
head-turner	1
approachable	1
people-oriented	1
party animal	1
young toy-boy	1
expensive commodity	1
Peter	1
guy	1

where Peter lexicalizes his own appearance in **positive** terms, for example 'pretty fit', 'head turner' and 'athletic', his clients fare largely unfavourably: he describes them, among other things, as 'repulsive', 'ugliest' and 'total dragons'. Peter is also described in terms of his appearance, but lexicalization of physical appearance is far more frequent and less flattering in relation to his clients, however, than in relation to him. The emphasis on women's appearance in the *Maxim* article is characteristic of men's glossy lifestyle magazines. Women are there to be looked at and are represented and judged according to their appearance, rather than their intellect or career as a man might be (and often is in these magazines). This bears out Lovering's identification (1995: 27) of a 'dominant discursive practice of subjecting the female body to the male and public gaze.' Further, representations of gender in men's magazines have a tendency to set up a contrast between 'ordinary women' and 'celebrity beauties'—the women represented in Peter's narrative are doubly transgressive because they have to pay to become the desired object of male focalization.

What (gendered/gendering) discourses 'run through' the text?

A strong commercial discourse is in evidence throughout the text, particularly in the first half. This is achieved through the use of phrases such as: 'cash before pleasure' (18) and 'I'm getting a grand for this, I can't afford to mess up.' (24). These are supported by the inclusion of details of Peter's earnings: 'most clients pay me about £100 an hour for sex' (26) and 'I clocked up £50k last year' (27). The choice of lexical items often associated with the business world builds up the discourse further, for example: 'assignment' (4), 'fee' (16), 'briefed' (57),

Table 2: Lexicalization of clients

Lexicalization of clients	Frequency
noun phrase including 'woman'	16
noun phrase including 'client'	16
after-dinner shag	1
all-nighter	1
wasn't unattractive	1
a bit hard-faced	1
not bad for her age	1
in good shape for a 38 year-old	1
noun phrase including 'ugly'	5
Gorgeous	1
Missus	1
referrals from friends	1
50 regulars	1
Cindy Crawford	1
women in their late 50s	1
didn't look their age	1
over 55	1
in very good shape	1
total dragons	1
Oldest	1
she was 60	1
Ugliest	1
tattoos and several teeth missing	1
Repulsive	1
she weighed in at about 17 stone	1
Kinkiest	1
she looked quite clean	1

'trade secret' (111) and the frequent use of the term 'client'. This 'commercial discourse' may function as one means of preserving Peter's power, glamour and apparent 'professionalism'.

Throughout the article there is also however a strong discourse of 'hegemonic masculinity' (Jewitt, 1997; Carrigan, Connell and Lee, 1987; Connell, 1995)— that is, a practice of masculinity which is the most widely (ie, in most contexts) acceptable (usually white, middle-class and heterosexual) and against which other forms of masculinity are measured. Peter is presented as heterosexual, tall, good looking, fit, in control and earning a good salary—all characteristics of hegemonic masculinity. Although his job does not prototypically fit this mould since he is 'at the service' of women rather than the other way round, neither does it go against it. He can still be successful because, as Connell (1995) points out, those white, heterosexual, middle-class men who do not quite embrace hegemonic masculinity, or do so rather problematically as is the case with Peter, are still tolerated because they are more accepted within Western society than subordinate masculinities such as black and gay.

The analysis of Peter's occupational practices is of interest for what these practices say about changing representations of masculinity. Importantly, the presentation of Peter's occupation as an escort would not be possible without the availability of a discourse of sexual liberation (for women as well as men), and a discourse of women's equality with men in the financial sphere—women can now pay for sex. Women expect equal pay and this can mean independence in all spheres of life. Yet the idea that women now exist who are both sexually and economically free to do what they choose (including asking men to go along with women's sexual preferences) is not necessarily an ideology consonant with dominant forms of masculinity and therefore not one with which male readers of *Maxim* and other 'men's lifestyle' magazines are entirely comfortable. The creator of 'Peter' seems to negotiate this dilemma by making sure that Peter is not only in control at all times (through careful grammatical and lexical choices, as well through what is strategically omitted), but also by ensuring that he is represented as 'supermasculine', being particularly expert and even heroic in the sexual sphere (see also Benwell, this volume). The reader is implicitly invited to be in awe of Peter, partly because of the inaccessibility (for most men) of his position. It is this very inaccessibility which means that the ordinary male reader need not feel negatively implicated.

Conclusion

Looking at language use as *choices*, the selection of one feature over another, allows us to explore particular representations of gender. Lexical and grammatical items in texts may contribute to discourses, which can reflect and construct social inequalities between men and women. Examining these items can thus help the analyst identify such discourses. In 'What's it like to . . . be paid to have sex: tales of a male escort', masculinity is presented as revolving around one particular discourse of male sexuality: the desirability of sexual relationships with no emotional ties. CDA has proved a useful tool for 'exposing' the ideological message of the text and for revealing a key discourse of masculinity—one that has 'intertextual' relationships with similar discourses in other texts. What might have been a highly transgressive text (men being paid to serve women sexually), and one which challenged the dominant 'gender order', becomes disempowered (from a feminist perspective) by its strategic language choices. Justification for Peter being paid to have sex is not seen to be needed and, as shown, any comparison between him and the female sex worker is conspicuous by its absence. This article is thus another example of the way hegemonic masculinity is able to adapt by flexibly accommodating alternative discourses, without actually compromising its strength and privilege, and a further example (see also Caldas Coulthard, 1996) of the way in which an at-first-sight apparently radical text may end up confirming the status quo in quite conservative ways.

Notes

1 SVO means that the activation and passivation is realized through a simple subject, verb, object construction. The numbers in parentheses refer to the line numbers in which the quotations appear in Appendix 1. Those marked with a (B) mean that the object is the 'beneficiary' of the action. PASS means that the grammatical object of the phrase becomes the subject, ie, 'doer' of the action but does not appear in subject position because of the passive voice.

References

Benwell, B. (2002) 'Is there anything "New" about these lads?: the textual and visual construction of masculinity in men's magazines': in Litosseliti, L. and Sunderland, J. (eds) *Gender Identity and Discourse Analysis*. Amsterdam: Benjamins.

Caldas-Coulthard, C.R. (1996) 'Women who pay for sex. And enjoy it. Transgression versus morality in women's magazines': in Caldas-Coulthard, C.R. and Coulthard, M. (eds) *Texts and Practices. Readings in Critical Discourse Analysis*. London: Routledge.

Cameron, D. (1990) 'Introduction: why is language a feminist issue?': in Cameron, D. (ed.) *The Feminist Critique of Language: A Reader*. London: Routledge.

Cameron, D. (1994) 'Problems of sexist and non-sexist language': in Sunderland, J. (ed.) *Exploring Gender: Questions and Implications for English Language Education*. Hemel Hempstead: Prentice Hall.

Cameron, D. (1995) *Verbal Hygiene*. London: Routledge.

Cameron, D. (1996) 'The language-gender interface: challenging co-optation': in Bergvall, V.L., Bing, J.M. and Freed, A.F. (eds) *Rethinking Language and Gender Research*. Harlow: Longman.

Carrigan, T., Connell, R.W. and Lee, J. (1987) 'Towards a new sociology of masculinity': in Brod, H. (ed.) *The Making of Masculinities: the New Men's Studies*. Boston and London: Allen and Unwin.

Connell, R.W. (1995) *Masculinities*. Cambridge: Polity.

Fairclough, N. (1989) *Language and Power*. Harlow: Longman.

Fairclough, N. (1992) *Discourse and Social Change*. Cambridge: Polity.

Fishman, P. (1983) 'Interaction: the work women do': in Thorne, B., Kramarae, C. and Henley, N. (eds) *Language, Gender and Society*. Cambridge, MA: Newbury House.

Huckin, T.N. (1997) 'Critical Discourse Analysis': in Miller, T. (ed.) *Functional Approaches to Written Text: Classroom Applications*. Washington DC: United States Information Agency.

Jewitt, C. (1997) 'Images of men: male sexuality in sexual health leaflets and posters for young people', *Sociological Research Online* 2(2). http://www.socresonline.org.uk/socresonline/2/2/6.html

Johnson, S. (1997) 'Theorizing language and masculinity': in Johnson, S. and Meinhof, U.H. (eds) *Language and Masculinity*. Oxford: Blackwell.

Kimmel, M. and Messner, M. (eds) (1995) *Men's Lives* (3rd edn.). USA: Allyn and Bacon.

Kress, G. and van Leeuwen, T. (1996) *Reading Images: The Grammar of Visual Design*. London: Routledge.

Lovering, K.M. (1995) 'The bleeding body: adolescents talk about menstruation': in Wilkinson, S. and Kitzinger, C. (eds) *Feminism and Discourse: Psychological Perspectives*. London: Sage.

Mills, S. (1994) 'Reading as/like a feminist': in Mills, S. (ed.) *Gendering the Reader*. Hemel Hempstead: Harvester Wheatsheaf.

Mills, S. (1995) *Feminist Stylistics*. London: Routledge.

Mills, S. (1997) *Discourse*. London: Routledge.

Sunderland, J. (2002) 'Baby entertainer, bumbling assistant and line manager: discourses of paternal identity in parentcraft texts': in Litosseliti, L. and Sunderland, J. (eds) *Gender Identity and Discourse Analysis*. Amsterdam: John Benjamins.

Sunderland, J. and Litosseliti, L. (2002) 'Gender identity and discourse analysis: theoretical and empirical considerations': in Litosseliti, L. and Sunderland, J. (eds) *Gender Identity and Discourse Analysis*. Amsterdam: John Benjamins.

Talbot, M. (1992) 'The construction of gender in a teenage magazine': in Fairclough, N. (ed.) *Critical Language Awareness*. Harlow: Longman.

Talbot, M. (1995) 'A synthetic sisterhood: False friends in a teenage magazine': in Hall, K. and Bucholtz, M. (eds.) *Gender Articulated: Language and the Socially Constructed Self*. London/NY: Routledge.

Talbot, M. (1998) *Language and Gender*. Cambridge: Polity Press.

Tiefer, L. (1993) 'In pursuit of the perfect penis: the medicalization of male sexuality': in Minas, A. (ed.) *Gender Basics: Feminist Perspectives on Women and Men*. California: Wadsworth.

Van Leeuwen, T. (1997) 'Representing social action', *Discourse and Society* 6(1): 81–106.

Van Leeuwen, T. (1996) 'The representation of social actors': in Caldas-Coulthard, C.R. and Coulthard, M. (eds) *Texts and Practices. Readings in Critical Discourse Analysis*. London: Routledge.

West, C., Lazar, M. and Kramarae, C. (1997) 'Gender in discourse': in van Dijk, T.A. (ed.) *Discourse as Social Action. Discourse Studies: A Multidisciplinary Introduction*. Vol. 2. London: Sage.

Appendix 1: 'What's it like to . . . be paid to have sex.' from *Maxim* (June 1998: 76–80)

1 Nothing's predictable in the escort game. Every woman's different and the
2 only sure fire way to tell if you're on the right track is in the bedroom—
3 once the client's had her first orgasm you know you're doing something
4 right. You wouldn't be human if you weren't a little nervous before an
5 assignment. But this one particular time I was more anxious than normal.
6 She wasn't the usual after-dinner shag. This was a big time client, an all-
7 nighter who I knew needed drinks and dinner at the Atlantic Bar, then on
8 to Browns for a nightcap, before I could even contemplate taking her back
9 to her place by the Thames. She ran a big PR company and wasn't unat-
10 tractive, a bit hard faced perhaps but not bad for her age. She was defi-
11 nitely in good shape for a 38-year-old: you find that most women with that
12 kind of earning power tend to look after themselves so there was no 'paper
13 bag' factor—just the prospect of an expensive night out, a night's shag-
14 ging in the lap of luxury and the next day, if it went as well as it had done
15 before, she'd probably throw in a shopping trip to Knightsbridge. The last
16 time we met she bought me a £90 Armani shirt as a tip. Which was a nice
17 touch considering she was footing the bill for the night out plus my fee
18 for the four or five times we had sex—a cool £1000 in an envelope that
19 she handed over when I picked her up at the office. I'd escorted her a
20 couple of times before so she knew the score—cash before pleasure. To be
21 honest, the mood of the evening wasn't that different from a night out
22 with someone you fancy; passionate but quite relaxed. That night she was
23 really into a lot of verbal foreplay, lots of teasing and whispering dirty
24 things while we were out, licking my earlobes, telling me she couldn't wait
25 to get me home . . . When you're actually getting down to it, one part of

26   you thinks, 'This is great,' but the business part thinks, 'Shit, I'm getting
27   a grand for this, I can't afford to mess up. It's 2am, there's a long night
28   ahead and the meter's got quite a way to run . . .' Mind you, the money's
29   not bad: most clients pay me about £100 an hour for sex on top of what
30   they pay for the night out. I clocked up £50K last year—not bad for a 25-
31   year-old who left school at 16. While you're working, you can never ever
32   relax and switch off completely, you're always very conscious of what
33   you're doing, running through the mental checklist in your head. Nuzzle
34   the neck, move down slowly but surely, make sure she's really aroused,
35   spend just the right amount of time—ten minutes is my advice—playing
36   with her top half, stroke her hair, then move on down . . . At the end of
37   the day, she might be moaning her head off but at some stage, she's prob-
38   ably thinking, 'I want my money's worth.' And I'm there to give it to her.
39   Whichever way she wants it. I use condoms every time, I'm not into taking
40   risks. Some guys can't make it as escorts because they can't deal with the
41   fact that, in this game, your preferences don't matter. So if she's ugly, you
42   have to act like she's gorgeous. You have to be careful not to be too false
43   though; she might pick up on it. You get to visit all sorts of expensive
44   show-off places but, like anything, the novelty of being paid to have a
45   good time around town can wear off. You do get blasé about it. I'm pretty
46   fit and athletic, 6 ft 3 in, fair-haired, blue-eyed and confident. I don't know
47   about being a head-turner but I certainly carry an aura of someone who
48   knows what he wants, though I like to think I'm approachable. An escort
49   has to be people-oriented—you have to get on with guys you meet in social
50   situations too. Tolerance has a lot to do with it. You can't be too much of
51   a party animal. I'm in the gym by 7am most mornings and I don't drink
52   much: you need total control for this game. You can't possibly survive
53   without being good at what you're doing. It's a cliché but practice makes
54   perfect if you're going to perform well and give a client her money's worth.
55   If your mind's not on the job in hand, it can show. Personal safety is at a
56   premium. There are husbands and boyfriends out there who'd go ballis-
57   tic if they knew what you were doing with their missus. Some clients will
58   go out and pay for an escort with hubby's money because they are con-
59   vinced he's having an affair. You might even 'accidentally' meet in a social
60   situation—in other words she's just hired you to 'get back' at him by
61   turning up to a function with a young toyboy in tow. That happens quite
62   a lot: I'm an expensive commodity really. In the situations where you
63   escort clients to functions you tend to get briefed in the car beforehand
64   about where you met, how long you've known each other, that sort of
65   stuff. You need a good memory. But the trick is to use the same story with
66   most of the clients—it saves time. I've never been caught by a husband or
67   boyfriend but I've hidden in a wardrobe once, in a client's house in Derby.
68   The husband came home because he'd forgotten something. We weren't
69   far off getting stuck into it. I tend to be very logical in situations like that:
70   I just kept calm and looked for somewhere he wouldn't spot me. After

71 about ten minutes he left. He never suspected anything. You could say I
72 love my work—I've certainly always loved women. At 17 I had a rela-
73 tionship with a 36-year-old, a very attractive blonde who was the aunt of
74 a friend. I'd been out with girls my own age but this was in a completely
75 different arena. She taught me a lot but in the end I shocked her with what
76 I could do. That really got me into older women. By the time I started
77 escorting, five years ago, I'd had lots of relationships with older women.
78 They know exactly what they want. In the beginning I used to work for
79 agencies but I stopped a few years ago—most successful male escorts work
80 on their own. The majority of my business is regular clients or referrals
81 from friends. I've got about 50 regulars—repeat business is what you're
82 always aiming for. I back that up with ads in papers or mags. I don't
83 mention money, just make it clear that I'm an escort for hire. You get very
84 good at judging women over the phone. That first conversation tells you
85 a lot—you can easily tell whether they've used escorts before. The golden
86 rule is not to try and be too seductive, it's more important to make them
87 feel at ease. I don't know why it is but ugly women tend to sound great on
88 the phone. So I never ever agree to have sex with someone there and then
89 if I don't know them. It's too dodgy. If they ask about a fee for sex I tell
90 them we can discuss that on the night. When you meet a client for the first
91 time, there's no set patter you use, the sooner you can play it by ear the
92 better, as far as her reaction to you goes. If I meet them in a bar I walk
93 up, smile and keep my body language very unthreatening; very open,
94 friendly, look them straight in the eye and say, 'Good evening, I'm Peter.'
95 Instant small talk usually works your way in. You have to follow their lead
96 a lot of the time, weigh the situation up. At first the atmosphere can be a
97 bit apprehensive, so it's up to me to create the mood. If they're nervous—
98 and quite a lot are—it's my job to make them feel relaxed. You generally
99 know within the first five minutes of meeting them for the first time if
100 you'll be up for sex or not. I've been to bed with women I didn't like, not
101 because of their looks but because of what they want to do. Don't get me
102 wrong, I've been whipped, scratched, bitten and I'm not fazed by S&M
103 or bondage but some women are a bit too dominant for my liking, espe-
104 cially when they start abusing you verbally. I can take a lot of things if
105 someone's paying me good money but I have a problem with being
106 insulted. Getting into bed with a woman who's had everything pierced is
107 also a no-no for me. No one's going to be a male escort and expect Cindy
108 Crawford on every date. But more often than not, the woman you wind
109 up in bed with is reasonably OK. There's a physical limit to who you'll
110 take on. I've been to bed with women in their late fifties but they didn't
111 look their age—I doubt if I could cope with someone over 55, they'd have
112 to be in very good shape. What do you do if she's really ugly? You can't
113 really fantasise successfully—you've only got to open your eyes. But give
114 me an ugly face and a nice body any day, rather than the other way round.
115 To be honest, a lot of my clients look better from behind! The way I deal

116 with really ugly clients is to explain that I do the escorting for the night
117 but that I never actually have sex because I'm married, my wife knows
118 what I do and the agreement is: no sex at the end. I've never actually said
119 I've got an infection, but I know guys who have. You do get women who
120 decide to hire you then change their mind. You have to be 100% under-
121 standing, you can't afford to be forceful about it. If they change their mind
122 and have already paid you, you have to do the honourable thing and offer
123 a refund. Most times they'll say keep the money. The big trade secret,
124 I guess, is to never ever show a client what you're thinking. If that comes
125 across, they'll pick up on it. But you don't spend your working life beating
126 off total dragons. Women who are totally self-conscious about their looks
127 wouldn't have the confidence to hire an escort. It takes balls for a woman
128 to pick up the phone and pay for a guy. On the other hand, there are a
129 lot of women who get a kick out of calling the shots. Sex: the ins and outs.
130 Worst jobs. Oldest: I suspect she was 60, though she said she was 45. I
131 managed because she kept her underwear on. Ugliest: She had tattoos and
132 several teeth missing. She was totally oblivious to the fact she was repul-
133 sive; I couldn't shag her for the life of me. Fattest: She weighed in at about
134 17 stone; I was terrified she'd get on top of me. Kinkiest: This one wanted
135 me to put on women's underwear, suspenders, high heels, full make-up, a
136 wig and a dildo. It freaked me a bit. Smelliest: She looked quite clean but
137 had the worst BO I've ever encountered. She wanted me to go down on
138 her—I tried it, but not for long. Most Expensive: I was new to the job.
139 I paid for the drinks and meal with my credit card, then she did a runner
140 out of the taxi into the hotel. I lost £100. It's never happened again. Secrets
141 of the trade. Don't start out with a set repertoire of all the tricks you can
142 turn on in bed; it's better to be adaptable to the situation and open to any
143 ideas they come up with. If they want a rough or rape fantasy scene,
144 always agree a codeword beforehand: once she says it, stop right there. To
145 be good in bed, you need a fantastic knowledge of oral sex. Be subtle
146 about talking dirty. Pick up on a semi-innocent remark but don't steam
147 in: most women who like really filthy talk will let you know anyway. Never
148 ever ask a client for a blow job. If she does it spontaneously, fine. But
149 you're not there to ask them to do anything. Never disagree with a client.
150 You've got to be interested in what they're interested in. In a social situa-
151 tion, at a party or a function, don't try to bullshit if you find you're out
152 of your depth with a group of brain surgeons. A good surface knowledge
153 of current affairs is fine, but don't make a wally of yourself. You won't be
154 asked back. To make a woman want you, you've got to operate on their
155 level—they don't want to know about your problems. And you can't come
156 on all mysterious either, they won't relate to that. If a client doesn't have
157 an orgasm, you're not doing the job properly. At the end of the day,
158 women pay good money for good sex. They can get crap sex anywhere.

As told to Jacky Hyams.

Part 4:
Comparative masculinities

Introduction: Comparative masculinities

The final three chapters of the book also focus (in part) upon language but are also united by their attention to widening the scope of our discussion of masculinities, by focusing upon what might be termed 'comparative masculinities' in a collection whose main object is a British, heterosexual and general lifestyle magazine masculinity.

'Lifestyle sport magazines: constructions of sporting masculinities' examines the important role that sport occupies in the construction of hegemonic male identity. Focusing in particular upon a sub-genre of lifestyle magazines that promote 'lifestyle' sports such as windsurfing and snowboarding, Wheaton charts the reflexive relationship between such publications and the construction of 'new lad', whose identity is highly dependent upon an alliance with sport and sporting activities. She uses a combination of methodologies by which to analyse constructions of masculinity within the lifestyle sports magazines, which reflect an ideal synthesis of the various sites of meaning production within the 'circuit of magazine culture' and which include semiotic analysis of images, general interviews with readers about their relationship to the magazines and habits of reading, and the elicitation of responses to particular articles and images within the magazines.

Wheaton concludes that the masculinities enacted in and around lifestyle sports magazines *draw* on elements of 'new lad' masculinity but are not entirely consonant with it either. Her analyses also highlight the advantages of audience research which, in the more nuanced and ambivalent responses she received, are suggestive that the constructions of laddish masculinity so lamented by the media 'oversimplif[y] the masculinities that readers actually articulated in and through reading their magazines' which often vary from or actively reinterpret the preferred meanings offered by the text.

Tanaka's chapter, 'The language of Japanese men's magazines: young men who don't want to get hurt' examines the men's magazine market in Japan and in particular, an emergent construction known as 'city boy' which has arguably displaced a more laddish predecessor. The construction of the 'city boy' offers a marked contrast to the British 'new lad': where 'new lad's' relationships with women are represented as casual and motivated purely by sex, 'city boy' is always interested to learn how to understand and please his girlfriend, magazines such as *Popeye* operating almost as a 'dating manual'. This is a construction remarkably consonant with that described by Toerien and Durrheim (2001) in their recent analysis of South Africa's *Men's Health*, in which men's identities are largely bound up with discourses of ignorance about women and 'what makes them tick'. Unlike *Men's Health* masculinity, these 'city boys' seem to accrue very little power from their construction and are arguably identities in which women have much more of a stake. Tanaka shows how the emergence of the 'city boy' actually coincided with a decline in the number of marriageable women and a new discourse of sexual assertiveness for women. The chapter then goes on to explore in detail differences between the language of men's and women's publications, such as the use of *kanji* (Chinese script) and *katakana* (syllabic script used for Western loan words) and concludes that young men's publications share more in common with women's magazines than with older titles aimed at men, such as *Playboy*, in their greater adoption of loan words and arguably more creative syntax.

In the final chapter of the book, 'No effeminates please: a corpus-based analysis of masculinity via personal adverts in gay magazines 1973–2000,' Baker uses a specific linguistic framework known as 'corpus linguistics' in order to analyse the representation of gay male identities in the personal ads in *Gay Times* across three decades. By arguing that personal ads are both a form of self presentation and description of ideal partner, he argues that they represent a likely site for an insight into cultural mediations of identity construction. After collating a large number of ads and processing them through a computer tagging programme, Baker's analysis of lexis reveals some striking and recurring patterns of how gay male identities are differently presented in each decade and he focuses, in particular, upon how masculinity is negotiated as a potentially desirable (but equally problematic) quality of this identity. Baker's results suggest that a clear pattern of markers of masculinity emerged in the advertisers' descriptions of themselves and their ideal partners in the early 1990s, and this definition tended to converge upon 'straight-acting', which tied masculinity explicitly to heterosexuality. Similarly, a high incidence of references to 'discreet' and 'discretion' leads Baker to conclude that this particular manifestation of gay male identity and negotiation of masculinity is directly related to the vilification of gay men in the tabloid press during the years leading up 1991, particularly in relation to the association of gay men with the spread of HIV that was being constructed and perpetuated in the media. Therefore it is possible that as male homosexuality became more stigmatized during this period, gay males were keen to distance themselves from an overt 'gay identity' and also to incorporate more obvious markers of a male *heterosexuality* which, Baker argues, was also reflected in patterns of appearance. Baker's chapter sheds useful light upon the way in which straight masculinity may function, just as gay male identities have in relation to men's style and fashion, as a form of cultural capital with which other types of male identity negotiate and define their own identities.

Lifestyle sport magazines and the discourses of sporting masculinity

Belinda Wheaton

Introduction: consuming masculinities

'Sport has become a symbol for our changing society' (Jacques, 1997: 18).

It is widely claimed that in late capitalist societies, such as Great Britain, there has been a shift in emphasis away from 'production' to a more fragmented social order, one where culture and consumption have central roles (Jameson, 1991; Lash and Urry, 1987; Hall and Jacques, 1989; Giddens, 1991). In this context the cultural industries and, particularly, new consumer and leisure activities play a more prominent role (Featherstone, 1991: 164). It has been asserted that these sites of consumption offer a potentially broader and more differentiated range of masculine identities from those traditional discourses and practices produced around work or career (Mort, 1988; Nixon, 1996; Edwards, 1997). As has now been well documented, the emergence and explosion of men's fashion and style magazines in the mid 1980s such as *GQ*, *Arena* and *Cosmo Man*, are linked to these wider debates about masculine identities being increasingly centred on and around leisure consumption practices (Nixon, 1996; Edwards, 1997; Mort, 1988; Mort, 1996). The 'New Man' was the ubiquitous media-driven label that embodied these 'caring and sharing' middle-class, white male consumers for whom, it was argued, a narcissistic concern with the body and fashion played a more central role in their sense of self (Craik, 1994: 249). Then the 'New Lad' emerged as a reaction to the 'New Man', a phenomenon centred around football, indie pop music and male 'general interest' or 'lifestyle' magazines such as *loaded, FHM* and *Maxim* (see Edwards, 1997; Craik, 1994).

Within this context of the centrality of leisure consumption practices in masculine cultures and identities, sport plays an important role. Historically, sport as a physical practice has been so closely identified with men, that it has become one of the key signifiers of masculinity in many western societies. Connell (1995: 54) goes so far as to claim that sport has become 'the leading definer' of masculinity in western culture. However, sport is increasingly experienced as a consumed 'leisure lifestyle', thus the meaning of masculinity is fought over in the playing, spectating *and* consumption of sport (Tomlinson, 2001; Boyle and Haynes, 2000). One just has to consider the changing nature of football fandom in Britain, particularly its increasing centrality in media culture from chat shows to sport style, to exemplify this trend. As Boyle and Haynes underline, on today's football terraces, 'a preoccupation with fashion sits alongside the more 'traditional' forms of fan identification' (2000: 136).

This chapter examines sport's enduring yet shifting association with masculinity as played out in the discourses in, and around, men's magazines. I explore the role of sport in the depiction of masculinity in men's lifestyle magazines. Then my empirical case study explores the genre of magazine that I have termed *lifestyle sport magazines*, publications *rooted* in the leisure lifestyles of lifestyle sporting activities such as windsurfing and snowboarding. I focus on windsurfing magazines, exploring the masculinities represented in and around the consumption of these magazines and the varied meanings made by readers, whose views I elicit from a series of ethnographic interviews. While the appeal of lifestyle sport magazines is much lower in terms of readership figures than men's lifestyle magazines, they are interesting sites for examining the circulation of discourses of masculinities beyond their centres in men's lifestyle magazines, and particularly for investigating claims about shifting masculinities such as whether the New Lad is the only representation and experience, of sporting masculinity.

Before turning to the lifestyle sports magazines, I will briefly illustrate the ways in which sport has become central to the masculinity embodied in men's lifestyle magazines, particularly the coupling of the new lad masculine identity with institutional sport and, specifically, with football.

Men's lifestyle magazines, embodied masculinity and sport

Given sport's pivotal place in discourses of masculinity, it is not surprising that sport is a key element of men's lifestyle magazines. In the first wave of men's magazines in the 1980s and early 90s, a central concern was with appearance, grooming and fashion, although health and fitness began to play an increasingly significant role in this 'reconstruction of masculinity' (Whannel, 2002: 71). Whannel (2002) outlines how the growing popularity of activities like jogging, aerobics and gym culture (encompassing an increasing range of activities from working-out to weight training) produced the 'fitness chic' of the 1980s in which sport and fashion converged. The body became seen as an (unfinished, malleable) identity 'project' (Shilling, 1993). Looking fit, and working hard to do so, became fashionable, fostering a 'competitive individualism' that echoed the themes of Thatcherism, namely 'individual self-reliance, hard work, enterprise, and self promotion' (Whannel, 2002: 131).[1]

New Laddism

Sport's most prevalent association, however, is with the 'New Lad,' a masculine identity commonly described as being based around cars, babe-watching, sex and booze, being self-centred, leering, and *obsessed with sport* (Edwards, 1997; Carrington, 1998; Whelehan, 2000; Nixon, 1996). The New Lad image originated in *loaded* but has subsequently been cultivated in a range of other men's magazines, and now pervades numerous areas of media culture (Whelehan, 2000). As Jackson *et al.* (2001: 46) suggest, magazines and New Lad identity have become linked intertextually with other cultural forms such as films, TV and music. Again sport is a defining feature. It headlines British television shows like *They Think It's All Over* and *Football Fantasy League*, has invaded music through the new genre of football songs, and is closely associated with the football writing of Nick Hornby's *Fever Pitch*.

However, 'sport' in these contexts is defined in a narrow way, focusing predominantly on the British nation's[2] love affair with football. Whelehan (2000: 127) claims that football creates a 'safe masculine haven' that 'offers the lad steadfast male cultural credentials' (2000: 104). Traditional institutionalized sports like football, and the associated practices and identities, have been widely exposed as important cultural sites in which hegemonic masculinities are created, shaped, and performed, involving the exclusion or control of women, and 'other' (for example, homosexual, and non-white) men (Connell, 1995; Messner and Sabo, 1990). Football, like most other high-level competitive and professional sport cultures, promotes and celebrates a masculinity that is marked by combative competition, aggression, courage and toughness. It also tends to be sexist and endorses violence often promoting homophobic and racist tendencies. For example, Carrington (1998, 1999) has illustrated how New Laddism can be interpreted as part of a wider process of reasserting a specifically *white, English* male identity, in which football (along with Brit pop) plays a central role. His illuminating analysis highlights the ways in which, during the build-up to Euro' 96, New Laddism became 'intertwined with the nationalist discourse' (Carrington, 1999: 77) allowing for an assertion of an 'aggressive, macho, xenophobic form of English nationalism' that was defended as a form of 'heroic working-class resistance' (Carrington, 1999: 83).

Likewise, despite women's increased participation in sport as fans, players and consumers, elite and professional sports, like football remain 'male preserves' and important proving grounds for masculinity. Despite claims about the feminization and gentrification of English football, (self defined) 'real' fans reject these new middle-class and female consumers. As Boyle and Haynes (2000: 136) argue, while 'fashion at the football ground may provide status and recognition among peers, it is still the assertion of hegemonic male relations through pride, honour and a sense of superiority that binds men to their particular communities.' Women can only enter at the risk of becoming the butt of sexual innuendo (Whelehan, 2000: 64), or sexist behaviour—of course meant ironically—as the chapter will go on to elaborate. 'Laddism has served merely to legitimize and increase the social acceptability of such behaviour among males' (Crolley, 1999: 65). Women in these sporting contexts are systematically objectified, commodified and sexualized, (re) establishing and naturalizing femininity as masculinity's binary opposite:

Female cheerleaders, topless dancers and swimsuit models reassure men that their true lustful feelings are properly channelled not towards the men whose heroic actions and sculpted bodies so excite them, but toward women, or caricatures of women' (Burton Nelson, 1996: 7).

Beyond the Lad: different sporting masculinities?

It is misleading, however to view 'sporting masculinity' either in its media representations or lived identities as essentialized and fixed. Like other masculinities it varies over time and cultural spaces, between men of different ages, backgrounds (particularly based on social class, ethnicity and sexual orientation), and is subject to a continual process of reinterpretation and revision. Research in different sporting contexts and cultures has illustrated that, while many traditional institutionalised British sporting cultures such as football, rugby and cricket remain entrenched within the traditional patriarchal colonial cultures that characterized them centuries ago (see Carrington, 1999; Carrington and McDonald, 2001), newer sports, especially alternative sport cultures are sites for more contradictory and potentially more progressive sporting masculinities (Wheaton, 2000b; Beal, 1996; Anderson, 1999). The period from the 1960s to the 1990s has seen an explosion in new and often individualized forms of sport in Great Britain, ranging from the fitness movement to alternative, extreme and 'lifestyle' sports such as surfing, skateboarding and windsurfing. With their roots in the counter-cultural social movement of the 1960s and 1970s (Midol and Broyer, 1995) many still retain characteristics that are different from the traditional rule bound, competitive and 'masculinized' dominant sport cultures. For example, ethnographic research conducted in the windsurfing culture illustrated that the prevalent lived masculine subjectivity—'ambivalent masculinity'—was less exclusive of women and 'other men' that many institutionalised sport cultures, or (middle class) work cultures (Wheaton, 2000b).

'Laddishness', particularly as played out through competitiveness over status, and masculine identification based on the subordination of women as passive, sexual objects, was largely confined to younger, elite men. Participants of both gender emphasized the supportiveness and camaraderie among men and women in the culture (Wheaton, 2000b).

These 'alternative' sporting activities, particularly risk or extreme sports, have become prominent in men's lifestyle magazines (Jackson *et al.*, 2001), providing a potentially different version of sporting masculinity. Two men's lifestyle magazines, *Xtreme* and *XL* are devoted to these outdoor and high-risk activities, including pieces on lifestyle sports such as surfing, windsurfing, mountain biking and kite-surfing. *Men's Health* and other similar niche titles such as *GQ Active*, also depict a somewhat different script about male physicality to the New Lad. Based around health, fitness, exercise and diet, these magazines offer a more 'middle-class aspirational discourse of body-maintenance' aimed at a slightly older male audience (Whannel, 2002: 36), but one that has also been extremely successful commercially with sales expanding from 130,000 early in 1996 to over 2,800,000 by the end of 1998 (Jackson *et al.*, 2001: 79). These titles contribute to the 'growing cultural centrality of sport' and masculine body-image awareness more broadly (Whannel 2002: 36).

Lifestyle sport magazines

Magazines that focus on a particular leisure pursuit or hobby have a long history in the consumption of men's magazines (Whannel, 2002; Jackson *et al.* 2001), and as such may not be considered to be part of this new trend in male consumption of magazines. Yet alongside the emergence of the general interest Men's Lifestyle magazines in the 1980s was an explosion in the range and consumption of other magazines marketed at men (Whannel, 2002; Carrington, 1999), with titles ranging from traditional male sports interests such as football and fishing to these 'lifestyle sports' and hybrid 'extreme' sport publications. By lifestyle sport magazines I am referring to both specialist magazines focusing on one particular sport, and hybrid publications such as *Extreme* that feature a range of high adrenaline sport activities, from base-jumping to motorcross. The range of titles is astonishing; surfing, skateboarding, snowboarding, windsurfing, kite surfing, mountain biking, in-line skating and wakeboarding all have at least two dedicated monthly or bimonthly magazines published in the UK alone. Additionally, magazines imported from Europe and the USA fill the shelves of newsagents, news-stands and sport shops.

Moreover, these lifestyle sport magazines fall somewhere between traditional sports or leisure interest magazines and the general men's lifestyle magazines. First, although their focus is on one activity, they emphasize 'sport style' (see Tomlinson, 2001) and the associated lifestyle. In these lifestyle sport activities the consumer is being sold a complete lifestyle package, that is saturated with signs and images that emphasize many of the aspirations of consumer culture. Secondly, unlike traditional sport titles, where readership tends to be clustered around focused age categories, the readers of lifestyle sport magazines are more varied. Although some, such as skateboarding magazines, are predominantly consumed by young teenage males, others like windsurfing and surfing magazines have a much wider age appeal, read (predominantly) by men from pre-teenage to middle age, with readers often owning magazine collections spanning several decades (Wheaton, 1997). Lastly, although readership of these titles varies dramatically, (they range from 5000 to 25,000)[3] and their circulation is considerably lower than the men's lifestyle magazines (which range from 100,000 to 800,000[4]), their enduring nature and proliferating range is indicative of their committed readership. As I will illustrate, these magazines are extremely significant in the (predominantly male) cultures surrounding these activities (Stranger, 1999) and play a central part in the way in which the sporting lifestyles and identities are learnt and displayed (Wheaton and Beal, 2003).

Cruising the pages: Action and Style

The content of the lifestyle sport magazines is based on comparable themes revolving around the sporting lifestyles, forms of consumption of the activity, (predominantly equipment reviews and tests, subcultural fashion and style), and 'how to do it' features ranging from beginner techniques to high action photo sequences of manoeuvres. Of course there are key differences based on the nature of the activities and their different forms of 'subcultural capital' (Thornton, 1995). For example, whereas snowboarding, surfing and windsurfing magazines emphasize travel locations, skateboarding magazines look at unique or challenging urban locations (Wheaton and Beal, 2003). Surfing and skating magazines often feature music scenes and reviews reflecting the larger teenage male audience.

Another key similarity is the style of the magazines. In all the lifestyle sport magazines, colourful and bright action photographs dominate the magazine content, with large telescopic lens and fast shutter speeds freezing and dramatizing the action. Windsurfers and surfers I interviewed discussed the importance of visual representations of these sports and their lifestyles: 'Surfing magazines have got it right because they have so much colour, [. . .] it is images of places, and people, and action' (James). This focus on visual images and the spectacular is not surprising given claims that 'visualization has become the central source of meaning within contemporary urban and consumer cultures' (Chaney, 1996, cited in Jackson *et al.*, 2001: 76). The significance of the visual in the appeal of both men and women's magazines is highlighted by Jackson *et al.* (2001: 76). They point to McRobbie's commentary about the female magazine *Jackie*, 'the dominance of the visual level reinforces the notion of leisure. It is to be glanced through, looked at and only finally read' (McRobbie, 1982). Windsurfers' and skaters' comments often focused on stylistic aspects such as design and layout, and read the magazines in a style best described as flicking or browsing (see also Jackson *et al.*, 2001). A minority of the windsurfing interviewees, all of whom were keen male windsurfers, said they read the entire text of a magazine. The majority did not admit to serious reading, and claimed photographs were often more meaningful than the written text, again accounting for readers browsing through the magazines. Nevertheless, the middle-class professionals who constituted the majority of readers also criticized the lack of 'decent content', for example, personality interviews that tended to be like those found in 'teen magazines.' This observation is replicated by Jackson *et al.*'s (2001) readers, who criticized men's lifestyle magazines as being glossy and 'nicely packaged' but 'lacking in substance.' Yet readers I interviewed favourably contrasted men's lifestyle magazines with windsurfing magazines, arguing that the former had more interesting interviews and a more professional looking style.

In many respects, similarities across lifestyle sport magazines are not surprising. Firstly, as noted, the cross-over, in terms of participation in these sporting activities, is mirrored in the magazine industry, with several magazines being produced in the same design house. For example, *Arcwind* have the same editorial team working on windsurfing, kite surfing and in-line skating magazines. Secondly, the majority of the lifestyle sport magazines in the UK rely on advertisers from within their sports. So, for example, windsurfing magazines are largely dependent on the manufacturers of windsurfing equipment to sustain the magazines. Many of these companies make equipment for several lifestyle sports, albeit under different brand names. For example the production of kite and windsurf sails take place in the same factories and wetsuits are produced for a whole range of water sports (surfing, windsurfing, wake boarding etc); snowboards and windsurf boards are manufactured by the same company. While many advertisers produce different adverts for each sport market, it is not always the case. For example, clothing companies like Quicksilver that sell to a range of lifestyle sport markets, have tended to use surfing as their brand 'image.'

The existence of female participants and consumers in all these lifestyle sport activities might suggest that these magazines purport to be unisex in appeal. Audience figures, however, suggest their readership is predominantly male and lower than actual participation rates. Similarly, those who have analysed the content of skateboard, surfing and windsurfing magazines have shown that their address is 'masculine' in style; male subjects dominate images, albeit to varying degrees, and a traditional or hegemonic masculinity is prevalent[5] (Rinehart, 1999; Treas, 1999; Wheaton, 1997; Stedman, 1997; Fiske, 1989; Beal and Weidman, 2003). Furthermore, images of these activities are dominated by white participants (Wheaton, 1997; Henio, 2000), which in North America are seen as potent symbols of whiteness (Kusz, 2001).

The next section explores and illustrates these discourses of sporting masculinity and their consumption in the context of the windsurfing magazines. The question underlying and structuring this discussion is whether windsurfing magazines perpetuate a culture of new laddism or a different version of male physicality, such as the masculinity encoded in the culture of the health magazine.

Windsurfing magazines

My discussion draws on several research projects that have collectively examined the production-to-consumption process in the 'circuit of the magazines culture.' Firstly, extensive ethnographic subcultural research involving participant observation and in-depth interviews was carried out in order to examine the windsurfing culture (Wheaton, 1997). This included making sense of the everyday consumption of windsurfing magazines in the lived culture. My 'insider' sub cultural role, which involved working as a columnist for a British windsurfing magazine, gave me valuable insights into the media production practices and the influence of the consumer industries more widely. This helped in considering the (sub)cultural economic and ideological forces that underpin the construction of media texts. Secondly, an analysis of the windsurfing magazine text (Wheaton, 1997), utilizing semiological analysis as well as a quantitative content analysis[6] to explore the image of the subculture in the two British windsurfing magazines *Boards and Windsurf* was carried out.[7] Lastly, and most recently, audience interviews involving participants 'reading' windsurfing magazine advertisements and images were conducted, as a part of wider project examining constructions of authenticity in lifestyle sports magazines (Wheaton and Beal, 2003).

Drawing on these different data sources, the analysis considers how producers, texts and consumers work together to construct the multiple meanings of the magazines. As Jackson *et al.* (2001) suggest, such an approach that identifies the 'circulation of discourses between the magazines and readers' and the wider, inter-textual influences that shape those discourses, helps avoid a linear and oversimplified approach to the 'encoding' and 'decoding' of media messages. I briefly sketch out the magazine's main story lines (image and narrative), and the ways they are consumed, to give readers a flavour of the windsurfing magazine subject matter, and their role in their community of readers. Then I illustrate the visual and narrative representations of masculinity coded in the magazines, going on to discuss how readers negotiate, contest and give meaning to these discourses of masculinity. My analysis examines whether individuals and groups of male and female readers viewed the magazines as exclusively laddish male spaces, exploring how their discourses constructed (or contested) women as Other particularly as fashioned in sexualized passive roles like the trademark 'beach babe' from the 'letch–fest' laddish TV series *Baywatch* (Whelehan, 2000: 49).

Addressing the (masculine) 'insider'

It was apparent, from the magazine content and their consumption, that windsurfing magazines served as both 'information bearers' and 'membership documents' informing readers about the windsurfers' value system and lifestyle, and particularly about forms of insider knowledge such as equipment, skills and techniques. Whereas men's lifestyle magazines tend to value leisure pursuits that can be mastered quickly and easily ('you can learn to windsurf in a day') (see Jackson *et al.* 2001), rarely do windsurfing magazine emphasize that windsurfing is a sport that is easy to do or address the 'outsider'. As the front cover of *Boards* magazine illustrates—'written by windsurfers for windsurfers'—the magazines interpellate the insider, the committed windsurfer, who was invariably assumed to be a male 'insider.' Participants' enthusiasm to read magazines was influenced by their level of involvement in the actual sport and lifestyle, with those who were actively procuring a subcultural identity being the most enthusiastic readers.[8] The significance of these magazines for participants was evident from the mass of ethnographic data that emerged, ranging from observations of people reading and buying magazines, to incessant conversations and debates about the magazines. Nevertheless, by no means all those who claim to windsurf in the UK read windsurfing magazines; buying magazines was the realm of the committed practitioner, not the occasional participant.[9] These windsurfers included men and women, aged from early teens to their late 50s, and representing a wide range of occupations. The typical windsurfer, however—and magazine reader—was male, middle-class and white, aged between 20 and mid 40s.

Like many men's lifestyle magazines, the address tends to be chatty and informal, conversing as a 'mate' (Jackson *et al.*, 2001: 76). The exception was in the discourse around equipment and learning techniques. Similarly to magazines like *Men's Health* with its focus on technical features, there is a clear and hierarchical divide between the magazine personnel, the 'expert' and his readers in need of advice (Jackson *et al.*, 2001: 77). Yet some interviewees—who often included female readers—said magazines were 'cliquey'; 'they talk to you as if you belong.' The prolific use of subcultural argot and jargon (particularly to describe windsurfer's equipment, manoeuvres and environment), the constant reference to 'names' and the world of the elite male windsurfer, and the journalistic style, excludes many readers, particularly women.

Nevertheless, despite describing magazines in negative ways or claiming not to buy them,[10] simultaneously these same individuals, I observed, regularly browsed through, borrowed, read, and bought windsurfing magazines. 'Diss-ing' the magazine, or claiming not to read them, was a way of displaying subcultural capital (Wheaton, 1997). This is supported by Jackson *et al.*'s (2001: 115) survey of readers which found that men distanced themselves from magazine reading. Their interviewees described themselves as 'casual' readers, and few were prepared to *admit* to being 'committed readers.' One of the reasons for this distancing, they suggest, is a reflection of men's view that magazine reading is a mundane and feminine activity that shouldn't be taken 'too seriously' (Jackson *et al.*, 2001: 114).

For the majority of magazine readers, the pleasure of the windsurfing magazine resided in illustrations of the windsurfing community and its lifestyle, rather than the material commodities. Although men fetishised, customized and individualized their windsurfing *equipment* (Wheaton, 2000a) many readers were very critical of the magazines' over-emphasis on advertising-driven content aimed at *buying* new equipment. Windsurfers saw their lifestyle as aspirational, but not one that had conspicuous consumerism as its guiding principle. Likewise, features about surf clothing, and 'style' advertisements were less prolific than in surfing and snowboarding magazines, or men's lifestyle magazines. The framing of masculinity around fashion was not one of the primary aspects of windsurfing masculinity (Wheaton, 2000a), nor magazine content. Yet this was not because these men were resisting the traditionally feminine realms of consumption and fashion; men did wear a recognizable 'Surf' style. However, men denied the significance of this form of sub cultural identification because they saw adopting surf fashion and clothing as the way *outsiders* and *novices* demonstrated their subcultural identity (Wheaton, 2000a). Furthermore, during the late 1980s when surf wear 'hit the high street'; the surfie image became incorporated into mainstream fashion, typified by its presence in men's lifestyle magazines. Surf style became a 'style', available to anyone to 'buy into.' So while windsurfers did buy and wear branded clothing, they didn't want to be *seen to be* buying into the surf image, coining terms such as 'fashion victims' and 'fashion surfers' to describe those individuals who tried to *display* their subcultural 'authenticity' via surf style (Wheaton, 2000a).

'Out there Action': Young, male and white

Windsurfing is denoted as an activity that is the realm of the young, blond, tanned and fit white male. 84 per cent of all the editorial photographs depicted men whereas only 9 per cent depicted women.[11] The sport was also represented as individualistic, the solitary male being by far the most common representation (only 7 per cent of photos depicted men and women together). There were no family groups in the editorial photographs, few male groups, and only 8.3 per cent of all the photographs portraying men and women together depicted any sports activity.

These young men are tanned but clearly signified as white. Where images of black subjects were used they tended to be as the native Other in a travel feature, or one of a handful of international windsurfing personalities, predominantly from the Caribbean or Hawaii. Traditional stereotypes of 'race' underpinned these magazines discourses, emphasizing cultural and 'racial' differences, such as (post) colonialized countries, and subjects, being more primitive than the 'civilized' west. For example, the Hawaiian windsurfers were often depicted as having a 'natural' affinity with the water. In consuming images of the exotic, a colonial mentality is reinforced that views the (post) colonialized Other as an exotic spectacle (Davis, 1997), and re-inscribes the *naturalness* of the windsurfer's (self) identity as a specifically *Western white* male.

Nevertheless, the photographic techniques used to dramatize the action also accentuated the lean muscularity of the fit, tanned, bodies, images that are open to sexualized readings.[12] A surprising number of photographs of men were classified as 'inactive' or 'windsurfing activity posed' (22 per cent of the editorial photos), a trend that had doubled between 1991 and 1997. This practice mirrors wider cultural representations of male bodies such as the New Man imagery in the early men's lifestyle magazines, in which men were represented in increasingly passive and sexualized ways (Nixon, 1996; Mort, 1988; Nixon, 1997), and the increasingly sexualized representations of male sporting bodies in other media forms (see Whannel, 2002).

However, the *dominant* image of the windsurfing lifestyle invokes the 'rhetoric of the beach scene' (Duncan, 1990) in which photographs of male *action* are interspersed with those of beautiful, nubile, tanned female bodies in bikinis, typified by *Windsurf* magazine's *Swimsuit Corner* (figures 1 and 2). Men dominated the photographs classified as advanced action, whereas women dominated in photos coded as beginners and inactive, posed photos. Editorial photographs of inactive men tended to depict them posing with their equipment, such as after winning a competition, to *suggest* sporting activity, their gazes 'steely' or averted

202

Figure 1: Swimsuit corner—Windsurf, July 1996, p. 123. Used with permission from Windsurf Magazine.

Figure 2: Swimsuit corner—Windsurf, May 2000, p. 141. Used with permission from Windsurf Magazine.

from the camera which as Dyer (1987) suggests in the context of male pins-ups, are techniques that suggests male dominance. On the other hand, women in close-ups smiled at the camera, gazing towards the imagined male voyeur; those photographed from a distance tended to look away, averting the gaze of the imagined heterosexual male spectator, while the camera accentuated their tanned, semi-naked bodies. These representations mirror Mulvey's (1975) analysis of the 'pleasure of looking' in narrative cinema, in which she suggests that the organization of spectatorship, in relation to Freud's scopophilic drives, is split between active/male and passive/female (Mulvey, 2000). These representations, the 'active masculine control of the look and the passive feminine object of the look' (Nixon, 1997: 319), reproduce positions of sexual difference maintaining this power relationship. Likewise, in magazine photos depicting men and women together, sexual difference is established by the female being depicted as *relatively* inactive, for example the male model holding a surfboard. Women's sexuality is signified in this as other sporting photographic texts by their youthfulness, thinness, tanned hairless bodies, and flowing (blonde) hair (Davis, 1997).

But this traditional lad mag discourse is not the whole picture. Over the past 10 years there has been a marked increase in the visibility of female performers in windsurfing magazines, both in the editorial and advertisements. In 1991, women in adverts were predominantly depicted as inactive (75 per cent), and shown in fewer roles than in editorial photographs. By 1997, the extent of female inactivity had decreased by 25 per cent (of all the photos of women), and my observations would suggest this trend has intensified since then. Alongside the 'babes in bikini'[13] photographs are those depicting women as active, competent, and advanced performers (Figure 3). During 2000–2001 the magazines ran several adverts for equipment manufacturers that starred elite female wave sailors. The photographs were action images emphasising women as embodied athletes.[14] For example, an advert for North sails (Figure 3) featured the world champion Daida Morreno in a high impact wave action shot in which the performer's identity and sex was barely visible. Only a secondary small photograph of her face identified the subject as female. Articles about women windsurfers I analysed were also more contradictory and ambiguous in terms of perpetuating the 'naturalness' of the ideological association between windsurfing and masculinity. On one hand, the articles tended to be shorter and less prominent than those about their male counterparts, however the text itself emphasized the women's identities as *windsurfers*, as performers.[15] Nevertheless in a cultural context in which 'sexual attractiveness' has been articulated with fitness (Hargreaves, 1993) these sportswomen are marked as unquestionably female and heterosexual. Photo captions and narratives reinforced the elite women's sexuality, such as commenting on their 'babe potential.' Yet even images of women depicted in active poses were often open to sexualized readings, particularly as the bikini is the 'chosen' beach attire for some female windsurfers, emphasizing parts of the body associated with female sexuality (breasts, buttocks etc). Professional women windsurfers I interviewed, eager to promote and exploit their

Figure 3: North sail advert—Boards, March 2000, p. 44.

commercial worth, were conscious that it was easier to get magazine coverage if they conformed to stereotypes of idealized femininity. They had to 'show their femininity—be aesthetic'; sell their sexuality as well as their athleticism.[16] Such media images of female athletes subvert the potential challenge these women pose to sport as a male preserve, re-establishing gender roles into a 'normative heterosexual regime' (Schulze, 1990: 78).

Bodily (ab)use: seeking risk and danger

The male windsurfing celebrities that dominate the magazine pages are represented as hedonistic pleasure seekers living exotic and carefree lifestyles. Articles titled 'The search' and the 'Big blue Odyssey' seduce the reader into a fantasy windsurfing lifestyle, illustrated with images of tropical beaches with crystal turquoise water and white sand beaches lined with palm trees. These magazines, like other popular media texts, use (post) colonialized countries as 'exotic backdrops for Western adventures, fantasies and tests of manhood' (Davis, 1997: 105). Whether Olympic racer or professional wave sailors, élite windsurfers are portrayed as nomads, travelling the world from one exotic event location to the next, their bodies vehicles for sensation-seeking activities, often involving flirting with danger, irrespective of the costs. Windsurfing injuries, particularly if gained by taking excessive risks, were banded like trophies. An article tracking the travels of a group of international male celebrities[17] illustrates this coding of masculinity based around hedonism, risk-taking and demonstrating sporting prowess. The group are depicted searching the world for the perfect wave sailing locations, travelling from one exotic beach to the next (writing such travel articles and making video documentaries). Jason Polalow, the world wave sailing champion, is framed not just as an elite sportsman, but as the most committed hedonist of the group, 'the hellman.' Jason's status in his masculine peer group is based on his windsurfing ability, but particularly his enthusiasm, 'attitude' and commitment to all adrenaline-seeking activities. Jason plays, parties and drinks 'the hardest'. As his peer wrote:

> I couldn't help but admire his energy and I have to admit he is definitely one of the most radical people I have ever met [..] pushing everything he does as hard as he can.[18]

The group's antics continually placed themselves and/or their equipment in dangerous situations. The narrative suggests that the person—who is clearly denoted as male—prepared to take the biggest risks has highest status within the group. Jason is respectfully described (by his peer) as 'One of the maddest, most manic human beings on the planet.' Similarly Beal (2002) argues that for skaters in North America, the ethos of risk-taking, particularly as embodied in 'street' skating, has become a sign of legitimacy that is equated with heterosexual masculinity.[19] She illustrates how female skaters are marginalized because of the assumptions that they are unwilling to take risks.[20] In this respect, the embodied hegemonic masculinity signified in the windsurfing magazines and—as I'll come on to illustrate—other lifestyle sport magazines, mirrors the *loaded* genre of men's magazines, which celebrate a 'high-risk culture of care-free consumption' (Jackson *et al.*, 2001: 102), disregarding the body by focusing on different types of excessive behaviour.

Such discourses of male physicality are different from dominant representations of sporting masculinity, both in traditional sports magazines, and men's lifestyle magazines such as *Men's Health*. The male body project underlined by *Men's Health* sees the body as a 'passport for the good life,' (Jackson *et al.*, 2001: 91). It requires a '*calculating* hedonism' emphasizing the co-existence of disciplined forms of 'body-maintenance' such as exercise and diet, with this more hedonistic conception of the body (Featherstone, 1982). So while the culture of the health magazines is narcissistic, such as the emphasis on the six-pack, it simultaneously reinforces bodily anxiety, particularly about ageing, contributing to an 'instrumental, calculative and individualized approach to the male body' (Jackson *et al.*, 2001: 102). The discursive codes of masculinity in windsurfing magazines portray men as uninterested in such issues of health, fitness, longevity and self-preservation. Where other sports activities were represented in the windsurfing lifestyle, they tended to be other lifestyle sports such as kite surfing, surfing, and snowboarding; men were rarely shown working at 'body maintenance' or undertaking any form of physical training. Likewise the ethnographic research illustrated that men windsurfed primarily for short-term gains, emphasizing immediate heightened experiences (Wheaton, 1997), and commitment to the 'felt' not 'displayed' body, more akin to the 1960s hedonism than the narcissistic 1990s body consumption practices.

Furthermore, contrary to those non-laddish men's lifestyle magazines that continue to emphasize the importance of work for men's sense of identity (Jackson *et al.* 2001; Whelehan, 2000), this leisure lifestyle was represented as a hedonistic separate world that rarely intruded into non-windsurfing issues, such as the world of work, or domesticity. Work and leisure are blurred, particularly for the professional windsurfer's whose 'working' life is one long hedonistic journey. There is no sense that work makes men 'complete' such as articulated in popular representations of masculinity like the film, *The Full Monty* (Whelehan, 2001). Employment in both surfing and windsurfing is represented as a lifestyle choice (Stedman, 1997; Wheaton, 1997). Nevertheless, men need the economic capital to buy the windsurfing equipment, and thus the lack of significance given to work needs to be read within a discursive practice rooted firmly in a *middle-class* hedonism.

Consuming images

Discussion with readers about this framing of masculinity and femininity was initiated by looking at some of the adverts depicting advanced action shots of female windsurfers. I expected that male readers would use their consumption of the magazines, particularly sexual representations of women, as a way to assert their hegemonic masculinity. For example, they might see 'real' windsurfing as what men do, constructing female performers as the less authentic Other, make 'jokes' about the female windsurfers such as 'not bad for a girl,' and centrally see consuming sexualized images of 'beach babes' as part of the windsurfing lifestyle.

Yet while male (as well as female) consumers did express a range of readings from conservative to pro feminist, most men did not feel the need to exclude—symbolically or otherwise—the *female windsurfer*. The majority of the men I interviewed were ambivalent about the photographic subject's gender, and only commented on the athlete being female when provoked.[21] They used the same criteria (style, quality of action photos, etc) to judge all the images I gave them, and while there was clearly an adoption of 'male as norm,' particularly the emphasis on images depicting power, strength and recklessness, they argued it was the quality of the windsurfing image that mattered, not *who* it was: 'It doesn't matter whether it's a woman or bloke really. I'd just still think it was a nice shot' (James). They were complimentary about 'good shots' irrespective of the photographic subject's gender, nationality, or ethnicity.

A few men, especially the older, professional males, criticized the male domination, and male perspective of the magazines. Simon, an advanced windsurfer in his early 30s suggested that 'The male-dominated media portrayal is an impression you can't fail to hide. [..] the impression of the sport the magazines gives you, is that you need to be fit and strong to enjoy sailing.' He highlights the magazine's emphasis on advanced windsurfing technique, noted in the magazine analysis, and illustrates the naturalness of the link between sport and masculinity. Occasionally, and perhaps surprisingly, men even wrote letters to the magazines criticising their portrayal of female sportswomen. As one reader suggested, 'So why the picture of a woman's backside and the gross innuendo? [. . .] Isn't it time that *Boards* took an interest in women as sailors rather then as decoration? You would make a good magazine far better by this.'[22]

The exception to this acceptance of elite female windsurfers were the younger (teenage and early 20s) elite, male windsurfers, who seemed more likely to resent the intrusion of female windsurfers into what they considered to be 'their' magazines, 'their' space. For these elite young men, the space of the magazines—like the sub culture itself—was a male world in which female performers were tolerated, but only if their presence didn't encroach sufficiently to challenge the male hegemony of elite sport, preserving their sport as a 'proving ground for masculinity' (Whitson, 1990).

Swimsuit Corner

However, men's attitudes to women portrayed in objectified, sexualized roles such as the Swimsuit Corner feature in *Windsurf* magazine, differed from those about *female athletes*. Swimsuit Corner was a half page or smaller photograph of a bikini clad female, which appeared in the news and gossip section of most issues (see Figures 1 and 2). The photographs were usually but not exclusively of models not female windsurfing celebrities, all of whom were white and typically photographed in sexualized poses. Younger men in particular welcomed these images reflecting the heterosexist laddish masculinity associated with both men's lifestyle magazines and more traditional sports magazines (Rowe, 1999; Boyle and Haynes, 2000; Davis, 1997). As Peter Howarth, editor of *Esquire* claims[23] 'Any good magazines must offer a balance of content, and part of that balance, if it is to reflect the interests of men, will inevitably be article on beautiful women.' Davis's (1997) investigation into the popularity of *Sport Illustrated Swimsuit Issue* in North America, suggests that men's identification with, and consumption of these images of women serves as a public declaration of their heterosexual status to secure or demonstrate their hegemonic masculinity.

Similarly the male windsurfers' consumption of these photographs was often very public—for example, 'drooling' over images with other young men, discussing their 'babe' potential, or sticking up pictures as 'pin-ups'—serving as public performances of their heterosexual status.

The diversity in the readings of one particular advert, however, (for a windsurfing shop) illustrates the *different* ways men consumed images of these 'beach babes.' The image (Figure 4) was an unusually sexualised image, depicting the torso and head of a woman in a swimsuit. The text read 'We shall not allow the use of inappropriate and or sexist imagery as a means by which to sell or promote our products and services.' Pete laughed and responded:

> Well this just reminds me of swimsuit corner really. I guess as a male I quite like to see women in swimming costumes—let's be honest [laughs] Not essential to have in a mag but, you know. [..] It's unique. Name another retail outlet or even a retail or manufacturer that has just been blatantly sexist in trying to sell their products. Very few of them have. It's the most old fashioned way of selling anything. And here we are— here we now finally have it in windsurfing and I haven't got a problem with that really, but then I'm a male.

His response can be read as a heterosexist display of masculinity, marking sexual difference, constructing the women as Other. However the words 'we now finally have it in windsurfing' also suggests that he previously thought of these magazines, and in this case their adverts, as somewhat *different* from other types of magazine advertising. Other readers similarly differentiated windsurfing magazines from other media sources, specifically seeing 'lads mags' as being 'different.'

Some male interviewees were more ambivalent or critical of the advert. Several did not really want to discuss the image at all saying they would 'just flip past.' A few claimed that it made them think 'more negatively' about the advertiser: 'I'm not—I don't go, wow look at that. I mean it's something I just— I don't think much of them. There isn't a particular need for it' (James).

Ironic sexism?

Despite claiming not to read men's lifestyle magazines, several interviewees commented on what they called the '*loaded*' style irony of the advert. As has been

Figure 4: 2XS advert—Windsurf, September 1999, p. 51. Used with permission from Windsurf Magazine.

widely commented on in both academic and popular sources, irony is one of the most pervasive features of 'new' men's lifestyle magazines, and wider media discourses around the New Lad (and Ladette) media identities (McRobbie, 1994).[24] How to *interpret* this widespread use of irony and parody, however, particularly to what extent irony supports or undermines sexual difference, is more widely disputed. A postmodern interpretation emphasizes the intertextual, multi-referential and playful way in which consumers encounter such images, suggesting that the reader plays the central role in interpreting their meanings. Thus sexist images can be used ironically, even deconstructing the original meaning of the image (Whelehan, 2001). In a consumer society saturated with (seemingly) playful provocative images, however, it is at the level of image and language that powerful ideological work is done. Hence many commentators interpret ironic laddism as a 'nostalgic revival of patriarchy' (Whelehan 2000: 6) that 'subverts political critique' (Jackson *et al.*, 2001: 78).

So how did the readers interpret the 'irony' in this image? For many there seemed to be an acceptance that irony reduced the ideological impact of the sexist image. Simon suggested the image wasn't really sexist as it was trying to 'use wit': 'So they're playing on it. So it's there for a reason, so in which case I don't think it is really that sexist' (Simon). As Jackson *et al.*, (2001: 78) argue, (one function of) irony is that it allows men to 'experience the contradictory nature of the magazines from a safe distance.' Men or women who take the sexism too seriously have missed the point of the joke (Jackson *et al.*, 2001: 78). Alison, who was extremely critical of sexist imagery in the magazines, articulated both the contradictory nature of the image and her own contradictory reading of it, unsure of whether it is as 'bad' as less playful sexist imagery:

> This is to me like a double-edged sword. On the one hand it's quiet sort of, (pauses) but on the other hand it's just as bad. It's sort of playing between the two. You know, I mean, at first you read it and you go, oh that's quite—and then when you think about it you go, eh, yeah, great, you know, same old scenario.

Alison suggested that the irony in the advert would be enhanced—the adverts would be 'cleverer'—by changing the photograph to a sexualized image of a man:

> The wording the whole text alludes to a woman anyway as it would do from conditioning, but to read that and then—I think that would be quite cool. Much cleverer than using the stereotype.

I asked the remaining male interviewees, who had mixed reactions. Some agreed with Alison, others argued that it didn't work without the sexism. As Mark put it:

> Well I think what's really sad about men is they are not very complicated when it comes to the other half, you know, as in the other sex. [laughing]. And if they see an attractive girl they're going to have a look. I'm sorry but that's just how it is.

As in men's magazines, irony allowed men to 'indulge in fantasies of successful manhood and consumer representations of beautiful women in a relatively comfortable and guilt free way' (Jackson *et al.*, 2001: 104).

Women speak out

The women I observed and interviewed (1997 and 2000) had differing and often unexpected attitudes to the magazines in general, and specifically the ways in which femininities were depicted. *Boards* magazine's own audience research (1997) suggests only 5 per cent of *Boards'* readership were women. This is lower than has been suggested read men's lifestyle magazines (around 10–15 per cent), and much lower than the percentage of actual female participants (somewhere between 10–25 per cent depending on location, degree of commitment etc), although this quantitative assessment may be misleading, as women I interviewed often read other people's copies. The less advanced female windsurfers interviewed were the group of consumers least likely to buy and read windsurfing magazine.

How these female consumers identified with the representations of windsurfing illustrates the ways in which some women contested the idea of windsurfing magazines as exclusively or 'authentically' laddish male spaces in which women's 'authentic' roles were as beach babes. Some women stated that they felt the magazines did not appeal to women. The excessive, and traditionally masculine 'techno babble' about equipment was cited as the main off-putting factor. Most women did not critique the emphasis on male performers in magazine content, arguing that articles about, or action photos of, women were not necessarily more interesting. As Helen explained, part of the appeal of the sport, and the magazines, was the exclusive male world she had successfully worked her way into.

Nevertheless, many female (non) readers were critical of the male control of windsurfing magazines and especially the sexist attitudes displayed by male editors and writers, such as the objectification and sexualisation of women in swimsuit corner. Rather than directly challenging or contesting these representations, women had adopted a range of often complex and contradictory reading strategies. One approach was ignoring the male producer's 'juvenile and sexist attitudes' using humour; 'having a giggle, just see it as a joke.' Some found looking at pictures of beautiful women pleasurable. As Sarah put it, 'politically it [swim suit corner] stinks, but yes I do like looking at pretty women.' Surprisingly hardly any of the women (and none of the men) commented on the magazines as an abundant source of image of 'hunky men', although they did allude to this sexual meaning in conversations about the windsurfing personalities, and the appeal of the lifestyle. Although the magazines do receive, and occasionally publish letters from women—and men—voicing gender protests, none of the women I spoke to considered writing a letter as a productive way of voicing a protest. They explained that there was no point in reacting to it, as 'the magazines are produced by men.' Furthermore women who did write letters were often mocked, either by other readers or at times by the editors.

Yet women seemed to be more willing to voice criticisms of advertisers using overtly sexualized images of women, particularly if they were images of women who were actually windsurfers. Kate claimed 'I find it really irritating. I find it very condescending. I just think, well stick this in the lad's mags.' Her comments suggest that she *didn't* see windsurfing and lads magazines occupying the same male space, moreover she felt some sense of ownership over windsurfing magazines.

Figure 5 TYR—Wahine, Vol. 3, No. 3, p. 57. Photograph by Lori Adamski-Peek.

One particular advert for swimsuits (Figure 5) provoked many comments about the 'inauthenticity' of the image from the men and women. The image depicts a 'posed' female, wearing a swimsuit, and holding a windsurf board that was resting on the sand.[25] Many women resented this objectified stereotype of femininity—the beach babe, being presented as the 'authentic' windsurfing woman:

> Hey, you know, 'if you want to be a windsurfing babe, you've got to be like a blonde stick.' You know? It's just all those stereotypes and I've just got no time for it quite honestly. (..) She's probably taken that board down to the beach for her boyfriend. It's just like—she *could* be a windsurfer, but I look at that and I doubt very much whether she is. I look at that and go 'she's not a windsurfer' (Claire).

She contrasted this image with other surf industry adverts for swimwear such as *Roxy*. Although their adverts did flaunt images of women wearing bikinis, they were depicting actual surfing or windsurfing (images that I've alluded to earlier in the discussion.). While acknowledging that women in bikinis will always be open to sexualized readings, the difference was the *pretence* of 'doing it'. 'There's no like, oh "let's find the tiniest bikini we can and pretend we're going to go out to surf the waves." [..] Because they're actually doing it' (Claire).

Sporting masculinities, New Lads, and men's magazines revisited

So how does this case study of windsurfing magazines inform our understanding of sporting masculinities, particularly the alliance between sport and the new lad that is prevalent in both men's magazines and the associated lived cultures? To summarize, the windsurfing magazines represent windsurfing as a predominantly male preserve. Men are depicted as young, able-bodied, white, heterosexual and with the commitment and financial ability to consume this hedonistic leisure lifestyle. Windsurfing masculinity, like other mediated sporting masculinities, is coded as being based on traditional markers of hegemonic masculinity such as sporting prowess, willingness to take physical risks, and enjoying consuming images of sexualized women (Messner *et al.*, 2000). However the representation and consumption of the female within their marginality was contradictory, ranging from the objectified and sexualized female body as espoused in 'swimsuit corner' to action images emphasising women as embodied athletes. Among female and male windsurfers there was a hesitancy to make gender central, or even a part of conversations and analysis about windsurfing. The participants wanted to discuss the 'generic' characteristics needed of a 'person' to be considered acceptable, characteristics that nevertheless invariably reflected values associated with hegemonic heterosexual masculinity, particularly risk-taking and sporting prowess. The beach babe remains a potent image in popular mythology about the beach, and it seems that consuming images of women as de-individualized 'heterosexualized commodities' (Messner *et al.*, 2000: 384) is an important way of demonstrating heterosexuality in this context, as in other male magazines. Nevertheless, readers did not necessarily read these images as the 'authentic' representation of windsurfing women, expecting and accepting the place of (high-action images of) female athletes. Although the magazines offer a relatively narrow image of sporting femininities and masculinities, the interviewees' *consumption* of those images reflect the diversity of both masculinities and femininities that exist in the lived culture (see Wheaton and Tomlinson, 1998; Wheaton, 2000b).

In this, and in other respects, windsurfing masculinity is not the same as the footy loving, beer-swilling, and predatory New Lad. Nor are they relics of the middle-class fashion obsessed 'New Men.' Although windsurfers simultaneously embrace and reject aspects of commercial culture, they particularly repudiate the fashioning of masculinity through style. Other differences lie in the absence of an explicit link between masculinity and paid work, and particularly attitudes to the body. Jackson *et al.* (2001: 95) claim that despite 'new' possibilities for the fashioning of masculinity around bodily consumption practices in men's lifestyles magazines, men's sense of identity is still largely secured through their ability to perform paid employment outside of home. Yet the discourse of work is largely absent from the windsurfing magazines; masculine identities are based around subcultural affiliation and commitment.

There are also differences in sporting masculinity between and within lifestyle sports, particularly in terms of the types and extent of the sexist imagery being used, authentic discourses of femininity, and how images of women as 'Other' were consumed. North American research on skateboard magazines has identified a heterosexist masculinity with an 'outlaw image' that—like surfing magazines—includes a clear separation from 'mainstream' standards or an anti-establishment stance. Unlike windsurfing and snowboarding magazines, women were very rarely presented as actual skaters (Wheaton and Beal, 2003), whereas pictures of women as heterosexualized commodities, objects to sell products, are much more common than in windsurfing magazines. As Rinehart (1999) has illustrated, most images of women were sexualized, and advertisers often use some extremely sexist and misogynistic images of women. Unlike the windsurfers, the majority of male skaters Beal interviewed relied on explaining sexist advertising and women in passive role as relatively unproblematic, 'a reflection of skate culture.'

Surfing magazines (in Australia) also portray females as passive, non-surfers (Fiske, 1989: 60). Male surfers demonstrate a predatory attitude to women mirroring the New Lad. As Fiske notes (1989) 'mastery' in the surfer's journals often alludes to women and waves; that is success with women is linked to sporting prowess. Stedman (1997), however, highlights that up until the 1980s, surfing magazines like *Tracks* gave much greater editorial support and recognition to women surfers. She (1997) suggests that one of the reasons for the Australian surfing media adopting such an *extreme* sexist attitude was a reaction to the increased commodification of their culture by 'mainstream society,'[26] which the surfing subculture has *constructed* as being tolerant of feminism, giving 'women an easy ride' (1997: 78). She argues—similarly to my claims about windsurfers' display of commitment—that surfers' 'attitude' is their way of demonstrating their collective identity,

The active construction of a deviant image through exaggerated sexism, therefore, is seen as an effective way of maintaining difference from what surfers define as the 'mainstream' (Stedman, 1997: 78)

For surfers, however, the consequence of this 'attitude' which has occurred *through* the surfing media in the 1980s was the increased 'masculinization of surfing and the progressive exclusion of women' and of gay men (Stedman, 1997: 81). As *Underground Surf* magazine (1994: 109) advocates: 'We should encourage surfing to be publicly dammed. People don't have to fear us—they just have to *not want to be us*, not want to identify with a label that spells sick, perverted, deviant' (cited in Stedman, 1997).

Furthermore these differences between lifestyle sport media are not surprising, given their different readership and locality. Skating and, to extent, surfing magazines are targeted at the teenage male, whereas windsurfing (and snowboarding) magazines include older and more affluent men. Age and social class, as well as gender and ethnicity, mediates the subcultural values expressed in the magazines content and particularly the coding of masculinity. Snowboarders and windsurfers are predominantly white *and* middle-class, and both welcome, even celebrate female participation (Henio, 2000). Skateboarding, on the other hand, is a 'tough street sport' that is accessible to those on lower incomes and thus is popular with lower-middle class young males, including (in North America) a greater range of ethnicities (Henio, 2000: 188).

Such discourses, however, are not fixed temporally or geographically. As discussed, Stedman's (1997) research has illustrated that media attitudes to women in surfing have changed quite dramatically over the past two decades. Arguably, since the late 1990s this hyper-masculinization of surfing has started to be reversed, with the boom in women surfing starting to penetrate into the surfing media (see Booth, 2001).

To conclude, this discussion of sporting masculinity in lifestyle magazines, both general and sporting, suggests that these magazines perpetuate narrow and stereotypical messages about gender, heterosexuality, and ethnicity. Particularly prevalent is the representation and consumption of women as heterosexualized commodities, which 'serves as one of the major linking factors in the conservative gender regime of the sport/media/commercial complex' (Messner *et al.*, 2000). In this cultural moment in which hegemonic masculinity is seen to be increasingly destabilized, male consumption of sexual representations of women, and sport spectatorship, continue to play an important part in defining hegemonic masculinity (Davis, 1997). However despite the permanence of certain masculine codes, as I have illustrated, a range of different, more complex, and shifting versions of masculinity exists within and between men's magazines, and particularly in relation to the more specialist 'lifestyle sport' magazines. The range of often-contradictory readings men and women windsurfers gave of the windsurfing magazines are indicative of the ambivalences, and instabilities of contemporary masculinities. The audience research supports Jackson *et al.*'s (2001: 19) claims that the media's focus on laddish masculinities over simplifies the masculinities that readers actually articulated in and through reading their magazines. It also reiterates that audiences actively interpret, draw on and create meanings that can vary and do differ from the preferred meaning offered by the texts. Although lifestyle sport magazines re-inscribe traditional hegemonic codes about masculinity, they simultaneously offer at least *the potential* for changes in gender relations and identities.

Notes

1 As discussed later in this chapter, magazines such as *Men's Health* continue to promote these attitudes to male physicality.
2 As Carrington (1989, 1999) and others have shown, nation, in this context, specifically refers to a *white* English affair.
3 Unofficial figures based on informal interviews with magazine editors.
4 According to Audit Bureau of Circulations in 2000 cited in Jackson *et al.* (2001: 30).
5 The last section of the chapter will illustrate these differences in the discourses of sporting masculinity and feminity, between (and within) these sporting publications, particularly in relation to the exclusion and objectification of women.
6 The main reason for the content analysis was to examine temporal changes in magazine content. A content analyses had been conducted in 1991.
7 However the 'formal' analysis was supplemented by the reading of magazines and images conducted during the audience research conducted in 2000.
8 Elite windsurfers, however, often found the content 'boring'; it was too wide-ranging to address their specific specialist interest on the 'hard core' elements of the sport, such as wave sailing.
9 The maximum (estimated) readership figures over the time period studied was 20–22,000, although a small percentage were sold abroad (*Boards* spokesperson). Only around 10% of those who defined themselves as 'regular windsurfers' in survey research bought windsurfing magazines.
10 Few of my interviewees would admit to regularly reading or buying *any* titles, other than *occasionally* buying other lifestyle sport magazines (mostly surfing and snowboarding magazines) or men's lifestyle magazines (*Men's Health* and *Esquire* were mentioned).
11 The remaining 7% were photos in which the subject was unclear. Fiske's (1989) analysis of Australian surfing magazines notes the importance of the 'de-individualized surfer,' that is, the photograph either had no surfer at all, or the surfer was so small, that s/he was just a speck on the wave, emphasizing the importance of the surfer's environment. Of all the photographs where the appearance of the subject was visible, 84% was a white subject, and in only 3% was the subject's appearance over 40.
12 For example Urry suggests the tanned skin signifies sexuality (Urry, 1990).
13 The terms 'babe' and 'girlie' were common ways of describing women, linguistic terms which, feminists have argued, infantilize women (see Whelehan, 2000).
14 One possible reason for this increased visibility of female athletes is the targeting of the female consumer by the surf clothing industry. Over the last 5 years, companies like *Roxy*, the female sector of *Quicksilver* surf clothing, have emerged as important players in the globalised surf and street wear markets (see also Booth, 2001). A positive spin off from this seems to have been the expansion in both sponsorship and media exposure for some female athletes in these sports.
15 They rarely adopted stereotypes of sportswomen evident in other sports media publications, for example that emphasise female identities as mothers, daughters and partners, and focuses on their non-sporting lives (Hargreaves, 1994; Duncan, 1990; Duncan and Messner, 1994).
16 Similarly Booth (2001) documents the tensions and contradictions around exploiting female sexuality in the history of the marketing of women's surfing.
17 *Boards*, August, 1995: 38–42.

18 *Boards*, August, 1995: 44.
19 Beal's (Beal, 2002) interesting analysis also outlines how risk-taking is related to social class. More privileged and regulated forms of skating, such as the ramp and vert, earn less respect as they are seen to be supervised or 'protected'.
20 It is interesting to compare this representation of masculinity to Neale's (1983) in his analysis of the cinematic gaze in male genres such as the 'action' film and western. Neal suggests that one way in which the narrative structure undercuts the possibility of an erotic masculine address is through wounding or injuring the male body, privileging a coding of masculinity that promotes toughness and control (Neale, 1983).
21 Of course my identity as a female windsurfer is a salient factor, and it is possible that men may have expressed different views in more informal contexts. As my ethnographic research demonstrated, however, in this subcultural context, my identity as an insider, a *windsurfer*, often displaced my gender identity (Wheaton, 2002; Wheaton, forthcoming).
22 Paul Wilson, *Boards*, May, 1990.
23 in Guardian, 25 November, 1996 cited in Jackson *et al.*, (2001: 77).
24 However Jackson *et al.* (2001) point out that how we understand irony is problematic; for example taking Rorty's (1989) claims about the different categories of (radical) irony, might suggest men's lifestyle magazines are not ironic at all (Rorty, 1989).
25 The advert was a swimsuit advert from *Wahine* magazine, a female water-sports magazine produced in North America.
26 As Stedman's analysis explores, the proliferation of identities and subject positions in postmodern culture makes categories such as mainstream and alternative increasingly problematic. She highlights the paradox that surfers are predominately white middle class men, thus representative of the 'mainstream'. Stedman claims that it is in response to this postmodern paradox that surfers in the 1980s attempted to reclaim their collective subjecthood via difference.

References

Anderson, K. (1999) 'Snowboarding: the construction of gender in an emerging sport', *Journal of Sport and Social Issues* 23: 55–79.
Beal, B. (1996) 'Alternative masculinity and its effect on gender relations in the subculture of skateboarding', *Journal of Sports Behaviour* 19: 204–220.
Beal, B. (2002) 'The shifting landscape of an alternative sport: Commercialization and the changing meaning of skateboarding'. Paper presented at Sport and the All-Consuming Cultures of [P]leasure, University of Surrey Roehampton.
Beal, B. and Weidman, L. (2003) 'Authenticity in the skateboarding world': in R. Rinehart and S. Sydor (eds) *To the Extreme: Alternative Sports Inside and Out*. Albany: SUNY Press.
Booth, D. (2001) *Australian Beach Cultures: The History of Sun, Sand and Surf*. London: Frank Cass Publishers.
Boyle, R. and Haynes, R. (2000) *Power Play: Sport, the Media and Popular Culture*. Harlow: Longman.
Burton Nelson, M. (1996) *The Stronger Women Get, the More Men Love Football: Sexism and the Culture of Sports*. London: The Women's Press Ltd.
Carrington, B. (1998) ' "Football's coming home" But whose home and do we want it? Nation, football and the politics of exclusion': 101–123 in A. Brown (ed.) *Fanatics! Power, identity and fandom in football*. London/NY: Routledge.
Carrington, B. (1999) 'Too many St Georges crosses to bear': 71–86 in M. Perryman (ed.) *The Ingerland Factor: Home Truths from Football*. Edinburgh: Mainstream publishing.
Carrington, B. and McDonald, I. (eds) (2001) *'Race', Sport and British Society*. London: Routledge.
Connell, R. (1995) *Masculinities*. Cambridge: Polity Press.
Craik, J. (1994) *The Face of Fashion*. London/NY: Routledge.

Crolley, L. (1999) 'Lads will be lads': 59–70 in M. Perryman (ed.) *The Ingerland Factor: Home Truths from Football*. Edinburgh: Mainstream Publishing.

Davis, L. (1997) *Hegemonic Masculinity in Sports Illustrated*. Albany: State University of New York Press.

Duncan, M. (1990) 'Sports photographs and sexual difference: Images of women and men in the 1984 and 1988 Olympic Games', *Sociology of Sport Journal* 7: 22–43.

Duncan, M. and Messner, M. (1994) *Gender Stereotyping in Televised Sports: A Follow-up to the 1989 Study*. The Amateur Athletic Foundation of Los Angeles.

Dyer, R. (1987) *Heavenly Bodies: Film Stars and Society*. London: Macmillan.

Edwards, T. (1997) *Men in the Mirror: Men's Fashion, Masculinity and Consumer Society*. London: Cassell.

Featherstone, M. (1982) 'The body in consumer culture', *Theory Culture and Society* 1: 18–33.

Featherstone, M. (1991) *Consumer Culture and Postmodernism*. London, Newbury Park, New Delhi: Sage Publications.

Fiske, J. (1989) *Reading the Popular*. Unwin Hyman.

Giddens, A. (1991) *Modernity and Self-Identity: Self and Society in the Late Modern Age*, Cambridge: Polity Press.

Hall, S. and Jacques, M. (1989) 'Introduction': 11–20 in M. Jaques (ed.) *New Times: The Changing Face of Politics in the 1990's*. London: Lawrence and Wishart in association with Marxism Today.

Hargreaves, J. (1993) 'Bodies Matter! Images of sport and female sexualisation': 60–66 in C. Brackenridge (ed.) *Body Matters: Leisure Images and Lifestyles*. Eastboune: LSA.

Hargreaves, J. (1994) *Sporting Females: Critical Issues in the History and Sociology of Women's Sports*. London and New York: Routledge.

Henio, R. (2000) 'What is so punk about snowboarding?', *Journal of Sport and Social Issues* 24: 176–191.

Jackson, P., Stevenson, N. and Brooks, K. (2001) *Making Sense of Men's Magazines*. Cambridge: Polity.

Jacques, M. (1997) 'Worshipping the body at altar of sport', *The Observer* 18–19.

Jameson, F. (1991) *Postmodernism or the Cultural Logic of Late Capitalism*. London/NY: Verso.

Kusz, K. (2001) '"I want to be a minority": The politics of youthful masculinities in sport and popular culture in 1990s America', *Journal of Sport and Social Issues* 25: 390–416.

Lash, S. and Urry, J. (1987) *The End of Organized Capitalism*. Cambridge: Polity Press.

McRobbie, A. (1982) 'The politics of feminist research: Between talk, text and action', *Feminist Review* 12: 46–57.

McRobbie, A. (1999) 'Pecs and penises: The meaning of girlie culture': 112–131 in A. McRobbie (ed.) *In the culture society: Art, fashion and popular music*. London: Routledge.

Messner, M., Dunbar, M. and Hunt, D. (2000) 'The televised sports manhood formula', *Journal of Sport and Social Issues* 24: 380–394.

Messner, M. and Sabo, D. (1990) *Sport, Men and the Gender Order: Critical Feminist Perspectives*. Champaign Illinois: Human Kinetic Books.

Midol, N. and Broyer, G. (1995) 'Towards an anthropological analysis of new sport cultures: The case of whiz sports in France', *Sociology of Sport Journal* 12: 204–212.

Mort, F. (1998) 'Boy's Own? Masculinity, style and popular culture': in R. Chapman and J. Rutherford (eds) *Male Order: Unwrapping Masculinity*. London: Lawrence & Wishart.

Mort, F. (1996) *Cultures of Consumption: Masculinities and Social Space in Late Twentieth Century Britain*. London: Routledge.

Mulvey, L. (2000) 'Visual pleasure and narrative cinema': 483–495 in R. Stam and T. Miller (eds) *Film and Theory: An Anthology*. Oxford: Blackwell.

Neale, S. (1983) 'Masculinity as spectacle', *Screen* 24: 2–16.

Nixon, S. (1996) *Hard Looks: Masculinities, Spectatorship and Contemporary Consumption*. London: UCL Press.

Nixon, S. (1997) 'Exhibiting masculinity': 291–330 in S. Hall (ed.) *Representation: Cultural Representations and Signifying Practices*. London: Sage.

Rinehart, R. (1999) 'Babes on boards: Women as co-opted sports models'. Paper presented at North American Sociology of Sport Association, Cleveland.

Rorty (1989) *Contingency, Irony and Solidarity*. Cambridge: Cambridge University Press.

Rowe, D. (1999) *Sport, Culture and the Media*. Buckingham: Open University Press.

Schulze, L. (1990) 'On the muscles': 59–78 in C. Herzog (ed.) *Fabrications: Costume and the Female Body*. New York: Routledge.

Shilling, C. (1993) *The Body and Social Theory*. London: Sage.

Stedman, L. (1997) 'From Gidget to Gonad Man: Surfers, feminists and postmodernisation', *Australian and New Zealand Journal of Sociology* 33: 75–90.

Stranger, M. (1999) 'The aesthetics of risk: A study of surfing', *International Review for the Sociology of Sport* 34(3): 265–276.

Thornton, S. (1995) *Club Cultures: Music, Media and Subcultural Capital*. Cambridge: Polity Press.

Tomlinson, A. (2001) 'Sport, leisure and style': 399–415 in D. Morley and K. Robins (eds) *British Cultural Studies Geography, Nationality and Identity*. Oxford: Oxford University Press.

Treas, S. (1999) 'Sports, space and in-your-face masculinity in skateboarding magazines'. Paper presented at *Pacific Sociological Conference*, San Diego.

Urry, J. (1990) *The Tourist's Gaze: Leisure and Travel in Contemporary Societies*. London: Sage.

Whannel, G. (2002) *Media Sport Stars: Masculinities and Moralities*. London: Routledge.

Wheaton, B. (1997) *Consumption, Lifestyle and Gendered Identities in Post-Modern Sports: The Case of Windsurfing*. Unpublished PhD, University of Brighton.

Wheaton, B. (2000a) 'Just Do it: Consumption, commitment and identity in the windsurfing subculture', *Sociology of Sport Journal* 17: 254–274.

Wheaton, B. (2000b) '"New Lads?" Masculinities and the New Sport participant', *Men and Masculinities* 2: 436–458.

Wheaton, B. (2002) 'Babes on the beach, women in the surf: Researching gender, power and difference in the windsurfing culture': in J. Sugden and A. Tomlinson (eds) *Power Games: Theory and method for a critical sociology of sport*. London: Routledge.

Wheaton, B. and Beal, B. (2003) '"Keeping it real": Subcultural media and the discourses of authenticity in alternative sport', *International Review for the Sociology of Sport*.

Wheaton, B. and Tomlinson, A. (1998) 'The changing gender order in sport? The case of Windsurfing', *Journal of Sport and Social Issues* 22: 252–274.

Whelehan, I. (2000) *Overloaded: Popular Culture and the Future of Feminism*. London: The Women's Press.

Whitson, D. (1990) 'Sport in the social construction of masculinity': 19–30 in M. Messner and D. Sabo (eds) *Sport, Men and the Gender Order: Critical Feminist Perspectives*. Champaign, Illinois: Human Kinetic Books.

The language of Japanese men's magazines: young men who don't want to get hurt

Keiko Tanaka

Introduction

Since the 1980s we have seen the rise of men's magazines, together with conspicuous consumption of men's fashion, in both Britain and Japan. These magazines, however, have propagated very different images in the two countries and they have contributed to confusing portraits of masculinity. British men's magazines initially developed various images of 'the new man', and then replaced them in the 1990 with 'the new lad' or 'men behaving badly' (Edwards, 1997: 82). In contrast, the growth market for Japanese young men can be summarized by the phrase 'the city boys'. The city boy is different from the new man, in that the former is typically apolitical (Inoue and Ebara, 1995: 210; Okabe *et al.*, 1997: 183). The city boy is also different from the new lad because he is unashamedly preoccupied with what his girlfriend thinks of him. As the term 'boy', as opposed to 'man', suggests, the city boy consumer is slightly younger than his British counterpart. Perhaps this has to do with the fact that, in Japan, even high school students have considerable disposable income, due to more generous pocket money. Kondo *et al.* (1988: 204) cite research showing that the average pocket money for college students stands at around $400 per month, in fact nearly as high as the average disposable income of a 'salary-man', or company employee, at $420 per month.

Men's magazines were identified as a growth market in the 1980s in Britain and Japan, but men's general interest magazines were not new. As Mort (1996: 19) argues, 'What was emphasized in the 1980s was the supposed originality of the men's magazine format'. As Edwards puts it, 'they weren't *called* men's magazines' (1997: 72, author's italics), rather they were called car magazines, hi-fi magazines and sport magazines. Indeed, such magazines, which target predominantly male interests, still exist and also prosper, according to Malkani (1999). In Japan, in addition to such specialist magazines whose target audience is men, there are a vast number of weekly magazines which cover general interests, that is social, political and economic issues, as well as sports and entertainment, equivalent to *Time* magazine, such as *Weekly Asahi*, *Weekly Shinchoo*, and *The Sunday Mainichi*. The readership of these magazines is largely, though not exclusively, male, and the average reader is in his early 40s.

Indeed, in Japan, an emerging male market does not seem to have received official recognition as a separate category, and magazines for men remain 'unmarked', while women's magazines are 'marked'. *The Japanese Publishing Year Book*, for example, refers to men's magazines in its general commentary, but puts magazines which target male readership, such as *Popeye, Brutus, Penthouse, Playboy Japanese Edition*, and *The Gay*, in the subcategory of 'general reading' under the category of 'literature', while magazines for young men, such as *Men's Club* and *Men's Non-No*, are in the category of 'women and fashion'. *An Advertiser's Guide to Magazines in Japan*, published by The Japan Magazine Advertising Association (hereafter JMAA), is more sophisticated. It uses the category 'men's fashion', as opposed to 'women's fashion & beauty'. However, where there are categories called 'women's general interest' and 'women's weekly', there are no male counterparts. Thus, magazines which are described as 'an entertainment weekly for men' or whose 'Readers are young urban males' (JMAA, 1998: 13) are all included in the 'general weekly' category.

Thus, magazines targeting women are defined by the gender of their readership, while their counterparts are categorized according to their contents. As Black and Coward (1990: 132) put it, 'The discursive formation which allows men to represent themselves as non-gendered and to define women constantly according to their sexual status is a discursive formation with very definite effects'. Such a discursive formation seems to be the absence of a category of 'men's magazines', and then subcategories within it.

The 'non-gendered' classification of what are really men's magazines is curious, given that the magazines are strongly gendered. Firstly, the target audience of magazines set by their publishers are mostly defined, at least in part, by gender, which more or less reflects actual readership. Inoue argues (2001: 122) that the gender segmentation of magazines is growing stronger. She argues that readers as young as junior high school students, aged between twelve and fifteen, read separate sets of magazines according to their gender. This tendency continues into adulthood. Thus, men and women read different sets of magazines and, although these sets are not mutually exclusive, there is not much overlap between the two. This finding could be used for the review of the category of 'general readership'.

I would argue that the contrast is less between 'general' magazines, which specifically target men, and women's magazines, than it is among various magazines targeting different segments of the male population. In many ways, Japanese magazines for young men have more in common with their female counterparts than with magazines for older men, an argument this chapter will seek to highlight. The focus of this chapter is on Japanese magazines, such as *Popeye, Men's Club*, and *Men's Non-No*, which are intended for young men in their late teens and early twenties.

The contemporary mass market for magazines in Japan

The popularity of men's magazines is part of what Kiyota (1987: 136) describes as 'the era of frivolity'. The matters these magazines deal with are inconsequential, although they are taken seriously, surprisingly so at times. The background to the comment by Kiyota is the success of magazines over books. Since the beginning of the 1980s, the turnover from magazines has constantly exceeded that from books and the gap has grown steadily. Between 1980 and 1992, over 2300 new magazines were launched or re-launched and nearly 1400 magazines were discontinued. That is equivalent to an average of 181 new magazines and 108 discontinued magazines per year. Parallel to this, as pointed out by Kiyota (1987: 136), has been the growing popularity of pocket-sized books, paperbacks, and comic strips. Magazines, comics and paperbacks together make up 87 per cent of the Japanese publishing industry in terms of the number of units, and nearly one third of the value of the $30 billion market (Katsura *et al.*, 1997: 64).

As I have argued elsewhere, the success of magazines over books is due not only to popular demand but also to the strategy of publishing companies and their advertisers (Tanaka 1998). As Japan grew as a consumer society, advertisers regarded magazines as an effective medium, as the target audience was defined relatively narrowly. According to Katsura *et al.* (1997: 68), in 1996 total magazine advertising revenue exceeded $4 billion for the first time. Cosmetics and toiletries, together with fashion and accessories, made up nearly 30 per cent of that. They note (1997: 69) that 45.9 per cent, nearly half, of fashion and accessories advertising expenditure is spent on material in magazines. The increased content of advertising in magazines was the result of severe competition among magazines. The more visually attractive the magazines became, the more production costs grew. The so-called visual magazines depended for one third of their revenue on advertising. Magazines and advertising in today's Japan are described as being 'in the same boat' (Kenkyuushuudan, 1985: 189).

A brief historical background to the contemporary magazines for young men in Japan has to start with the launch of *An.An* by Heibon Shuppan, now called Magazine House, in 1970. Although it is a women's magazine, it set various trends relevant to the men's magazines discussed here. Now a weekly magazine, *An.An*'s has a target readership of women in their early twenties and a circulation of 580,000 (JMAA, 1998: 97). *An.An* was a new women's magazine, targeting the first generation of baby-boomers. The format was large and the visual aspect was important; *An.An* was truly a magazine to be 'looked at', rather than 'read'. It was a major advertising medium and it introduced 'tie-up' features, which looked like editorials but were paid for by advertisers. The focus was on consumerism, hedonism, and practical matters. Lastly, it had a foreign-sounding title. Thus, *An.An* epitomized all the points which Kawai (1987: 155) lists as features common to today's popular magazines in Japan. It is noteworthy that these features are also shared by the Japanese magazines for young men discussed here, though not by magazines for older men, such as *Playboy Japanese Edition*.

An.An was followed by other magazines for young women, such as *Non-No* (1971), *JJ* (1975), and *More* (1977). *Non-No* is published by Shuuei-sha twice a month. In terms of its readership, '20 per cent are less than 17 years old, 50 per cent between 18 and 20, and 30 per cent are over 21' (JMAA, 1998: 99). *JJ* is a monthly publication by Kobun-sha, and is 'geared to female college students and office workers in metropolitan areas' (JMAA, 1998: 26). *More* is published by Shuuei-sha, and more than 90 per cent of its readership are in their 20s. (JMAA, 1998: 99). These magazines have all survived to date, and their circulation is over 860,000, 700,000, and 720,000, respectively, with *Non-No* being 'the number one selling women's fashion magazine in Japan' (JMAA, 1988: 99).

The success of *An.An* was followed not only by women's magazines brought out by other publishers but also by other magazines targeting different segments of the population by *An.An*'s publisher, Heibon Shuppan, which launched a male counterpart to *An.An* called *Popeye* in 1976, followed by *Croissant*, for women who are slightly older than *An.An*'s readership, in 1977, and then *Olive* for girls at high school in 1982.

Heibon Shuppan/Magazine House could be described as a trend-setter in the Japanese publishing industry for decades. *An.An* is still regarded as an influential magazine today (JMAA, 1998: 97). *Popeye* is said to have heralded the beginning of the subculture known as 'the city boy' (Okabe *et al.*, 1997: 183, etc.) whilst *Croissant* now targets married, albeit more independent, women and is a 'new-family' magazine, which has been claimed to be responsible for what is known as 'the *Croissant* syndrome' (Matsubara, 1988), 'an ironic description of the fate of those who had waited too long to get married whilst pursuing their independence and thus missed the boat' (Ochiai, 1994: 116). These magazines can be claimed to be responsible for having given rise to a subculture named after them, which is discussed below.

Given the importance of advertising revenue to the publishers, it is not at all surprising that the success of women's magazines with heavy advertising content[1] was followed by the launch of similar magazines for men. The catch-phrase for *Popeye* was 'a new magazine to reconsider men's city life', giving rise to phrases such as 'the city boy' and 'the city magazine'. It is published twice a month, and its circulation is 310,000. It has been claimed that 'for more than a generation [*Popeye*] has guided young Japanese men through their college years, featuring stories on fashion, fun and girls' (JMAA, 1998: 38).

Just as *An.An* was followed by other magazines for young women, *Popeye* was followed by other men's magazines by different publishers, such as *DonDon* in 1977 and *Hot-Dog Press* in 1979. *The Publishing Year Book* 1983 even called 1983 'the year of men's magazines', saying that both *Popeye* and *Hot-Dog Press* were doing well. *DonDon* has since been discontinued, but *Hot-Dog Press* has survived with a circulation of 360,000. Published twice a month by Kodan-sha, it 'offers advice to young male readers on various aspects of daily life' (JMAA, 1998: 36). It is worth noting here that the role of 'guiding' and 'advising' is of utmost importance to these magazines—a theme that will be developed shortly.

Magazine House could be said to have set yet another trend when it launched *Brutus* in 1980, as it was regarded as the first 'lifestyle' magazine for men. The 1980s were noted for advertising moving from product-based advertisements to 'lifestyle' ones in Britain as well (Chapman, 1996: 229). The catch-phrase of *Brutus* was 'the lifestyle magazine for men who live in the new era', and it did well, particularly in urban areas (*The Publishing Year Book* 1981). It is published twice a month and its circulation is 130,000. According to Saito, the editor-in-chief of *Brutus*, whilst *Popeye* catered for college students in the cities, his magazine was for men who work in the cities, and that his magazines was about 'happy consumption' (1998). Thus, it could be said that 'lifestyle' magazines were a variation on 'city magazines', and that lifestyle was defined by consumption.

Men's magazines were the focus of attention in the Japanese publishing industry in 1987 again, when 'men's fashion magazines' were launched (*The Publishing Year Book* 1987). In May 1987, Shuei-sha, which had already followed Magazine House by bringing out *Non-No* after *An.An*, both for young women, brought out a monthly magazine called *Men's Non-No*, targeting college students and young adults in their 20s. The first edition sold out within a few days of the launch. Later in the same year in October, Koobun-sha, the publisher of *JJ*, brought out *JJ Boys*. In the following year, *Men's An.An* was published by Magazine House. While *JJ Boys* and *Men's An.An* are published irregularly, *Men's Non-No* is published monthly, with a circulation of 400,000. It is claimed that, like its sister publication *Non-No*, *Men's Non-No* is 'the number one selling fashion magazine for men in Japan' (JMAA, 1998: 96). As the titles suggest, these magazines were all male versions of popular women's magazines. Many of the Japanese men's magazines discussed here were brought out as male versions of the existing, successful female magazines. *Men's Club*, also described as a men's fashion magazine, was launched in 1954 by Fujingaho-sha. First called *Otoko no Fukushoku (Men's Fashion)*, it was originally brought out as a special issue of *Fujin Gahoo (Women's Gazette)*. It was an early magazine for men, which was brought out as a male counterpart to an existing and successful women's magazine. It is claimed to be 'a veritable textbook of fashion' (JMAA, 1998: 96). Published monthly, its readership is in the 18–25 years range, and its circulation is over 172,000.

This format has been tried and failed in the UK, according to Chapman (1996: 231). *Cosmopolitan* launched a sister (sic) publication *Cosmo Man* in 1984, but the venture was deemed unsuccessful. Chapman (1988: 231) sees the failure of *Cosmo Man* as instructive. The premise behind its launch was that 25 per cent of its 360,000 monthly circulation was male. Chapman talks of a 'metamorphosis' in the first issues of *Cosmo Man*. The original idea had been to cater for the audience who had already been reading *Cosmopolitan*, and who were meant to be 'emotionally literate and fluent' and 'devoted fathers and lovers'. However, *Cosmo Man* quickly changed its orientation, and became focused on yuppie males, preoccupied with status. Chapman concludes, 'the nurturant tadpole had become a narcissistic toad' (1988: 232). She also points out, suggestively, that the failure of *Cosmo Man* came only a couple of years earlier than the launch of *Arena*, the success of which, she argues, was 'predicated on a synthesis of the *Playboy* ensemble'.

The circulation of these Japanese magazines for young people varies from 130,000 for *Brutus* to *Non-No*'s 860,000, but it could be argued that their influence is even wider than such figures suggest, as contemporary magazines have been closely associated with subcultural lifestyles. 'Subculture groups' are described by Bestor (1989: 15) as being distinguished by their tastes in clothing, music, pastimes, 'hangouts', and demeanour. I have argued elsewhere (Tanaka, 1998) that there are subcultures directly associated with women's magazines, such as 'the *An-Non* tribe' (*An.An* and *Non-No*), 'the *JJ* girl', 'the *Hanako* tribe', and 'the *Olive* girl'. In a similar vein, there are subculture groups inspired by young men's magazines, such as the '*Popeye* boy' and the '*Non-No* boy'. Moreover, there are subcultures indirectly associated with young people's magazines, such as 'the city boys' mentioned above. 'The city boy' and 'the *Popeye* boy' have been used interchangeably. Akurosu Editorial Room (1995: 184) further points out that the *JJ* girl and the *Popeye* boy are the topic of the 1981 novel by Yasuo Tanaka *Somewhat Crystal*. This novel in turn gave rise to the term 'the *Crystal* tribe'.

Having described the history and terrain of the lifestyle magazine market in Japan, I shall now go on to describe the defining characteristics of contemporary Japanese men's lifestyle magazines.

Contemporary men's magazines

Edwards (1997: 75–6) lists five characteristics of British men's magazines, which are also applicable to Japanese men's magazines. Firstly, they are relatively expensive, ranging from about $4 for magazines published twice a month to $6 for monthly magazines. The second characteristic is 'the overt legitimization of consumption itself', related to the large number of advertising features. Thirdly, all these men's magazines have an implied dependence on an urban environment, though it could be said that in the case of their Japanese counterparts it is overtly claimed. A fourth point, which Edwards considers to be the key issue, concerns 'aspirationalism'. This can be defined as upward social mobility through consumption patterns, a point which I have made about Japanese women's magazines elsewhere (Tanaka, 1998), and which I would argue is valid for their male equivalents.

While the first four points are all true about Japanese counterparts, it is less certain whether Edwards' fifth point also applies to Japanese men's magazines. Edwards asserts that British magazines exhibit a strong heterosexuality, 'often with a near-defensive vengeance'. He suspects that this is due to 'the felt necessity of off-setting the near-pornographic and homoerotic nature of much of the imagery used to advertise products or illustrate features on fashion and style'. According to Beynon (2002: 118), this applies to the 'new lad', but not the 'new man', whose sexuality is more 'ambivalent'.

In the case of the Japanese magazines for young men discussed here, hetero-sexuality is also apparent, but essentially through the repeated proposition of the need to better oneself in order to keep one's girlfriend. It could be argued that there is some ambivalence about sexuality, in that the models in Japanese magazines for young men look rather feminine, and certainly far from macho. Indeed, one could sometimes mistake them for images in certain gay magazines. Subcultures known as 'kamao'(Mr. Gay) and 'femio' (Mr. Feminine), which emerged late in 1993, involve young men whose build and choice of outfit are feminine. And yet, according to Okabe *et al.* (1997: 185) these men are not homosexual but simply want to look feminine. This difference may reflect a lack in Japan of the 'rise of a visible and partially more socially acceptable gay mas-culinity' attributed to Britain (Edwards, 1997: 73). Or, perhaps, there might be less stigma attached to men looking feminine in Japan.

Japanese magazines for young men carry features on how to clip eyebrows, with detailed illustrations, like their counterparts for women. Discussing a special feature in the first edition of *Men's Non-No* titled 'We want to wear pink!', Ueno (1987: 23) talks of fashion becoming unisex. She says that women had already been consuming men's fashion and that men were belatedly start-ing to wear things which had been regarded as feminine. Her conclusion is that, for the young, the distinction between feminine and masculine is a constraint that they could do without. In contrast, Field (2000) reports on the use of pastel colour in men's fashion in Britain. His argument is that wearing pastel colours such as 'powder-pink, baby-blue, . . . [and] lemon-yellow' is the privilege of men whose masculinity and virility are not in question, his examples being David Beckham and Brad Pitt. However, if one is otherwise inclined, one sticks to tra-ditional macho looks, such as 'black leather, denim and rottweiler collars as necklaces'. The fear of being regarded as homosexual seems ever-present in the UK, but is less felt in Japan.

Furthermore, the timing of the launch of young men's 'fashion' magazines such as *Men's Non-No* and *JJ* Boys coincided with the beginning of the increased consumption of cosmetics and grooming products by men in Japan. Okabe *et al.* (1997: 184) describe 1987 as the year when men's cosmetics were popular, while 1988 was noted for the increase in men undergoing plastic surgery for cosmetic purposes. This, apparently, was not a short phase which Japan went through. Ten years on, the 21 December 1998 edition of *Nikkei Weekly* reported rising sales of grooming products to male consumers, as well as a surge of demand for beauty salons by men, despite the continuing decline of the Japanese economy. The booming of the cosmetics industry has also been reported in the UK around the same time (Cook, 1999, Hughes, 1999, and Snoddy, 2001) However, this does not necessarily mark a change in the attitude of British men. Cook reports a suggestion by a Clinique's PR manager that much of the products are bought by women.

Noting that *Popeye* did not do as well as expected initially, despite Magazine House's large investment in its advertising campaign, *The Publishing Year Book 1977* hinted that this might have been because *Popeye* did not contain photographs of nude women. With hindsight, however, one could argue that this was the beginning of magazines which young men did not have to hide from their girlfriends. The sales figures rose over time, and by 1983, *Popeye* had become successful and influential, being appreciated by young men for providing a 'date manual', a regular feature giving detailed information and advice on where to take a girl on a date. Okabe *et al.* (1997: 183) describe *Popeye* as a magazine for men 'who do not want to get hurt'. This was a new kind of magazine, which helped men to learn how to keep their girlfriends happy, and in turn keep themselves happy.

Popeye's formula of a publication of which women could approve was gradually taken up by competitors, such as *Men's Non-No* (1986) and *JJ Boys* (1987). Inoue and Ebara (1995: 190) argue that Japanese women are generally more likely to read men's magazines than the other way round and it is probable that the publishers of such men's magazine also target young women, as in the case of the earlier *Popeye*. Saito (1998) also claims that over 40 per cent of the readership of his magazine were women. Women are important purchasers of men's fashion, while the reverse is not the case in either the UK or Japan.

The overt success of Japanese magazines for young men stands in contrast with the more covert consumption of British men's magazines. While titles such as *FHM* and *loaded* boast a circulation of 580,738 and 309,041 respectively (Audit Bureau of Circulation figures 2002), their 'visibility' is open to question (Sweet, 1997). Their readers do not generally look at them on public transport or let them be seen by their girlfriends. One of my informants, explaining that he would not have such a magazine lying around when his girlfriend came to visit, put it this way, 'It's all right with guys, but not with my girlfriend'. These magazines, reflecting a 'babes 'n' booze' ethos, are not to be paraded on coffee tables. This may explain the sentiment demonstrated by one of my (male) students who was alarmed to see copies of those British men's magazines on the floor of my office and, having heard my explanation that they were for research purposes, offered to go and buy them himself for me if I ever needed to get any in future. It has also been suggested (Thorpe, 1997) that 'lifestyle' magazines, such as *loaded*, were replacing 'soft-porn' magazines, such as *Mayfair*, *Penthouse*, and *Men Only*.

The background to the launch of *Popeye* was what Ootsuka (1991: 94) describes as the age when boys' dreams had vanished. The high economic growth of Japan had peaked, then came the oil crisis in 1973, followed by high unemployment. Traditional masculinities were losing their appeal, and the father figure his respect. Okabe *et al.* (1997: 183) argues that 'the city boy' epitomised by *Popeye* was a reaction to the student movement in the mid 60s to early 70s and anti-establishment 'punk' movement. They go on to claim that young men who felt out of tune with those movements became 'city boys' who were 'devoid of any ideology, and wanted to be cheerful and have fun in the company of girls'.

This change in the 1980s in terms of the assessment of traditional mas-culinities as well as men's magazines has also been noted in Inoue and Ebara (1995: 210). They point out that *Playboy Japanese Edition*, which had once been extremely successful, was no longer so popular. *Penthouse*, launched by Kodan-sha in 1983, was discontinued, although it was later re-launched by another publisher called Bunka-sha. *Heibon Punch*, which could be called the original Japanese laddish magazine, was launched in 1964. It covered sex, cars, fashion, and was noted for carrying nude photos of women in colour for the first time (Shiozawa, 1998: 180) but it was discontinued in 1986. In contrast, new magazines, which had more in common with their female equivalents, were flourishing. Thus, in Japan, the city boy's magazine was replacing the lad's magazine.

Morohashi (1998: 215) claims that some Japanese men's magazines have become 'feminized', as the market for them has altered, a change also noted by Inoue and Ebara (1995: 210). Inoue *et al.* (1989) note that in magazines such as *Men's Non-No* and *JJ Boys*, about 50 per cent of the content concerned fashion, and that the overall content analysis demonstrated that these young men's maga-zines were extremely similar to their female counterparts, namely *Non-No* and *JJ*. Thus, the content of these men's magazines has more in common with their female equivalents than with magazines for older men, such as *Playboy Japanese Edition* and *Penthouse*. Firstly, the young men's magazines have a higher proportion of advertising content. According to Morohashi (1998: 215), the 10 June 1995 edition of *Popeye* carried more than 50 per cent of advertis-ing content, including so-called 'tie-up' features, while that of the 6 June 1995 edition of *Playboy Japanese Edition* was just over 13 per cent. Furthermore, many young men's magazines are concerned with fashion and beauty. Together with their female counterparts, they have been described as 'catalogue' and 'manual' magazines (Okabe *et al.* 1996) full of colour photographs of fashion and beauty items, with detailed information on where to buy them and how to use them.

Another way in which Japanese magazines for young men differ from other magazines targeting male readership is that they contain little on politics and economics. According to Inoue (2001: 134), there are two distinctive interest areas among traditional Japanese men's magazines targeting older men, such as *Playboy Japanese Edition*: sex on the one hand, and politics and the economy on the other. The magazines which are the focus of this chapter carry no women's nude pictures and little on political or economic concerns, in common with Japanese magazines for young women. The attitude towards women por-trayed in the Japanese magazines for young men, Morohashi (1998: 216) argues, is not all that different from that of 'the old man' in that women are regarded as the object of desire. However, the difference lies in the fact that the young men who are the assumed audience are passive. He goes on to say that the readers of these magazines are waiting to be instructed as to exactly what to do in their relationships with women. This theme will be taken up again in the concluding sections of the chapter.

Another marked difference between Japanese magazines for young men and their British counterparts is Japanese seriousness. The contrast is particularly stark with 'lad's' magazines such as *loaded*. As one founder of the magazine recalls:

> I remember Tim [another founder] saying that given a choice *loaded* would rather interview George Best than Gary Lineker. That was the really important thing about the magazines, way before the whole Lad thing happened. It was about having a laugh—about self-depreciation. I mean there I was, nervous as fuck, pissed out of my brains and about to interview Bruce Willis. You could never get pissed before interviewing Bruce Willis for *The Times*. (Southwell 1998: 73–4)

Neither could you do such a thing writing for Japanese magazines for young men, presumably. The issues dealt with by Japanese magazines could be described as inconsequential, in that they are more likely to do with fashion or how one's eyebrows should be clipped. Indeed, they could well be described as frivolous and trivial. There is no hint of self-depreciation, however, in the manner in which such issues are treated. Indeed, the whole issue of the role of humour in Japanese popular magazines remains to be researched.

Men's magazines, consumption, and sexual politics

Consumption by men has been described in terms of the feminization of men. Traditionally, production has been associated with masculinity and consumption with femininity. As men have become consumers, and as women have become producers, such traditional boundaries have become blurred. It could be argued that magazines simply reflect such changes in society, involving a reassessment of masculinity. Chapman (1988: 234) quotes Ehrenreich as saying:

> What had been understood as masculinity, with its implications of hardness and emotional distance, was at odds with the more feminine traits appropriate to a consumer orientated society; traits such as self indulgence, emotional liability and a soft receptivity to whatever is new and exciting. (Ehrenreich 1983)

Consumption of fashion has been regarded as particularly feminine, but this is changing, as shown in popular men's magazines. Among British men's magazines, for example, the proportion of fashion advertising is anything between 40 per cent and 70 per cent. Edwards argues that fashion is no longer simply feminine in terms of consumption and masculine in terms of production, 'as more men now consume it and more women produce it or directly influence it as designers or retailers' (1997: 118). Chapman goes on to add other female traits involved in the consumption of fashion:

Moreover, in order to sell products, advertising had to sell men, to capture them between the covers of designer magazines. And the process of doing that rendered them the recipient of the gaze, passive and therefore female. (p.229)

This change of men into objects to be seen, rather than people who watch women, has a number of implications. Edwards (1997: 73) claims:

. . . most significantly of all I think, it has become more socially acceptable for men to be consumers *per se* and, more importantly, to be consumers of their own masculinity or, in short, to look at themselves and other men as objects of desire to be bought and sold or imitated and copied. At least some male narcissism is now socially approved.

As has been pointed out by Beynon (2002: 104), both Mort (1996) and Edwards (1997) see these changes as the result of commercial pressures, rather than sexual politics:

Men's style magazines have very little to do with sexual politics and a lot more to do with new markets for the constant reconstruction of masculinity through consumption: buy this to be that; own a double-breasted suit, portable CD player or BMW and be a man! (Edwards 1997: 82)

Things may be slightly different in Japan. Yamazaki (1995: 53) argues that around 1980, when he was involved with the editorial of *Popeye* launched in 1976, it was narcissistic and asexual. It later became more heterosexually-oriented, however, guiding young boys in their relationships with girls. His argument is that *Popeye* was originally about boys' cultures of consumption. It started off notably devoid of sex, and Yamazaki (1995: 53) ponders that perhaps it was a kind of experiment to see whether boys could be consumers in their own right, independent of their relationship with girls. He goes on to comment that the only time that girls appeared was when *Popeye* had an annual feature entitled 'Thank you Olive: Give us these for Christmas', providing some ideas to girls (Olive being a partner to Popeye in the eponymous American comic story) as to what they should get for their boyfriend. He adds that it now seems incredible that it should have been boys making such demands on girls. Yamazaki (1995: 54) notes that the change came around 1983, when the population of boys aged 18 came to exceed that of girls, heralding the phenomenon of the shortage of girls. Noting that 40 per cent of the readership of *Popeye* in its early stage was girls, for whom *Popeye*'s publisher intended to cater by launching *Olive* in 1982, he concludes that boys' consumption had never been independent of girls' after all.

Yamazaki (1995: 55) argues that the success of *Men's Non-No*, which followed *Popeye*, firmly established what it had started, that is young men consuming in ways that made them objects of desire for young women. *Men's Non-No* has also been described as 'men's fashion magazines seen through the eyes of women' (*Publishing Year Book* 1986).

Inoue and Ebara (1995: 210) and Morohashi (1998: 215) mention the tendency to put an emphasis on men 'being seen' in Japanese men's magazines.

However, the reason seems to have to do less with narcissism than with appeal to other people, particularly women. Kodan-sha launched *FRaU* to target young women in 1991, and followed up with *FRaU Homme*, in 1998. The catch-phrase for the latter was 'Make men beautiful! Then women will be beautiful. Then the relationship will improve!' Japanese magazines for young men have regular features with titles such as: 'This month's date spot', 'Tell me what kind of flowers girls would like', 'Tell me what kind of stationery is currently popular with high-school girls'.

These changes might best be described as meeting the assumed needs of men to shape themselves as acceptable and desirable to women. The popularity of these publications represent a response to the changing relations between men and women. As women have become better informed and more choosy, aided by magazines for young women, men have needed their own prop in order to keep up.

In Japan, the late 1980s have been noted for the advent of a culture in which women judge and choose men, rather than the other way round (Okabe *et al.*, 1997: 186). At around the same time, a set of desirable criteria for a 'Prince Charming' was elaborated, known as 'three highs'. This meant a high income, defined as an annual income of $100,000 or over, a high level of education, and a height over 180cm. Increasingly demanding, young women have added the 'three goods' as further hurdles: namely, good looks, good character, and good breeding. Yonekawa (1996: 153) notes that a common characteristic of phrases which emerged in the 1980s to describe young men, such as 'the city boy', 'the *Popeye* boy', and 'the *Non-No* boy', is that they express women's assessment of men. Commonly cited phrases include 'Mr. Chauffeur', 'Mr. Meal', and 'Mr. Gift', that is men who provide goods or services to women by driving them around, taking them out to restaurants, and showering them with gifts. These expressions all have a derogatory tone.

It could be argued that sexual politics have changed in Japan, not so much because of feminism, but more as a consequence of demographic shifts. Towards the end of the 1980s, the shortage of marriageable women was becoming a social problem. According to the National Census conducted in 1985, there were 7.5 million unmarried men aged 20–34, while the figure for women was 4.9 million. In the 30–34 age group, the ratio of unmarried men to unmarried women is almost two to one (Inoue and Ebara, 1995: 15). The importation of foreign brides was no more than a palliative.

The change also reflected women's deliberate choice. Women no longer felt that they had to marry. The various demands which women made on Mr. Right were not just a bluff. A collection of essays by Shiho Tanimura entitled *The I-May-Not-Get-Married Syndrome* was published in 1990, and it became a best-seller. The trend was also reflected in TV dramas. In 1991, two popular series called *25-Years-Old: Marriage* and *The 101st Proposal* both depicted men who wanted to get married and were trying to win over unwilling women. As Kashima (1989: 104) puts it, 'Men have gone into the era of being chosen'.

In her exploration of the background to falling birth rates in Japan, which made headlines when it hit 1.46 per woman in 1993, Jolivet (1997: 141) discusses the *Hanako* syndrome, so named after a magazine for young women in their twenties in the Tokyo metropolitan area. The women who are targeted by the magazine have a high disposable income, as they have a job and yet live with their parents, paying little, if any, board. Being in a comfortable situation, their material expectations from a future partner are high, and there are few young men who satisfy various criteria that women have set. She quotes an article in the *Asahi* newspaper (17 June 1992), 'Women *could* marry but they don't: men *would like* to marry but they can't' (Jolivet, 1997: 146).

Around the same time, women were starting to take the initiative in sexual matters. *An.An* picked up this trend quickly and made its own contribution by having a regular annual feature, from 1986, entitled '*Men we want to go to bed with: The readers' choice*'. This change then spread to television drama. A successful TV series in 1991, called *Tokyo Love Story*, became noted for the heroine saying to her partner, 'Let's have sex'. This was regarded epoch-making, for it had not been seen as acceptable for women to initiate sexual relations. Representations of men talking about desirable lovers among themselves predated this considerably in the world's first novel, the eleventh century *The Tale of Genji*, by the female author, Murasaki Shikibu.

How masculine is the language of Japanese magazines for young men?

As the content of magazines for young men has more in common with that of their female equivalents, the language of young men's magazines is also not dissimilar to that of young women's magazines. It has some characteristic features of traditional male speech, while displaying others which have usually been regarded as feminine.

The Japanese language is noted for distinctive differences between male and female speech (Shibamoto, 1985). At the lexical level, these would include personal pronouns and sentence-final particles, where men and women use different sets of them. A particular sentence-final particle, for example, may sound distinctively feminine or masculine. Moreover, women are said to use Sino-Japanese forms less frequently, and thus use fewer Chinese characters when writing (Shibatani, 1990: 374).

Reynolds-Akiba (1989) discusses differences between male and female speech, based on data drawn from a few selected Japanese magazines, namely *Non-No*, *Cosmopolitan*, and *Housewife's Friend* for women, and of *Playboy Japanese Edition* for men. She concludes that traditional male and female speech differences persist in these magazines. More specifically, the traditional distinction between male and female speech is indicated by the fact that men's magazines use more Chinese characters [*kanji*] than women's magazines; 53 per cent as opposed to 40 per cent. My impression is that this does not apply to young men's magazines, although I have not attempted a statistical count. They appear to use Chinese characters less, perhaps in quantities similar to those in *Non-No*. Further research on this point is awaited.

Another criterion used by Reynolds-Akiba is how much magazines use *katakana*, syllabic script mainly employed for Western loan words. Her conclusion is that men's magazines use less *katakana* than those for women, 20 per cent versus 30 per cent. While I would not dispute Reynolds-Akiba's findings about the particular magazines which she surveyed, the language used in magazines for young men, as discussed in this chapter, actually has more in common with that of *Non-No*, which is intended for young women. Magazines for young men, for instance, are full of fashion and beauty features, two subjects which are associated with *katakana* words due to Western influence. In the examples that follow, Western loan words written in *katakana* are underlined:

<u>Return</u> to <u>basic</u>	Return to basics
Haru no <u>East</u> <u>boy</u> <u>men</u>	East boy men in spring
Itsuka mita eiga no <u>one</u> <u>scene</u> no yoona	Like a scene from a film I once saw
<u>Image</u> ni nokoru, ano <u>scene</u> to ano fuku	The images remain, that scene and those clothes
Boku-tachi no <u>real</u> <u>clothes</u> wa	Real clothes for us
Itsumo <u>American</u> <u>casual</u> datta	have always been American casual
	(*Men's Non-No*, April 1997)

The third point Reynolds-Akiba raises has to do with the way in which *katakana* is used. She argues that while over 70 per cent of *katakana* in the women's magazines concerns fashion terms, generally of a descriptive nature, *Playboy Japanese Edition* is more likely to employ *katakana* for what she calls 'essay-like commentary', which might be glossed as 'pontificating'. Her implication is that women's magazines give a detailed description of fashion items, whereas men's magazines attempt something more critical and creative. Given that the men's magazines discussed here, such as *Popeye* and *Brutus*, have been described as 'manuals' and 'catalogues', they are more likely to contain descriptive features on fashion than 'essay-like commentary'.

Another major difference between male and female speech, according to Reynolds-Akiba, concerns how a sentence ends. A 'perfect' sentence in Japanese should end with a predicate, verb or adjective in the 'final' form. Any other sentence is 'imperfect'. She argues that whereas women's magazines use from 63 per cent to 71 per cent of imperfect sentences, *Playboy Japanese Edition* has only 38 per cent such sentences. She goes on to show that over 90 per cent of imperfect sentences found in *Playboy Japanese Edition* end with a noun, and the rest end with a verb in the te-form, which is not a final form. *Playboy Japanese Edition* does not contain a single imperfect sentence other than these two types. In contrast, women's magazines have ending such as:

Simple and beautiful with a black scarf [*Kuro no <u>scarf</u> de sukkiri utsukushiku*]. (adjective in non-final form)
A little like a lycéenne [*Chotto <u>lyceenne</u> fuuni*]. (adverbial phrase)

Reynolds-Akiba's observation that *Playboy Japanese Edition* strikes a more masculine tone, by using few imperfect sentences and of a particular type, does not extend to Japanese magazines for younger men. Many imperfect sentences are found, as can be seen in the following:

> A delicate knit with nylon 100% [*Nylon 100% no delicate-na knit*]. (April 1997, *Men's Non-No*) (noun-ending)
> Don't go easy on the belt. [*Belt ni mo ki wo nukanaide*]. (April 1997 *Men's Non-No*) (te-form ending)

In magazines for young men, there are other imperfect endings, of the kind that Reynolds-Akiba has not found in *Playboy Japanese Edition*:

> As this item is see-through, [wear] a T-shirt inside [*Sukeru node in ni T-shirt wo*]. (*Men's Non-No*, April 1997)
> A shirt with vivid colours in a slim and formal shape [can be] worn with the bottom tucked in (to trousers) [*Vivid-na iro to hosomi no kacchirishita tsukuri wa, tack in-shite kite mo*]. (*Men's Non-No*, April 1997)

Reynolds-Akiba refers to the use of *tai*-form (would like to) as a characteristic of *Non-No*. She argues that there are only a small number of examples found not only in *Playboy Japanese Edition* but also in *Cosmopolitan* and *Housewife's Friend*. The *tai*-form is frequently found in other magazines for young women, as I have shown elsewhere (Tanaka, 1998), as well as in magazines for young men:

> If there is something you like, it is a good idea to get it straight away [*Kiniitta mono ga areba sugu teniire-tai*]. (*Men's Club,* May 1997)
> It is a good idea to use your favourite colour as an accent [*Kiniitta iro wo isshoku accent ni shi-tai*]. (*Men's Club*, May 1997)

Reynolds-Akiba singles out *Non-No* for using 'cutish' language. She points out that there is a tendency to use 'childish' language, as in *daisuki tomato* (my favourite tomato), which should read *daisuki-na tomato*. This habit of dropping the endings of adjectives seems to be shared by young men's magazines, as in:

> Go to Rocky for extremely sweet chocolate [*Mecha ama (i) choco wa koko Rocky e*] (*Men's Club*, May 1997)

Moreover, when it comes to 'cute' objects, which have been regarded as being in the domain of young women (Kinsalla, 1995), young men seem to value them as much:

> Both the colour and the shape are pop and cute [*Iro mo katachi mo pop de cute*]. (*Men's Non-No*, April 1997)

It is worth noting here that, according to Morii (1998), editor of magazines for young mums, the language employed by *Non-No* is called 'Non-No speak', and that it tends to be copied by other women's magazines. Evidently it gets picked up by magazines for young men as well.

Despite this, there are certain areas where young men's magazines are more typically masculine. The first has to do with direct imperatives, which are associated with men's speech in Japanese. These are rarely found in women's magazines, or in any other form of written communication. They are even rare in manuals or recipes, where they would be the norm in English equivalents (Tanaka, 1998). However, imperatives are frequently found in young men's magazines:

> First start with brand goods this spring! [*Haru wa brand kara semero!*] (*Men's Non-No*, April 1997)
>
> To find out what you really want to wear, check these shops! [*Hontooni kitai mono wo mitsukedasu niwa kono shop gun wo check se-yo!*] (*Men's Club*, April 1997)

However, direct imperatives, while still rare, are on the increase in women's magazines, as in:

> Look for your own long-legged trousers! [*Watashi-tachi dake no ashinaga pants wo sagase!*] (*With*, November 1998)

The second point concerns sentence-final particles. Among sentence-final particles in Japanese, *zo* is regarded as a male particle, and it is often encountered in young men's magazines:

> There is no good reason for missing this [*Kore wo nogasu te wa nai-zo*]. (*Popeye*, 25 April, 1997)

That said, this is precisely the area in which women's language has been observed to be moving towards that of men. Young women have increasingly been using what has been traditionally regarded as male sentence-final endings, including *zo*. This phenomenon can be seen in young women's magazines:

> You would lose out if you don't know it [*Shiranai to sonsuru-zo*]. (*Non-No*, June 1998)

Taken in conjunction with the increasing use of imperatives by women, this suggests that there may be a convergence between male and female speech in magazines for young people. The use of imperatives in both male and female magazines contribute to what might be termed their prescriptive character.

A prescriptive approach

I have demonstrated elsewhere that a strong unifying theme that runs through Japanese women's magazines is the didactic approach that they adopt towards their readers (Tanaka 1998). They share a tone which can be described as blunt and hectoring, and which thus contrasts with the alleged Japanese concern with politeness (Lakoff 1973). Like their female equivalents, Japanese magazines for young men are similarly characterized by their prescriptive approach. The use of direct imperatives, discussed above, is one example. Japanese magazines for young men are full of expressions such as 'You mustn't miss it!', 'This is absolutely essential', 'You should buy it now'. However, given the popularity of such magazines, this tone is presumably not seen as patronising or condescending.

I have argued elsewhere that the language of Japanese magazines for young women resonates with that of the classroom (Tanaka 1998), and this feature is also common in Japanese magazines for young men:

> The styling of eyebrows. The great equation. (*Men's Non-No*, April 1997)
> It is a correct answer to buy leather goods at traditional old establishments. (*Men's Club*, May 1997)

One of my informants confirmed my claim about a prescriptive approach in Japanese magazines for young men. She spent nine months from the autumn of 1997 living in Tokyo, doing various odd jobs, including a stint at the editorial of *DonDon* targeting young male college students. One of her assignments was to help an editor write a feature on how to take out a Western woman on a date, describing which restaurant to take her to, what to wear, and even what topic of conversation to broach. Her piece, apparently, kept being sent back by the editor with the specific demand that she should make it more prescriptive.

The didactic tone is also present in the Japanese men's 'lifestyle' magazines for a slightly older generation. When I conducted the interview with the editor-in-chief of *Brutus* (Saito 1998), it was just after the May 1998 edition had been published. There was a special feature entitled 'Textbook on Italian Wine', and this title was splashed in large letters in the middle of the front cover. Asked if he had considered that his audience might mind this 'classroom talk', he responded by saying, 'I know exactly what you're getting at, and I agree with you entirely. I think myself that the best advice would be to say that the most important thing is that you enjoy your wine, and that you should have whatever you fancy'. He went on, 'However, my readers would not be happy if we said that. They would like to be told in great detail exactly what to do'. He explained that his audience would not simply try out different wines themselves and see what they liked best or what went best with various dishes. They would like to read up on the subject and 'study' before going to a restaurant and ordering wine. Asked if he thought that his readers generally liked 'studying', he said, 'Oh, yes. Japanese people love studying!'

Magazines work on creating a niche for themselves and maintaining their relation with that segment of the population. To give a lesson on Italian wine is one thing, as wine is relatively new to Japan; that however would not be enough to keep the publication going. Thus, they create a myth that the world is full of things that readers do not understand and therefore need the magazine to assist them with. Japanese magazines for young men give much advice on fashion matters. *Popeye* (April 1997) ran a special feature entitled, 'Vintage jeans: Do you really think you know it all? Be an expert!' The magazine thereby urges readers to believe that they do not know enough about something they might not have ever imagined they needed to know about, and suggests that there is much more to find out, a task with which it is happy to assist.

British men's magazines share some of these characteristics. Edwards (1997: 83) argues that magazines reinforce the perception that fashion is complex, and that readers thus require guidance:

> ... the didactic or educational as well as entreatment functions of men's style magazines were seen as equally important. For example, explaining the virtues of wool suits over polyester ones was cited as indicative of such didacticism rather than as a ploy for random unmitigated consumption and, as Nick Sullivan, fashion director at *Esquire*, pointed out to me: 'On one level it is about buying but, really, it is to make sure the reader spends rightly or makes the right choices. It's more about *how* to spend it and not waste it' (author's italics).

Holidays abroad are a particularly sensitive topic. Young Japanese women are regarded as generally having more experience than men in this field, and yet expect men to take the initiative when they are on holiday abroad together. This is evident in one of the derogatory terms for young men, *domeokun*, or 'Mr Domestic', meaning a man of little or no experience abroad. Itoo (1996: 43) cites research on student life at Osaka University in 1995 showing that 46.5 per cent of female undergraduates had been abroad, while only 25.3 per cent of their male counterparts had done so. Among the graduates, the figures were 75 per cent and 46.8 per cent. The discrepancy has also given rise to what is known as 'Narita divorces' (Itoo, 1996: 43). Narita is Tokyo's international airport, where a young woman, back from her honeymoon, initiates a divorce on arrival, because her newly-wed husband did not handle the social side of the honeymoon overseas according to her standards.

The magazines are on hand to help. *Men's Club* (May 1997) ran a feature presenting the situation of a male reader going on a trip to Hawaii with his girlfriend. It tells him that his girlfriend is a 'repeater', meaning that she has been to Hawaii on a number of occasions. Thus, the young man is at disadvantage, which he must overcome. The feature goes on to tell him that most flights to Hawaii from Japan arrive early in the morning, and then sets a question, supposedly asked by a reader, 'There arises a problem! Check-in time at hotels are usually 3 o'clock. What shall I do?' The feature offers answers by giving a detailed response, mingled with a constant reminder that he may fail at any stage, such as 'If you are unprepared and end up asking your girlfriend what to do she would be appalled', or 'Doing things like this might put her in a bad mood'. It also offers some reassurance, with comments such as, 'There are lots of places to which women will like to go' and 'When your girlfriend sees it, she will smile'.

Conclusion

Japanese magazines for young men have much in common with their female equivalents, while differing considerably from Japanese magazines for older men. Japanese magazines for young men have a high advertising content, are full of features on fashion and accessories, and show little interest in current affairs. They also share with their female equivalents the role of authority figures, giving lessons to their readers, and mimicking the language of educational institutions.

At the same time, they differ in some significant ways from their British counterparts, for reasons which remain to be determined. In particular, the tone of Japanese magazines for young men is more authoritarian, with a greater tendency to infantilize the readers. Going together with this is a marked lack of self-deprecation, which may be a particularly British (or English) trait. These characteristics are reminiscent of familiar national stereotypes but more research is needed to establish whether they reflect broader cultural features.

Japanese magazines for young men reinforce the perception that there are many areas where readers need guidance, which editors are only too happy to provide. They take a lot of space to tell their male readers what women want, which parallels the notion in Japanese women's magazines that women and men are completely different creatures (Morohashi, 1995: 70, see also Toerien and Durrheim, 2001 for a similar discussion of South Africa's *Men's Health*). The success of both sets of magazines implies that neither young men nor young women really know what they want. Further research is needed to explore the roots of this insecurity, particularly as it would appear to be greater than that of their British counterparts.

Young Japanese men seem to be in need of great help in relationships with women. Jolivet (1997: 165) mentions that schools for bridegrooms-to-be have been opened, complementing the traditional schools for brides-to-be, to counter the difficult situation of bachelors. However, this phenomenon may not be unique to Japan, as the first male finishing school has opened in London (Thompson, 2001). A far larger number of Japanese men respond to their difficulties in relationships with women by buying the magazines discussed here.

There has been a suggestion that gender differences are breaking down both in language and in fashion. This is not at all new. The languages spoken by women and men at school and college have always been less distinctive than at the office, just as many women wear jeans at college but start wearing a skirt again at work. Further research is necessary to establish whether the convergence which can be seen in contemporary magazines will have lasting effects when readers grow older.

Recent convergence seems to be moving from male to female, though not exclusively. According to Okabe *et al.* (1997: 185), the motivation for young men dressing in a manner that can be described as feminine is their envy of women. Women, the magazines seem to suggest, are simply more fun to be with, and it is much nicer to be a woman than a man. Perhaps, they reflect a realization that, although the world is not perfect for women, it is tough to be a man.

Note

1 Katsura *et al.* (1997) cite the figures from a survey in 1996 showing that, in terms of volume, 49 per cent of advertising expenditure was on women's weekly and monthly magazines. Furthermore, the advertising cost per page is higher in women's magazines. The advertising rates per page for *An.An* and *Non-No* are $20,000 and $28,000 respectively, while those for *Weekly Asahi* and *Playboy Japanese Edition* are $16,000 and $18,000 respectively (JMAA 1998).

References

Bestor, T. (1989) 'Lifestyles and popular culture in urban Japan': 1–37 in Powers and Kato, *Handbook of Japanese Popular Culture*. Westport, Connecticut: Greenwood Press.

Black, M. and Coward, R. (1990) 'Linguistics, social and sexual relations: a review of Dale Spender's Man Made Language': 111–133 in Cameron, D. (ed.) *The Feminist Critique of Language*. London: Routledge.

Beynon, J. (2002) *Masculinities and Culture*. Buckingham: Open University Press.

Chapman, R. (1988) 'The great pretender: variations on the New Man theme': 225–248 in Chapman, R. and Rutherford, J. (eds) *Male Order: Unwrapping Masculinity*. London: Lawrence and Wishart.

Cook, E. (1999) 'Who's a pretty boy, then?', *Independent on Sunday*, 4 July.

Edwards, T. (1997) *Men in the Mirror: Men's Fashion, Masculinity and Consumer Society*. London: Cassell.

Field, M. (2000) 'Pretty in Pink', *Independent on Sunday*, 23rd January.

Hughes, J. (1999) 'Milk baths on tap for beauty parlour man', *Independent on Sunday*, 21 November.

Inoue, T. *et al.* (1989) *Josei zasshi wo kaidokusuru: Comparapolitan-Nichi, Bei, Mekishiko hikaku kenkyuu (Deciphering Women's Magazines: Contrastive Studies of Japanese, American and Mexican Magazines)*. Tokyo: Kakiuchi Shuppan.

Inoue, T. and Ebara, Y. (eds) (1995) *Josei no data book dai-2-han: sei, karada kara seijisanka made (Women's Data Book 2nd edition: From Sex and Body to Political Participation)*. Tokyo: Yuuhikaku.

Inoue, T. (2001) 'Gender to Media' (Gender and Media): 118–139 in Suzuki, M. (ed.) *Media literacy no genzai to mirai (The Present and the Future of Media Literacy)*. Tokyo: Sekai Shisoo-sha.

Itoo, K. (1996) *Danseigaku nyuumon (An Introduction to Men's Studies)*. Tokyo: Sakuhin-sha.

Japan Magazine Advertising Association. (1998) *An Advertiser's Guide to Magazines in Japan 1998–1999*. Tokyo: The Japan Magazine Advertising Association.

Jolivet, M. (1997) *Japan: The Childless Society?* Originally published in French in 1993, translated by Glasheen, A. London: Routledge.

Kashima, T. (1989) *Otoko to onna: kawaru rikigaku (Men and Women: Changing Power Politics)*. Tokyo Iwanami Shoten.

Katsura, K. *et al.* (eds) (1997) *21 seiki no masukomi vol. 4: Shuppan: shuppan bunka no hookai wo kuitomerareruka (Mass Communication in the 21st Century vol. 4: Publishing: Is it Possible to Prevent Breakdown of Publishing?)*. Tokyo: Ootsuki Shoten.

Kawai, R. (1987) 'Shuppan: shoseki to zasshi' ('Publishing: books and magazines'): 146–155 in Yamamoto and Fujitake (eds) *Zusetsu Nihon no mass communication* dai-3-han *(Illustrated Japanese Mass Communication* 3rd edition*)*. Tokyo: NHK Books.

Kenkyuushuudan Communication (1990) (eds) *Masukomi no asu wo tou vol. 2: Shuppan (Questioning the Future of Mass Communication vol. 2: Publishing)*. Tokyo: Ootsuki Shoten.

Kinsella, S. (1995) 'Cuties in Japan': in Skov, L. and Moeral, B. (eds) *Women, Media and Consumption in Japan*. Richmond: Curzon Press.

Kiyota, Y. (1987) 'Shuppan: gaikan' ('Publishing: an overview'): 136.145 in Yamamoto and Fujitake, *Zusetsu Nihon no Mass Communication* dai-3-han (*Illustrated Japanese Mass Communication* 3rd edition). Tokyo: NHK Books.

Kondo, M. *et al.* (1988) *88-nen trend ga mietekuru* (*88 Trends*). Tokyo: Koosaidoo.

Lakoff, R. (1973) 'The logic of politeness: or, minding your p's and q's', *Proceedings of the Ninth Regional Meeting of the Chicago Linguistics Society*: 292–305.

Malkani, G. (1999) 'Riding high on a growing appetite for specialist entertainment', *Financial Times*, 13 December.

Matsubara, J. (1988) *Croissant shookoogun* (*The Croissant Syndrome*). Tokyo: Bungeishunjuu.

Morii, M. (1998) Interview conducted in Tokyo, Japan, on 15 April.

Morohashi, T. (1998) 'Nihon no taishuuzasshi ga egaku jendaa to kazoku' ('Gender and family depicted by Japanese popular magazines'): in Muramatsu, Y. and Gossmann (eds) *Media ga tsukuru gender: nichi-doku no danjo, kazoku-zoo wo yomitoru* (*Gender Created by Media: Reading Men, Women and Family in Japan and Germany*). Tokyo: Shin'yoo-sha.

Mort, F. (1996) *Cultures of Consumption: Masculinities and Social Space in Late Twentieth-Century Britain.* London: Routledge.

Ochiai, E. (1994) *The Japanese Family System in Tradition: A Sociological Analysis of Family Change in Postwar Japan.* LTCB International Library Collection.

Reynolds-Akiba, K. (1989) 'Josei zasshi no kotoba' ('The language of women's magazines'): 209–227 in Inoue *et al.* (eds) *Josei zasshi wo kaidokusuru: Comparapolitan-Nichi, Bei, Mekishiko hikaku kenkyuu (Deciphering Women's Magazines: Contrastive Studies of Japanese, American and Mexican Magazines).* Tokyo: Kakiuchi Shuppan.

Saito, K. (1998) Interview conducted in Tokyo, Japan, on 15 April.

Shibamoto, J. (1985) *Japanese Women's Language.* New York: Academic Press.

Shibatani, M. (1990) *The Language of Japan.* Cambridge: Cambridge University Press.

Shiozawa, M. (1998) *Hikaku Nihon no kaisha: Shuppan-sha (Comparing Japanese Companies: Publishers).* Tokyo: Jitsumu Kyooiku Shuppan.

Snoddy, J. (2001) 'The new face of cosmetics', *Independent on Sunday*, 2 September.

Southwell, T. (1998) *Getting Away with It: The Inside Story of Loaded.* London: Ebury Press.

Sweet, M. (1997) 'Men's magazines: who reads em?', *Independent on Sunday*, 15 June.

Tanaka, K. (1998) 'Japanese women's magazines: the language of aspirations': 110–132 in Martinez, D. (ed.) *The Worlds of Japanese Popular Culture.* Cambridge: Cambridge University Press.

Tanaka, Y. (1981) *Nantonaku kurisutaru* (*Somewhat Crystal*). Tokyo: Kawade Shoboo Shin-sha.

Thompson, J. (2001) 'Gentlemen: how changing your underwear can change your life'. *Independent on Sunday*, 7 October.

Thorpe, V. (1997) 'Out goes porn, in come "lifestyle" mags: so what's the difference?', *Independent on Sunday*, 25 May.

Toerien, M. and Durrheim, K. (2001) 'Power through knowledge: Ignorance and the "Real Man"', *Feminism and Psychology* 11(1): 35–54.

Ueno, C. (1987) *Watashi sagashi game* (*Looking-for-myself Game*). Tokyo: Chikuma Shoboo.

Yamazaki, K. (1995) '*Men's Non-No, Popeye, Hot-Dog Press* ga otoko no fukoo wo shoochoo shiteiru'('*Men's Non-No, Popeye*, and *Hot-Dog* Press represent the unhappiness of men!'): in Inoue *et al.* (eds) *Dansei gaku (Men's Studies).* Tokyo: Iwanami Shoten.

Yonekawa, A. (1996) *Gendai wakamono kotoba koo* (*Study of the Language of Young People Today*). Tokyo: Maruzen.

No effeminates please: a corpus-based analysis of masculinity via personal adverts in *Gay News/Times* 1973–2000

Paul Baker

Introduction

> Attractive looking, late forties, mature, fit, non-scene, non-smoking, straight-acting seeks similar or younger (21+) masculine guys for uncommitted friendship. Any country, no effeminates please.

Magazines aimed solely at either gay or heterosexual men can often share more similarities than differences. Both tend to include features based on health, fashion, exercise, consumer goods and sex, an ironic, irreverent style of writing is frequently applied, and they often use attractive semi-clothed male models in advertising or other features. However, for gay men such images can play a dual role. As with heterosexual men, they present aspirational ideals of consumption, grooming, fitness and masculinity which invite the reader to identify with, reject or compare himself to, but gay men may also find the same representations of masculinity to be sexually desirable. The depiction of 'ideal' or new masculinities in gay lifestyle magazines is therefore doubly compelling for the target audience—object cathexis (the desire to possess) merges with object identification (the desire to become).

One of the most significant differences between magazines that are aimed at heterosexual men and those marketed towards gay men is that the latter are likely to include a section for personal adverts, allowing its readership to engage socially, romantically or sexually with each other. In the West, the personal advert represents a quest for a romantic partner or perfect mate (Nair, 1992) with partner selection being anticipated via descriptions of the self, other and desired relationship (Erfurt, 1985). Personal columns are a kind of 'colony text' (Hoey, 1986) made up of numerous separate entries which may be categorized in different ways, (eg, men seeking women vs. women seeking men) although the meaning of each entry is not affected by the order in which they appear. The personal advert is a minimalist genre (Nair, 1992), often with non-essential items such as function words being omitted (Bruthiaux, 1994). They tend to have an informal, spoken style, often featuring lexical vagueness (Crystal and Davy,

1975: 111–14), eg, imprecise references to age or approximations via the suffix—
ish (*tallish, youngish* etc.).

The lonely hearts advert has always been a popular feature of gay magazines,
and for decades has been one of the ways that gay men have made contact with
each other, sometimes meeting another openly gay man for the first time. While
Shalom (1997: 187) notes that people feel ambivalent about using personal
adverts, as it brings their personal world into the public sphere, this is not usually
the case with gay men, whose minority status in society has meant that they have
had to use less mainstream means to make romantic and sexual contacts.[1]

Harris (1997) gives an historical overview of gay personal adverts in America
from the 1940s onwards. His qualitative analysis focuses on the ways that advertisers became more specific about the qualities of their prospective partners over
time, as well as increasingly drawing upon narratives of gay pornography. He
notes that the history of the assimilation of gay men into mainstream society
can be charted by the fact that euphemisms such as 'special friend', which were
common to adverts of the 1950s, were replaced by terms such as 'husband' in
the 1990s.

Other approaches to personal adverts have involved a quantitative analysis
of a larger set of adverts, sometimes using a corpus linguistics approach (eg
Shalom, 1997). Corpus linguistics involves using a large, representative sample
(or corpus) of electronically annotated text, which can be used in conjunction
with computer software in order to discover linguistic patterns and trends.[2]
While corpus linguistics offers a form of quantitative analysis, often in terms of
making frequency information available about a particular set of texts, it can
also help to pinpoint trends or unusual features of the texts, which allow for
more detailed qualitative analyses of smaller extracts. In addition, a corpus can
be used to uncover associations or *collocations* between different lexical items—
for example, if the words *flamboyant* and *homosexual* often occur near to each
other in a particular text, then they can be said to be strong collocates of one
another. Collocational information can be extremely useful in revealing underlying discourses and assumptions in a text.

Shalom (1997) carried out a corpus-based analysis of personal adverts in
London's *Time Out* magazine. Her data was taken from a five-month period over
1995. While ambitious, in examining the most frequent lexis of four groups of
advertisers (gay and heterosexual men and women), only 155 adverts were
placed by gay males. The aim of this chapter, then, is to carry out an analysis
of gay male personal adverts which combines Shalom's corpus-based study,
using a larger sample, with the diachronic analysis used by Harris in order to
look at how gay men use language to construct identities in the personal ad
genre, and how such identities have changed over time.

I chose to focus on personal adverts from a single magazine (*Gay Times,*
formerly *Gay News*), as it has not particularly changed its focus—providing a
balance between reporting on political developments concerning the legal and
social status of gay men, as well as acting as a lifestyle magazine, giving
information about gay-related media (films, television, books and latterly

websites etc.). It is also the longest-running gay magazine in the UK and perhaps the most mainstream, being available in many newsagents. *Gay News*
was founded in 1972 as a bi-monthly newspaper, connected to the emerging Gay
Liberation movement in the UK[3] and relaunched in 1983 as a magazine. By
1985 it had become the monthly *Gay Times*, and it survives to the present.

While a corpus-based approach to personal adverts will not explain why gay
identities have (or have not) changed over time, they will at least provide a
representative set of linguistic snap-shots. It is my intention to link the
longitudinal patterns found in the corpus to other types of socio-cultural
data such as attitudinal data or an analysis of representations of homosexuality and masculinity in the media over time. This multidisciplinary approach will
enable hypotheses about changing constructions of gay identity to be explored
more fully.

Once I had collected and annotated my corpus, it became clear that there
were numerous ways of approaching the research—for example, by examining
patterns relating to the age of the advertiser and the age of the desired partner
or by looking at the ways that ethnic identities were constructed in the adverts.
However, for the purposes of this chapter, I choose to focus on the ways that
advertisers negotiate masculine gay identities, both for themselves and in the
sort of person they desire to meet.

Masculinity, as a gendered practice, is often stereotypically associated with
heterosexual men. While Johnson (1997: 19–21) notes that there are many ways
of being masculine and we should therefore think in terms of masculinities
rather than there being a single masculine identity, Connell (1995: 76) stresses
the importance of recognizing relations among masculinities, pointing to
hegemony, subordination, complicity and marginalization as four of the
practices and ways of regulating the main patterns of Western masculinity.
Masculinity is often viewed as a desirable trait by gay men, a fact which will
become clear in the analysis below; yet stereotypically, homosexuals have been
represented as camp or effeminate, via folk myths and in the media over the
twentieth century.[4] Thus the relationship between homosexuality and masculinity is potentially complex. Gay male personal adverts would therefore function
as a possible site where desires and fantasies surrounding masculinity are foregrounded, negotiated and contested. As Connell (1995: 41) states, 'Gay men's
collective knowledge . . . includes ambiguity, tension between bodies and identities, and contradictions in and around masculinity.'

Methodology

One problem with studying personal adverts over a long period of time is that
different magazines cater for different audiences or the same magazine may
change its target audience over time. Therefore diachronic change in adverts may
be a result of a magazine attracting different sorts of people at different points
in time, rather than any wider social factors. In order to address issues of data

representativeness it would have been useful to build a very large corpus which sampled dozens of different magazines but, due to constraints of time, this was not an option.

As all of my data is derived from *Gay News/Times* it is therefore important to note that any findings should only relate to the readers of this magazine who placed adverts and not be generalized to all gay men in the UK. The mainstream and popular status of this magazine, however, suggests that these findings can be more credibly generalized as being representative of gay men in the UK than adverts in, say, a gay magazine which caters for a more specialist audience such as *bears*.[5] Possibly the magazine's emphasis on current events, social issues and arts reviews may mean that it attracts a more mature audience than youth-oriented publications such as *Attitude* and *Boyz*. It should also be noted that in 1973 *Gay News* was probably one of the few options for gay men who wanted to place a personal advertisement. By 2000 there are many more sites that carry gay personal ads in the UK: numerous gay magazines, mainstream publications such as *Time Out* and the *Guardian*, specialist websites and telephone dating. So it should be taken into account that some of the men who placed an advert in *Gay Times* in 2000 would have done so because they did not have access to, or did not like to use, other types of advertising. This may possibly make the 2000 dataset a more homogenous sample than those who posted adverts in 1973, where less choice was available.

Although *Gay News* was founded in 1972, the earliest issues that I obtained were published in 1973. As I carried out the study in 2000, I decided to sample the data over nine year periods, from 1973, 1982, 1991 and 2000. As Harris (1997: 44–5) notes, the personal advert is a continuously evolving form of discourse. One reason for this could be that when people engage in writing an advert they are likely to emulate what they find desirable in those that they have already seen. Therefore certain phrases or words will become increasingly popular, while others will die out. One way of demonstrating this is that when terms become very popular, they are acronymized. This abbreviation of a longer phrase such as *good sense of humour* is both convenient and cost-effective—it is cheaper to post an advert saying GSOH than one which writes out the phrase word by word. So, by taking a 'snapshot' of the state of personal adverts from the same magazine at nine-year intervals it should be possible to see how constructions of gay identity within *Gay News/Times* have changed over time.

For each year that was sampled, four issues of the magazine were used, although adjacent issues were not sampled in order to prevent the likelihood of repetitions of the same advertisement. Approximately 2000 words of adverts were collected from each issue. In this way almost 8000 words of adverts were collected for each year, resulting in a total corpus of 31,788 words (1350 adverts in total, with a mean advert length of 24 words). In terms of modern corpus building this represents a small corpus. However, the personal advert is characterized by a high degree of repetition which allows patterns to be observed even with a small sample of data.

So that the description of the advertiser could be analysed separately from the description of the sort of person the advertiser was looking for, the corpus was marked up in the following way:[6]

‹me›London. Professional guy (30) slim fair short hair‹/me› seeks ‹you›similar active guy over 21‹/you› for a real relationship. Photo please. Box 255.30

Using the computer corpus analysis package *WordSmith Tools* it was possible to derive frequency information, concordances (a context-based list all of the occurrences of a particular word or phrase) and collocations (pairs of words that often occur next to or near each other) on either the data as a whole, or just by focussing on different parts of it, eg, just the data from the year 1991, or just the parts of the adverts where advertisers described themselves. The adverts should not be read as revealing any 'truths' about the advertisers but, instead, can tell us the ways in which gay men chose to present their identities to potential partners, by constructing the most attractive possible image of themselves in order to ensure a large number of responses from people whom they considered to be desirable. As a result, the constructions, both of the advertiser and of what he desires, are likely to be fuelled by ideals and fantasies, which are possibly embodied within the pages of the magazine, for example, via images of the attractive men used in commercial advertising.[7]

Analysis

About 60 per cent of the advertisers used an identity-based noun, usually to describe either themselves or what they were looking for. Often these nouns were preceded by a list of adjectives. Table 1 shows the most frequently used noun labels in the corpus.

Overall, the most popular noun used was *guy*, followed by *male* and *man*. These terms were often preceded by adjectives such as *young, professional, active, slim* and *masculine*. These three terms, being so popular, were relatively neutral descriptors of identity. In contrast, *gent* or *gentleman* were paired with words

Table 1: General male identity-based nouns

	1973	1982	1991	2000	*All*
Bloke	1	1	1	8	11
Chap	3	5	0	0	8
Fellow	1	0	0	1	2
Gent(leman)	3	7	6	6	22
Guy	86	169	144	151	550
Lad	1	0	4	17	22
Male	68	15	5	30	118
Man	38	19	19	32	108

Table 2: The most popular adjectives used to refer to the self

	1973	1982	1991	2000	All
1	young (52)	slim (74)	slim (52)	slim (71)	slim (244)
2	slim (47)	attractive (47)	non-scene (49)	professional (53)	attractive (146)
3	attractive (33)	young (33)	straight-acting (40)	caring (34)	professional (132)
4	good-looking (24)	tall (32)	professional (34)	attractive (31)	young (116)
5	lonely (33)	non-scene (30)	attractive (33)	tall (30)	tall (105)
6	active (22)	professional (30)	good-looking (27)	good-looking (26)	non-scene (100)
7	tall (19)	active (22)	tall (24)	fit (25)	good-looking (93)
8	professional (17)	quiet (18)	young (23)	affectionate (24)	active (55)
9	sincere (15)	good-looking (16)	intelligent (22)	non-scene (20)	caring (55)
10	affectionate (13)	sincere (16)	sincere (18)	GSOH (19)	sincere (55)

like *mature, elderly, refined* and *retired*. A chi-squared test on this data, as described in Kilgarriff (1996a, b) showed a difference between frequencies of these words over time at the 5 per cent level of significance. In 2000 *blokes* and *lads* had become more popular than in previous years, suggesting a more masculine, working-class identity, with words like *skinhead, horny, muscular* and *rugby* occurring as common left-hand collocates.

Overall, the most common adjectives used in the adverts were *slim* (305), *similar* (284), *young* (217), *attractive* (176), *active* (155), *sincere* (155), *professional* (147), *genuine* (133), *non-scene* (133) and *tall* (119). Descriptions of the self, however, differ somewhat from descriptions of the other, as Tables 2 and 3 reveal.

While advertisers were much more likely to refer to themselves as *slim, attractive, professional, tall* or *young*, they tended to be seeking someone who was *younger, genuine* or *similar*. Shalom (1997: 195–6) also notes that *similar* was the most popular word used in her corpus of personal adverts. While Shalom, however, concludes that in her corpus of male, female, gay and straight adverts, *similar* could often be used to refer to *parts* of the advertiser's self-description, particularly sexuality in the case of gay male advertisers, I would argue that in the case of adverts placed in a more specialist magazine where it is already assumed that all of the advertisers and readers are gay, then *similar* is more likely to be used in conjunction with other non-sexuality based adjectives.

The most common adjectival collocates occurring within four places to the left or right[8] of *similar* in order of collocation strength were: *non-scene* (19),

Table 3: The most popular adjectives used to refer to the desired other

	1973	1982	1991	2000	All
1	similar (61)	similar (73)	similar (80)	similar (62)	similar (276)
2	active (47)	active (26)	young (30)	younger (20)	active (96)
3	sincere (31)	younger (24)	younger (26)	active (17)	younger (91)
4	younger (21)	sincere (22)	slim (17)	slim (14)	sincere (71)
5	non-camp (13)	young (22)	straight-acting (17)	young (13)	slim (61)
6	attractive (10)	slim (20)	smooth (13)	non-scene (12)	genuine (46)
7	non-effeminate (10)	genuine (15)	clean shaven (11)	caring (11)	non-scene (34)
8	slim (10)	discreet (12)	genuine (11)	genuine (11)	non-camp (31)
9	genuine (9)	non-camp (12)	non-scene (10)	sincere (10)	attractive (30)
10	masculine (8)	non-scene (12)	black (9)	intelligent (9)	intelligent (28)

sincere (17), *genuine* (15), *straight-acting* (13), *younger* (12), *gay* (11), *attractive* (10), *discreet* (10), *slim* (9) and *young* (9), suggesting that these tended to be generic attributes which many advertisers claimed to both possess and desire.

From Tables 2 and 3, it can be seen that different lexical strategies were used at different times to refer to masculine identities: *straight-acting, non-camp, non-effeminate* and *masculine* occur at different periods as popular adjectives. An analysis of all of the adjectives in the data revealed that there were other, less frequently occurring words or phrases that referred to masculinity. Table 4 shows the ways in which the uses of these words changed over time, across all of the data.

A chi-squared test carried out on this data (Kilgariff 1996a, b) revealed that there were differences in the ways that masculinity-based words were used over time at the .001 per cent level of significance.[9] In 1973 advertisers were most likely to refer to masculinity by using *anti-types*—words which stated a lack of a particular trait. So terms such as *non-camp, non-effeminate* and *not camp* were most commonly used (comprising about 56 per cent of overt masculinity lexis in this year). By 1982, three differing strategies fought for dominance: *non-camp* was still used, as was *masculine*. Comparisons to stereotypical male heterosexual gender norms, however, (eg, *straight-looking*) were also beginning to be used more frequently. In 1991 the situation had changed again. *Straight-acting* had become by far the most dominant term, used in 47 per cent of cases where men wanted to overtly refer to masculine gendered behaviour. In 2000, *straight-acting* continued to be the most frequently used marker, having being acronymized as SA. The term was not as popular, however, as it had been in 1991, with the older terms, *masculine* and *non-camp* returning as alternatives. The use of *straight-acting* resonates with Butler's theory of gender performativity (1990), the idea that gender is what we do, rather than who we are. As gay identities have traditionally being associated with notions of effeminacy, it may be the case that gay men have been more likely to dwell on their own performances of gender, resulting in a reconceptualization of gender *as* performance, something that can be subject to change in different contexts. For example, some gay men may 'act butch' at times through fear that their sexuality may be exposed, while others may 'camp it up' when in private groups of gay friends; both cases may be considered in terms of performance in particular contexts, rather than a lasting, crystallized state.

Interestingly, the figures for overt masculinity lexis in 1991 are much higher than in the other three time periods that were sampled, (this relationship between time period and identity construction is examined in more detail later in the discussion section). In 1991 the connection between heterosexuality and masculinity as an ideal resulted in adverts such as the one below:

> Normally straight? Just happened to be looking at these pages? Clean-shaven, non-smoking young-looking guy (21+) wanted by straight-acting totally non-scene male 28. Fun/friendship. London Box 6611

The main adjectival collocates of the words which refer to masculinity (taken as a whole) in Table 4 are: *non-scene, slim, similar, attractive, professional, active, tall, clean-shaven, intelligent* and *young.* A discussion of the strongest collocate, *non-scene,* is perhaps useful here. The term *gay scene* roughly refers to the commercial side of gay culture: particularly bars and nightclubs but also incorporating cafés, restaurants, charity and sporting events or specialist clubs relating to hobbies or sexual fetishes. To be *non-scene* is therefore to claim to have either minimal contact with other gay people or to only meet gay people in non-gay establishments. *Non-scene* is not present in the 1973 data, occurs 42 times in 1982, rising to 59 times in 1991 (when explicit references to masculinity are also highest) and decreases to 32 times in 2000. The pairing of *non-scene* and terms such as *straight-acting* is interesting, perhaps implying the belief that social contact with other gay men is emasculating.

Another concept which occurred most frequently in 1991 is that of discretion. In 1991 the words *discreet* or *discretion* occurred 37 times, whereas this figure appeared 30 times in 2000, 29 times in 1982 and only seven times in 1973, six years after the decriminalization of homosexuality. Perhaps everyone was expected to be more or less discreet in 1973, so there was less need to state it as a requirement. The higher number of references to discretion, however, in 1991 (when compared to 1982 and 2000) again suggests a desire to be covert about gay identity during this period.

Table 4: Adjectives referring to masculinity

	1973	*1982*	*1991*	*2000*	*overall*
butch	3	0	1	1	5
manly	0	0	2	0	2
masculine	15	21	19	18	73
no camp	2	0	0	0	2
no campers	1	0	0	0	1
no effems/effeminates	3	2	2	0	7
no fem	1	0	0	0	1
non-camp n/camp	20	19	8	5	52
non-fem non-fm	0	1	1	0	2
non-effeminate	15	3	2	0	20
not camp	8	0	0	0	8
outwardly straight	0	1	0	1	2
real man	0	0	1	0	1
straight-acting	0	1	57	19	77
straight type	1	1	1	0	3
straight appearance	1	2	2	0	5
'straight'	0	0	3	0	3
straight	1	0	3	0	4
straight life(style)	0	0	4	0	4
straight-living	0	1	0	0	1
straight looks	0	1	0	1	2
straight-looking	6	14	14	2	36
straight-talking	0	1	0	0	1
SA	0	0	0	20	20
SL	0	0	0	9	9
ungay	0	0	1	0	1
Total frequency	77	68	121	76	342
Total % of sample	0.96	0.85	1.54	0.94	1.07

One of the most obvious ways to construct a masculine identity is via the body, particularly by exercising the body in order to make it stronger, and therefore more muscular and defined. The following advert from 1991 wishes to trade muscularity (among other things) as physical capital:

> Black guy. Tall, muscular build, broadminded, good humour, seeks tall dominant heavyweight bodybuilders/rugby guys for fun and friendship. All nationalities welcome. Photo with letter ensures quick reply. Box 6405

Words which suggested a masculine body (eg, *well-built, athletic, muscular, fit, trim, strong, hunk*) were lowest in 1973 (with fourteen occurrences) and increased over time, rising to 69 in 2000. Also, references to traditionally male sports such as wrestling, rugby and football slowly rose over time, from six in 1973 to fifteen in 2000.

Table 5: Terms relating to musculature

	1973	*1982*	*1991*	*2000*
rugged	2	1	0	0
well-built	0	3	0	0
athletic	1	8	3	12
muscular	2	7	16	12
muscle	0	2	2	0
fit	0	6	22	30
trim	0	1	4	1
strong	2	1	2	2
gym-trained/toned	0	0	1	3
sturdy	0	1	0	0
body-builder	4	0	0	0
good/nice/firm/physique	3	10	4	6
good/nice body	0	1	0	2
defined body	0	0	0	0
masculine body	0	0	1	0
hunk	0	0	1	1
Total	14	41	56	69
Total % of sample	0.17	0.51	0.71	0.86
Slim	58	93	82	86
Total % of sample	0.72	1.16	1.04	1.07

Bourdieu (1978) conceptualizes the body as a form of commodification or physical capital in modern societies, a theory which has particular resonance with the genre of personal adverts. Indeed, the personal advert becomes a part of the commodification process of gay identity, with its descriptors converging on ideals of masculinity and muscularity. Whereas, in the past, muscular male bodies were a form of physical capital, exchanged via manual labour for wages (Bourdieu, 1986: 246), or when middle-class gay men paid working-class 'trade' for sex, what is now on offer in exchange for a muscular male body, is simply another muscular male body—a non-financial 'trade', in an increasingly competitive market.

The other popular body type which is often mentioned in the adverts is *slim*, which had a sharp rise in occurrences between 1973 and 1982. Even in 2000, *slim* was used more often than all of the other muscularity words combined together but it is definitely the case that descriptors of mesomorphic (muscular) bodies are catching up.

Words which collocate with *slim* include: *smooth, boyish, clean-shaven, affectionate, caring* and *sincere*, while words which collocate with the muscularity words in Table 5 include: *hairy, straight-acting, masculine, similar, mature* and *handsome*. These collocates define two poles of desirable masculinity. Slimness

Table 6: Body hair

	1973	1982	1991	2000
		Presence of body hair		
long hair	3	0	0	0
hirsute	6	8	6	2
beard(ed)	2	9	10	0
moustache	1	5	2	0
tache	0	0	2	0
hairy	4	8	11	4
hairy chest	1	0	4	3
Sub total	17	30	35	9
		Lack of body hair		
clean shaven	6	13	20	11
skin(head)	4	2	4	6
smooth	2	8	22	9
crop	0	0	3	1
bald	0	2	0	1
short hair	0	1	0	3
shaved	0	0	3	0
sub total	12	26	52	31
		totals		
Combined total	29	56	87	40
% of sample	0.36	0.70	1.11	0.49

is associated with youth, a lack of body and facial hair and a softer, caring personality, whereas muscularity is linked to age, body and facial hair and masculinity.

Another way in which masculinity is constructed through some personal adverts is via reference to hair (see Table 6). This occurs either by referring to hair colour[10] or to the length or amount of hair a person has (or would like their prospective partner to have). References to hair (in terms of its quantity) are also highest in 1991—both for terms which refer to the presence of hair (particularly male hair—*hairy chests, beards, moustaches*) and for terms which refer to a lack of hair (eg, *smooth, skin, clean shaven, shaved*).

In 1973 and 1982, terms which refer to presence of hair are slightly more frequent than terms which refer to removal or shortening of hair. This trend is reversed in 1991 and 2000. Overall references to both presence and non-presence of hair, however, are highest in 1991. If, as is suggested by the analysis so far, 1991 was a year in which masculine identities were particularly popular, then perhaps it is the case that the maintenance of body hair is one way in which gay masculinity can be indexed. Removal of body hair allows a

Table 7: Expressive artefacts and concrete objects

	1973	1982	1991	2000
tattoo	1	1	1	1
leather	31	14	17	4
denim	17	5	2	0
sportswear	0	9	2	0
jocks	0	1	2	1
briefs	0	11	4	2
boots/booted	2	1	5	0
breeches	0	2	0	0
cigarettes	0	0	3	0
pipes	0	0	1	0
motorbike	0	0	1	1
Total	51	44	38	9
% of sample	0.63	0.55	0.48	0.11

muscular body to be more clearly seen, whereas shaving the head (*skin head* or *zero crop*) has had associations with working-class masculinity over the 20th century. A lack of body hair may also signify youthfulness. However, the presence of body hair emphasizes males as being different from females—being able to grow a beard or moustache or possessing a hairy chest are also signifiers of masculinity. The following advertiser from 1991 uses *manly, hairy, muscular* and *non-scene*—all indicators of the masculine identity he is trying to project:

> South Wales. Manly 28 year old, 5′10″, dark, hairy and muscular, non-scene, professional, seeks taller, straight-acting, very hairy guy 25–35 with good physique for companionship and maybe more. Sense of humour as valid as hairy legs and chest! Box 9356

Blachford (1981: 192) points out that one way in which gay men came to construct masculinity during the 1970s was via *expressive artefacts* and *concrete objects*. This refers to particular types of clothing: work boots, tight jeans, chaps and leather, as well as tattoos, handle-bar moustaches, cropped or short hair, uniforms or objects associated with masculinity such as pipes and motorbikes. As other references to masculinity appear to have increased since the 1970s, perhaps we would expect to see even more of these types of words appearing in gay personal adverts, particularly in 1991.

However, while sexual fetishes relating to masculinity, such as leather, denim and sportswear became increasingly unpopular since 1973 (see Table 7), the fetishisation of masculine identities, especially those which relate to 'real-world' traditionally male occupations (eg, fireman, police, ex-army, trucker) is at its highest in 1991 (Table 8).

Perhaps another way in which masculinity can be expressed in personal advertisements is by reference to a successful career or material possessions (eg,

Table 8: Masculine occupations

	1973	*1982*	*1991*	*2000*
punk	0	1	3	0
biker	0	4	4	2
ex(forces)	0	0	24	1
ex(services)	0	0	3	0
fireman	0	0	2	0
police	0	0	3	1
security guard	0	0	1	1
soldier	0	0	2	0
(ex)navy	1	0	2	2
(ex)army	0	0	1	1
construction	0	0	1	0
sailor	0	0	0	1
labourer	0	0	0	2
truck(er)	1	1	2	1
Total	2	6	28	12
% of sample	0.002	0.007	0.03	0.01

car, home). Traditionally it has been the male who has been the 'bread-winner' in the past, so it could be theorized that by demonstrating financial security, an advertiser is implicitly making a statement about his 'success' at being a man. O'Kelly (1994: 23) quotes Dunbar as saying that people indicate wealth by 'identifying what job they do, whether they are educated, or what kind of car they drive.' Shalom (1997: 200) notes that in her corpus of personal adverts, *professional* was one of the three most commonly occurring adjectives used, and it was gay men and heterosexual women who were most likely to include it in their adverts. So, would it be the case that in the *Gay News/Times* personal advertisement corpus, references to profession would also occur as indicators of masculine success?

Claims about holding down particular 'professional' jobs (*doctor, lawyer, executive, director* etc.) peaked in 1973 (see Table 9), while references to owning a car and/or home were highest around 1982 and decreased thereafter, possibly because home/car ownership was becoming increasingly taken for granted. Interestingly, the inclusion of the words *solvent* and *professional* gradually increased over time, being most common in the 2000 data. Taken as a whole, however, references to a successful career or material possessions are highest in the 1982 data and lowest in the 1991 data (although this difference was *not* statistically significant)—a finding which is at odds with the fact that other ways of expressing masculinity are highest in 1991. Perhaps it is the case that in 1982, with UK unemployment at a high level, career status became a more relevant issue for advertisers.

Paul Baker

Table 9: Indicators of success

	1973	1982	1991	2000
successful	1	4	2	3
solvent	0	1	1	11
professional	17	32	36	62
car	19	18	7	2
home/pad/flat	35	45	14	2
doctor/lawyer/executive/director/graduate	20	8	14	9
Total	9	109	74	89
% of sample	1.15	1.36	0.94	1.11

Discussion

Why were advertisers more concerned with markers of masculinity in 1991 and why had their definition of gender at this time converged upon *straight-acting*, a term which ties masculinity to heterosexuality, implying an association between effeminacy and homosexuality? To 'act straight' is to act like a 'real' man. 'Acting', however, implies a performance—something not real.

One way to provide an explanation for this observation is to examine the ways that gay and heterosexual men in the UK during 1991 and the years leading up to it, were perceived by mainstream society, including the government and the media.

During the 1980s in the UK, gay men had been blamed for the spread of HIV and consequently AIDS by a number of tabloid newspapers, including *The Sun* which consistently stated that AIDS is a 'gay disease', *The Daily Mail* and *The Daily Express* which followed the line that homosexuals were to blame for the appearance and spread of HIV (Sanderson, 1995: 46). The introduction of Clause 28, in 1988, which stated that a local authority should not 'promote homosexuality or publish material for the promotion of homosexuality ... promote the teaching in any maintained school of the acceptability of homo-sexuality as a pretended family relationship by the publication of such material or otherwise' placed a further legal stigma upon gay lifestyles. Unsurprisingly, negative attitudes towards homosexuality rose during the 1980s[11], peaking in 1987 (see Table 10), the year before the introduction of Clause 28.

While gay men were increasingly represented negatively during the 1980s, however, images of heterosexual masculinity had begun to be increasingly represented as sexually attractive in the media and advertising (Bronski, 1998: 105). For example, a 1985 television advertisement for Levi's 501 jeans which featured the model Nick Kamen undressing to his boxer shorts increased sales by 800 per cent (Simpson, 1994: 97). While it could be argued that these images had been appropriated from ideals of male beauty in the gay media, it was the first time that such directly sexualized images of the exposed male body had

256 © The Editorial Board of the Sociological Review 2003

Table 10: Percentage of respondents answering 'always wrong' to the question 'What about sexual relations between two adults of the same sex?' Data derived from *British Social Attitudes* 9th, 13th, 16th and 17th reports (Jowell *et al.*, 1992: 124, 1996: 39, 1999: 348, 2000: 112).

Year	1983	1984	1985	1987	1989	1990	1995	1998	2000
%	50	54	59	64	56	58	55	38.5	37.5

been used on mainstream audiences. Physical fitness also became more mainstream over the 1980s, represented in film by body-building actors such as Sylvester Stallone and Arnold Schwarzenegger. At the same time, some gay men turned to body-building as a response to AIDS (Harris, 1997: 93–4). The gay media has been increasingly likely to employ images of unclothed muscular (and therefore by implication, masculine) men in a variety of advertising and other features (Dotson, 1999: 135–140), particularly since the 1980s.

During the 1980s, as male homosexuality became more stigmatized and male heterosexuality became eroticized, it is possible that gay males felt the need to distance themselves from appearing obviously 'gay'. This would have led to an emphasis on 'discretion' and a gender performance most usually associated with heterosexual males—stereotypically masculine, or 'straight-acting'. It would have also led to a focus on the shape of the male body; since the 1980s the mesomorph is increasingly defined as an ideal body shape for males, both heterosexual and homosexual. Hair is also seen as an important signifier of gay masculinity—either by shaving the head and body (in order to make muscles more defined) or by possessing hair characteristics associated with males (hairy chest, beard, moustache)—both being ways of emphasizing the masculine body. With the emphasis on masculine constructions being overtly concerned with appearances—the body and the gender performance—at the same time the association of masculinity with success is downplayed in 1991, perhaps because it is not as easy to demonstrate (or manufacture) as other indicators of masculinity.

In conflict with the above findings, identities based around leather and denim were relatively unpopular in 1991, although masculine occupational identities such as fireman and ex-army were at their most popular at this time. As Blachford (1981) notes, however, the leather and denim identities had developed in the 1970s. Perhaps by the 1990s they were seen as unfashionable by mainstream gay men, or too 'obviously gay', a theory which holds with the idea that gay men wanted to distance themselves from appearing explicitly gay in 1991. On the other hand, identities connected to stereotypically masculine occupations were possibly seen as more authentic and therefore attractive because of their association with masculinity but not specifically homosexuality.

One factor which was discussed earlier is that as the 20th century progressed, the number of possible sites for placing personal ads for gay men in the UK increased (particularly with the popularity and availability of the internet). So it could be the case that the apparent decrease in interest of *Gay News/Times* advertisers in 'expressive artefacts and concrete objects' (Table 7) by 2000 is the result of such interests being catered for by niche magazines and websites which concentrate on particular fetishes or newer constructions of gay masculinity. Such men may advertise elsewhere, feeling that *Gay Times* is too mainstream or its advertisers place the wrong amount of emphasis on physical appearance and masculinity for their tastes. I limited the source of my corpus because I wanted to concentrate only on the construction of identities within the relatively unchanging and long-running *Gay News/Times*, but a larger corpus of personal adverts, which is both longitudinal, and takes samples from multiple sources may result in different findings. I would argue that we may be able to generalise the patterns found in the *Gay News/Times* personal adverts over the last 30 years to other representations of identities found in the (mainstream) gay media, particularly as personal adverts are often expressions of idealistic desire. The patterns elicited from the personal advert data, however, may not reveal the range of possible identities that are constructed by gay men away from the media, or they may foreground certain constructions of gay masculinity at the expense of others.

So, it may be the case that other factors can explain the preoccupation with the appearance of heterosexual masculinity in the early 1990s by the advertisers in *Gay Times*. The plausible thesis remains, however, that some gay men, feeling stigmatized as disease spreaders and potential proselytisers by a hostile government and media, suffered an identity crisis, becoming increasingly fixated on the idea of stereotypical heterosexual masculinity. Therefore, this research suggests that the negative treatment of a minority group by mainstream society can have far-reaching consequences in the ways that members of the minority group perceive themselves, ultimately attempting to appropriate and exaggerate alternative identities that are viewed as more acceptable by mainstream society.

Notes

1 For example, the UK magazine *Films and Filming*, while not being an explicitly gay magazine, regularly featured 'coded' advertisements from 'bachelors' seeking friendships with other men in the 1950s and 1960s.

2 See McEnery and Wilson (1996) Kennedy (1998) and Biber, Conrad and Reppen (1998) for more information on corpus linguistics.

3 Gay liberation paralleled and was connected to the Civil Rights, students' and Women's Liberation movements of the 1960s/70s. It was linked to the struggle against 'sexism' (Young, 1972:7) and was one of the first movements to instil a sense of pride for gay men and lesbians.

4 Russo (1987) gives numerous examples of effeminate representations of homosexuality in the cinema, while Sanderson (1995) focuses on such constructions in the popular British press.

5 Bears are gay men who generally possess one or more of the following traits: a hairy body, beard and/or moustache, large or tubby build, muscular development and masculine behaviour.

6 Corpora are often annotated in order to encode additional information. Such annotations (or tags) can often take the form of sgml (standard generalized mark-up language) codes.

7 It is beyond the scope of this chapter to carry out a full analysis of the relationship between gay personal adverts and the images found in gay magazines, but Dotson (1999: 125–137) gives an analysis of representations of the male body within the gay magazine genre.

8 The mean sentence length in the corpus was eight words. For this reason, unless stated, collocates were calculated on the basis of occurring four words to the left and four words to the right of a target word.

9 Differences across time based on frequency data presented in Tables 5–8 were also significant at the .001% level.

10 In terms of hair colour, *blonds* are cited most often (27 times as opposed to 15 times for *dark* hair, the next highest category).

11 It would have been useful to extend the range of this survey to look at attitudes in the 1970s. 1983, however, was the first year that this question was added to the British Social Attitudes survey.

References

Biber, D., Conrad, S. and Reppen, R. (1998) *Corpus Linguistics: Investigating Language Structure and Use.* Cambridge: Cambridge University Press.

Blachford, G. (1981) 'Male dominance and the gay world': 184–210 in Plummer, K. (ed.) *The Making of the Modern Homosexual.* London: Hutchinson.

Bourdieu, P. (1978) 'Sport and social class', *Social Science Information* 17(6): 819–40.

Bourdieu, P. (1986) 'The forms of capital', *Theory and Society* 14(6): 723–44.

Bronski, M. (1998) *The Pleasure Principle. Sex, Backlash and the Struggle for Gay Freedom.* New York: St Martin's Press.

Bruthiaux, P. (1994) 'Functional variation in the language of classified ads', *Perspectives: Working Papers of the Department of English, City Polytechnic of Hong Kong* 6(2): 21–40.

Butler, J. (1990) *Gender Trouble: Feminism and the Subversion of Identity.* New York: Routledge.

Connell, R.W. (1995) *Masculinities.* Polity: Cambridge.

Crystal, D. and Davy, D. (1975) *Advanced Conversational English.* London: Longman.

Dotson, E.W. (1999) *Behold the Man: The Hype and Selling of Male Beauty in Media and Culture.* New York: Harrington Park Press.

Erfurt, J. (1985) 'Partnerwunsch und Textproduktion: Zur Strujtur der Intentionalitat in Heiratsanzeigen', *Zeit für Phonetik, Sprachwiss und Kommunikforsch* 38(3): 309–20.

Harris, D. (1997) *The Rise and Fall of Gay Culture.* New York: Ballantine Books.

Hoey, M. (1986) 'The discourse colony: a preliminary study of a neglected discourse type': 1–26 in *Talking about Text,* Discourse Analysis Monograph no. 13, English Language Research, University of Birmingham.

Johnson, S. and Meinhof, U.L. (eds) (1997) *Language and Masculinity.* London: Blackwell.

Jowell, R., Brook, L., Prior, G. and Taylor, B. (1992) *British Social Attitudes, the 9th Report.* Aldershot: Ashgate Publishing.

Jowell, R. (1996) *British Social Attitudes, the 13th Report.* Aldershot: Ashgate.

Jowell, R., Curtice, J., Park, A. and Thomson, S. (1999) *British Social Attitudes, the 16th Report: Who Shares New Labour Values?* Aldershot: Ashgate.

Jowell, R., Park, A., Thomson, K., Jarvis, L., Bromley, C. and Stratford, N. (2000) *British Social Attitudes, the 17th Report: Focusing on diversity.* London: Sage.

Kennedy, G. (1998) *An Introduction to Corpus Linguistics.* London: Longman.

Kilgarriff, A. (1996a) 'Using word frequency lists to measure corpus homogeneity and similarity between corpora'. Information Technology Research Institute, University of Brighton, 18 April.

Kilgarriff, A. (1996b) 'Corpus Similarly and Homogeneity via Word Frequency', *EURALEX* Proceedings, Gothenburg, Sweden, August.

McEnery, T. and Wilson, A. (1996) *Corpus Linguistics.* Edinburgh: Edinburgh University Press.

Nair, B.R. (1992) 'Gender, genre and generative grammar: deconstructing the matrimonial column': 227–54 in M. Toolan (ed.) *Language, Text and Context: Essays in Stylistics.* London and New York: Routledge.

O'Kelly, L. (1994) 'Kiss a few frogs, land a prince', *Observer*, 10 July, p. 23.

Russo, V. (1987) *The Celluloid Closet.* New York: Harper and Row.

Sanderson, T. (1995) *Mediawatch.* London: Gay Men's Press.

Shalom, C. (1997) 'That great supermarket of desire: attributes of the desired other in personal advertisements': 186–203 in Harvey, K. and Shalom, C. (eds) *Language and Desire.* London: Routledge.

Simpson, M. (1994) *Male Impersonators.* London: Cassell.

Young, A. (1972) 'Out of the closets, into the streets': in Jay, K. and Young, A. (eds), *Out of the Closets.* New York: Douglas.

Notes on contributors

Paul Baker is a lecturer in the Department of Linguistics at Lancaster University. He has published numerous articles on the teaching of linguistics via the internet and is also pursuing his research interests in identity theory, gender, queer studies and conversation/ discourse analysis. He is the author of *Polari— The Lost Language of Gay Men* (Routledge, 2002).

Bethan Benwell is a lecturer in English language and linguistics in the Department of English Studies at Stirling University. Her research interests include language and gender, educational linguistics and discourse analysis and she has published journal articles and chapters on masculine discourse in men's lifestyle magazines and (with Stokoe) student identity in tutorial discourse. She is currently co-writing a book *Discourse and Identity* with Elizabeth Stokoe (Loughborough University) for EUP and continues to research popular cultural realizations of masculinity.

Kate Brooks is a lecturer in media studies at the University of the West of England. She has worked on a number of projects investigating popular leisure practices, including cinema goers, magazine readers, and second hand shoppers. She is the co-author of *Knowing Audiences* (University of Luton Press, 1998) and (with Jackson and Stevenson) of *Making Sense of Men's Magazines* (Polity Press, 2001) and has most recently published work on the changing culture of volunteering.

Ben Crewe is a Nuffield Foundation New Career Development Fellow at the Institute of Criminology, University of Cambridge. His current research interests are prison culture and masculinity. The chapter in this volume came out of PhD research submitted in 2001 under the title 'Representing Men: Cultural Production and Producers in the Men's Magazine Market'. A book based on the thesis will be published by Berg in 2003.

Tim Edwards lectures in the Department of Sociology at the University of Leicester and has lectured and published widely on topics relating to masculinities, fashion and consumption. Recent publications include *Men in the Mirror* (Cassell, 1997) and *Contradictions of Consumption* (Open University Press, 2000). He is currently writing a book for Routledge on masculinity and cultural theory.

Rosalind Gill is a lecturer in Gender Theory at the London School of Economics and Political Science. She has recently worked with Karen Henwood and Carl McLean on a study of British young men's embodied identities, and is currently conducting interviews in Australia for a comparative project on a related theme. Her other areas of interest are in media and new technologies, and she is editor of *The Gender-Technology Relation* (with Keith Grint), Taylor & Frances, 1995, and author of *Gender and the Media* (Polity, in press).

Peter Jackson is Professor of Human Geography at the University of Sheffield. His research focuses on the geography of consumption and on the cultural politics of identity. Recent projects include an ethnography of two shopping centres in North London (published as *Shopping, Place and Identity,* 1998); a study of transnational commodity culture; and new work on retail competition and consumer choice. Other recent publications include an edited collection on *Commercial Cultures* (Berg, 2000) and a co-authored book on *Making Sense of Men's Magazines* (Polity, 2001).

Bill Osgerby is a Senior Lecturer in Cultural Studies at London Metropolitan University and has written widely on British and American cultural histories. His key publications include *Youth in Britain Since 1945* (Oxford: Blackwell, 1998, *Playboys in Paradise: Masculinity, Youth and Leisure-Style in Modern America* (Oxford: Berg / New York University Press, 2001) and a co-edited anthology, *Action TV: 'Tough Guys, Smooth Operators and Foxy Chicks'* (London: Routledge, 2001).

Nick Stevenson is the author of *Understanding Media Cultures* (2002), *The Transformation of the Media* (1999), *Culture, Ideology and Socialism* (1995) and the editor of *Culture and Citizenship* (2001). He is also the joint author of *Making Sense of Men's Magazines* (2001) written with Peter Jackson and Kate Brooks. 2003 will see the publication of *Cultural Citizenship:Cosmopolitan Questions* and he is currently working on a book-length project on the celebrity David Bowie.

Jane Sunderland is a Lecturer in the Department of Linguistics and Modern English Language, Lancaster University, where she is responsible for the Gender and Language MA course as well as the PhD in Applied Linguistics by Thesis and Coursework programme. She has published widely on gender and language, especially in a language classroom context. She has recently co-edited *Gender Identity and Discourse Analysis* with Lia Litosseliti (John Benjamins, 2002).

Keiko Tanaka is a senior research fellow at Oxford Brookes university. She is the author of *Advertising Language: A Pragmatic Approach to Advertisements in Britain and Japan* (Routledge 1994, paperback edition 1999). She has also published a number of articles on advertising in women's magazines and has a number of articles and chapters forthcoming on representations of masculinity in Japanese men's magazines.

Yolande Taylor is a freelance editor. She completed her MA in Language Studies at Lancaster University in 1998. The chapter for this volume originates from a comparison of two articles about sex workers which was the subject of her MA dissertation focusing on Language and Gender.

Belinda Wheaton is a Research Fellow at the University of Brighton's Chelsea School Research Centre. Her research and publications examine the consumption of sport and leisure cultures, focusing on alternative sport. She has been a contributer to various specialist sports magazines, and is editing a book for Routledge on Lifestyle Sport Cultures.

Index

fatherhood 13, 18, 34–5
feelings 4
femininity 9, 11, 17: consumption
   associated with 58–9, 60, 61, 62, 64,
   75, 142
feminism 12, 20–1, 101; backlash to
   15–16, 42–3, 47–8, 128; and men's
   magazines 155–6; and women's
   magazines 112–13
FHM 3, 121, 133, 138, 141; content 120;
   new lad and 13; sales 25, 95–6, 118,
   119, 132, 144, 229; in USA 25
Field, M. 228
Fielding, Helen, *Bridget Jones' Diary* 51
Fight Club 2
Fiske, J. 216
Fitzgerald, Scott, *The Great Gatsby* 65
flexible specialization 114
Focus 92
football 52–3; 96–7, 99, 193, 195
fops 4
Foucault, M. 35, 36
fragmentation 19, 22
France, new petite bourgeoisie 74–5
Franks, S. 47
FRaU Homme 233
Front 13, 138, 139
Frosh, S. *et al* 41

gadget magazines 96
gangsters 64–5, 143
Gardiner, J.K. 9, 10, 11
Gay Blade 78
gay liberation 45–6
gay men 46, 243; construction of
   masculine identities 192, 245, 247–55,
   257–8; negative representations of 256
Gay News 245, 246
gay scene/non-scene 250
Gay Times 244–5; personal adverts in
   246–58
gender 9, 11; abolishing 9–10; biology
   and 10, 17; discursive account 8–9,
   151–2; fetishization of 11, 15; language
   use and 169–70
gender differences 9, 17, 50–1; in Japan
   240
gender relations 2, 11
Gent 78

Gentlemen's Quarterly 78
Giddens, A. 11, 90, 115–16
Gill, R. 33
Gingrich, Arnold 57, 66, 67, 69
Goodwin, J.A. 48
GQ 6, 49, 120, 123, 132, 133, 157; Brown
   and 107; content 94, 118, 121, 141;
   'heroes' 162, 165–6; new man and 94,
   104, 106; sales 119
GQ Active 196
Gray, J. 17, 50–1
Greenfield, J. *et al* 74
Greer, G. 139
Guardian, The 102

hair, and gay masculinity 253–4, 257
Halberstam, J. 10
Hall, S. 18
Harris, D. 244, 246
Hartley, J. 37
Haynes, R. 195
health and fitness titles 96, 133, 196, 208
hedonism 106; masculinity and 61–2, 65,
   207, 208; of 'new bourgeoisie' 75, 78
Hefner, Hugh 76, 77
hegemonic masculinity 60, 181–2;
   lifestyle sporting magazines and 195,
   199, 207–8, 208–9, 210, 215, 217; of
   new lad 20, 47, 195
Heibon Punch 230
heroes 47, 157–8, 165–6; and anti-
   heroism 157–60, 162
heterosexual relations 115–16
heterosexuality 90, 138, 156, 215–16,
   227–8; and consumption 71, 75, 77;
   eroticization of 256–7; masculinity and
   38, 143, 145, 192, 256; readership and
   118, 121–2, 210
Hi Life 78
hidden consumers 61
historical development of masculinity
   59–60
historical perspective 24, 58–81, 133
HIV/AIDS 46, 53, 256
homoeroticism 46, 69, 139, 156
homophobia 13, 18, 195
homosexuality (*see also* gay men) 18,
   139; stigmatization of 256, 257
honesty 11, 100, 123–4

masculine identity 58–61, 74, 76–8,
81–3, 139–40, 143, 231; of new man
18, 44–5, 144
male escorts 174–82
male gaze 139, 156
male physicality 47–8, 207–8
male subjectivities 5, 34, 39–41
Man About Town 81–2
Man Show, The (TV) 25
manliness 1–2, 60
market for men's lifestyle magazines 92,
94, 117–22, 132
masculine identities 60, 108; constructed
by gay men 245, 248–55, 257–8
masculinity 34, 38, 133–4; changing
constructions 13–14, 115–16, 122, 125,
127; cultural shifts in 39–41; markers
of 192, 249–55; meanings of 60; new
19–22; style and 141–4
mass culture, in information age 113–17
Maxim 17, 118, 132, 133, 141, 171;
circulation 95, 96; and new lad 13,
120, 121, 138; representation of male
sex workers in 174–82, 184–7; response
to feminism 16
Mayfair 81
McRobbie, A. 21–2
media, and production of new lad 48–9,
125, 137–8
Men Behaving Badly (TV) 137, 138
Men Only 74, 80
Men's An An 226
Men's Club 223, 226, 239
Men's Health 118, 126, 132, 196, 208;
ambivalence about reading 126;
circulation 96, 119; expert status of
120–1
men's health movement 43, 194
Men's Non-No 223, 226, 230, 232
Messner, M. 171
middle-class culture 74, 78, 81
middle-class identity 75–6, 98, 104
Middleton, P. 122
Millionaire 78
misogny 16, 101
Modern Man 76
modernity 127–8
Moore, S. 46
More 225

Morohashi, T. 230, 232
Mort, F. 23, 45, 80, 135, 222
Mulvey, L. 205
muscular heroes 47
music, and masculinity 45
music press 103

narcissism 83, 90, 141–4, 145, 208;
historical perspective 61, 72; in Japan
232–3; new man and 13, 48, 140,
193
naturalness 11, 124–5
New Deal 67–8
new father 34–5
new journalism 102–3
new lad 25–6, 141, 144; backlash against
feminism 47–8; characteristics 124–5;
constructions of 36–9, 90; as discourse
39, 47–54; and fashion 140; and
football 52–3; future of 25; irony of
121–2, 137, 210–12; lad lit 51–2; media
production of 48–9, 125, 137–8;
nationalist discourse 195; popularity of
loaded 6, 91, 93–4, 121–2; psychology
and 49–51; reaction to new man 13,
14–19, 92–3, 140, 171, 193;
representations of masculinity 138,
144–5, 157; sexuality and 138–9; and
sporting masculinities 191, 194–5, 196;
and style magazines 144–5, 210; and
women 92–3, 137–8
new man 36–8, 104, 124, 141, 193, 222;
and consumption 18, 44–5, 144; as
discourse 39–41, 42–6, 53–4; feminism
and 13, 42–3, 101–2; and gay
liberation 45–6; psychology and 43;
music and 45; rejection of 16, 156,
171; sexuality and 100, 138–9; and
style press 43–4, 92, 135, 137
new masculinities 19–22
new social movements 42
New Success 67
new technology 114
Next 45
Nixon, S. 23, 44, 121–2, 135
NME (New Musical Express) 97, 98,
103, 104
Non-No 225, 235, 236
Nugget 78

Lightning Source UK Ltd.
Milton Keynes UK
UKOW06f1013081013

218653UK00006B/208/A